Boston and the Making of a Global City

Boston and the Making of a Global City

James C. O'Connell

University of Massachusetts Press
Amherst and Boston

Copyright © 2025 by University of Massachusetts Press
All rights reserved

ISBN 978-1-62534-862-3 (paper); 863-0 (hardcover)

Designed by Jen Jackowitz
Set in Minion Pro
Printed and bound by Books International, Inc.

Cover design by adam b. bohannon
Cover photo by Carol M. Highsmith, *Aerial view of the skyline of Boston, Massachusetts*, 2019. Courtesy Library of Congress Prints and Photographs Division.

Library of Congress Cataloging-in-Publication Data
A catalog record for this book is available from the Library of Congress.

British Library Cataloguing-in-Publication Data
A catalog record for this book is available from the British Library.

Contents

Illustrations and Tables vii
Preface ix
Acknowledgments xiii

Introduction 1

Chapter 1
What Makes Boston a "Global City" 11

Chapter 2
The Port of Boston: Gateway to the Global Economy 33

Chapter 3
How Boston Financiers Bolstered an Innovation Economy 56

Chapter 4
The Evolution of the Global Information Network 76

Chapter 5
Jet Age Global Node 98

Chapter 6
How Greater Boston Global Supply Chains Operate 119

Chapter 7
How the Cambridge-Boston Life Sciences Ecosystem Works 134

Chapter 8
The First Waves of Migrants Reshape Boston Society 164

Chapter 9
Post-1965 Immigration Becomes Truly Global 187

Chapter 10
Fashioning a Global City Image   203

Chapter 11
Inequality and Global Cities   221

Chapter 12
Global Cities in an Age of Disruption   238

Notes   249
Index   293

Illustrations and Tables

FIGURES

Figure 1: Map of Metropolitan Boston Communities   15
Figure 2: "Boston, Capital of the United States of North America"   36
Figure 3: Map depicting destinations of freight and passenger steamships sailing from Boston, 1928   51
Figure 4: Logan Airport International Terminal E expansion, 2023   101
Figure 5: Venture Café, Cambridge Innovation Center   151
Figure 6: Ray and Maria Stata Center, 2004, MIT   162
Figure 7: San Rocco Procession, North End, 1971   171
Figure 8: Chinatown, ca. 1950   179
Figure 9: Rendering of proposed Boston Expo '76   208
Figure 10: Rendering of proposed Boston 2024 Summer Olympics Stadium   216

TABLES

Table 1: Global Cities Ranking Studies Evaluating Boston   25–31
Table 2: United States, Boston, and New York Imports and Exports, 1821–1860   43
Table 3: Cost of Sending Messages through Different Communications Media   90
Table 4: Leading International Destinations for Passengers Flying to and from Logan International Airport, October 2022–September 2023   102
Table 5: Largest Biopharma Employers in Massachusetts   142
Table 6: Institutions Supporting the Greater Boston Life Sciences Ecosystem   150
Table 7: US Percentage Foreign-Born, 25 Largest Metropolitan Areas, 2016   165

Table 8: Black (Non-Hispanic) Population in Boston, 1800–2020   183
Table 9: Percentage of Foreign-Born in Selected Boston Suburbs, 2010   191
Table 10: Percentage of Immigrant Workers in Massachusetts, by Occupation, 2019   192
Table 11: Shares of US Income by Economic Tier, 2010   225
Table 12: Income, Assets, and Net Worth of Boston Racial/Ethnic Groups   229

Preface

The purpose of this book is to spark a dialogue about the role that Boston plays in the global urban network that has been developing since the 1980s. The globalized economy that emerged during this period has integrated most of the entire world into a single capitalist market, driven by instantaneous telecommunications and world-spanning airplane service. With globalization, markets, workforces, and investments have expanded through worldwide networks, opening up new opportunities for metropolitan areas like Boston. The cities that have made the most of the flows of trade, investment transportation, telecommunications, tourism, and migration have become referred to as "global cities" for the fundamental role they play in the world economy. Some of the largest established cities, such as New York and London, are at the center of the management and financing of global trade, while mid-sized knowledge hubs like Boston also have global reach.

I have pursued this topic because the focus of my research and writing has always been on exploring overlooked aspects of the cities and regions where I have lived. As both an urban historian and an urban-regional planner, my goal has been to reveal these cities and regions in a new light to spark reflection and debate about their histories and how they may develop going forward. I wrote an earlier book, *The Hub's Metropolis: Greater Boston's Development from Railroad Suburbs to Smart Growth* (2013), out of a desire to get beyond a preoccupation with the history of the core city of Boston and understand the planning and development of the entire metropolitan area. The overlooked story that this book, *Boston and the Making of a Global City*, relates is how Boston has taken advantage of intensifying global connections and technological innovation to invigorate its economy. This book has arisen from my fascination with Boston's renaissance of recent decades, how a stagnating city reversed its fortunes and joined the ranks of dynamic global cities.

Using the "global cities" lens helps us recognize that Boston's particular trajectory builds upon a long history of global engagement compared to most other American cities. Boston's involvement with global exploration, trade, and migration dates from its establishment as an English colony in 1630. Right up until the Civil War, Boston's economy was primarily based on international trade. After the next century of being industrially based and oriented to the domestic market, Boston again became more globally aligned, driven by higher education and world-class innovation sectors in life sciences, healthcare, information technology, robotics, and climate technology. Aspects of the story have been described, but the impacts of globalization have been obscured. By examining how globalization has been playing out in Boston—with its businesses, universities, entrepreneurs, immigrants, and the rest of us—this book can provide a new perspective on Boston's strengths and challenges.

Viewing Boston in a global context has exposed me to the academic subject area of "global cities," which, while robust in other countries, is less studied in the United States. A major reason is that cities in European and Asian economies are far more invested in export markets than the US and have a strong interest in enhancing competitiveness with their peers. This country has so many large cities and a mature market system that it is not as reliant upon connections to international cities. Exports from United States make up 10% (2020) of the economy, while China's exports are 20%, India's are 20%, Canada's are 30%, Germany's are 47%.[1]

The framework for my book has been influenced by two of the foremost sociological scholars of "global cities," Saskia Sassen (Columbia University) and Manuel Castells (University of Southern California). They were influenced by the European perspective, having grown up in the Netherlands and Spain, respectively. It is also noteworthy that leading researchers of global cities have been concentrated in sociology, geography, and economics. Some of the most probing research being done on the most competitive "global cities" has been taking place at think tanks, academic research centers, and consulting firms. Institutions in this field that stand out are the Organisation for Economic Co-operation and Development (OECD), Globalization and World Cities (GaWC) Research Network at Loughborough University (UK), Chinese Academy of Social Sciences, and UN World Intellectual Property Organization. In this country, the Brookings Institution has led the way in studying global cities and the consequences of globalization on communities. My book has drawn upon many global city ranking studies (some of which can be gimmicky) to identify globalizing factors that influence the development of cities. Many of these studies have ranked Boston high among global cities, usually citing the importance of its world-renowned higher education, healthcare, and technological innovation clusters. There are a number of books that examine specific global cities and how they achieved that status. Some valuable books that have influenced my approach include Stephen Chiu and Tai-Lok Lui, *Hong Kong: Becoming a Chinese Global City*; Greg Clark, *The Making of a World City: London, 1991–2021*; and Steven P. Erie, *Globalizing L.A.: Trade, Infrastructure, and Regional Development*.

Acknowledgments

The seeds of this book lie in my previous work *The Hub's Metropolis*. I intended to use that book as the basis for a course about Boston's history of planning and development, which I ended up teaching at Boston University (BU). As the course evolved, I realized that globalization's impacts on Boston were an important story that was overlooked. It could be a course unto itself. Boston University's City Planning and Urban Affairs Program Director Madhu Dutta-Koehler supported the idea of a new course and advised me to make sure I took into account "global cities" in general and not concentrate exclusively on Boston. I have done that in a BU course on Global Cities: Through Boston's Experience. During the COVID-19 pandemic, that period of isolation gave me time to start turning the research for my course into this book. I am particularly grateful to the Land Economics Foundation, an ancillary, research-oriented organization to Lambda Alpha International, for the financial support it has provided to the publication of this book.

A significant aspect of this book project has been input from people who have read or discussed parts of this book with me. I am grateful for their feedback. UMass Press editor Brian Halley has played a critical role in bringing this book to publication. He encouraged me to focus on Boston's experience first and foremost and use discussions of globalization in an ancillary role. Boston University Professor and Director of the Initiative on Cities Loretta Lees has been another important supporter. She urged me to view this book as a vehicle for stimulating debate about the status of Boston in the global urban network. Others who commented on various aspects of the book include Ed Allard, John Avault, Carlos Balsas, Dan Dray, Dick Garver, Roger Harris, Marilynn Johnson, Bob Krim, Brian Ladd, Marc O'Brien, Amaryah Orenstein, Jim Pasto, Andy Robichaud, Charlie Ryan, Robin Scheffler, and Ted Van Dyke. I interviewed a number of people about topics covered in this book. They include James Colimon, City of Boston; Rick Dimino, A Better City; Scott Kirsner, Boston Globe; Mike Lake, Leading Cities; Rodrigo Martinez, Cambridge Innovation Center; Mark Sullivan, Massachusetts Office of International Trade & Investment; Yuxi Wang, City of Boston; and Mary Yntema, World Affairs Boston. Yesim Sungu-Eryilmaz, Program Director of the Boston University City Planning and Urban Affairs Program, has strongly supported my course on Global Cities: Through Boston's Experience, which has produced many insights incorporated in this book. Boston University students who took this course deserve credit for the insights about global cities and Boston that they have provided in class discussions and written assignments. Garrett Dash Nelson, President of the Leventhal Map and Education Center at the Boston Public Library, was very helpful in identifying maps and illustrations that convey Boston's global role. My wife Ann Marie has helped immeasurably, reading and commenting on the entire book draft as well as counseling me on all matters of research, publication, and personal morale.

Boston and the Making of a Global City

INTRODUCTION

Boston is an entirely different place today than it was a few decades ago. It is more prosperous, less provincial, more tolerant, more appealing, more confident. The region's economy is far more dynamic due to the vitality of its innovation sectors—life sciences, health care, information technology, robotics, and advanced manufacturing. Its financial sector and professional services, such as law, accounting, management consulting, insurance, design, and engineering, also play a critical role in the economy. As a college town, Boston is less a contemplative grove of academe and more a beehive of transformative research and learning. The key to the economy is the area's highly skilled talent base, much of it developed at local colleges and universities. Almost half of the area's adults over twenty-five have at least a bachelor's degree. Boston's Puritan and Yankee legacies contribute to the work ethic that motivates its workforce. Metro Boston is an avatar of the world's knowledge economy. The story of this urban metamorphosis is an important one. It has been told piecemeal in various ways. Yet, there is a broad context of Boston's urban development that has been overlooked—it is related to the process of globalization that has been sweeping the world and reshaping every city.

With the globalization of recent decades, the flows of international trade, capital, and knowledge exchange have multiplied. Free market capitalism has supercharged the drive for global markets. Investment, production, and consumption are no longer nationally oriented. They operate in a global marketplace. Financial and advanced professional services and technological innovation have superseded manufacturing as the foremost functions of global capitalism. These economic functions are concentrated in "global cities," places where financial and management decisions are made and cutting-edge research institutions and entrepreneurs are located. These cities are nodes in networks of investment, trade, knowledge exchange, telecommunications, transportation, travel, and migration, which have significant social and cultural impacts as well as economic effects.[1] The measure of a global city is the extent of the international networks with which it is connected. Because of this, the globalized urban network is resolutely competitive, as cities strive to be more prosperous, influential, and attractive.

The great financial centers of New York, London, Paris, and Tokyo, which offer the broadest range of business services, are at the apex of this urban hierarchy. As the economies of China and the rest of East Asia have grown, Beijing, Shanghai, and Seoul have also assumed positions of primacy. Cities specializing in functions that propel the world economy also have prospered. Los Angeles is a focal point for entertainment, technology, and shipping. Washington, DC and Brussels are headquarters of government. Frankfurt, Zurich, and Singapore are important financial cities. Mexico City, Sao Paulo, Mumbai, and Johannesburg are command posts for economies of the Global South.

Boston is one of the foremost hubs of technological innovation, along with San Francisco-Silicon Valley, Seattle, Toronto, Paris, and Tel Aviv. Studies ranking urban economic performance, published by such entities as UN-Habitat, World Intellectual Property Organization, Japan's Mori Memorial Foundation, and the international real estate firm Jones Lang LaSalle (JLL), rate Boston's innovation and higher education sectors among the top ten in the world. Technology innovation hubs are strategic sites in the global economy. They possess dynamic entrepreneurs, leading-edge research institutions, highly educated talent, and highly connective transportation and telecommunications infrastructure. Innovation hubs have become critical since they are creating new products that are driving the global economy. With the informationalization of the economy, their workforces are involved with generating great flows of information and ideas. The role of large metropolitan areas has been magnified, as places where economic opportunities proliferate. They are sites of culture, entertainment, tourism, real estate, and consumption. While attracting international markets, a city like Boston also plays a significant economic role in the US and serves as the business and cultural hub for New England.[2]

To comprehend Boston's evolution as a "global city," this book is structured with specific chapters tracing the flows of trade, supply chains, capital, information and ideas, transportation, and migrants that connect the city to the rest of the world. From its founding in 1630, Boston played a significant trading role in the British Atlantic Empire. The port shipped furs, cod, and lumber to England and Europe. Boston merchants sold food and supplies to the West Indies for the enslaved people who were harvesting sugar. In return, they obtained molasses, which they made into rum and sent to England for manufactured products and to West Africa in exchange for enslaved Africans, who were transported to Caribbean islands to work the plantations. Referred to as the "triangle trade," these were some of the most profitable supply chains of the colonial era. Many of the cities that are considered "global" today, including London, Paris, Lisbon, Amsterdam, and Hamburg, built their economies on similar far-flung colonial trade connections during this era. They developed financial institutions, legal structures, and business customs which continue facilitating commercial exchange today.

After the United States gained its independence, Boston merchants pursued trade the world over, particularly with the rich market of China. During the nineteenth century, Boston was the second leading US port to New York. Boston's maritime trade earned substantial capital, which was subsequently invested in textile mills and railroads, the cutting-edge endeavors of the early industrial age. After the Civil War, manufacturing became the dominant economic activity in New England. Boston remained one of the world's leading entrepôts for wool and cotton, which were the basic materials of New England's textile mills. To support the region's shoe factories, it was a global center for trading and processing animal hides and leather. The port was also a major importer of sugar and molasses from the West Indies for supplying its sugar refining and confectionery industries. The region's manufacturing economy flourished until the 1920s, when textile mills started to move to the South. New England became the first region to experience deindustrialization, a process that was later repeated in other parts of the country. By midcentury, Boston's economic condition and population numbers were in decline, though its academic and medical institutions remained highly regarded. Boston's economic malaise was exacerbated by socio-political struggles between urban ethnic Democrats, who controlled City Hall, and suburban Republicans, who controlled the State House. In the city's neighborhoods, ethnic divisions and racism poisoned efforts at civic cooperation.

The economic picture changed entirely during the 1980s, when globalization kicked into gear, the high-tech knowledge economy began to take off, and an urban revival got underway in Boston and other cities. Metro Boston's per capita income, which ranked jumped #31 in the US in 1980 soared to #4 by 2021.[3] Higher education attracted many of the country and the world's best minds as teachers, researchers, and students. The resultant innovation sectors have made the Boston-Cambridge area a key node in some of the foremost circuits of global knowledge exchange. Life sciences, robotics, 3-D printing, climate technology, and artificial intelligence (AI) are innovation sectors participating in global flows of research and development (R&D) dissemination. Much of the research originates at the foremost universities, particularly MIT, hospitals, and research institutes. Some of the commercialization and manufacturing of technology inventions occurs in the Boston area, but much of it takes place around the world, sometimes under the management of Boston-based companies.

To explicate how innovation ecosystems operate, this book focuses on the area's life sciences (a comprehensive treatment of all of the region's innovation sectors would require a book of its own), with special attention to the global supply chain utilized for developing COVID-19 vaccines. The Moderna, Pfizer, and Beth Israel Deaconess Medical Center/Johnson & Johnson vaccines have been either researched or manufactured in Greater Boston. These efforts exemplify the flows of scientific knowledge and pharmaceutical materials across the world. An integral part of the life sciences story is the supporting ecosystem provided by universities, venture capital, incubator spaces, contract laboratories, law firms, accountants, real estate developers, trade organizations, and government agencies.

Boston also plays an important role in global flows of investment. Its current standing among the world's leading financial centers is based upon decades of wealth accumulation and financial innovation. Boston's greatest claim to financial prominence is its investment management experience. It goes back to the formation of trusts designed to manage wealth gained from the China trade and other mercantile markets. Other financial innovations included investment banks and brokerage houses, such as Kidder, Peabody and Lee, Higginson in the nineteenth century; the invention of mutual funds in the 1920s; and the development of venture capital after World War II. The availability of astutely managed capital provided by varied financial mechanisms in recent years has been a critical factor in Boston's development as an innovation hub.

For investment and economic activity in general to flourish, it is essential to maintain highly efficient flows of information. This book traces the historical evolution of the global information network, as it relates to Boston, from mail service to the telegraph, telephone, wireless/radio to the internet. Today, digital telecommunications have made information, streaming entertainment, music, and inter-personal communication available across the world virtually for free. The book explains the impacts of communications breakthroughs by discussing the contributions of such locally related innovators as Samuel F. B. Morse (telegraph), Alexander Graham Bell (telephone), Ray Tomlinson (person-to-person email), and Tim Berners-Lee (World Wide Web).

The development of modes of transportation from sailing vessels to jet airplanes has also played a fundamental role in facilitating a global reach. Although Logan International Airport has been an international air hub since the beginning of the Jet Age in the 1960s, it reached a new level during the 2010s, when nonstop flights connecting Tokyo, Hong Kong, Seoul, Dubai, Qatar, Istanbul, Panama City, São Paulo, and other far-flung locations were introduced. With a nonstop flight or a single transfer, one can fly to almost any major city in the world from Boston. The availability of flights to and from Boston has fueled both business travel and tourism. With international accessibility and an increasing array of cultural and entertainment attractions, the public has become drawn to global cities like Boston.

Besides tourism, another flow enabled by Logan Airport has been air freight. It has expedited trade for items ranging from high technology to seafood. Massport, the state agency that operates Logan Airport, also manages the Port of Boston and its global container ship facility, which connects to ports around the world.

A different type of global flow comprises immigrants, who have increased in number in recent decades. A 2007 study of the top 25 immigration destinations found that metropolitan Boston ranked #25 in the world and #10 in the United States.[4] Boston has been a major immigrant destination since the mid-nineteenth century. Migration by the Irish, Italians, East European Jews, Chinese, and other ethnic groups reshaped the society of Greater Boston. Since the US Immigration Act of 1965 immigrants from non-European countries, particularly those in Central America, the Caribbean, and East Asia, have settled in Greater Boston. Two types of immigrants reside in global cities like Boston. There are the highly educated and entrepreneurial, who are attracted to innovation and education hubs. These cities are home to the majority of skilled foreign talent in any given country. The second group is made up of less-resourced workers who fill such service jobs as custodians, landscapers, nannies, and restaurant workers. Although immigration is politically controversial, it does provide needed workers and boosts demographic growth. These newcomers play a role in repopulating declining cities and neighborhoods. If it were not for them, Lawrence, Brockton, and other older cities would be distressed and their economies would be stagnant. Immigrants have also made a meaningful impact on local politics, assuming public office and reorienting public policy in recent years. They have contributed to cultural exchange through their ethnic foods and restaurants, their festivals and music.

Besides the flows of people, products, and information, global cities must have supporting infrastructure. Before we note the significant amount of urban infrastructure built in recent decades, it is important to recognize that the functional setbacks of the Massachusetts Bay Transit Authority make a mockery of any "world-class" claims. The physical plant has been deteriorating, and reliability has been on the decline. One hopes that remedial steps being taken by General Manager and CEO Philip Eng are successful and that state government will finally step up and fund the agency at the levels that are necessary to provide the service that a flourishing metro area require. Despite this, Boston has made many infrastructure improvements, including the Boston Convention Center, TD Garden, refurbished and expanded Fenway Park, burial of the Central Artery/I-93 and replacing it on the surface with the Rose Kennedy Greenway, Ted Williams Tunnel, harborfront Institute of Contemporary Art, and gleaming new towers on the skyline. New developments have been springing up all across the metropolitan area. Cambridge's Kendall Square is one of the world's leading centers of technological and biotech R&D. Assembly Row has sprouted in the last decade as a sleek, upscale multi-use district of working-class-bohemian Somerville. In Brighton, the behemoth complex of New Balance, the practice facilities of the Celtics and Bruins, and the headquarters of WGBH looms over the Massachusetts Turnpike. In nearby Allston, Harvard is developing a tech campus emulating MIT's involvement with Kendall Square. New developments combining tech companies, multifamily residences, restaurants, and entertainment can be found in the Ink Block, South Bay, Quincy, Watertown, Everett, and other communities.

The area of Boston that most vividly expresses the forces of globalization is the burgeoning Seaport District. Located directly across the harbor from

Logan International Airport, this area has become a zone for businesses and residents desiring transnational connections. Once covered with warehouses and parking lots, the area provided a tabula rasa for creating a new neighborhood. The Seaport District has adopted a signature "glass box" style of architecture that appeals to multinational corporations. Real estate in the Seaport has become a magnet for foreign investment. Although the Seaport marks Boston as a globally competitive place, its aura is that of an exclusive place that embodies local class and racial divides. To locals it is a cautionary tale about the inequalities that accompany globalization.

All the urban attributes contributing to Boston's case for being a global city described here are tangible. Yet, perceptions are also important in determining a city's international status. Boston's reputation is somewhat unsettled. There are skeptics who wonder how such a relatively small city can be considered "global," in league with New York, Los Angeles, London, and Tokyo. The city of Boston ranks #25 in the country for population (2022), though the Boston metropolitan statistical area (MSA) ranks #11 (2023), never mind how it compares with the surging urban agglomerations in the rest of the world. Observers note that Boston can feel like a "small town." Some might regard this as a handicap, but its moderately-sized scale is probably an advantage, since Boston has a strong sense of face-to-face civic life, one of a handful of American cities with such a quality. Combined with the 30 plus surrounding communities inside the Route 128/I-95 beltway, Boston forms an extensive walkable urbanized fabric. The compact scale of Boston generates energy and makes it easy to "bump and connect," a key element for sharing and testing ideas. As urbanist Jeff Speck contends, "there is mounting evidence that dense, walkable cities generate wealth by sheer virtue of the propinquity that they offer. This is a concept that is both stunningly obvious—cities exist, after all, because people benefit from coming together." Observing the palpable vibrancy in Boston, *Condé Nast Traveler* has opined that it is "a city that's always on the move."

Besides the issue of its size affecting Boston's claim to being a "global city," some might think a reputation for provincialism might also weaken its case. The charge of provincialism covers many shortcomings. It has been reflected in the tribal attachments and prejudices of Boston's neighborhoods and ethnic groups. There are the old jokes about the self-satisfied parochialism of local Brahmins. For example, there was the Beacon Hill matron who, when reproached for her lack of interest in travel, responded, "Why should I travel when I'm already here?"⁵ Such a mindset impeded social and economic progress and played a role in Boston's stagnation during much of the twentieth century. In recent years, the bid to host the 2024 Summer Olympics fell apart, and cynics argued this failure demonstrated that Boston could not be considered a "global city."

Boston's portrayal in films can support the notion of the area's provincialism. Such films as *Good Will Hunting*, *Mystic River*, *The Departed*, and *The Friends of Eddie Coyle* project a gritty, lived-in, working-class persona. Yet these films do not diminish Boston's reputation—they complicate its highbrow image and demonstrate a sense of authenticity that works well in publicizing the area.

As a counterweight to provincialism, there have always been cosmopolitan influences at work in the city and the region. Boston has consistently had dynamic entrepreneurs in science and technology, business, social and health care reform, progressive politics, and intellectual attainment. The impacts of their achievements have been evident across the world. The changing social makeup of the city has also tilted it in a more urbane direction. The deep-seated rivalry between the established Yankees and European ethnic groups has released its grip. Boston is full of newcomers—tens of thousands of college students, all kinds of people seeking to further their careers, immigrants from around the world. Imagine what it means that Michelle Wu, daughter of Taiwanese immigrants could become mayor, after the Irish and, then, Italian American Tom Menino had a lock on the position for a century.

Boston has accomplished a great deal in recent decades. It has been extolled for being the first city to successfully employ "a formula for the post-industrial city."⁶ To continue in this productive vein, it must address the daunting challenges ahead. A significant feature of global cities like Boston is socioeconomic inequality, exemplified by a bifurcated occupational structure with sizable numbers of high-income workers counterbalanced by larger numbers of low-income service workers. Those with "knowledge"—human capital—have a superior position to those with less. Free market libertarianism has played a role in accelerating inequality through tax policies that favor capital accumulation, corporations, and the wealthy, while reducing social support for ordinary citizens. In 1973, the share of the US national income for the wealthiest 1 percent of the population was 9 percent. By 2015, their share had risen to more than 22 percent, reducing the amount of wealth held by the rest of society. People with access to capital have prospered, while wage earners saw their incomes stagnate. The ruptures in the socioeconomic fabric of communities pushed millions of middle- and working-class families into more vulnerable circumstances. There has also been an economic gap between thriving global cities and less competitive postindustrial communities. Richard Florida calls it "winner-take-all urbanism." In Boston, a majority of low-income earners are Black and Latino, reflecting long-term disadvantages for people of color. Metropolitan Boston has been ranked #7 for inequality in the United States, according to the Boston Foundation. Housing costs, which are among the most expensive in the nation, are a significant contributing factor. A major challenge in mitigating the impacts of inequality is increasing the production of housing that can be affordable for all levels of society and promoting homeownership among minorities and the wealth accumulation that accompanies it.

Boston's efforts to create a more equitable and resilient community while maintaining economic prosperity are being imperiled by ominous trends. Transformational advances in communications, transportation, and trade have made it difficult for cities to evade the consequences of troublesome events that arise in other parts of the world. Wars, political unrest in a wide range of countries, and climate change are having global repercussions. Globalization and its benefits, which have accrued to Boston, are being questioned. For the region to maintain its economic vitality and quality of life in the face of such disruptions, it will depend upon how effectively its knowledge-based economy and its capacity for governance adapt to significant challenges within the global context. By stimulating debate about Boston's role as a "global city," this book seeks to prod Boston and its region to constructively appreciate its identity and potential.

CHAPTER 1

What Makes Boston a "Global City"

"We can no longer consider a city global if it is not at the forefront of entrepreneurship and innovation."

A.T. Kearney, *2020 Global Cities Report*

In 1980, the 350th anniversary of Boston's founding, Mayor Kevin White proclaimed that Boston was a "world-class city." As part of the celebration, Mayor White organized the Great Cities of the World Conference to highlight Boston's urban revitalization achievements and discuss strategies for redevelopment with other international cities. Under his mayoralty and that of his predecessors, John Hynes and John Collins, Boston had launched many high-profile projects intended to reverse decades of decline in population and economic vitality. Although many observers declared that older cities were in a downward trajectory, the optimistic Kevin White believed that Boston was turning the corner in a long-term rebirth.

To make his point, Mayor White had the chutzpah to gather mayors and delegations from thirty-six major world cities, including Athens, Hong Kong, Dublin, Paris, Rome, Jerusalem, Bombay, London, Istanbul, and New York, for a week-long conclave held at Faneuil Hall, MIT, and Harvard's Kennedy School of Government. Mayor White's keynote address maintained that Boston had vaulted itself into the category of "great cities" with the widely heralded redevelopment successes of the 1960s and 1970s. Recalling the Puritan admonishment for Boston to be a "city upon a hill," White declared that all the participating cities were striving for that goal.[1]

Some mocked the Great Cities Conference. A *Boston Globe* editorial entitled "A Great Dirty City" read: "Despite all the fancy hotels, the glass highrises, and developments on the drawingboard, Boston is a city run down at the heels. And so long as this is true, maybe Kevin White better scratch all-inclusive references to some kind of worldwide urban renaissance."[2] *Globe* columnist Robert A. Jordan wrote: "Mayor Kevin H. White has shown that he can do two things well—win re-election and make Boston look better to visiting delegations than it really is." He chided White for camouflaging "Boston's social and racial problems, its dirty streets and its poorer neighborhoods," as well as Boston being "an unfriendly, even hostile city."[3] School department employees protested a school budget crisis and poor morale by picketing 350th anniversary events to tell "all of Kevin's friends throughout the world that whatever they think of him, we don't think he's doing a good job for the Boston schools."[4] Criticism even came from outside of Boston. Ada Louise Huxtable, architectural critic for the *New York Times*, registered her own captious reaction: "It takes more than hype from City Hall to make cities great again.... The recent Boston meeting seemed short on urban affairs and long on political hurrah."[5]

The visiting mayors and public officials took away disparate impressions. Jerusalem Mayor Teddy Kollek thought that Boston had developed a template for revitalizing center cities through shopping and entertainment. The deputy governor of Bangkok was impressed by Boston's trees. Montreal Mayor Jean Drapeau was disturbed by the graffiti at Boston's subway stations. Nairobi's mayor was struck by Boston's clean streets. The Parisian deputy mayor thought that Boston still had not "learned the commercial value of making the city comfortable for the pedestrian." A Dakar representative witnessed a fight between a Black youth and a white youth in Harvard Square. The chairman of the Hangzhou Municipal Revolutionary Committee diplomatically praised Boston for its friendliness.[6]

Mayor White sensed important changes were happening to his city. There were such things as "world-class cities"—and he thought that Boston should be part of the discussion. Yet even Kevin White could not have foreseen the remarkable transformations ahead. Just as Boston had been one of the first American cities to industrialize and then suffer the loss of its industries, it became one of the first to adapt to the high-tech and service economies and secure a foothold in the emerging global economy.

WHAT IS A "GLOBAL CITY"?

During the 1980s, supercharged globalization started to impose massive changes on all cities. Flows of international trade, investments, and knowledge exchange multiplied. Multinational corporations utilized advances in telecommunications and computer power to intensify information exchange and organize complex international production processes and supply chains. "First World"-based corporations took advantage of low-cost labor in less developed countries. The deregulation of finance accelerated the flow of capital. Markets for investment, production, and consumption were no longer nationally grounded. By the time that China opened its economy and the Cold War ended, free market capitalism (sometimes referred to as "neoliberalism"), with a minimum of government oversight, was the preferred path for economic development around the world.[7]

Cities that were plugged into globalizing trends benefited enormously. Urban planning professor John Friedmann is credited with identifying, in his 1986 article "The World City Hypothesis," a network of "key cities throughout the world" that were bases for capitalism to manage the global marketplace.[8] Sociologist Saskia Sassen followed with a comprehensive explication of "global cities" in her book *The Global City: New York, London, Tokyo* (1991). She argued that the leading economic activity of global capitalism was no longer manufacturing but the financial and advanced professional services that help manage complex, far-flung economic activities. Large, established cities that already provided many professional and financial services emerged as command-and-control centers for overseeing worldwide economic networks. Sassen initially focused on New York, London, and Tokyo, but also identified Boston, Los Angeles, Chicago, San Francisco, and Washington, DC, as cities involved in propelling the world economy. Some might assume that global cities are synonymous with the enormous megacities and great national capitals, and smaller, knowledge-economy-oriented metropolitan areas like Boston, Seattle, Amsterdam, and Frankfurt would not qualify. This is definitely not the case, as such cities have meaningful global influence. Going further, Sassen and other urbanists have made the point that the urban hierarchy, in which "superstar" cities have the greatest extent of global interactions and influence, goes for cities everywhere. Postindustrial cities, less developed Global South metropolises, all "ordinary cities" also participate in the global economic system and have globally oriented connections.[9]

The term "global cities" is sometimes used interchangeably with "world cities." Yet, some urbanists make a distinction between the two, arguing that "global cities" are defined by the intensity of their participation in contemporary economic networks, while "world cities" have been traditional centers of political power (Washington, DC, and imperial London) and culture (artistic Paris and religious centers such as Rome and Jerusalem), as well as trade. In this book, "global city" is used to hew to Saskia Sassen's definition and to maintain a sense of clarity and consistency.[10]

A primary force behind the development of global cities has been the ascendance of the financial and professional services complex. Financialization of the world's economy has enabled the financial sector to reap super-profits, while the previous preeminent economic function—manufacturing—could not compete in profit-making and has become a subordinate sector. Industrial companies have shrunk in profitability and size, and industrially dominant cities have lost population and status. This has occurred as multinational corporations took advantage of low-cost labor in less developed countries and countries like China became go-to places for setting up supply chains, which were managed from global business centers.

Besides finance and professional business services, the contemporary global economy also depends upon centers of high-tech innovation. These are strategic sites in the global economy which possess dynamic business clusters, strong research institutions, highly educated talent, and transportation and telecommunications infrastructure connectivity to compete globally in the highest value-added economic sectors. These factors enable cities to manage far-flung global supply chains and innovation operations.[11]

According to a 2016 Brookings Institution report, knowledge economy centers have the highest nominal GDP per capita ($69,000) and GDP per worker ($136,000) of any type of city in the world. Between 2005 and 2017, the superstar innovation cities of Boston, San Francisco, San Jose/Silicon Valley, Seattle, and San Diego accounted for 90% of the US innovation sector growth.[12] According to economist Enrico Moretti these global "brain hubs" are where "good jobs and salaries increasingly come from the production of new ideas, new knowledge, and new technologies." Global innovation centers have become so dynamic that, according to Moretti, "attracting a scientist or a software engineer to a city triggers a multiplier effect increasing employment and salaries for those who provide local services."[13]

It is startling how the fortunes of American cities have shifted since the decline of manufacturing and the rise of the knowledge economy. In 1980, only three of the ten wealthiest metropolitan areas in terms of per capita income were located on the East and West Coasts. San Francisco, Seattle, and San Jose were not in the Top 10; Boston and New York were not even in the Top 20. Five of the ten wealthiest metro areas in the country were in Michigan, as the auto industry remained strong, even in the face of Japanese competition. At this time, economic prosperity was more widely distributed in communities across the country than it is today. By 2016, nine of the ten wealthiest cities were located on the coasts, testimony to their heady combination of top-flight research universities and medical centers, dynamic innovation clusters, and

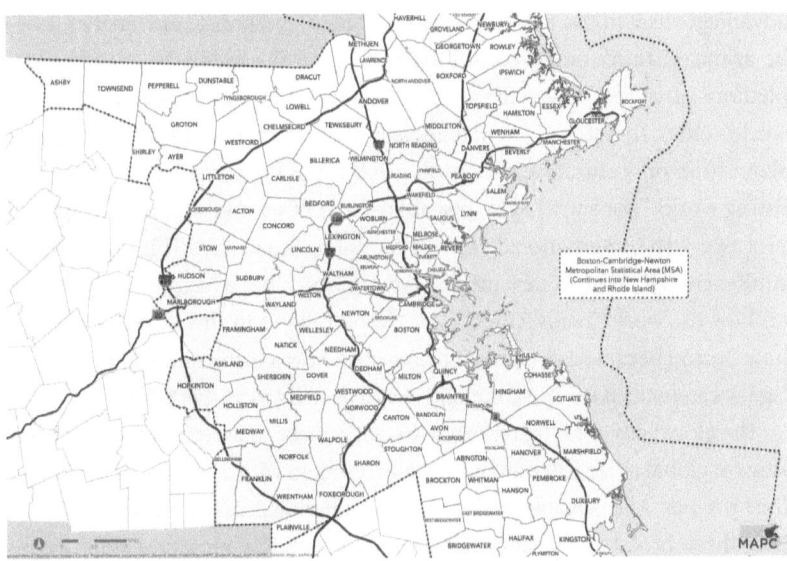

Figure 1. Map of Metropolitan Boston Communities, which are included in the Metropolitan Area Planning Council (MAPC) jurisdiction. Communities considered part of the US MSA stretch beyond these boundaries to the north, west, and south.—Courtesy of Metropolitan Area Planning Council.

flourishing capital finance. Metro Boston's per capita income ranking jumped from #31 in 1980 to #4 in 2021.[14]

The continuation of this trend is not assured, however, as the global economy and political order are entering a new phase beset by major disruptions that are shaking people's faith in the advantages of globalization. Such disruptions are evident in increasing tensions between the US and China, Russia, and other ambitious powers. Other perils include climate change and epidemic disease. These challenges are intensified by the global connectivity that has fueled the rise of global cities. As these threats loom, Boston and other global cities are continuing to pursue success. In this endeavor, it is necessary to understand the factors promoting urban economic and community development and how Boston can maintain its status as a globally influential innovation center.

ASSESSING THE ATTRIBUTES OF GLOBAL CITIES

Cities, nations, and businesses have been scrambling to position themselves advantageously in the new global cities order. In response, universities, public agencies, think tanks, consulting firms, and the media have authored a plethora of studies that evaluate the characteristics and performance of the world's cities. Investors in companies and real estate use these studies to target acquisition opportunities. The most insightful of these studies go far beyond listing world "hot spots," they reveal business flows and urban development processes. The international real estate management firm JLL asserts these studies contribute to a "new urban science," which has a "significant influence on how the world 'reads' cities."[15] This book follows in this vein in exploring how Boston became a global city. It considers how a forthright embrace of this legacy can make it a more competitive and socially inclusive place.

The global city ranking reports are a good place to ascertain the characteristics of global cities. Though they should be taken with a grain of salt, together they provide a reasonable basis for analyzing global cities. These studies fall into three broad categories. The first set of studies measures interactions between cities, tracing trade, capital investment, information exchange, travel, and population movement. These studies track the actual flows of globalization. The second type of reports assesses the production factors that drive economic exchanges and overall urban performance. For an innovation center like Boston, these measures survey institutions of higher education, workforce skills, finance and business services, investment, and governance. The third type compares urban traits that create a supportive environment for global exchange. These studies cover quality of life, local infrastructure, culture, environmental sustainability, and social equity. This book examines Boston's status as a global city in light of key global city attributes identified in these benchmarking studies.

Some of the most suggestive research argues that global cities are defined by their interactions with other cities. These studies follow the lead of urban sociologist Manuel Castells, who has argued, in *The Rise of the Network Society* (1996), that "our society is constructed around flows. Flows of capital, flows of information, flows of technology, flows of organizational interaction, flows of images, sounds, and symbols."[16] In the global "space of flows," major cities are the primary economic control hubs and nodes of the worldwide transportation and information infrastructure.

In 1998, Loughborough University's (UK) GaWC Research Network set out to measure these flows with the first social science-based model depicting the network of world cities. This study traced the provision of corporate services by tracking over 177 million connections between world cities made by 175 leading multinational professional firms. Their services included finance, insurance, legal services, accounting, advertising, management consultancy, real estate, architectural design, engineering, sourcing, and marketing. Some of the most ubiquitous are the Big Four international accounting firms— KMPG, PWC, Deloitte, and Ernst & Young, which maintain a significant presence in most global cities, including Boston. These firms and those in other professional sectors connect cities through workflows involving professional know-how, plans, strategies, and data exchanges.

The GaWC index ranks New York and London as the leading economic centers, followed by Hong Kong, Beijing, Singapore, and Shanghai. Boston ranks #57 out of 708 cities on the volume of global business connections, indicating that Boston is a mid-tier global city in terms of overall business connections. At first blush, this ranking does not look impressive. But GaWC explains that American cities are underrepresented in its study because the US market is so large that domestic exchanges far outpace international transactions. In measuring the connections between world cities, the GaWC report determined that Boston's most intensive business links are with New

York, followed by London, Chicago, and San Francisco. Other cities with which Boston has strong connections include Hong Kong, Paris, Los Angeles, Shanghai, and Sydney.[17]

DHL, the German-based global logistics company, has published some perceptive studies of globalization of its own, subtly making the case for the value of its logistics services. Its *Global Connectedness Index 2016* focuses on international interactions between cities, tracking trade (35% of score), capital investment (35%), information flow (15%), and foreign migrants, tourists, and students (15%). Harvard economist Dani Rodrik has said of DHL's globalization report that "there is no better index that measures the overall global connectedness of nations—encompassing flows of goods and services, capital, people, and information across borders."[18] According to DHL, Boston ranks #58 out of 113 cities on the volume of its international interactions related to trade, capital, information, and people. Boston is in the middling ranking because, like all American cities, it has such a large proportion of domestic market transactions that it is not as reliant upon international connections.

Two of the "people" factors that DHL measures for connectedness are foreign tourists and international students attending local universities. In foreign tourism, Boston ranks #10 for American cities, behind San Francisco (#7), Honolulu (#8), and Houston (#9). The number of foreign tourists (not including Canada and Mexico) visiting the Hub increased from 475,000 to 1.7 million between 1991 and 2017. China and the United Kingdom have been the leading sources for Boston's international visitors. During the 2022–2023 academic year, Massachusetts enrolled 79,751 students from foreign countries, including 20,637 at Northeastern University, 13,281 at Boston University, 7,236 at Harvard, and 5,290 at MIT.[19]

BOSTON'S GLOBAL ROLE AS AN INNOVATION HUB

The GaWCResearch Network and DHL acknowledge that their reports measuring global flows tend to overemphasize giant financial and corporate management centers and underestimate cities that play more specialized functions, particularly related to technological innovation. Boston is a perfect example. It is a world leader in higher education, technological R&D, medicine, and life sciences. Its highly skilled workforce, strong financial and professional services, entrepreneurialism, air transportation and telecommunications infrastructure, and urbane culture have enabled its knowledge economy sectors to thrive. Different factors driving innovation hubs are described below.

Categorizing Innovation Cities

The Brookings Institution's Global Cities Initiative's report *Redefining Global Cities* (2016), which organizes global cities into seven types, places Boston in its "knowledge capital" category. All but two of Brookings's nineteen knowledge capitals are in the United States (including San Francisco, Austin, Washington, DC, and Chicago), with the two others being Stockholm and Zurich. With highly skilled workforces and elite research universities, these cities are at the world's innovation frontier. Brookings points out the knowledge capitals have the best educated workforces and the highest productivity levels. These cities are frequently moderately sized and, because of their wealth, have a desirable quality of life.[20]

Another typology of global cities has been offered by the international commercial real estate services firm JLL's *Universe of City Indices* (2018). The JLL categorization of global cities confirmed the Brookings Institution findings when it classified Boston in its "innovator" group. The eleven other "innovators" include Silicon Valley, Austin, Dublin, Berlin, and Tel Aviv. These cities attract the most real estate investment relative to their economic size, with Boston being the leading destination for external real estate investment. Innovation cities also tend to generate the most per capita airline trips of any type of city. In a 2022 study ranking dynamic innovation hubs, JLL rated Boston #4 for innovation (including tech companies, finance, R&D) and #2 for talent (universities, percentage of college-educated workers, percentage of workers in tech sectors).[21]

Economic Competitiveness

One of the most widely followed global cities reports is the UN-Habitat and Chinese Academy of Social Sciences-produced *Global Urban Competitiveness Report*. UN-Habitat sponsors the study as a means of tracking progress on how cities are achieving the seventeen interlinked Sustainable Development Goals that were adopted by the United Nations in 2015 to guide urban development policies. This biannual study tracks the progress of more than 1,000 world cities in achieving economic and social competitiveness. The most recent report ranked Boston #14 for overall economic competitiveness and #6 for technological innovation and #9 for business environment. The top five most economically competitive cities were New York, Singapore, Tokyo, London, and Munich.[22]

Scientific Research

Metrics that indicate innovation tend to focus on scientific research. The World Intellectual Property Organization, a United Nations agency, ranks Boston #6 in the world for patents and scientific papers. Its *Global Innovation Index* has observed that, if San Jose/San Francisco or the Boston area were countries, they would top most nations' scientific research.[23] Patents and scientific papers signify much of the knowledge being generated in innovation hubs. The flow of ideas is an important driver of Boston's economic performance. Besides the documentary information distributed in reports and studies, technical and business knowledge is exchanged at technology conferences and forums, many of which are held in Boston. Shared workspace, structured knowledge exchange, and informal interactions that are fostered by such entities as the Cambridge Innovation Center and MassChallenge spur much technological innovation. So respected is the reputation of these organizations that cities elsewhere in the world have invited them to open branches in their cities in efforts to replicate Boston's entrepreneurial achievements.

Highly Skilled Talent

Highly trained researchers and entrepreneurs are fundamental to tech innovation sectors. Former New York Mayor Michael Bloomberg maintains that the value of a talented workforce cannot be overemphasized: "Many newly successful cities on the global stage have sought to make themselves attractive to businesses based on price and infrastructure subsidies. Those competitive advantages can work in the short term, but they tend to be transitory. For cities to have sustained success, they must compete for the grand prize: intellectual capital and talent."[24] For advanced industries, lower labor costs are secondary to a skilled workforce.

One of the leaders in recognizing this aspect of economic development has been urban sociologist Richard Florida, author of *The Rise of the Creative Class* (2002). According to Florida, the "creative class" includes educated workers in the knowledge-oriented sectors of business and finance, technology, healthcare, law, education, and architecture and design. He estimated that the American "creative class" numbers 40 million (30% of the United States workforce). Florida has ranked American cities on a Creativity Index, which measures the three "T's"—the key ingredients needed for cities to attract the "creative class": talent (highly trained workers, usually educated at local universities), tolerance (diverse community, with a relatively large LGBTQ population and openness to foreign-born persons), and technology (patents and up-to-date physical infrastructure). The Creativity Index rated Boston #3 in the United States overall, behind Boulder, CO, and San Francisco. Boston came in at #9 for talent, #9 for technology, and #20 for tolerance.

Of the leading US metropolitan areas with adults over 25 having at least a bachelor's degree, Boston (49.3%) ranks #4 behind San Jose (52.7%), San Francisco-Oakland-Berkeley (51.4%), and Washington, DC (51.4%). Harvard economist Edward Glaeser argues that a highly educated workforce is the most important factor for economic development. He points out that the key ingredient in Boston's economic performance over its 400-year history is its skilled, resourceful workforce.[25]

Financial Investment

Another critical element of an innovation city is the availability of financial backing for entrepreneurs. Traditionally, it has been difficult for startup technology businesses to obtain seed financing. Investors usually are seeking to make bets with limited risk. Boston became the first place to develop an approach for investing in risky yet promising startup enterprises. In 1946, officials from MIT, Harvard Business School, and the Boston Federal Reserve Bank formed the American Research and Development Corporation (ARDC) to provide what is considered the first example of venture capital. Since then, the venture capital sector in Boston has played a decisive role in tech development. In 2021 alone, Boston entrepreneurs attracted $35.2 billion in venture capital, ranking only behind San Francisco and New York. A 2023 study by the innovation research consultancy Startup Genome maintains that the key indicators for an urban startup ecosystem are venture capital investment and the maturation of startup companies. For these factors, Boston ranks #6 in the world, following Silicon Valley, London, New York, Los Angeles, and Tel Aviv.[26]

Overall foreign direct investment (FDI) in the United States, much of which is invested in technology and manufacturing companies, is another measure of economic dynamism. Massachusetts trails only California in FDI (2021) with $53.8 billion in investment, following California's $64 billion. These numbers well surpass the next three states: New York ($34.8 billion), Pennsylvania ($30.1 billion), and Illinois ($21.1 billion).[27]

For overall financial clout and expertise, Boston is also well regarded. Since 2005, Z/Yen Partners and the China Development Institute have been publishing the semiannual *Global Financial Centres Index*. This report has continually recognized Boston for its financial sector's capabilities. In 2024, it ranked Boston #22 as an international financial center. Boston has been a leading center for investment management, having invented the mutual fund and playing a significant role in private equity and hedge funds. Fidelity Investments, State Street Corporation, and Putnam Investments are major players in managing investments.[28]

Urban Infrastructure

For a city to flourish in the world economy, it requires more than strong business and innovation sectors. It must have a resilient physical and socioeconomic infrastructure. This is especially important as cities face climate change, economic crises, and health epidemics. Many comprehensive city benchmarking studies take into account a broad range of factors, including such elements as transportation, water and sewer systems, the electric grid, and telecommunications. Boston receives mixed grades for these factors, with the deteriorating public transit service provided by the Massachusetts Bay Transportation Authority being singled out. For example, the *IESE Cities in Motion Index*, which ranks Boston #24 overall as a competitive global city, rates it #109 for mobility and transportation.[29] For these measures, European and Canadian cities tend to surpass US cities, which have not maintained their physical infrastructure at a high functioning level.

Socioeconomic Inequality

A holistic study about global cities is published by Arcadis, an Amsterdam-based global design and engineering firm. Its *Sustainable Cities Index* evaluates the sustainability of 100 leading world cities related to three pillars—People (social mobility, opportunity, and quality of life), Planet (management of energy use, pollution, and emissions), and Profit (business environment and economic performance), each aligned with the United Nations Sustainable Development Goals. At the core of these goals is the concept of "Leave No One Behind," which requires prioritizing the needs of the most vulnerable and impoverished populations. Arcadis tracks several indicators in measuring facets of inequality and suggesting how to remedy social inequities. Boston came out #22 in the 2022 Arcadis *Sustainable Cities Index*. The most sustainable cities are Oslo, Stockholm, Tokyo, Copenhagen, and Berlin. Boston's highest ranking was for "profit" at #3, while it ranked #54 for both "planet" and for "people." "People" factors where Boston has been found wanting include income inequality and housing affordability.

Other studies have picked up on the importance of socioeconomic inequality in affecting the future of cities. Such inequality occurs when there is a sizable number of people earning high incomes in R&D, entrepreneurship, and business services, while a substantial population is working in low-pay services in hospitality, retail, domestic services, and security. Although there are plenty of jobs in the less-skilled services, the cost of living is high in Boston, particularly for housing. The economic stress is consequential. In his book *The New Urban Crisis*, Richard Florida argues that income inequality has become the most serious problem facing cities across the world. He explains that just as cities have been making a comeback, "a host of new urban challenges—from rising inequality to increasingly unaffordable housing and more—started to come to the fore." This created "a new kind of urban crisis."[30] Florida goes on to explain how the lack of affordable housing, transportation failures, and environmental degradation exacerbate inequality in cities.

Concerns about inequality have become so widespread that even the Knight Frank *Wealth Report: The Global Perspective on Prime Property and Investment*, which is targeted toward high-wealth investors, calls out social equity as an issue that the rich should be concerned about, stating that "inequality will fuel risks to wealth accumulation." Surveyed international wealth managers and private bankers "expect the growth in income inequality to fuel demand for policies aimed at curbing imbalance—specifically wealth taxes."[31]

Boston officials and policy mavens are alert to the problems created by inequality. The Boston Foundation Indicators Project, which has been tracking regional socioeconomic indicators since 2000, highlighted the underside of the knowledge economy in *Boston's Booming . . . But for Whom?: Building*

Shared Prosperity in a Time of Growth. The Boston Foundation reported that metropolitan Boston ranks #7 for income inequality in the United States. Housing costs in Greater Boston rank #13 in the nation, with $793,400 (second quarter, 2024) being the price of the median existing single-family house. San Jose was #1 with an astonishing $1.75 million for a single-family home.[32] Income inequality and affordable housing have become central issues in Boston and Massachusetts. There is a clear awareness that the area's socioeconomic weaknesses must be addressed.

City Reputation

A city's "reputation" is also considered to be a factor in analyzing its status. Does a reputation confirm the genuine global connections and influence that a city enjoys? Many evaluations of urban reputations use superficial criteria related to popularity, often conveyed through social media. The international brand management consultancy Resonance's *World's Best Cities Report* is, perhaps, the most scrupulous in its methodology. It gauges city "reputations" using twenty-three indicators, with half being numerical measurements of urban performance and half measuring the popularity of the city's attractions, restaurants, nightlife, culture, and shopping as expressed by visitors and locals on Google, Facebook, Instagram, and Tripadvisor. Resonance believes that travelers and potential residents are attracted to a city more based on subjective opinions and recommendations than by indicators employing hard data. Resonance has rated Boston #24 among the "world's best cities," with a #1 ranking for its higher education and #8 for its GDP per capita. The umbrella category that measures Boston's "relative vibrancy and quality of place," referred to as "lovability," relies upon online recommendations and rates Boston #58. This benchmark, as superficial as it might seem, is worth noting because it reflects how Boston's overall attractiveness as a city does not match the reputation of its universities or the level of its wealth.[33]

The Boston Consulting Group measured the opinions of local residents about their cities in *Cities of Choice: Are People Happy Where They Live?* (2023). Assuming that the world's educated workforce is more mobile than ever, the report set out to was to evaluate the desirability of cities to live in. In its category of thirty "cruiser weight" cities (between three and ten million population), Boston ranked #6. It ranked #6 in both economic opportunities and quality of life and #22 in the interestingly conceived factor of the "speed

Table 1: Global cities ranking studies evaluating Boston

Below are some of the leading global city benchmarking studies that evaluate Boston. To learn about their methodologies and how different cities rate for specific factors, examine individual reports.

Author	Report	Boston Global Ranking with Selected Factors	Other Selected Ranked Global Cities	Focus of Global Cities Studies
Global City Typologies				
Brookings Institution	*Redefining Global Cities* (2016)	1 of 19 "Knowledge Capitals"	"Knowledge Capitals" – Atlanta, Austin, Baltimore, Boston, Chicago, Dallas, Denver, Hartford, Houston, Minneapolis, Philadelphia, Portland, San Diego, San Francisco, San Jose, Seattle, Stockholm, Washington DC, Zurich	Think tank classifies 123 global cities in seven categories by evaluating economic characteristics, tradable clusters, innovation, talent, & infrastructure connectivity.
JLL & The Business of Cities	*The Universe of City Indices* (2018)	1 of 12 "Innovator Cities"	"Innovator Cities" — Austin, Berlin, Denver, Dublin, Milan, Munich, San Diego, Seattle, Silicon Valley, Stockholm, Tel Aviv	Global real estate consultancy identifies ten types of global cities, in which peer groups share similar advantages, sector specializations, talent they seek to attract, and requirements to maintain competitiveness.
Global City Economic Dynamism				
A.T. Kearney	*The 2022 Global Cities Report*	Overall #20 Top Universities #1'	New York #1 London #2 Paris #3 Tokyo #4 Beijing #5	Report analyses capacity of cities to sustain their economies in the face of mounting global crises.

Table 1: Global cities ranking studies evaluating Boston (*continued*)

Author	Report	Boston Global Ranking with Selected Factors	Other Selected Ranked Global Cities	Focus of Global Cities Studies
UN-Habitat & Chinese Academy of Social Sciences	*Global Urban Competitiveness Report* (2021–2022)	Tech Innovation #6 Business Environment #9 Economic Competitiveness #14 Living Environment #15	Tech Innovation: Tokyo #1 Beijing #2 New York #3 London #4 Seoul #5	Report studies urban economic & sustainability competitiveness of 1,000+ cities in achieving UN 2030 Sustainable Development Goals. Most academically rigorous study of urban competitiveness. Published since 2005.
JLL Global Research	*City Momentum Index* (2018)	Future-proofing #5	San Francisco #1 Silicon Valley #2 New York #3 London #4 Los Angeles #6	Global real estate firm analyzes short-term economic "momentum" as well as "future-proofing" to identify desirable cities for their clients' investments.
Knight Frank	*The Wealth Report* (2018)	Overall #13 Future #7 Lifestyle #21	Future: New York #1 London #2 Tokyo #3 Los Angeles #4 Paris #5	International real estate consultant ranks "cities that matter to the wealthy, now and in the future." The report uses composite index for health, wealth, and innovation to identify best cities to invest and live in.
Oxford Economics	*Global Cities Index 2024*	Overall #11 Economics #12 Human Capital #10	Overall: New York #1 London #2 San Jose #3 Tokyo #4 Paris #5	Global business consulting firm ranks 1,000 cities, assessing best places to do business. Ranked factors include economics, human capital, quality of life, governance, & environment.

Author	Report	Boston Global Ranking with Selected Factors	Other Selected Ranked Global Cities	Focus of Global Cities Studies
Schroders	*Global Cities Index 2022*	Overall #2	Overall: San Francisco #1 London #3 New York #4 Melbourne #5	Global asset management company rates strongest economies globally.
Mori Memorial Foundation	*Global Power City Index 2022*	Overall #27 R&D #5 Economy #21 Accessibility to World #28 Cultural Interaction #40 Livability #42	R&D: New York #1 London #2 Los Angeles #3 Tokyo #4 San Francisco #7	Japanese think tank tracks performance of Japanese cities & their global competitors. Assesses economic health, livability, ecology, & cultural interaction with other cities.
IESE Business School, University of Navarra	*IESE Cities in Motion Index (2022)*	Overall #24 Human Capital #2 Economy #12 Governance #15 Technology #29 International Profile #43 Urban Planning #59 Social Cohesion #78 Transportation #109	Human Capital: London #1 New York #3 Washington, DC #4 Paris #5 Los Angeles #6	European business school's *Index* is intended as tool for policymakers to make their cities more efficient, sustainable, & prosperous.
Global Connectedness				
DHL	*DHL Global Connectedness Index 2016*	"Giant Index" (cities with largest international flows) #58	Singapore #1 New York #4 San Francisco #24 San Jose #59 Washington, DC #60	Global logistics firm tracks actual international interactions of cities related to trade, capital investment, information flows, workers, & tourists.

Table 1: Global cities ranking studies evaluating Boston (*continued*)

Author	Report	Boston Global Ranking with Selected Factors	Other Selected Ranked Global Cities	Focus of Global Cities Studies
GaWC	*Globalization and World Cities (GaWC) Research Network* (2018)	Beta+ ("important world cities that are instrumental in linking their region or state into the world economy") #57	London Alpha++ #1 New York Alpha++ #2 Hong Kong Alpha+ #3 Beijing Alpha + #4 Singapore Alpha+ #5	First mapping of global city network, in 1998. GaWC rankings trace provision of corporate services by 175 leading professional service firms, tracking over 177 million connections between pairs of world cities.
Innovation & Talent				
World Intellectual Property Organization (WIPO)	*Global Innovation Index* (2022)	Science & Technology Intensity #6	Cambridge, UK #1 Eindhoven #2 Daejeon, South Korea #3 San Jose-San Francisco #4 Oxford, UK #5	UN organization measures innovation intensity by dividing patent and scientific publication shares by population.
KMPG	*Changing Landscape of Disruptive Technologies* (2018)	Overall #12	Silicon Valley #1 Shanghai #2 Tokyo #3 Bangalore #9 Tel Aviv #9	Multinational accounting firm tracks innovation centers & their industrial clusters.
INSEAD (Institut Européen d'Administration des Affaires)	*Global City Talent Competitiveness Index* 2022	Overall #2 Growing Skilled Workforce #1 Global Knowledge Skills #3 Enabling Workforce #8	Overall: San Francisco #1 Zurich #3 Seattle #4 Lausanne #5 Singapore #6	French business school ranks European cities highest for talent.

Author	Report	Boston Global Ranking with Selected Factors	Other Selected Ranked Global Cities	Focus of Global Cities Studies
Hickey & Associates	*Global Innovation Hubs: 2022 Report*	Overall #1 Biotech #1 Pharmaceutical #1 Nanotechnology #1 Medical Science #4 Fintech #9 Aerospace #9	Overall: San Francisco #2 Los Angeles #3 Seattle #4 New York #5 London #6	As a global leader in business location strategy & logistics/supply chains, Hickey evaluates cities with the greatest innovation potential.
JLL Global Research	*Innovation Geographies; Resilience and Recovery (2022)*	Innovation #4 Talent Concentration #2	Innovation: San Jose #1 Tokyo #2 San Francisco #3 Talent: San Jose #1 New York #19	Future-oriented analysis of 100+ cities identifies leading innovation ecosystems & talent hubs.
Startup Genome	*Global Startup Ecosystem Report 2022*	Overall #4	Silicon Valley-San Francisco #1 New York #2 (tie) London #2 (tie) Beijing #5 Los Angeles #6	Measures factors that create dynamic urban startup ecosystems, focusing on venture capital and maturation of startup companies.
Z/Yen Group	*Smart Centres Index 6 (2022)*	Overall #6 Innovation Support #6 Creative Intensity #10 Delivery Capability #6	Overall: New York #1 London #2 Zurich #4 Cambridge, UK #7 San Francisco #9	Employs 134 factors to evaluate Innovation Support, Creative Intensity, and Delivery Capability.

Table 1: Global cities ranking studies evaluating Boston (*continued*)

Author	Report	Boston Global Ranking with Selected Factors	Other Selected Ranked Global Cities	Focus of Global Cities Studies
Financial Sector				
Z/Yen Partners with China Development Institute	*The Global Financial Centres Index 33* (2023)	Overall #9 Human Capital #6 Financial Sector Development #8 Business Environment #9	Overall: New York #1 London #2 Frankfurt #17 Tokyo #21 Zurich #22	Leading financial center ranking, undertaken by entities crafting financial development strategies.
Livability & Urban Planning				
Arcadis	*Arcadis Sustainable Cities Index: Prosperity beyond Profit* (2022)	Overall #22 Profit (economic) #8 Planet (environmental) #29 People (social) #44	Overall: Oslo #1 Paris #2 Stockholm #3 Copenhagen #4 Berlin #5	Amsterdam-based consulting firm promotes sustainable design with its evaluation of city sustainability based on reinforcing economic, social, & environmental factors.
Economist Intelligence (EIU)	*The Global Liveability Index 2022: Recovery and Hardship*	Overall #45	Vienna #1 Copenhagen #2 Atlanta #26 Chicago #41 San Francisco #46	Analyzes 172 cities for stability, healthcare, culture & environment, education, & infrastructure. The quality of public transport & the high cost of healthcare & housing marks US cities down, with Atlanta being the leading US city.

Author	Report	Boston Global Ranking with Selected Factors	Other Selected Ranked Global Cities	Focus of Global Cities Studies
Resonance	*World's Best Cities: A Ranking of Global Place Equity 2024*	Overall #24 Universities #1 GDP per Capita #8	London #1 Paris #2 New York #3 Dubai #6 San Francisco #7	Resonance report advises "where to live, work, invest and visit." Report gauges city "reputations" subjectively with twenty-three factors, with thirteen related to popularity of the city's attractions, restaurants, etc. on Google, Facebook, Instagram, and Tripadvisor.
Boston Consulting Group	*Cities of Choice: Are People Happy Where They Live?* (2023)	("Cruiser Weights" category, 3–10 million pop.) Overall #6 of 30 Interactions with Authorities #3 Speed of Change #22	"Cruiser Weights" Washington DC #1 Singapore #2 San Francisco #3	Interviewed 50,000+ people in 79 world cities on factors affecting satisfaction with their cities. Report analyzed increasing mobility of people between cities based on desirability.

Source: Reports that have been identified.

of change."[34] This finding demonstrates that Bostonians, while well aware of their prosperity, recognize that their city could slip from its perch as an innovation hub if municipal and state government ploddingly attempt to tackle the most pressing problems.

The global city benchmarking reports cited here sketch out a framework for analyzing Boston's status in the global network of cities. The following chapters will pursue the story by examining each of topics the reports have identified. These discussions will provide a composite view of Boston and its status in the world, with an evaluation of its current strengths and vulnerabilities.

CHAPTER 2

The Port of Boston: Gateway to the Global Economy

"The past and present are reminders that all cities enter globalization with their own unique set of assets, and must pursue global opportunities from that basis, rather than copying other cities."

Brookings Institution, *The 10 Traits of Globally Fluent Metro Areas*

Globalization, in the sense of worldwide trade, started with demonstrations by Columbus, Magellan, and other European explorers that all parts of the world were available for economic enterprise. The seafaring European nations of England, Portugal, Spain, Holland, and France were galvanized to develop trade routes, ports, and colonies on all continents.[1] Boston, established in 1630, quickly became an English colonial port, planting the seeds of its destiny as a global city.

Even though its Puritan founders considered Boston to be a model Christian commonwealth, it was formally governed as a crown corporation under the charter of the Massachusetts Bay Company. This company was established to finance the new colony while providing profits for its shareholders. Beginning during the reign of Queen Elizabeth I, the English Crown utilized private joint-stock companies like the East India Company to promote trade around the globe. The settlers of New England relied upon financing from the London-based stockholders as well as investors who were migrating to New England. From the settlement's establishment, Boston and other budding

New England communities supported themselves by providing building materials and domestic supplies to the thousands of new immigrants fleeing the Stuart monarchy in England. The rise of a Puritan-dominated Parliament and the coming of the English Civil War in the 1640s ended the flow of immigrants, necessitating the Puritans to come up with alternative products that they could trade to the mother country for manufactured goods to sustain their colony.

The settlers at Boston took advantage of the commodious and well-protected harbor to develop an economy based on international trade. The New England landscape was unsuitable for growing high-value agricultural commodities like the tobacco of Virginia or sugar of Barbados. The first exports were dried fish, which were traded to Spain and Portugal for wool that could be sold in England. Beaver pelts acquired from Indian trappers, which were used in making coats and hats, were another export product. The big breakthrough took place in the 1640s, when the Puritans discovered a market in the West Indies.

Sugar was emerging as the premier cash crop on Barbados and, later, Jamaica, Antigua, Nevis, St. Kitts, and Montserrat. The British increased sugar imports from the Caribbean a hundred-fold between 1660 and 1717. The British, both in Europe and America, consumed large amounts of sugar in rum, molasses, hot drinks, and pastries. In 1731, the Royal Navy adopted a policy of serving a half pint of rum daily to seamen.[2] Essential to sugar cultivation, which entailed grueling labor-intensive work, was the enslavement of thousands of Africans. Boston recognized it could profit from the sugar trade by selling food and supplies for the enslaved workers. The first New England export to the West Indies was dried cod, which was caught off the Grand Banks. So profitable was the codfish trade with Caribbean and Catholic Europe that, in the late eighteenth century, the Massachusetts state government hung a five-foot carved wooden cod in the legislative chambers. The "Sacred Cod" still hangs in the State House.

New England ship captains discovered that they could transport enslaved Africans to Caribbean islands and carry sugar to Europe, while supplying the Sugar Islands with food, clothing, and work implements for the enslaved labor force along with lumber and manufactured European goods. The colonial shipping arrangements became known as the "triangle trade." With sugar—"white gold"—being the most profitable commodity imported from the New World, it made no economic sense to dedicate land in the West Indies to cultivating food for enslaved persons, so the planters imported low-quality dried fish, corn, and meat from New England. With thousands of enslaved Africans in the West Indies by the late seventeenth century and over 1.2 million transported there between 1700 and 1775, there was an enormous market to be served by Boston (also by New York and Philadelphia).[3] This arrangement benefited Boston because the revenues obtained from selling provisions in the West Indies allowed for purchasing manufactured goods from England (the colonies were prohibited from manufacturing many products by the British Navigation Acts). Massachusetts also had enslaved Africans of its own, with about 400 in the 1720s and 1,400 by the 1740s (6.5% of the population).[4]

New England made a specialty of building and supplying ships. As early as 1631, shipwrights were building vessels at harbors along the coast, including Boston, Medford, Salem, Gloucester, Ipswich, and Newburyport. These ships transported people and supplies between England and its colonies. They carried on the triangle trade, and they formed the fishing fleet. The high quality of building materials, including pine for spars and masts and oak timbers for the ship bodies, attracted markets in England and other colonies for New England shipbuilders.[5]

Massachusetts and other British American colonies were deeply enmeshed in capitalist trading and credit networks centered on the mother country. During the colonial period, there were no banks or standardized investment vehicles as we know them. Trading enterprises were financed through partnership arrangements with other Atlantic world merchants and investors. As they built these relationships, New England merchants discovered that conducting trade could be an exportable service. According to economic historian Mary Ellen Newell: "Carrying cargoes for other colonies and nations netted ship owners extra profits. Processing foreign goods for re-export created yet more value, and New Englanders became expert at turning waste products such as molasses into cash commodities like rum. In this way, New England's very lack of a staple proved to be a long-term economic advantage."[6]

Mark Peterson maintains that "the pursuit of overseas trade *was* Boston, or at least an indispensable part of it. . . . Boston required the freedom for its merchants to act as though Massachusetts were a free state, trading not just as a colonial dependency within England's mercantile system, but widely across the empires of the Atlantic world." Peterson goes on to argue that Boston developed the identity of a "city-state," with a hinterland that embraced all of New England. This mindset originated at the colony's settlement, when the

Puritans carried the royal charter of the Massachusetts Bay Company with them to the New World instead of leaving it in London, where corporators there would oversee the colony, under the shadow of the Crown and Parliament. This action allowed the Boston-based corporators to take charge of the governance of the new colony. The Puritans got used to governing themselves, with the Crown making intermittent efforts to direct local policy. Peterson asserts that Boston's sense of autonomy became so strong that it persisted from the establishment of the United States government during the Revolution right up until the Civil War.[7]

In theory, Boston merchants were constrained by the British Navigation Acts, which required all of the colonies' imports to originate in Britain and be transported on British ships. These laws were not strictly enforced because of Boston's remoteness. Along the routes of the triangle trade, Boston ship captains traded with other countries, including possessions of the French, Dutch, Portuguese, and Spanish Empires. This experience demonstrated Boston's global commercial reach. When Parliament tried to exert more stringent control over the colony's free-wheeling trading during the 1760s, it generated tensions that fueled the Revolutionary War. John Hancock, one of Boston's

Figure 2. "Boston, Capital of the United States of North America." This French engraving of Boston Harbor was made in 1778 to depict the supposed "capital"— Boston—of the new country that the French government had made an alliance with in support of American independence. Notice the ship flying the flag of the thirteen "Stars and Stripes."—Image copyright © The Metropolitan Museum of Art. Image source: Art Resource, NY.

richest merchants, ran afoul of the British government by smuggling Dutch tea and Portuguese wines into Boston. When British officials impounded one of his ships and charged him with smuggling, it infuriated Bostonians, who believed the Parliament was interfering with their traditional mercantile practices. Such enforcement actions combined with increased taxation levies ultimately pushed the colony to rebel against British rule.

Besides producing a wide array of goods for the West Indies and outfitting ships, the triangle trade prodded the development of a nascent global financial network, as merchants sought capital investment, insurance, and legal assistance. They engaged correspondents across the Atlantic world to provide credit, dispose of cargo, collect debts, and provide reliable news about crops, prices, weather, and politics.[8]

Massachusetts was ingenious at financial innovation. Flouting the Crown's monopoly on minting currency, the Massachusetts General Court, in 1652, became the only colony to coin its own currency. It was intended to circulate only in New England. The Puritan settlers desired small coins, namely silver shillings, to facilitate local exchange because its economy was based on numerous face-to-face exchanges. Mark Peterson has argued that, because of the availability of local currency, New England residents "may have been more deeply enmeshed in market enterprises, producing goods for overseas marketing and in need of ready cash to pay for imported goods, than their counterparts in England."[9] Another financial initiative originating in Boston was issuing insurance for ocean voyages against storms, piracy, and losses at sea. Joseph Marion started a maritime insurance business in 1724. He organized wealthy Boston merchants to pool their resources to insure their voyages instead of relying on London and the likes of Lloyd's for maritime insurance.

URBAN COMPETITION

From its early years, Boston's leading North American competitor port was New York. The Dutch founded their New Amsterdam trading post four years before Boston's establishment, in 1626, when Governor Peter Minuit obtained Manhattan Island from the Indians. The English and Dutch settlements were very different places. As the Massachusetts Bay Colony was intended to be a model Christian community, it attracted thousands of Puritan settlers from England. Within less than a decade, they had established communities in

Connecticut, Rhode Island, and New Hampshire. The Puritans had long-term settlement ambitions. Meanwhile, the Dutch West India Company was basically interested in trading with the Indians, mainly for furs. The company had outposts at New Amsterdam and farther up the Hudson River at Fort Orange (later Albany). The Dutch established a fortified trading post on the Connecticut River at today's Hartford, CT, but were quickly pushed out by aggressive Puritans. The English also settled the eastern part of Long Island, leaving the western part, near New Amsterdam, to the Dutch.[10] The New England towns were homogeneous communities grounded in radical religious dissent, while Dutch villages had a disparate mix of people from different ethnic backgrounds, classes, and religions. In 1664, New Amsterdam was seized from the Dutch by the English Duke of York (subsequently King James II) and was renamed New York. Even though New York became an English colony, it maintained its heterogeneous society and ambitious trading spirit, which has shaped its development ever since.

Boston was the leading population and trading center of the British colonies through most of the colonial era. After London and Bristol, it was the third most important port in the British Empire. As of 1700, Boston port supported 1,000 ships and 63 wharves. The town's population grew from 1,200 inhabitants in 1640 to approximately 4,500 by 1680. A burst of growth brought the population to 6,000 by 1687 and 12,000 by 1720. The number of residents peaked in 1740 at 17,000.[11] During the years leading up to and during the Revolution, Boston's trade was brought to a standstill and the population shrank. Philadelphia and New York caught up to Boston in population. New York grew from 13,046 in 1756 to 21,863 in 1771, picking up business that Boston was losing in its struggles with the British Crown. New York's trade with the West Indies eventually surpassed Boston's partly because it was located a one-week sail closer to Barbados and ten days closer to Jamaica.[12] Coming out of the American Revolution, Boston, in 1790, had only 18,320 people compared with Philadelphia's 42,520 and New York's 33,131. Though Boston grew and prospered during the antebellum period, its population was 61,392 in 1830 and 177,840 in 1860 compared with New York's 202,589 and 813,669 and Philadelphia's corresponding 86,462 and 565,529 people during the same years.

The great East Coast cities—Boston, New York, Philadelphia, and Baltimore—in the years between the Revolution and the Civil War, gained their wealth as commercial ports, shipping and merchandising a wide range of goods. As merchants scoured the globe for products that Americans wanted to buy, they needed goods to trade with international destinations. This usually meant natural resources and agricultural products, as American-manufactured products tended to be less competitive with European-made products.

By the 1820s, New York asserted its commercial primacy as the middleman, through which most cotton from the South and grain from the North and Midwest passed on its way to Europe. In return, New York funneled capital, labor in the form of immigrants, and manufactured and cultural goods to the rest of the United States.[13] New York merchants shipped raw cotton bales from the major southern ports of Charleston, Savannah, and New Orleans through their city on its way to the great British cotton textile port of Liverpool to feed England's voracious textile mills. Gotham also tapped into the hinterland of Upper New York State and the Great Lakes for grain, at first, and manufactured goods as Upper New York State grew. The key to developing this market was the opening of the state-financed Erie Canal in 1825. The canal connected the Hudson River with Buffalo and Lake Erie. Philadelphia and Baltimore also built canals and, later, railroads to tap the markets west of the Allegheny Mountains

Boston, with its limited New England hinterland, never had an easily exportable supply of products to send to other countries. During the colonial era, Boston scraped together furs, fish, lumber, and whatever else it could trade for—sugar from the West Indies, slaves from Africa, wool from Spain, and manufactured goods from England. After the achievement of American independence, Boston, with neighboring Salem, opened up trade with China, India, Russia, and Latin America.[14] The admonition to their captains was to "try all ports." The initial China-bound commodity was sea otter furs acquired from Indigenous people in the Pacific Northwest. To obtain the furs, Boston merchants traded copper, iron tools, nails, and clothing. The furs were transported to China to exchange for tea, porcelain, and silk. When the supply of otter furs became depleted, Boston merchants started shipping opium from India and the Ottoman Empire.

Perhaps the most extraordinary export was ice. Frederic Tudor, a merchant trading with the West and East Indies, needed ballast to fill his ships because Boston lacked exportable staples. He used rocks from Boston's Harbor Islands and ice cut from its frozen ponds. Tudor discovered that ice could be a marketable commodity in warm climates when he made a shipment to French Martinique in 1806. Tudor gradually increased shipments of ice to the Caribbean. He used sawdust to insulate the ice in his ship's hold. A trip as far as

Calcutta, which lasted more than four months, lost only about one-third of the cargo to melting. Calcutta residents were dazzled by first shipment of New England ice, but, when the ice melted, they requested a refund. The remaining ice was bought up by European expatriates, who used it to chill their drinks. The ice trade grew so much that, by the 1850s, Boston ice exporters were shipping 140,000 tons of ice each year to Calcutta, Bombay, and Madras.[15]

Ice and other Boston exports allowed the city to dominate American trade with India until the Civil War. As late as 1857, 96 of 110 ships sailing from Calcutta to the United States were bound for Boston. The cargoes of these ships were varied, as evidenced by an 1826 voyage of William H. Boardman, Jr's *Arabella*, which shipped to Calcutta such motley products as cigars, paint, currant jelly, shaving soap, cider, oakum, ham, pineapple, and cheese. The Works Progress Administration guide *Boston Looks Seaward* described this approach of opportunistically trading different types of cargoes as "the many-cornered and unspecialized trade typical of the period."[16]

The world was Boston's mercantile oyster. The first voyage to Buenos Aires took place in 1791. A decade later, William P. White established a trading operation there. The leading nineteenth-century merchant trading with Argentina was Samuel B. Hall, who operated as many as forty-six ships. Hall exchanged manufactured goods and lumber for hides, wool, and sheepskin used to manufacture shoes and textiles. On the Pacific Coast, at Valparaiso, Chile, Boston merchants obtained copper ore, nitrates, wool, hides, and goatskins in exchange for soap, lumber, candles, kerosene, refined sugar, boots, shovels, picks, machines, textiles, and pianos.[17]

Boston ships were actively trading in the Mediterranean after Barbary pirates were pacified in the early 1800s. They traded textiles and rum for dried fruits, wines, wool, corkwood, and olive oil. Smyrna, in Turkey, was the leading Mediterranean market for obtaining figs, coarse wool, carpets, and, for the China trade, opium. St. Petersburg and other Baltic ports traded hemp and Swedish steel for West Indies sugar, cotton, whale oil, and manufactured goods, and cotton.[18]

The China trade was one of the greatest generators of fortunes in Boston. Maritime historian W.H. Bunting wrote that it ranked "among the most durable and influential sources of capital in American history." Canton, which was the only Chinese port open to foreign merchants, had warehouses referred to as "factories" where America and seagoing European countries were able to trade their goods for those of China. The wealthiest merchant of early nineteenth-century Boston was Thomas Handasyd Perkins. His nephew John Perkins Cushing managed his business in Canton for twenty-five years. Besides trading goods, Cushing owned and sold ships, provided insurance and banking services, and kept accounts for other merchants. He played a significant role in developing strategies for smuggling opium into China and manipulating the opium market to sideline competitors.[19] After he returned to America in 1828, he became the wealthiest man in the country. He gradually shifted his investments out of foreign trade and into textile mills, railroads, municipal bonds, and other domestic investments. Perkins nephews John Murray Forbes and Robert Bennet Forbes also made fortunes in the China trade. Robert was a sea captain, who managed the opium business. John Murray used his Canton-earned nest egg to branch out into railroad development after returning to America. The experience of the Perkins family and other China traders demonstrates how global maritime investments provided experience in entrepreneurship and worldwide financial connections, which proved valuable in future foreign and domestic investment dealings.

The physical configuration of Boston's harborfront reflected the growing international importance of the port. Substantial wharves proliferated along the shoreline at the city center, Charlestown, East Boston, and South Boston. Architect Charles Bulfinch's Commercial Wharf (1819) featured a one-quarter-mile-long, three-story brick warehouse with three large auction rooms, multiple counting rooms, and fifty-four wholesale stores.[20] Ships set sail from there to the Caribbean, Cape of Good Hope, China, and (Mexican) California. India Wharf served ships destined for India, China, and southern US ports. Ships sailed from Russia Wharf to the Baltic. The Granite Wharf, the first all-stone dock, served ships bound for the East Indies and South America. Frederic Tudor's Wharf in Charlestown shipped ice to warmer climates. Along all the harbor's wharves there were immense warehouses, many of them built of brick and granite blocks, where goods were stored and products were assembled.[21]

The scope of Boston's global trade was exemplified by S.S. Pierce, the region's foremost grocer and importer of fine foods. Samuel Stillman Pierce, with Eldad Worcester, established a firm supplying food provisions to ships setting sail from Boston. Down on the docks, Pierce bartered with ship captains to bring him foreign food products, which he sold to Boston consumers. He billed himself in the 1831 Boston city directory as "a dealer in East India goods."[22] In the barter exchange, Pierce often offered New England rum. Very quickly, the firm established itself as a leading food importer and grocer in the city and, later, across the country. Pierce started publishing a catalog that pioneered the marketing of imported foods, wines, spirits, and tobacco products. The catalog was published continuously until the 1960s. The company popularized Russian caviar, French paté, macaroni and lasagna from Italy, pineapple from Singapore, Russian reindeer tongues, java and mocha beans from Arabia, Chinese teas, French and German wines, and Havana cigars. The S.S. Pierce catalog grew from 265 items in 1849 to over 5,000 by 1910. Gradually, S.S. Pierce moved beyond bartering with ship captains and established formal importing arrangements with foreign merchants. For example, S.S. Pierce maintained a close trading relationship with the noted Bordeaux winemaker A. de Luze et Fils starting in the 1840s. The wines were shipped in casks. S.S. Pierce employees would bottle the wine for consumers. The company was said to have introduced more international grocery products to America than any other business.[23]

Like its East Coast rivals, Boston looked to the West as a source of exportable products. During the 1820s, business leaders considered building a canal to the Hudson River, but the elevations reaching up to 3,000 feet in the Berkshires and Taconics posed a daunting engineering challenge. Boston businessmen became early adopters of the new-fangled steam railroad, opening the first westward stretch of track to Worcester in 1834. Eight years later, the Western Railroad connected Worcester with Albany and the Hudson River, with rail connections on to Buffalo. This put Boston a decade ahead of its East Coast rivals in reaching the West by railroad. In 1844, the Western Railroad carried 300,000 barrels of flour to Boston, increasing to 515,000 barrels three years later.[24] Much of these cargoes were exported from the port. Boston's business acumen, resourceful sea captains, and advanced shipping supply and maintenance infrastructure enabled it to thrive as America's second port to New York until after the Civil War. Philadelphia and Baltimore focused less on foreign exports and more on serving the agricultural and mining sectors of their hinterlands and building up their own industries. Robert Albion, in *The Rise of New York Port, 1815–1860*, observed: "Boston, of all the cities in the United States, was least likely to come under New York's domination because it was exceedingly enterprising itself.... Boston was the only port to compete strongly in New York's specialty of importing. In some regions, such as the Baltic, the Levant, and India, it traded more heavily than New York throughout our period."[25]

Between 1821 and 1860, Boston handled 21.9% of US foreign exports and 15.7% of imports, while New York processed 58.6% of foreign exports and 60.3% of imports. During this period, Boston's share of US imports declined from 22% to 11%, while New York's increased from 37% to 68%. Boston's proportion of exports dropped from 18% to 4%, while, New York's exports expanded from 18% to 36% (Table 2). These numbers indicate that Boston ships continued to bring in a wide range of cargoes from markets across the globe, while New England products had difficulty finding significant foreign markets. New England's burgeoning industrial production mainly served the domestic market.[26]

Table 2. United States, Boston, and New York imports and exports, 1821–1860

Imports	US	Boston	New York
1821	$62 million	$14 million (22%)	$23 million (37%)
1840	$107 m	$16 m (15%)	$60 m (56%)
1860	$362 m	$41 m (11%)	$248 m (68%)
Total Percentage, 1821–1860	—	15.7%	60.3%
Foreign Exports			
1821	$64 m	$12 m (18%)	$13 m (18%)
1840	$132 m	$10 m (7%)	$34 m (25%)
1860	$400 m	$17 m (4%)	$132 m (36%)
Total Percentage, 1821–1860	—	21.9%	58.6%
Immigrants	—	7.1%	68.6%

Source: Robert G. Albion, in *The Rise of New York Port, 1815–1860*.

New England played a major role in developing New York's port. New York lacked sufficient experienced ship captains, crews, and counting-house support to expand its shipping activities. It drew this talent from New England, especially from Connecticut. Albion explained: "New Englanders captured New York port about 1820 and dominated its business until after the Civil War. . . . They built and commanded most of the ships engaged in New York's ever-increasing commerce. They were, moreover, the leaders among the merchants and shipowners who set those ships in motion and made fortunes from their goings and comings."[27]

Boston's commercial experience entailed the development of sophisticated business services, including banking, insurance, accounting, legal services, and business management. This stood the city in good stead for developing additional business ventures to maritime trade. Boston was a major center for shipbuilding. The swift, three-masted, clipper ships its shipyards built marked the apogee of the Age of Sail. Clipper ships could sail 250 miles a day, while conventional schooners sailed 150 miles. The clippers were designed to carry high-value products, like tea from China or mining, construction, and domestic supplies to California during the Gold Rush. The country's foremost builder of clipper ships was Donald McKay, whose East Boston shipyard built the fastest clipper ships between 1845 and the Civil War. His *Flying Cloud* set the record for the fastest time for a sailing vessel (which lasted until 1989)—from New York to San Francisco in eighty-nine days and eight hours. McKay's *Great Republic* was the largest wooden clipper ship ever built. Of the 350 clipper ships built in the United States between the 1840s and the 1860s. Boston built 140 and owned 163, while New York shipyards built 53 clippers and owned 116.[28]

Boston was also a pioneer in steamship travel, which supplanted sailing vessels during the mid-nineteenth century. Because the early steamships were expensive to operate, they required a subsidy to sail from Europe to North America, which the British government provided to facilitate delivery of the mails. Samuel Cunard's North American Royal Mail Steam Packet Company inaugurated the first regularly scheduled transatlantic steamship mail and passenger service in 1840, between Liverpool and Boston. Cunard chose Boston as the first American destination because it was a day closer to Britain and the Halifax native had trained in a Boston counting house. Cunard's *Britannia* departed Liverpool on July 4, 1840, both Samuel Cunard's and America's birthday. The ship arrived fourteen days later, including a stop in Halifax, amid general rejoicing at the East Boston waterfront. Steamships could travel 3½ times faster than sailing ships, and they were not prey to the caprices of the winds.[29] Going forward, Cunard used a fleet of four steam sidewheelers to ensure that his ships departed on schedule every two weeks.

New York caught up with Boston, when Cunard introduced service between Liverpool and New York in 1848. The United States government wanted to encourage American-owned shipping lines and provided a mail subsidy to the New York-based Collins Line, which began competition with the Cunard Line two years later. New York soon surpassed Boston as the primary American gateway for passenger and freight ships. An important factor was New York's more enthusiastic embrace of steamships than Boston. By 1857, Boston's steamer tonnage was 8,100 compared to New York's 84,662 tons.[30] Boston was a dominant force in the Age of Sail, a peer of such maritime centers as Amsterdam, Hamburg, and Bristol; but it lost the comparative advantage provided by its skilled sailing workforce when steamships became widespread.[31]

THE POST-CIVIL WAR PORT

Boston's glory days as a sailing port ebbed after the Civil War. Though international trade declined, coastal trade, much of it on sailing ships, still thrived, carrying commodities like sugar, coal, wool, grain, and lumber. The city's economy was transitioning from being an opportunistic entrepôt to being oriented to manufacturing and serving the booming domestic market. Boston's railroads played a transformative role. The city upgraded its harbor by dredging it and laying railroad tracks to docks along the waterfront. The New York & New England Railroad (subsumed by the New Haven Railroad in 1898) bought 2.5 million square feet of South Boston tidal flats from the Boston Wharf Company and gradually filled them, developing rail yards that facilitated inland transport of goods landed at Fan Pier. Other railroad companies built tracks to wharves in East Boston and Charlestown. Railroads connecting Boston to the Midwest farm belt made the city a major exporter of beef and grain.[32]

Though its international trade was in decline, growing domestic and Canadian shipping drove Boston's port growth. In 1900, its $180 million in foreign trade surpassed #3 Baltimore by 50%.[33] Boston Harbor played a pivotal role in the global supply chain for wool and leather. The entrepôt obtained the materials for the region's leading industries—raw wool from England and Australia for textiles (it became the world's second largest wool market after London) and animal hides from India, Turkey, South America, and Australia for leather and shoes. Boston maintained its role as America's second busiest port into the 1920s.[34]

The importance of this global trade is physically displayed in the Fort Point Channel warehouse district. The Boston Wharf Company built out this district primarily between the 1880s and 1915 (the company filled the harbor mudflats of the Fort Point area between 1837 and 1882). Today, more than eighty of the original five- to nine-story masonry loft buildings remain extant. During their heyday, which lasted up through World War II, the dense ensemble of warehouse structures provided infrastructure for Boston to function as an international port and manufacturing center. The lofts stored, processed, and distributed sugar and molasses, wool, and leather, usually brought by ship and sent on via rail. So important was the wool trade that half of all the loft space in the Fort Point Channel district was devoted to the industry through the 1940s (by 1963, wool warehousing had virtually disappeared in Fort Point).[35]

One of the most profitable mercantile enterprises was started by Cape Codder Lorenzo Dow Baker, who brought in Boston's first cargo of bananas, from Jamaica in 1870. The fruit was so popular that Baker ended up creating a major import business, with bananas becoming known as the first "global fruit." In 1885, Baker joined with produce wholesaler Andrew Preston to form the Boston Fruit Company, which undertook trade operations in Jamaica, Cuba, and Santo Domingo. Fourteen years later, Boston Fruit Company merged with the businesses of Minor C. Keith, which operated banana plantations in Costa Rica, Colombia, and Panama and ran steamships to Central and South America, into the United Fruit Company. During the late nineteenth century, steamship improvements drastically reduced the cost of freight shipment, which resulted in lower food prices, creation of a global food market, and, ultimately, a revolutionized human diet.

The development of the United Fruit Company in Boston is a surprising occurrence because Boston was the most distant from the Caribbean of United States banana ports.[36] The city is between 1,400 and 2,400 miles away from banana-growing regions. In cold weather, bananas freeze and go bad, so Boston originally could not match a warm-water port like New Orleans. Yet the Yankee canniness of Preston and Baker built their enterprise into a virtual banana monopoly through developing a superior supply chain and capably exploiting consumer markets. Baker, who spent a lot of time at his plantation in Jamaica, was in charge of the shipping, while Preston, from his perch at the head of Boston's Long Wharf, secured distribution channels and created a vertically integrated corporate structure. The company had the fastest and the earliest refrigerated ships plying the Caribbean. In 1901, Preston developed a relationship with British importers Elder and Fyffes to provide them with bananas. Within the decade, Elder and Fyffes became a United Fruit subsidiary, distributing bananas across Europe as far as Russia.

In order to ensure a steady supply of bananas, the Boston-based fruit merchants established plantations, built railroads in Central America to bring the products to port, and maintained a Great White Fleet of eighty steamships, which, at one point, was the largest shipping line in the world. Within a decade of United Fruit's founding, it had established a virtual monopoly in the fruit-producing regions of Central America and the West Indies. Historian Marcelo Bucheli maintained that Guatemala, Honduras, and Costa Rica "virtually surrendered sovereignty over the company's areas of operation," allowing rampant exploitation of agricultural workers.[37] United Fruit was the banana business counterpart of the monopolies and trusts that came to dominate the American economy in the early twentieth century.

United Fruit held sway over Latin American and Caribbean countries, employing bribery, extortion, and occasional US military interventions. In the early 1900s, Guatemala hired United Fruit to operate its postal and railway systems. The CIA-inspired 1954 coup in Guatemala, intended to protect United Fruit's investments, was the foremost example of running a "banana republic." Because of its tentacles into Central America and Caribbean countries, United Fruit was nicknamed "El Pulpo," or "The Octopus." In 1970, United Fruit was merged with meat packer AMK-John Morell to become United Brands (today called Chiquita Brands International). Though headquartered in Boston's Prudential Center until the 1970s, the company's banana boats had long since stopped docking in the port city.

Another commodity trade that flourished in Boston was sugar imported from the West Indies. During the colonial era, sugar and its molasses byproduct was a critical link in the triangle trade. New England merchants shipped molasses, the dark, caramelized goo left over from the process of crystallizing sugar, from the Sugar Islands to their home ports. New Englanders turned the molasses into rum, which was sent to West Africa, where it was exchanged for captive Africans who were transported to the West Indies, where they made up the enslaved workforce on sugar plantations. Merchants reportedly paid 150 gallons of rum for a male and 95 gallons for a female.[38] There were thirty-six rum distilleries in Boston alone at this time. After the Revolution, the production of rum continued, though it dropped off during the nineteenth century due to the rising popularity of grain whiskey made in the Midwest and South. Nevertheless, Daniel Lawrence & Sons Company continued to produce high-quality dark, full-flavored Old Medford Rum into the twentieth century. Even with the decline in rum-making, New Englanders still found many uses for molasses, using it to sweeten gingerbread, brown bread, baked beans, pumpkin pie, and other dishes.

The most notable episode in Boston's molasses business was the Great Molasses Flood of 1919. Over the years, inventors found a way to manufacture industrial alcohol from molasses. It was used for cleaning products, solvents, dyes, lacquers, and smokeless gunpowder and high explosives for the military. During World War I, the United States Industrial Alcohol Company, built a 2.3-million gallon, 50-foot-high tank on the North End waterfront to hold molasses it was importing from the West Indies to be refined into industrial alcohol. The molasses was siphoned directly from cargo ship into the holding tank. Because of shoddy construction, the tank gave out in 1919, flooding the North End, killing 21 and injuring 150.[39]

During the nineteenth and much of the twentieth century, Boston continued to import large amounts of sugar for consumer use. Its sugar producers were absorbed into New Yorker Henry Osborne Havemeyer's Sugar Trust (1887), one of the first of the great industrial monopolies. In 1901, Havemeyer's trust took on the brand name of Domino Sugar, named for the domino-shaped cubes that it manufactured. The following year, Domino built a large refining plant on Fort Point Channel, where the company refined sugar cane transported from Cuba and elsewhere around the Caribbean. In 1958, the company moved to a new refining plant in Charlestown on the Mystic River, where it operated until 1988. There was also a Revere Sugar Refinery located in Charlestown, which operated until 1984. Revere Sugar had been a subsidiary of United Fruit, which transported the raw sugar cane to Boston via its Great White Fleet.

The sugar refineries fed many candy-making companies, which made Boston and Cambridge one of the leading candy centers in the country. These included the New England Confectionery Company (NECCO; 1847), which invented the first candy-making machine and popularized penny candy with its NECCO wafers; James O. Welch Company (1927), which introduced Sugar Daddies, Junior Mints, and Poms Poms; and Schrafft's, which operated the world's largest candy plant in Charlestown (1928). These days, Boston still has a sweet tooth, though it has no more sugar refineries or large candy manufacturers.

Prior to World War I, Boston did significant commerce with West Africa. Merchants traded extensively with the Gold Coast, which was an African dependency of Great Britain. Ships carried rum, lumber, flour, and supplies and Bibles for missionaries in exchange for palm oil that the Lever Brothers plant in Cambridge used to make soap. The Gold Coast, instead of the human beings it exported during the colonial era, also shipped mahogany and cacao beans to Boston.[40]

Another significant import was animal hides used to make leather. A fascinating *Boston Globe* article from 1904, "Leathers from Many Lands Sold in Boston," reported that Boston's leather tanning business earned $155 million a year. Boston imported the most skins and hides of any city in the world. The article reported on the buyers of animal skins and hides, who extended their reach as far as India, Persia, Turkey, Russia, Central Asia, South America, and Australia. Tanneries in Woburn, Peabody, and Norwood not only produced leather for New England shoe manufacturers they also exported leather to England, Russia, and other countries.[41]

In 1900, Boston still ranked #2 to New York in total imports, when it handled 9% of the nation's imports and 9.7% of its exports. By 1922, Boston's port ranked #6 in the country, with 6.3% of imports and only 1.3% of exports. Nevertheless, it maintained a fairly strong import business until after World War II. Its imports ranged from the commonplace, like wool, cotton, and hides, to delicacies, such as tea, silks, dried fruits, and spices. As late as 1939, Boston imported twenty-four million pounds of black teas like Formosa, Oolong, and orange pekoe, primarily from Ceylon, Java, and Sumatra. Boston promoted American preferences for black teas over the green Chinese and Japanese teas which flowed into the ports of San Francisco and Seattle. Boston was the second largest American tea port after New York and the fourth largest coffee port. Coffee and tea processors, such as Chase & Sanborn, operated near the docks.[42]

The big challenge lay in the port's difficulty in securing exportable products. Its major bulk export was grain carried by railroad from Midwestern states. Boston also exported smaller cargoes of leather, footwear, packinghouse products, and cotton waste. In 1929, import shipments outnumbered international exports by ten to one. Boston's volume of exports was so low and its operational inefficiencies so great that shippers were discouraged from using the port. Boston's acquisition of grain from the US farm belt also suffered from federally mandated railroad rates which made it less competitive with other cities. By the time the Supreme Court ruled the rail transport rates for Boston to be discriminatory in 1963, it was too late. The opening of the St. Lawrence Seaway allowed Great Lakes States to ship grain and other products directly to world markets without having to use eastern ports as intermediaries. The last grain shipment left Boston in 1965. Scrap metal, which had become a major export to such places as Japan, Italy, Great Britain, and Romania before World War II, replaced grain as Boston's foremost export by the late

1960s, constituting 80% of Boston's exports. Today, scrap metal and paper and paperboard waste are the city's largest seaborne exports.[43]

Boston was the second busiest port for passenger traffic between the Civil War and World War II, though it lagged far behind New York. Steamships, transporting both passengers and freight, proliferated in the late nineteenth century. The Cunard Line (the Cunard Steamship Lines Building at 126 State Street, erected in 1901, was evidence of the steamship line's long-term commitment to serving Boston) was joined in linking Boston with Europe by the White Cross, Allan, and Anchor Lines. By the early 1900s, Boston enjoyed regular sailings between Liverpool, Bristol, Hull, Copenhagen, and Bremen. Inbound passengers grew from 40,905 in 1900 to 138,000 by 1913, with about two-thirds being immigrants.[44] During the 1920s, tourism increased dramatically, as US immigration restrictions greatly reduced the amount of immigrant traffic and steamship companies retooled their ships to attract middle-class tourists. The Cunard and White Star (owner of the Olympic-class RMS *Titanic*) Lines offered weekly service to and from Liverpool. During the summer, Italian, French, and Dutch lines provided sailings to their respective countries. The Great White Fleet of United Fruit operated year-round passenger service on its banana boats to the West Indies, Panama, Rio de Janeiro, and Buenos Aires. Steamship lines even connected Boston to the Far East, Australia, and West Africa.

The WPA guide *Boston Looks Seaward: The Story of the Port, 1630–1940* (1941), which provided an insightful overview of the evolution of the Port of Boston, tried to make the case for its continued prosperity. The WPA guide was published in coordination with the Boston Port Authority, a precursor to the Massachusetts Port Authority/Massport (established 1956). The Boston Port Authority was seeking to reinvigorate the port, which suffered during the Depression. Its optimism for the future was belied by the postwar experience, when the port collapsed into obsolescence. The leading foreign imports into Boston were wool, hides, cotton, jute, and hemp, which fed industries that were entering a steep decline and eventually would no longer require those materials. Even Boston's fishing fleet was in decline because of over-fishing and more convenient ocean access from Gloucester and New Bedford.

The transportation revolutions wrought by trucks and by airplanes did in Boston's port. The region's electronics and technology products were high-value, low-volume goods that were transported by truck, rail, or even air.

The Port of Boston: Gateway to the Global Economy   51

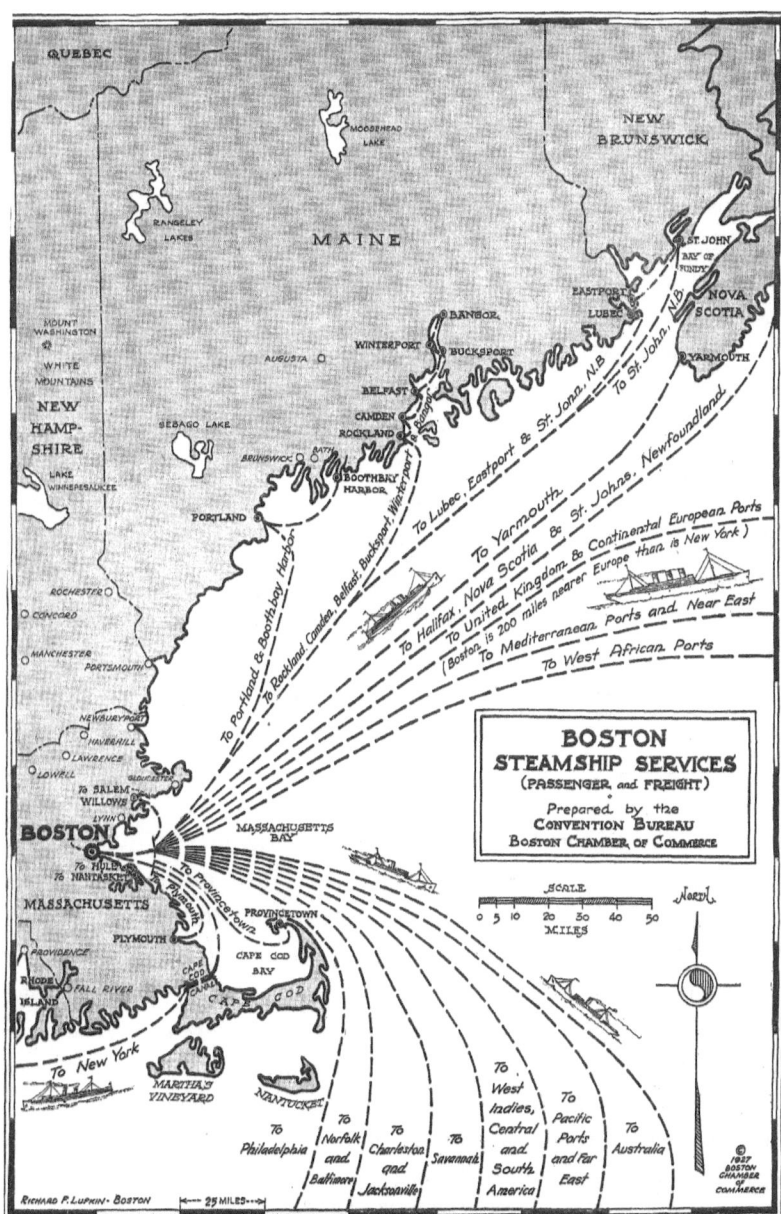

Figure 3. Map depicting destinations of freight and passenger steamships sailing from Boston in 1928. It is striking how many shipping routes radiated from Boston as late as the 1920s.—Courtesy of author's collection.

Boston was also hurt by poor management of the port, deteriorating wharves, and inadequate funding for needed improvements. New York drew an increasing proportion of leisure passengers from New England. When jet planes became common during the 1960s, most travelers stopped taking ocean liners to Europe. Only with the surge in leisure cruises by the late twentieth century did Boston revive as a passenger port. The number of passengers using the cruise terminal grew from 11,723 in 1986 to 373,203 in 2023. The cruise ships serving Boston primarily sail to Bermuda and along the New England and Canadian coasts.[45]

Container ships, which were introduced in 1956, changed the way shipping freight was done. Ports needed large open areas, special cranes, and many fewer longshoremen. Because of longshoremen's union opposition, Massport did not open its first container facility, at Castle Island, until 1970. Export products continued to be a long-term conundrum for the Port of Boston. Historian William Fowler wrote in a 1985 epilogue to *Boston Looks Seaward*: "Economies of scale demand large container ships, which to reduce costs and maximize efficiency can only call at ports where they are likely to find full cargoes. Boston is not such a port."[46]

By the third decade of the twenty-first century, Boston Harbor seems to have found a niche. Improvements to the container facilities, combined with harbor dredging, have enabled Boston to attract service from twelve of the world's fifteen largest shipping companies. In 2023, Boston handled 236,975 containers (the technical term is twenty-foot equivalents or TEUs), placing it as the #25 container port in the United States. There are expectations that container traffic should grow after the 2021 completion of a $350 million harbor dredging project for accommodating super cargo ships. Over 1,600 local companies use the South Boston Conley Container Terminal, including Jordan's Furniture, L.L. Bean, and International Forest Products. In addition to containers, Boston imports substantial volumes of liquefied natural gas (LNG), oil, road salt, wines, and approximately 40,000 Subaru automobiles each year. Yet, the relative importance of the cargo port to Boston's status as a global city is insignificant. The total freight handled by the combined ports of Los Angeles and Long Beach was over 100 times greater than Boston, and New York's total was 54 times larger.[47]

It is noteworthy that the majority of cargoes exported from the Port of Boston are waste materials. Seven of the leading twenty cargo categories consisted of some type of waste, scrap, or worn materials. In 2017, waste materials to be used for recycling represented 76.5% of Boston's seagoing exports, the majority of which was headed to China. The other leading exports included gravel, sand, wood, and paper products. These low-value commodities were exports because container ships from China and other Asian countries were seeking cargoes to carry to the Far East and charged such low rates that they attract recycled material shipments to fill their empty carriers.[48] With such a low level of exports, Boston struggles to compete with other harbors and is basically a niche port.

BOSTON INDUSTRIALIZES

The Industrial Revolution set the stage for changing Boston's economic trajectory from being a mercantile port. During the antebellum decades, Boston investors sought to complement maritime trade by introducing mechanized industry and textile manufacturing to America. Textiles had kick-started England's industrial development, and they would do the same for New England. In 1814, Francis Cabot Lowell opened the country's first integrated textile mill on the Charles River at Waltham. This mill used water-powered looms to mass-produce finished cloth from raw cotton.

From the 1820s until the Civil War, an elite group of Boston investors, referred to as the Boston Associates, erected mills to take advantage of waterpower on rivers and streams across New England. Lowell (1822), named for the textile entrepreneur, who had died in 1817, became the country's foremost cloth manufacturing city. Within a decade of its founding, Lowell had 7,000 mill workers, mainly New England "farm girls." Led by the Lowell and Waltham mills, New England's production of textiles mushroomed over the years:

1805–46,000 yards of cloth (prior to mechanization)
1830–142 million yards
1860–857 million yards
1880–1.8 billion yards.[49]

During the decades leading up to the Civil War, mill owners, who depended upon slave-grown cotton from the South, favored tolerant relations with the South. Those of this persuasion were called Cotton Whigs. Even as public opinion in New England swung heavily against slavery by the 1850s, the mills continued to rely upon southern-raised cotton.

The roles that the city of Boston played in this industry included financing and management. The port received cotton from the South and exported textile goods around the country and the world. The actual manufacturing took place at water-powered mills at such towns as Lowell, Lawrence, Chicopee, and Manchester, NH. New England enjoyed continuous industrial growth until the Panic of 1857 struck. Textile investors realized that there were limits to its growth and the wealth it could produce. Challenges mounted when the Civil War broke out, and cotton from the South became unavailable. After the war, investors sought new opportunities (though they continued to develop textile mills until the 1920s). Boston and New England took advantage of growing US market opportunities and became more integrated into the national industrial economy.

Employment in the region's manufacturing sector, led by textiles and shoes, doubled from 647,000 to 1,350,000 between 1880 and 1920.[50] The region's proportion of urbanized industrial workers led the country, even though the pace of New England's overall industrial growth lagged the mid-Atlantic and Midwestern states, which were becoming the heartland of advanced heavy industry. During America's industrial "golden age" between 1900 and 1970, New England was never a major player. As western and southern states grew in population, New England's peripheral geographical location made it less competitive, and the number of industrial jobs started declining in the 1920s.

Textile employment in Massachusetts shrunk from 182,000 in 1923 to 84,000 by 1939. It increased temporarily during World War II. By 1960, textile jobs had dropped all the way to 16,000. Southern states surpassed New England in textile manufacturing during these years. In the early twentieth century, the South based its industrial emergence on textile manufacturing. There were myriad factors in the textile decline, including New England's unionized labor force, high wages, obsolescent factories and equipment, and relatively high taxes and electricity costs. Southern states wooed textile companies with financial subsidies, a lack of unions, and low wages, taxes, and power costs. Southern states picked up on the invention of synthetic fibers more readily than traditional New England factories did. Employment in the Massachusetts shoe industry followed a similar downward trajectory—from 69,000 jobs in 1923 to 45,000 jobs in 1939.[51] Starting in the 1960s, the shoe industry entered its ultimate demise, being challenged by competition from foreign imports. During this period, Greater Boston's status as a globally significant city abated.

After the industrial losses of the 1920s and the Depression years, the region was stagnating. Yet this collapse ended up working for New England's benefit. In the introduction to his book, *New England Comes Back* (1940), Lawrence Dame wrote that the region's story "will be reported over and over again in all parts of the Union. Just as sure as the sun shines, Steel will one day leave Pittsburgh, Motors will one day leave Detroit, Chicago will not always have its stockyards. . . . New England, after a somewhat terrible period, is indubitably on the up-swing. Not all of the United States has yet been through a like cycle."[52]

Lawrence Dame must have had a crystal ball, as he foresaw the rise of new products and technology that would propel the New England economy. The region responded to economic blows by supporting the development of high-value industries like chemicals, machinery, instruments, and fabricated metals. These sectors flourished during World War II and the postwar boom. Electronics was the most dynamic industry. Almost all the action occurred along the Route 128 corridor, with such companies as RCA, Raytheon, Polaroid, Sylvania, Xerox, Hewlett-Packard, General Electric, Honeywell, and Thermo Electron. Also developing at this time were minicomputer companies Digital Equipment and Data General. Much of the innovation and many of the researchers came out of MIT, Harvard, and other colleges and universities. These technology businesses were supported by some of the country's earliest venture capital. The development of technologically innovative industries paved for way for Massachusetts to become more competitive as the world entered the knowledge economy era, a story that will be pursued in subsequent chapters on technological innovation.

CHAPTER 3

How Boston Financiers Bolstered an Innovation Economy

"The deep economic history of a place and the specialized economic strengths it can generate increasingly matter in a globalized economy."

Saskia Sassen, *Cities in a World Economy*

Some of the most important contributions that Boston mercantile and industrial sectors made to the regional economy were synergistically giving birth to dynamic financial institutions that bankrolled technological innovation. Boston's current-day financial sector, in the competition among global cities, ranks surprisingly high. The 2023 *Global Financial Centres Index 33*, published by Z/Yen Partners and the China Development Institute, ranked Boston #9 as a financial center—ahead of Frankfurt (#17), Zurich (#20), and Tokyo (#21). Boston was recognized for its "established international" financial ecosystem with strengths in human capital (#6) and financial sector development (#8).[1] These attributes reflect Boston's clout as a premier center for investment management.

Financial capacity is an important building block for global cities. Saskia Sassen has argued that the leading economic activities in global capitalism are finance and the advanced professional services of accounting, law, insurance, and management consulting. These services facilitate the development of businesses with global reach, such as, in Boston's case, life sciences, medical equipment, and information technology.

During the current wave of globalization, the leading financial centers and business hubs are cities that tend to have long had flourishing banks and insurance companies. It is difficult for cities to develop and maintain strong financial sectors from scratch. Their historical experience in finance has afforded a competitive advantage to London, New York, Hong Kong, and Tokyo.

Boston also has an established leading-edge financial sector. Building on its colonial era financial practices, Boston developed a culture of innovative investment and successful wealth management during the nineteenth century that has persisted to this day. The heirs of this legacy and the pillars of Boston's current financial clout include Fidelity, State Street, Putnam Investments (subsidiary of Franklin Templeton Investments), Bain Capital, and myriad venture capital and private equity firms.

Boston's financial proficiency in the Early Republic was founded upon the establishment of the Massachusetts Bank (today's Bank of America, which, because it has absorbed the Boston-based successor institutions of the Massachusetts Bank, calls itself the oldest continuously operating bank in the country). Opened in 1784, it was the first federally chartered joint-stock owned bank in the United States. The Massachusetts Bank counted John Hancock, Paul Revere, Samuel Adams, and Henry Knox among its early investors. In 1786, the Massachusetts Bank financed the first US mercantile voyage to China, by the *Columbia*. Five years later, it financed the first voyage of an American ship to Buenos Aires, creating a beachhead for long-term trade and investment in Latin America. The bank's successor, the First National Bank of Boston, eventually became the leading foreign bank in several major Latin American cities.

Boston's foremost financial function was amassing capital and managing investments. This has continued to be the city's forte to this day. In order to build the mills, canals, and railroads that spearheaded the Industrial Revolution in America, significant capital investment was needed. Much of it was obtained from seagoing merchants. Two of the founders of the first integrated textile mill, in Waltham (1815), were Francis Cabot Lowell and Patrick Tracy Jackson, who both had accumulated wealth in maritime trade. The twenty-seven investors they attracted to build the first mill in Lowell in 1822 also had accumulated their wealth from international shipping. The profits from the textile plants earned capital that could be reinvested in manufacturing expansion. The initial Lowell factory, the Merrimack Mill, earned approximately 19% a year over its first decade and almost 15% per year in the following decade. By 1845, a tight community of eighty investors, referred to as the Boston Associates, owned thirty-one New England textile mills. The profits from these factories, combined with profits from mercantile trade and railroads, helped establish Boston as a leading investment center. The accumulated wealth spawned banks and insurance companies, which ultimately invested in many national industrial and infrastructure enterprises. The profits also supported the area's charitable, cultural, and educational institutions, which ultimately earned world-class distinction.[2]

The first significant institutional investor in the textile industry was the Massachusetts Hospital Life Insurance Company, the state's first life insurance company. It was founded in 1818 to provide income support for Massachusetts General Hospital. Like other insurance companies, it needed to invest its premiums. Textile mills became the first big beneficiary. The company's board formed interlocking directorates with the mill owners. Within a dozen years, the Massachusetts Hospital Life Insurance Company was the largest financial institution in New England. The insurance company established a model for other Boston insurance companies to make strategic investments, paving the way for such major insurers as John Hancock, Liberty Mutual, and New England Mutual Life.

In 1834, Boston businessmen established the Stock & Exchange Board to serve as a market for financing New England's textile mills and other industrial and utility enterprises. It was the country's leading stock exchange for industrial stocks until the end of the nineteenth century. The New York Stock Exchange, which was established in 1819, for a long time refused to list industrial stocks because its directors believed that industrial companies, which were prone to failure during periodic recessions, were too risky to list. When the New York Stock Exchange started listing industrial firms in the 1890s, it curtailed Boston's dominance in industrial financing. Still, Boston remained a financial center. According to historian Joshua Rosenbloom, Boston was buttressed by "the development of a dense and sophisticated network of financial intermediaries capable of mobilizing savings and channeling them into productive activities." The number of banks and deposits was greater in New England than elsewhere, leading to lower interest rates than those available in the rest of the country by two or three points. The flow of interest and dividend payments into New England from successful financing ventures helped achieve the region's primacy in average personal income.[3]

INVESTING IN THE WEST

Since much of Boston's wealth was earned in maritime commerce, especially the China trade, investors had valuable experience in far-flung investments and the management of novel, risky enterprises. By the 1840s, some audacious Bostonians were placing their bets in other regions of the country. The Midwest was both the country's breadbasket and, ultimately, its industrial heartland. The Great Plains, the Sierra Nevada and Rocky Mountains, and the Pacific Coast formed a potential empire ripe with natural resources. As the West lacked capital to exploit this potential, the investment opportunities for investors in the East in railroads, stockyards, and mines seemed boundless.

Railroad investment became a Boston specialty, building on the financial and entrepreneurial experience of New England railroad development starting in the 1830s. Historians Arthur M. Johnson and Barry E. Supple claimed that, "in the mid-1840s Boston was the center of railroad capital in the United States," playing "a dominant role in eastern financing of new western lines."[4] John Murray Forbes (1813–1898), who started his business career in the China trade, spent much of his life investing in and managing railroads. After working in China for a decade, Forbes returned to Boston, where he continued to manage a fleet of twenty ships while opening an investment management firm. One of his first investors was the wealthy Chinese merchant Houqua, with whom he had worked in Canton. Houqua had become disappointed with his dealings with the London-based Baring Brothers merchant bank and transferred much of his business to Forbes to invest in US securities. The Forbes firm, which still exists, estimates that Houqua's investment was approximately $500,000, which would amount to more than $10 million today.[5] Another prominent Forbes client was French political analyst Alexis de Tocqueville.

John Murray Forbes started his involvement in railroads when he and other Boston investors bought shares in the nascent Michigan Central Railroad. Forbes, like subsequent Boston railroad investors, was not a passive investor, but actively directed development of the Michigan Central and other railroads. He ended up serving as president of the line between 1846 and 1855. As railroad presidents, board members, and engineers, Bostonians cultivated expertise in the strategic development of complex transportation systems, which informed their investment culture. Forbes boasted in 1847 that "whenever any coal mines are to be made accessible, or ill managed Rail Roads made available, or indeed any scheme that requires Capital & intelligence they come to Boston for help."[6]

The Michigan Central Railroad became the main connector between Northeastern cities and Chicago. It opened up the mineral and timber resources of Michigan's Upper Peninsula. Forbes bought the land there that became the Calumet and Hecla copper mine. The mine yielded its great wealth years later, under the direction of Boston capitalist Henry Lee Higginson. In addition, Forbes's business also built the Sault St. Marie Canal, which connected Lake Superior with the rest of the Great Lakes. Perhaps Forbes's most significant railroad venture involved routes running west from Chicago. He started investing, with other Bostonians, in several small railroads in Illinois. In 1856, he worked to combine these railway lines into the Chicago, Burlington & Quincy Railroad, for which he served as a director 1857–1898 and as president 1878–1881. The Burlington Line reached Denver in 1882 (the first rail link to the Mile High City) and St. Paul four years later. Just as he had done in Michigan, Forbes acquired sizable real estate holdings along the rail lines of the Burlington.

Boston businessmen Oakes (1804–1873) and Oliver, Jr. (1807–1877) Ames, played a pivotal role in opening of the West. Their North Easton, Massachusetts shovel company made a fortune selling shovels and picks to miners during the 1849 California Gold Rush. This alerted the Ames brothers to opportunities in the West, and they became the primary financiers for the construction of the transcontinental railroad, funneling a great deal of Boston-based capital into the project. The railroad was chartered in 1862 by President Abraham Lincoln in an effort to tie California more effectively into the Union. Crews building the Ames brothers' Union Pacific Railroad started working west from Omaha, while crews were working east from Sacramento on the Central Pacific Railroad, which was under the management of San Francisco-based interests. The two rail lines met in 1869 at Promontory Summit in Utah, where a celebratory final "Golden Spike" was hammered to mark the completion of the transcontinental railroad.

Not only did the Ames brothers lead the financing of the Union Pacific Railroad, Oakes, who also served as a congressman from Massachusetts, oversaw its construction, including the provision of shovels and other construction tools. Oliver served as president and fiscal manager of the Union Pacific. The construction company that Oakes ran was the Credit Mobilier. Overcharging the federal government for construction, the Credit Mobilier garnered profits of almost 100% of costs. The company justified the substantial profits because of the remoteness of tracks from any settlement or supplier. In order to hush up any note of impropriety, Oakes Ames bribed thirty Congressman and Senators with discount-priced shares in Union Pacific. The scandal became public during the 1872 presidential election. Ames was censured by the House of Representatives and died less than three months after.

Despite the Credit Mobilier scandal, railroads remained an important business to the Ames family. Oliver, Jr.'s son Frederick Lothrop Ames (1835–1893) served on boards of forty different railroad lines, including the Union Pacific. As he also owned considerable Boston real estate, including the Ames Building, the city's first skyscraper, Ames was considered the richest man in Massachusetts, according to his obituary in the *New York Times*.[7]

The Union Pacific Railroad remained a Boston project. Charles Francis Adams, Jr. (1835–1915) acted as president of the Union Pacific between 1884 and 1890. After serving as a decorated lieutenant colonel in the Union Army, he was named to the Massachusetts Board of Railroad Commissioners (1869–1879). This state board was a pioneer in government regulation of business in America. Adams wrote an influential book, *Railroads, Their Origins and Problems* (1878), which argued that railroads were necessarily monopolies and, therefore, needed to be regulated to make sure that they served the public in a responsible way. Adams's expertise attracted the attention of Congress, which urged his installment as president of the Union Pacific Railroad. He managed the railroad out of the Ames Building in Boston. Besides financing the Union Pacific, he owned stockyards in Kansas City, with Philip Armour, and in Denver. In addition to these investments, Adams invested in real estate in San Antonio, Houston, Portland, Oregon, Seattle, and the mining towns of Helena and Spokane.

Bostonians also played a major role in the development of the Santa Fe Railroad. Chartered as the Atchison, Topeka & Santa Fe Railway, the company ran out of funds before it could complete the short fifty-mile route between Atchison and Topeka, KS. The flailing railroad reached out to the Boston investment bank of Kidder, Peabody & Co. to market its shares. The initiative was successful, and, under Boston management, the railroad expanded its trackage and bought up other lines to ultimately link Chicago with the Pacific Coast at Los Angeles and open up the Southwest territories of New Mexico and Arizona. Boston textile magnate Thomas Jefferson Coolidge served as president of the railway during the 1880s.[8] For a number of years Santa Fe securities were listed only on the Boston Stock Exchange and were owned entirely by Boston interests.

Even the Northern Pacific Railroad had roots in Boston. In 1864, Boston businessmen, led by President Josiah Perham, received a federal charter for a rail line that stretched from Minnesota to Puget Sound in Washington State. The inclusion of the word "Pacific" in the names of the transcontinental Northern Pacific, Union Pacific, and Central Pacific Railroads implied a desire for the settled Eastern United States to connect with the Pacific Ocean and the markets of East Asia. Josiah Perham maintained that his railroad provided "the direct and nearest routes to the great Pacific emporiums of Russia, China and Japan." This vision for Pacific trade was a logical extension of the China trade successfully pursued by Boston merchants.[9] Unfortunately for Boston interests, the board of directors could not raise the funding necessary to for the ambitious construction project, and Philadelphia banker Jay Cooke took control.

Perhaps the most ambitious Boston-backed railroad effort was the Mexican Central Railway (its headquarters was in Boston and nine of its thirteen directors were from Massachusetts), which grew to become that country's largest rail network as well as the foremost foreign-owned corporation in Mexico. The Mexican Central Railway (1880) was controlled by the same investment group as the Atchison, Topeka, and Santa Fe Railway, with which it connected at the US-Mexican border at El Paso. The railway stretched to Mexico City and crisscrossed the country from the Pacific to the Gulf of Mexico. Because of the underdeveloped nature of the Mexican economy, the investments did not pan out. In 1906, the Mexican government nationalized the railroad. Looking back on Boston's far-flung investments in railroads, it seems ironic that a city on the periphery of North America would be such an important player in developing the continental railroad system.

INVESTMENT BANKING

By 1890, the western railroad network had become mature. Boston capitalists were moving on to investments in new industries like utilities, chemicals, steel, and petroleum. Investment banks played a significant role in assembling capital and deploying it in the form of stocks and bonds for the use of corporations and governments. In underwriting new debt and equities, investment banks pledged to buy unsold stock and bonds and sell them to other investors. They were essential middlemen in facilitating mergers and acquisitions and the establishment of new corporations.

Between the Civil War and World War I, two of the country's leading investment banks were Kidder, Peabody & Co. and Lee, Higginson & Co. These two firms, along with New York-based J.P. Morgan & Co., Kuhn, Loeb and Co., First National Bank of New York (now part of Citibank), and the National City Bank, have been credited with creating the large-scale industrial US economy that emerged at the end of the nineteenth century.[10] They provided financing for burgeoning industrial enterprises, arranging initial stock offerings and selling shares to investors or to intermediary bankers in foreign cities.

The Kidder, Peabody firm descended from one of Boston's earliest private bankers, John Eliot Thayer, who specialized in foreign exchange and brokerage starting in the 1820s. Three of his employees—Henry P. Kidder, Francis H. Peabody, and Oliver W. Peabody—started their own investment banking firm in 1865. Kidder, Peabody attracted European capital and directed it into American railroads, manufacturers, and real estate. Their connection to the London's Baring Brothers was strong, as Boston-bred Joshua Bates (1788–1864) and Russell Sturgis (1805–1887) served as senior partners at the British firm during the mid-nineteenth century. Under their leadership, Baring Brothers funneled significant European capital through Boston into development of the American West.

Some of Kidder, Peabody's most noteworthy work involved organizing and financing some of the great corporations that emerged at the turn of the century. It played a central role in creating the Santa Fe Railway, Procter & Gamble, and P. Lorillard Tobacco Company. Kidder, Peabody collaborated with New York banking magnate J.P. Morgan in effecting the merger of the Thomson-Houston Electric Company, of Lynn, with the Edison Electric Company to create General Electric. The firm also collaborated with Morgan in forming the United States Steel Company, the New Haven Railroad, and the American Sugar Refining Company trust (Domino Sugar).[11]

Following Alexander Graham Bell's invention of the telephone in 1876, Kidder, Peabody played a key role in establishing the Bell Telephone Company. One of the leading investors was John Murray Forbes, whose son William Hathaway Forbes served as president of Bell Telephone Company for a decade. In order to build the first long-distance network, the Bell Company created a subsidiary named the American Telephone & Telegraph (AT&T) in 1885. The Bell Company headquarters remained in Boston, while AT&T was chartered in New York. In 1902, AT&T became the parent company of the Bell system and moved the corporate headquarters to New York. Nevertheless, Kidder, Peabody was the leading underwriter of AT&T bonds through the 1920s.[12] According to Richard R. John, "No other financial institution enjoyed as long a relationship with Bell or played a more central role in the all-important financing of its big-city operating companies. . . . Kidder, Peabody and not J.P. Morgan became the deus ex machina that explained why Bell and not independents prevailed."[13]

Although the corporate development engineered by Kidder, Peabody and the profits earned for its investors were significant, its local employment impact was relatively small. Its Devonshire Street office had fewer than fifty employees prior to World War I. The executives tended to be family members or associates from a tight social circle.[14]

Kidder, Peabody suffered from increased competition in the 1920s, as the lure of Wall Street escalated and new, aggressive retail brokers entered the field. While most other investment banks were located in New York, Kidder, Peabody remained in Boston. Conservative senior partner Robert Winsor (nicknamed "The J.P. Morgan of Boston" for his work with Morgan on many deals) retained much of the firm's holdings in older New England companies that it had originally financed. When the value of these businesses plunged in the 1929 stock market crash, Kidder, Peabody's fortunes crashed as well. Winsor died of a heart attack three months after the crash. The firm reorganized under the direction of the House of Morgan and moved its headquarters to New York two years later.

The other leading Boston investment banking firm of this era was Lee, Higginson & Co., which was established in 1848 as a broker and foreign exchange dealer. After the Civil War, when the son of founder George Higginson— Henry Lee Higginson—returned from service as an officer in the Union Army, the firm blossomed into one of the nation's leading investment banks. Perhaps the firm's most successful investment was in the Calumet and Hecla Copper Mine in Upper Michigan. For decades the Calumet Mine, which was managed by Harvard-educated scientist Alexander Agassiz, was the largest copper producer in the United States. Henry Lee Higginson made 400% profit on the initial investment in the copper mines; in fact, Boston investors in general made greater profits from mines than Western railroads.[15] Higginson used his wealth to support many causes, including Harvard University and the Boston Symphony Orchestra, which he founded.

The Lee, Higginson firm was as active as Kidder, Peabody in financing railroads and mines and after, the year 1900, national manufacturing and utility companies as well. Lee, Higginson played the lead role in underwriting the merger of twenty-five paper mills (sixteen mills located in Holyoke, MA) into the American Writing Paper Company in 1899. Lee, Higginson, which served as banker for Thomson-Houston Electric Co., arranged with J. P. Morgan and Kidder, Peabody the merger with Edison Electric Co. to create General Electric. Lee, Higginson even played a role in getting the Detroit auto industry off the ground. Partner James Storrow, Jr. served as chairman of General Motors between 1910 and 1915, leading efforts to modernize management of the corporation.

As the demand for capital and the public's taste for investing accelerated after the turn of the century, Lee, Higginson and Kidder, Peabody pioneered the use of retail stockbrokers to sell stocks and bonds to small investors, something the New York investment banks did not do for years after.[16] By the Roaring Twenties, when small investors fueled the stock market boom, Boston boasted a phalanx of stock brokerage houses. The local firms of Hayden, Stone; Hornblower & Weeks; Kidder, Peabody; Paine, Webber; Tucker, Anthony; and Jackson & Curtis all opened offices around the country. Between the 1960s and 1980s, these brokerage houses ended up being acquired by larger national financial institutions.

Like Kidder, Peabody, Lee, Higginson was slipping during the 1920s and was forced into liquidation during the Great Depression. The death blow came from the notorious swindle by Ivar Krueger, the "Swedish Match King." Lee, Higginson had advised the purchase of $250 million of Krueger's International Match Corporation securities without doing due diligence. The collapse of the match corporation led to the collapse of Lee, Higginson. The firm was reorganized and moved to New York in 1932, but it was a shadow of its former self.[17]

INNOVATIONS IN MANAGING INVESTMENTS

Much of Boston's edge in business and technological development can be attributed to innovative investment management practices. Trusts and the laws that enabled them have provided the basis for such alternative investment instruments as mutual funds, venture capital, private equity, and hedge funds. The development of these financial vehicles has helped establish Boston as a foremost investment center.

Since colonial times, Boston had a cadre of lawyers, accountants, and businessmen who managed finances for merchants who were away on trading voyages. By the early decades of the nineteenth century, the relationships became formalized in trusts, which were used to keep estates intact after a producer of wealth died. The trustees managed the investments and paid income to beneficiaries, who did not play a role in investment decisions. The "Boston trustee" established the professional means for managing and transferring intergenerationally a family's wealth. Such wealth has done much to further the region's business development and its remarkable range of philanthropic institutions. The status of "Boston trustees" was legitimized by the Massachusetts Supreme Judicial Court's 1830 decision in the *Armory* case, which granted trustees of estates flexibility in making investments as long as they were prudent. This doctrine, which allowed trustees to steer a middle ground between making the most conservative investments and undertaking the riskiest speculations, became known as the "prudent man rule." The state developed a trustworthy investment culture that served not simply formal trusts but all investment clients. The reason that such money management services started in Boston is that, with New York and Philadelphia, it was among the first American cities to generate large financial fortunes that required sound multi-generational stewardship.

For many years, the trustees were usually attorneys, with entire law firms set up to manage trusts and their investments. They even paid bills and made charitable contributions. Companies purposely established to manage trusts appeared after the Civil War, when the New England Trust Company (1869) and the Boston Safe Deposit and Trust Company (1875) were established. These trust companies and others that followed also provided banking services such as making loans and enabling check-writing. The "golden age of trusts" occurred between the 1860s and World War II. During the 1930s, leading Boston trustees E. Sohier Welch, Robert H. Gardiner, and Philip Dexter each managed over $100 million in investments. A related concept to trusts is the "family office," which has had a long history in Boston. Both trusts and family offices manage wealth that can be transferred across generations. Family offices offer more comprehensive services and can manage multiple trusts.

Since 2000, there has been an explosion of family offices elsewhere in the world, providing wealth management for ultra-high-net-worth clients who have benefited most from the global economy.[18]

Despite the financial rewards enjoyed by many trusts, there was a feeling that conservative trust investments were responsible for Boston's economic stagnation during the mid-twentieth century. As an investment institution that had served Boston's old-line families for a long time, many trustees had grown overly cautious. They tended to avoid risky new enterprises that might boost economic growth.

Ward Just, in his short story about a Boston attorney, "About Boston," described the tangled ends to which trusts could be dedicated: "The trusts are of breathtaking ingenuity, the product of the flintiest minds in Massachusetts, and of course facilitated over the years by a willing legislature. . . . the trust . . . was originally devised to avoid taxes or to punish a recalcitrant child or to siphon income to 'protect' an unworldly widow or to reach beyond the grave to control the direction of a business or a fortune or a marriage."[19] This may have been the case earlier in the twentieth century; but, after the knowledge economy developed in the years after World War II, trust companies became active investors in the dynamic technology sector, which has spurred significant economic growth.

Mutual Funds

Mutual funds were a pivotal Boston innovation. During the 1920s, America transitioned from being a debtor nation to being a creditor. The country's financial institutions increased their efforts to match available capital with appropriate investment opportunities. Small investors were drawn into the market by the growing availability of professional investment advice and accessible Boston-based brokerage houses such as Paine, Webber, Tucker, Anthony, and Hornblower & Weeks. This led to New England having more shareholders per capita than any other region.[20]

In 1924, the Massachusetts Investors Trust, established by bond salesmen Charles H. Learoyd, Hatherly Foster, Jr., and Edward G. Leffler, offered the first open-end mutual fund, which allowed small investors to own shares in a professionally managed, diversified portfolio of stocks. The mutual fund allowed shareholders to redeem their shares on demand at net asset value rather than having to petition the fund to buy back shares or try to sell them to another party. This mutual fund built upon the concept of the Boston trust, in which trustees managed all investments and paid income to beneficiaries. On the heels of the Massachusetts Investors Trust, mutual funds opened under State Street Investment Corporation (1924) and Incorporated Investors (1925). During the 1930s and beyond, Boston-managed mutual funds proliferated.

The foremost mutual fund, Fidelity Fund Inc., was founded in 1930. Within a decade, it was the tenth largest fund in Boston, with $4 million in assets under management. In 1943, Attorney Edward C. Johnson II became president, launching Fidelity on a growth trajectory that made it the eleventh largest mutual fund in the US by 1959, with $491 million in assets. Fidelity's assets exploded to $2.3 billion six years later. Fidelity and other mutual funds benefited from the interest in growth stocks in the "Go-Go Years" of the 1960s.[21]

Fidelity became the country's leading mutual fund after Edward ("Ned") C. Johnson III took over the company in 1972. Ned Johnson was noted for his marketing talents. In 1974, Fidelity offered the first money market fund with check-writing privileges. Johnson bypassed third-party sales agents with direct toll-free phone service. He even expanded his offices to other countries. Fidelity and mutual funds in general thrived during the stock boom of the 1980s and beyond. US mutual funds grew from $49 billion in assets under management in 1980 to $4 trillion in 2000, as the Dow Jones Industrial Average rose from 777 points to 11,900 and the NASDAQ skyrocketed from 166 to over 5,000.[22] Fidelity's star performer was the Peter Lynch-managed Magellan Fund, which grew from $5.4 billion in assets in 1978 to $75.3 billion nine years later. Between 1990 and 2009, Fidelity had the most assets under management of any mutual fund company. Much of this growth was driven by the introduction of Individual Retirement Accounts (IRA), 401(k) plans, and other personal retirement investment vehicles. Today, Fidelity's family of mutual funds ranks #5 with $4.88 trillion in assets under management.[23]

State Street Global Advisers is one of the world's largest managers of institutional assets, with a specialty in index funds. Its mutual funds manage $4.1 trillion in assets for #4 place in the world. State Street's Global Services division is the largest custodial bank in the world. State Street has $43.7 trillion under custody. Going back to the 1920s, State Street has played a custodial role for mutual fund and pension funds that it does not directly manage. It holds securities, keeping track of their market values, apportioning holdings to various accounts, and issuing account statements.[24]

Other leading Boston mutual fund companies include Putnam Investments (subsidiary of Franklin Templeton Investments), Wellington Management, and Eaton Vance (under Morgan Stanley Investment Management).

Venture Capital, Private Equity, and Hedge Funds

The most significant investment initiative for local economic development has been venture capital. It originated during the 1940s, when New England was trying to pull out of its manufacturing slump. There was an awareness that the region had to replace the outmoded textile and shoe industries. Since the 1920s, MIT, under the leadership of President Karl Compton and Engineering School Dean Vannevar Bush, had been promoting research that could produce technological breakthroughs and economic development. One of the problems new technologies encountered was securing adequate financing once they had been developed.

In 1946, Compton, joined with Boston Federal Reserve Bank President Ralph Flanders, and Harvard Business School's Georges Doriot, to form the American Research and Development Corporation (ARDC) for financing promising startup enterprises. ARDC sought to create a capital pool of $4 million with funds from institutions, insurance companies, and wealthy individuals. ARDC was the world's first venture capital fund as well as the first one to be publicly traded. ARDC gravitated toward businesses related to science and technology research. Its most celebrated investment was in the Digital Equipment Corporation. ARDC invested $70,000 in 1957 and cashed out with $355 million 11 years later, for an amount over 500 times greater.[25]

Jane Jacobs cited the significance of the ARDC in *Cities and the Wealth of Nations*. She argued that Boston's conservative trusts had contributed to the area's economic stagnation: "The old textile, shoe, and railroad fortunes were tied up in routinely invested trusts, the city as a whole had become an exporter of capital, not a place in which capital was being put to work productively and diversely." ARDC investments in startups launched a process of creative development that Jacobs described as a positive breakthrough: "upon the multiplying suppliers of materials, instruments, tools and services that served the new enterprises and thus were supported by them and by one another, the Boston regional economy was stunningly rejuvenated."[26]

The majority of venture investments flowed into technology hardware and business applications, while steering clear of software and consumer applications. Silicon Valley venture capitalists, meanwhile, dove into the consumer sector, and that region became the world's dominant tech innovation center. Silicon Valley's venture sector surpassed Massachusetts during the 1980s and is several times larger today.[27]

Boston has fostered the creation of many private venture capital funds starting in the mid-1960s and taking off in the 1980s. They included Greylock, Charles River Ventures, and Fidelity Ventures. Banks such as First National Bank of Boston and New England Merchants Bank (both subsumed by Bank of America) started investing in startups. New England Merchants was notable for its stake in Continental Cablevision, the early cable television leader in New England (assimilated by Comcast). Boston Celtics lead owner Wyc Grousbeck has been a partner at Highland Capital Partners, a global venture firm with investments in more than 225 companies, including Sybase and LevelUp.

Venture capital has been one of the primary reasons for Boston's current standing as a center for technological and life sciences innovation. The venture capital news website PitchBook reported that Boston ranked #4 for venture capital, behind San Francisco, New York, and Los Angeles, between 2017 and 2023 with $99.2 billion invested. Because of Boston's high level of venture capital investment, urbanists Richard Florida and Ian Hathaway have ranked Boston as one of six "Superstar Global Startup Hubs" with San Francisco, New York, London, Beijing, and Los Angeles.[28] A detailed discussion of life sciences venture capital funds is included in Chapter 7: How the Cambridge-Boston Life Sciences Ecosystem Works.

In addition to venture capital funds, Boston has also developed private equity and hedge funds, cutting-edge financial instruments that promise higher returns than can be achieved through conventional stocks and bonds. Private equity firms are limited partnerships that invest in companies that are not traded on a stock exchange. After buying a company, a private equity firm usually restructures it for resale and a significant profit. This often entails breaking a large corporation into more profitable stand-alone units. Private equity funds grew exponentially from $4.7 billion to $400 billion in assets during the 1980s and 1990s, when federal law allowed pension funds to invest in private equity firms. The total of private equity assets under management (February 2024) is an astonishing $11.7 trillion.[29]

Perhaps Boston's best-known private equity firm is Bain & Company. In 1973, Bain started as a management consultancy which preferred to take an equity position in a company instead of receiving a consulting fee. It created Bain Capital (1983), which was led by US Senator Mitt Romney, to buy up underperforming companies, reorganize them, and sell them at profit. Some of Bain's noteworthy acquisitions were Staples (which started in Brighton), Dunkin' Brands, and Sealy Mattress. A former co-chair of Bain Capital is Stephen Pagliuca, who is also a co-owner of the Boston Celtics. Bain Capital manages $180 billion in private equity.[30]

Another pioneering private equity firm is TA Associates (1968). The 500+ companies that TA Associates have invested in include Biogen, Federal Express, Ameritrade, and numerous small technology firms. TA Associates, like Bain, has offices around the world both raising investment funds and acquiring business positions. The firm of Thomas H. Lee & Co. (1974) has focused on technology, healthcare, financial services, and consumer businesses whose operations it would upgrade in exchange for an equity position. Its investments have included General Nutrition (GNC), Snapple, Fisher Scientific, Dun and Bradstreet, and Experian Information Solutions. Other leading Massachusetts private equity firms include Advent International, Audax Private Equity, Berkshire Partners, Summit Partners, and HarborVest Partners.[31]

Hedge funds are known by the general public as opaque entities that seem to generate fabulous wealth. The original idea behind hedge funds, when the first US hedge fund was established in 1949, was to "hedge" investment risks by taking both long and short positions. More recently, hedge funds have pursued a wide array of bold investments tempered by sophisticated risk management strategies. Hedge funds can have dramatic upside potential because they are able to use leverage that is not permitted for mutual funds and other publicly traded investments. Much of the mystery surrounding hedge funds exists because they are only open to big-money investors and institutions.

The first Boston hedge fund, Essex Investment Management Company, opened in the late 1970s. Some of its major clients were from Switzerland, where there was an appreciation of hedge investing techniques. By 2000, there were many Boston-based hedge funds, building on the investment management experiences that asset managers had acquired in mutual funds, venture capital, and private equity firms.[32]

Leading Boston-based hedge funds, as of 2023, included Arrowstreet Capital, Baupost, Bracebridge Capital, Rockpoint Group, and Wellington

Management. Because of a tradition of prudent investing, the number of Boston hedge funds and private equity firms is the fourth largest concentration behind only New York, California, Greenwich, CT, and Chicago.

The surge in recent decades of sophisticated investment vehicles like venture capital, private equity, and hedge funds has been driven by an explosion of Information Age wealth garnered by tech executives, prodigious pools of institutional portfolios, and the fortunes made by actors, celebrities, and star athletes. As the market for investment management boomed a good deal of business has come to Boston.

THE EMERGENCE OF FINTECH

Financial technology (fintech) usually comes in the form of software deployed by financial institutions in a way that seems imperceptible to consumers. It does not receive the same enthused attention attracted by biotechnology, 3-D printing, or robotics. Yet, overlooking fintech is a mistake. It has been combining innovative business models with technology applications to enhance and create new ways to pay, save, invest, and manage money.

Boston has its share of fintech innovators, as indicated by the 2023 *Global Financial Centres Index 33*. This report, which ranked Boston #9 globally as a financial center, rated it #10 for fintech. There are over 350 fintech companies headquartered in Massachusetts, most of them around Boston. The Hub trails only London (1,076 fintech companies), San Francisco (910 fintechs), New York (771 fintechs), and Montreal-Toronto (521 fintechs). In 2022, the state's firms raised more than $1 billion in venture capital, placing it fourth behind California, New York, and Florida.[33]

Boston's fintech expertise is based on developments in payments, insurance, asset management, cybersecurity, crypto currency, and blockchain. Innovations are being driven by AI, big data, and advanced analytics. Fintech firms have been building off the region's highly regarded financial institutions, the renowned universities, and the deep pool of finance and technology talent.[34]

A sampling of leading fintech companies in the area includes the following:

Sovos Compliance—Globally oriented service for tax determination and tax reporting.

Financial Recovery Technologies—Governance solutions for asset owners and managers to identify eligibility, file claims, and collect funds made available in securities class action settlements.

Flywire Corp.—Global payments software company, facilitating complex, large-sum transactions through cutting-edge payments platform and proprietary global payment network.

Kensho Technologies—Data analytics and machine intelligence company combining natural language search queries and cloud computing to create analytics tools for investment professionals.[35]

Besides the presence of such fintech firms, the cluster depends upon many supporting institutions. In 2021, state government, private companies, and academic research institutions formed the Mass Fintech Hub to strengthen the fintech cluster and make it appealing for fintech entrepreneurs from around the world to locate here. The organizations set out to escalate collaboration within the cluster and provide more visible branding, as the fintech cluster lacks the clout of the Greater Boston biotech sector. The nonprofit trade organization convenes a host of networking and outreach fintech programs, including a mentorship program, fintech "bootcamps," and angel investor education.[36]

The DCU Fintech Innovation Center, located in Boston's Financial District since 2016, seeks to accelerate seed-stage startups from the "proof of concept" stage to developing products with a potential market by offering a year of workspace, mentoring, and networking through relationships with DCU's 600 plus bank and credit union customers. MassChallenge FinTech, which is located in donated space in Mass Mutual's Seaport office building, offers a comparable accelerator program, with cash awards up to $250,000. Another key player in the fintech cluster is the Boston-based FinTech Sandbox, a nonprofit founded in 2014 to support fintech startups by offering no-cost financial data feeds (market and otherwise) for six months, before requiring payment for membership. The organization also offers networking and mentorship opportunities for investors, institutions, and others in the fintech community.[37] Many of the leading universities in the state, including MIT, Boston University, Northeastern University, UMass-Amherst, and Worcester Polytechnic Institute, are now offering master's and certificate programs in fintech. These programs are expanding the local talent base for fintech.

BOSTON'S REPUTATION AS AN INVESTMENT CENTER

In some sense it is remarkable that Boston continues to thrive as a financial center. Boston's leading commercial banks, some in existence for more than two centuries, were merged out of existence toward the end of the twentieth century. This process originated in the 1980s, when federal deregulation permitted unlimited interstate banking and the creation of nationwide banks. Further impetus for bank mergers came with the late 1980s collapse of banks that were overextended by risky loans and burdened by debts incurred by mergers. Boston banks that disappeared included First National Bank/Bank of Boston, New England Merchants/Bank of New England, Shawmut, and Baybank. State Street Bank & Trust sold off its commercial operations to Citizens Bank. Fleet and Citizens, two Rhode Island-based banks, ended up taking over these Boston banks in various mergers. Fleet, in turn, was absorbed into the Bank of America in 2004. This megabank is headquartered in Charlotte, the nation's center for retail banking.

Because of the talent and financial ecosystem in Boston, the new megabanks kept many jobs in Boston. Bank of America CEO Brian Moynihan, who started his career at FleetBoston, explained Boston's persistence as a financial center: "Boston has the kinds of people you want, a critical mass, and there's a locus of talent we can build around."[38] Boston financial institutions have maintained a sterling reputation for managing trillions of dollars in investments. A 1959 *Business Week* article observed the relative strengths of Boston and New York, which still hold today: "New York's financial community handles a much bigger amount—but Wall Street, money market to the nation and the world, is as much a banker and broker as it is an investor. Boston is pre-eminently an investment center, and its State Street community claims more experienced investment men per capita than any other city in the country."[39] (An updated characterization of Boston's talent pool would include women.) Paul Cabot, co-founder of State Street Investment Corporation, explained the difference between the two cities: "I think there was a feeling on the investors' part that they didn't trust the New Yorkers quite as much as they did Boston because Boston had the reputation of the old Boston conservative trustee and New York had the reputation of the slick Wall Street fellows who take the shirt off your back."[40] Boston has been able to maintain a distinctive investment management culture based upon proficient financial research and judicious investment decision-making. This approach has rubbed off on the more speculative investing done by venture capital, private equity, and hedge funds. A culture of prudent investment management has given Boston a competitive edge in the global economy.

Despite the advantages enjoyed by Boston's financial sector, the city should be wary of the fallout from the adoption of remote work that has taken place in the wake of COVID-19. Financial services are a sector more prone to telework than others. Partially empty office buildings in Boston's Financial District testify to this reality. It is uncertain how this situation will affect Boston's financial ecosystem.[41]

CHAPTER 4

The Evolution of the Global Information Network

"The single most important component of economic success, either for a business or for a worker, is access to networks of all kinds: job networks, money networks, idea networks, and networks of vendors and services."

Peter Calthorpe and William Fulton, *The Regional City*

Of all the factors driving globalization, telecommunications is the most pervasive. The Internet Revolution, brought about through a marriage of telecommunications and the computer, has provided instantaneous speed and unparalleled versatility in communications. Like innovations in communications over the last 200 years, the Internet has revolutionized how all aspects of society operate. Remarkably, Boston has played an important role in developing many transformative communications breakthroughs.

From its beginnings, Boston was situated in a global communications network. As the colonial economy strove to find trade outlets for its commodities, information had to be exchanged. Sea captains would carry mail, which included political and business news. Ship journeys from England took at least six weeks and often many more, depending upon the weather. In 1639, only nine years after Boston's founding, the General Court of Massachusetts designated the port's first postmaster, Richard Fairbanks. It cost one penny, usually paid by the sea captain delivering a letter from England, to deposit a letter with the postmaster. Missives from government officials were carried gratis. Fairbanks owned a tavern at the foot of Long Wharf. When ships arrived from London and Caribbean islands, merchants and other interested people would gather at his tavern to read the mail and share relevant news. This was British America's first post office.

Since letters and newssheets conveyed news from England and beyond, it ultimately made sense for someone to collect the news and publish it in the form of a newspaper. In 1690, Boston printer Benjamin Harris became the first American to put out a newspaper, *Publick Occurrences, both Foreign and Domestic*. It included shipping news and public notices gleaned from arriving vessels. The colonial government shut down the paper immediately because of reporting it deemed unfavorable. In 1704, the Massachusetts government licensed John Campbell, who was both Boston's postmaster and a printer, to publish the first government-licensed weekly, the two-page *Boston News-Letter*. This newspaper lasted, and it circulated in other colonies, inspiring newspapers in New York and Philadelphia. The *Boston News-Letter* was basically a compilation of business news, government communications, and advertising. The first newspaper with an independent, local perspective was James Franklin's *New England Courant*, first published in 1721. Franklin, Benjamin's older brother, added satirical essays on local affairs that were modeled on *The Spectator*, published by Londoners Richard Addison and Joseph Steele. As a teenager, Benjamin, who was a poorly treated indentured servant to his brother, anonymously submitted sarcastic essays under the pen name "Silence Dogood," before he ran away to Philadelphia. Because of his paper's free-lancing opinion, James Franklin was eventually charged with libel and jailed and his newspaper was shut down by the authorities.[1]

To create a functional land-based network for sharing news and official and personal communications, a postal system was necessary. Colonial authorities, in 1673, laid out a roughhewn Post Road between Boston and New York (also called the King's Highway), following forested Indian trails. By the 1690s, colonial governments introduced formal mail service, first by a private franchise, later under Crown control. The service resembled the later Pony Express, with post riders galloping from station to station (usually inns). It took a week to travel between the two cities. By 1729, there was weekly mail delivery at thirteen post offices between Boston and Philadelphia. At Philadelphia, printer Benjamin Franklin was named postmaster. Bringing to bear his first-rate organizational skills, Franklin introduced night post riders. This reduced the travel time between Boston and Philadelphia to three days.[2] When the thirteen American colonies endeavored to improve their coordination at the Albany Congress of 1754, they named Franklin co-postmaster for the colonies. One of his most important actions was permitting newspapers to be carried at a lower postage rate than that charged for private letters. Under this policy, newspaper publications flourished, helping influence the colonies' movement for independence. Because of Franklin's achievements in facilitating mail communication, the Second Continental Congress named him postmaster general of a new Post Office Department of the United States in 1775. The Post Office was charged with providing secure communications between government and the military and fostering the exchange of information in the emerging nation.

The US Constitution invested Congress with the power "to establish post offices and post roads," endorsing the notion of a postal service as a public amenity. The ensuing Post Office Act of 1792 ensured that the Post Office would be the first major federal agency with facilities and services throughout the country. In accordance with the nation-building vision of President George Washington, the Post Office was directed to allow anyone to use the mails, not just the wealthy or those living in cities. The Post Office authorized low-cost delivery of newspapers to foster the diffusion of knowledge and create an informed citizenry. By 1801, the country had 200 newspapers using the postal service.[3]

Over the ensuing decades, there was a growing desire to send personal letters, which was expensive. In 1843, it cost 19 cents to send a half-ounce letter from Boston to New York. Mailing a letter across the Appalachians cost more. Public demand for "cheap postage" swelled. The Post Office Act of 1845 set a price of five cents to mail a letter with an unlimited number of sheets (prior to that, each sheet was priced separately) less than 300 miles and 10 cents to mail it farther. Six years later, Congress set a uniform rate of three cents per half ounce for prepaid mail throughout the country.[4] The three-cent first-class rate remained the same for a century. In 1847, in order to standardize first-class mail service, the Post Office introduced the first postage stamps, following the example of Great Britain, which produced the world's first adhesive stamp, a "penny post" with an image of Queen Victoria in 1840. The US Post Office put portraits of Benjamin Franklin on the five-cent stamp and George Washington on the ten-cent stamp.[5]

The use of the mails for personal correspondence increased exponentially after the establishment of cheap uniform rates and prepaid stamps. Most letters were mailed from the East Coast cities, with a sizable volume headed to Europe pertaining to business dealings. By 1830, Americans mailed 14 million letters, averaging one letter per person per year (excluding Indigenous people and enslaved Black people). By 1856 and the reduction of postal rates, the post office handled 130 million letters, averaging 5.3 letters per person per year. Boston was one of the leaders for sending private correspondence, averaging forty-one letters per person. New Yorkers averaged thirty letters per person. Such rural states as Indiana and North Carolina averaged three and one and a half letters per person, respectively.[6]

The US Post Office created a postal system unmatched in the world, generating an insatiable appetite for speedy, efficient communications. The number of post offices in the country mushroomed from 75 in 1790 to 8,450 post offices in 1830. In America, every rural village had a post office with a postmaster, while, in Europe, post offices were located mainly in cities and towns. As steamboats and steam railways started plying routes in the 1830s, the mails became speedier. By 1835 it became possible to send the mail between Boston and Washington, DC, by a combination of railroad and steamboat within a mere thirty-seven hours. The mail was sent by train from Boston to Providence, by steamboat from Providence to New York, by a mix of railroad and steamboat to Philadelphia, by another mix of train and steamboat to Baltimore, and a final leg to Washington, DC, via railroad.[7]

The efforts to make the US mail more efficient and less costly came at the same time when international mail delivery was being transformed. During the late eighteenth and early nineteenth century, it could take between six weeks and three months for a letter to make its way to America from England.[8] The first regularly scheduled transatlantic "packet" service (so named because they carried "packets" of mail), the Black Ball Line, started operating between New York and Liverpool in 1818. These sailing ships departed every two weeks whether they were carrying full cargoes or not, or whether the weather was fair or foul. The Boston-Liverpool Line for packet ships was operating by 1824. In the age before the telegraph, ships were the sole source of news from Europe and the rest of the world. Just as in the seventeenth century, ship officers brought newspapers and correspondence to places where merchants and other interested persons gathered to receive the news. During the 1810s and

1820s, the Boston Exchange Coffee House, the city's leading hotel, played this role. It was called the Exchange Coffee House because it served as an informal exchange for news and business dealings.⁹

In 1840, Canadian steamship entrepreneur Samuel Cunard introduced the first regularly scheduled steamship service between Great Britain (Liverpool) and the United States (Boston). His service was subsidized by the British government to facilitate international mail. Cunard's steamship *Britannia* delivered the mail from Britain to Boston in two weeks, beating the time of the fastest sailing packets by two to four weeks. With Cunard employing four ships on the Liverpool-Boston run, he was able to deliver transatlantic mail weekly to Boston. By 1844, the Cunard Line was carrying 60,000 letters a month to England. Boston was assuming a role as intermediary between America and Europe. Historian Richard John maintained that "No longer was the Boston post office the back door to Europe; it had become instead a gateway between Europe and the transappalachian West."¹⁰

Even though steamships speeded international mail, it was still complicated and costly to mail letters. Separate postage was charged for each leg of transoceanic mail—the domestic route, the maritime route, and the overland route in Europe. Each country had its own postal policies, so countries needed to make treaty arrangements to exchange mail. Traditionally, European states, negotiated a postal treaty with each country it sent mail to. With the development of transatlantic steamship service, the United States established a convention with Great Britain in 1847 to facilitate prepaid mail. By 1870 the postage rate between the two countries had been reduced from twenty-four cents to six cents for a half-ounce letter—two cents for the transatlantic route and two cents for each overland segment. In 1874, the major European countries and the United States sorted out the chaotic international postal arrangements by forming the General Postal Union (later renamed the Universal Postal Union). This Union created a universal treaty that any nation could subscribe to. The Universal Postal Union members agreed to flat mail rates and equal treatment for foreign and domestic mail. Under these new arrangements, Americans could mail a letter to Europe for five cents and pre-stamped postcards and newspapers for two cents. With the fastest steamships traversing the Atlantic in seven days, the mails were intensifying the pace of globalization.¹¹

The next significant advance in international mail was airmail. The US Post Office inaugurated scheduled airmail service in 1918, using government aircraft on the New York-Philadelphia-Washington route. Within a couple years, it opened the first transcontinental route, between New York and San Francisco, stopping at thirteen places along the way.¹² In 1925, Congress directed the Post Office to contract with commercial airlines to deliver airmail, thereby boosting the airlines that became United, Eastern, American, TWA, and Pan American. In 1927, Colonial Air Transport, a predecessor of American Airlines, flew the first airmail route from Boston. It traveled to Hartford and New York, with connections there to the rest of the country. In 1926, domestic airmail rates were ten cents, dropping to five cents two years later. Airmail service became more widespread and reliable during the 1930s. The Post Office authorized the first international airmail route in 1928, between New York and Montreal. The next year, routes were opened between Miami and Caribbean islands and between Brownsville, Texas, and Mexico City. Transpacific airmail routes opened to the Philippines in 1935, Hong Kong in 1937, New Zealand in 1940, and Australia and China in 1947. The first transatlantic airmail service started in 1939, on Pan Am Yankee Clippers, which flew a route from New York to Bermuda-Azores-Lisbon-Marseilles- and on through Europe. During World War II, service opened on the New York-Newfoundland-Greenland-Iceland-London route.¹³ Airmail became broadly deployed by the 1950s and the coming of the Jet Age. For domestic service, the specific category of airmail was dropped in the 1970s; and first-class mail was sent by air whenever it would have been more expeditious than surface delivery.

TELEGRAPH

Mail delivery provided the only form of distance communication before Samuel F. B. Morse's introduction of the electric telegraph in 1844. Telegraphy and electric technology revolutionized communications and, with it, how businesses operated and individuals connected with one another.

Morse's telegraph, like many other groundbreaking inventions, built on the work of earlier inventors. The precursor of Morse's telegraph was an optical "telegraph" invented by French engineer Claude Chappe during the early 1790s. Chappe built a series of towers called "telegraphs" topped by a pair of T-shaped signaling arms (called "semaphores"), which could be arrayed in approximately 200 positions to transmit a code that spelled words alphabetically. The first electric telegraph used for commercial communication was developed by Englishmen William Fothergill Cooke and Charles Wheatstone. The receiver had needles that were manipulated by electromagnetic coils to point to letters on a board that spelled out messages. Both modes of communications were problematic to operate.

In America, Charlestown, MA native Samuel F. B. Morse, who was making a career as an artist, became fascinated with the budding concept of electric telegraphy and developed a practical method of conveying language through electric wires. In coding messages, Morse originally tried to use the ten cardinal numbers to stand in for the twenty-six letters of the alphabet, but that method proved too complicated for operators to transcribe. He made a conceptual breakthrough when he developed a code that used short dots and longer dashes to indicate letters, dramatically simplifying the task. Morse obtained funds from the US Congress to construct a 44-mile line of electric wires along the tracks of the Baltimore & Ohio Railroad between Baltimore and Washington. It got the attention of the political class when his first telegraphic message announced the vote of the Whig Party national convention taking place in Baltimore, which chose Henry Clay to be its 1844 presidential nominee. Morse followed up with a message sent directly to the Supreme Court room in the US Capitol, exclaiming "What hath God wrought." Morse hoped that Congress would fund a government-operated telegraph system similar to the Post Office. President James Knox Polk, who stood by the Democratic platform plank opposing "internal improvements," implacably resisted government management of a telegraph network. The measure did not pass Congress.[14]

Samuel Morse, who envisioned connecting the whole world through telegraphy, next sought private investment. Within a couple years, his company and others were operating telegraph lines connecting New York to Boston, Philadelphia, Washington, Buffalo, and communities in between. Boston used the new network to relay news from Europe received from Cunard steamships docking in its harbor to New York and beyond.[15]

For speculators, mastery of the news flow via telegraph could be invaluable. Boston entrepreneur Daniel H. Craig figured that by obtaining early news of European grain commodity prices he could make lucrative futures transactions. As soon as the Cunard steamship docked, he wired the commodity news to a collaborator in New York, then had the local telegraph wire cut to handicap New York investors in receiving the news. New Yorkers learned the trick and tried cutting the wire to Boston. This practice was no long-term solution for anyone. Craig realized that he could get a better jump on the news by sailing to Halifax and meeting the Cunard ship heading for Boston, reading the European papers during his two days on board, writing out important news on tissue paper, and sending it by carrier pigeon to Boston once it was about 100 miles from the port. This beat the steamship itself and gave Craig and his clients the advantage.

In 1846, the Boston-New York telegraph line opened. Five of the leading New York newspapers banded together to hire a representative in Boston to telegraph news received from Europe to New York. This arrangement followed an initiative of New York newspapers to form a reporting pool for gathering news related to the outbreak of the Mexican–American War. This arrangement became known as the New York Associated Press. The New York Associated Press went on to develop a relationship with Boston entrepreneur Daniel H. Craig to provide news gathered from European-originating ships docking at Halifax to be conveyed as quickly as possible to New York. In 1851, the newspaper consortium hired Craig to move to New York and run the entire organization.

Prior to the development of the telegraph, newsgathering relied upon rehashing newspapers from other places that were received through the mail. The telegraph enabled newspapers and other parties to receive and report news almost instantaneously. By the late 1850s, the Associated Press (which dropped the "New York" prefix) was sharing information simultaneously throughout the country. To serve the whole country equitably, the Associated Press introduced objective reporting, which vastly improved the quality of newspapers. For decades, the foremost user of telegraphy services was the Associated Press.[16]

Transatlantic ships were the only means for transmitting European news to the United States before 1858, when Cyrus Field laid the first transatlantic cable, between Valentia Bay, Ireland, and St. John's, Newfoundland, which was connected to Boston and New York by telegraph. There were celebrations on both sides of the Atlantic. Queen Victoria sent President James Buchanan a congratulatory cable, and Boston and New York batteries fired 100-gun salutes. But the cable failed within one month because of poor design and materials. Ships remained the sole information link to Europe for another eight years, when a functional underwater transatlantic cable was secured. By the 1870s, the telegraph linked the United States, Europe, India, Australia, and

Japan, providing businesspersons with real-time prices and supply information and enabling them to optimize decision-making.[17]

The American telegraph system grew rapidly after Morse opened his first lines. The country had 2,000 miles of telegraph wire by 1848, 12,000 miles by 1850, and 33,000 miles by 1853, connecting hundreds of cities and towns. The telegraph, which the Western Union Company extended to California in 1861, was considered vital to nation-building for the role it played in keeping the Golden State and the Mountain West attached to the Union during the Civil War. Morse's telegraph made a deep impression upon his contemporaries. In 1846, *De Bow's Review* called it "the greatest revolution of modern times."[18] Tom Standage has called the telegraph the "Victorian Internet" for its revolutionary impact of creating an instantaneous global communications network.

Besides disseminating news, the telegraph served mainly businesspeople and public officials. From its inception, the telegraph was used to communicate stock and commodity prices and other aspects of business dealings, facilitating the rise of industrial capitalism. In 1888, the minimum charge for sending a Western Union telegram between Boston and New York or other Northeast cities was $.25 for 10 words or less. The rate between Boston and Chicago and other Midwestern cities was $.50 for 10 words. The rate between Boston and San Francisco was $1.00. Transatlantic cables to London cost $2.50 for a ten-word telegram. After 1910, the price of telegrams was reduced, encouraging the general public to send telegrams announcing births, deaths, and other important moments of life. The heyday for personal telegrams lasted from the 1920s through the 1940s. Cheaper, easier-to-use long-distance phone service eroded the market for telegrams. Western Union delivered its last telegram in 2006.[19]

One of the best-known telegraph operators in Boston was Thomas Alva Edison, who worked there between 1867 and 1869. Edison was a prodigy at transcribing the messages as rapidly as they appeared. He was attracted to Boston because, in the words of Peter Hall and Paschal Preston, "it was then the unique centre of scientific and electrical research in the USA."[20] On the side, Edison rented space for a lab in a downtown electrical equipment shop, where he undertook experiments and exchanged ideas with other inventors. His first successful invention was a stock ticker for Western Union that relayed commodity and stock prices. This reinforced the role of the telegraph in disseminating business information. For greater business opportunities, Edison relocated to New York.

In the early years of international telegraphy, the systems of different nations could be incompatible. To remedy this, the United States and European countries founded the International Telegraph Union (a forerunner of the International Postal Union) in 1865 to create international protocols for telegraph equipment. The Union formally adopted the Morse code, common accounting regulations, and the right of all to use international telegraph networks. When wireless radio communication was developed at the turn of the century, twenty-nine countries joined to establish the International Radiotelegraph Union (1906). In 1932, the International Telegraph Union and the International Radiotelegraph Union merged into what is now called the International Telecommunications Union (ITU). The ITU assigns global radio spectrum and satellite orbits and establishes technical standards for telecommunications technologies.

As the use of electrical telegraphy grew, wireless (or radio) telegraphy began to change the nature of communications. The first person to successfully send an electrical wireless message was Alexander Graham Bell, who used a beam of light to transmit a message in Washington, DC, in 1880, four years after patenting the telephone. Bell called his invention the photophone. Because of difficulty achieving reliable transmission, this invention never caught on.

The foremost inventor in the field was Italy's Guglielmo Marconi, who sought to develop applications for using radio waves, which had been discovered by German physicist Heinrich Rudolph Hertz in the late 1880s. Hertz maintained that electromagnetic currents radiating from an antenna traveled through the air at the speed of light, a million times faster than sound waves. When Marconi was 21, he used radio waves to send signals several miles. In 1901, he sent the first wireless transatlantic message—in Morse code—between Ireland and Nova Scotia. The following year, he initiated transmission between England and Wellfleet, MA, on Cape Cod (the remains of the Marconi Wireless Station can be visited at the Cape Cod National Seashore). He introduced regular wireless service between Great Britain and the US two years later.

The first transmission of the human voice via radio waves was accomplished by Brazilian priest Roberto Landell de Moura in 1900. On Christmas Eve, 1906, Reginald Fessenden made the world's first radio broadcast of violin music and a Bible reading from Brant Rock in Marshfield, MA. Marconi refined these wireless discoveries to convey voice communications over his wireless network. The first systematic application of wireless voice communication took place during World War I, when the combatant navies employed it for communicating between ships. This paved the way for civilian broadcast radio after the war. Several commercial stations started broadcasting in 1920, with Westinghouse Electric's KDKA in Pittsburgh taking the lead. Television followed, with the first experimental US broadcasts taking place in 1928. Ten years later, NBC initiated regularly scheduled programming; the medium took off after World War II. Other wireless communications innovations of the 1920s led to the development of wireless telephone and Internet service and the radical transformation of global telecommunications.

TELEPHONE

Perhaps the most impactful invention to come out of Boston was Alexander Graham Bell's telephone. Bell came to Boston in 1872 to serve as professor of Vocal Physiology and Elocution at the Boston University School of Oratory. Like Edison, he was drawn to Boston because it was country's leading center for technological research. On the side, he taught deaf students and experimented with the transmission of the human voice through telegraph wires. Bell became interested in the operation of sound waves from his research on deafness and hearing. At MIT, he saw a "mechanical ear." This apparatus inspired his realization that an artificial diaphragm in a telephone could carry sound as the diaphragm does in the human ear. The electrical currents used with the telegraph could carry sound waves.[21] While researching voice transmission in a downtown building where Thomas Edison had experimented with the telegraph, Bell came up with a process for electrically transmitting sound. In 1876, Bell was tinkering with his telephone, when he called to his assistant Thomas Watson, who was in another room: "Mr. Watson, come here—I want to see you." Watson heard it over the wire and came running. The two men kept avidly working to improve the equipment and held the first two-way phone conversation, between Cambridge and Boston, seven months later. Before the end of 1876, they displayed their invention at the Centennial Exposition in Philadelphia. It caused a sensation, and Bell set out to commercialize the invention.

With funding from a small group of Boston investors, including his eventual father-in-law Gardiner G. Hubbard and the Forbes family of China trade fame, he established what became known as the American Bell Telephone Company. Although other companies sought to compete with American

Bell, it was able to maintain a monopolistic grip on the American market until 1894 by enforcing its patent, through supportive rulings of the US Supreme Court.

Skeptics wondered what the new "toy" would be good for. Alexander Graham Bell retorted with the prediction that "it is conceivable that cables of telephone wires could be laid underground or suspended overhead, communicating by branch wires with private dwellings, country houses, shops, manufactories, etc., etc., uniting them through the main cable with a central office where the wire could be connected as desired, establishing direct communication between any two places in the city."[22] The first city to be licensed by Bell Telephone to have a telephone exchange was New Haven, in 1878. Boston followed later the same year. During the 1880s, the company set up exchanges in every significant city. At each exchange, there were switchboards, analogous to the servers currently used for Internet traffic. Customers would phone in their calls to the exchange, where operators (phone companies were early employers of women, since women seemed to be more patient and polite with callers than men) would switch their call to the line of the designated destination. It was not until the 1920s that direct-dial service became widely available. Long-distance callers had to rely upon operator assistance until direct-dial was introduced in the 1950s.

Boston was the home of the American Bell Telephone Company—the city was an early adapter of the telephone. The regional subsidiary New England Telephone and Telegraph Company proclaimed: "Boston has become telephonically one of the best developed cities of the United States—it ranked first among the six largest cities in 1902." A survey four years later reported that the Boston Metropolitan District, with a population of 1,307,022, had 63,110 telephone subscribers or 4.8 subscribers per 100 people. By 1910, the Boston telephone exchange had 120,769 subscribers, ranking fifth in the world, after New York, Chicago, Berlin, and London.[23]

In the early years, almost all calls were local. Most customers were businessmen, physicians, and other professionals. There was little demand for residential use until after 1900. The first pay telephone was installed in Hartford, CT, in 1889. William Gray invented the pay phone in order to make phone service available to everyone, not just to customers who could pay a hefty annual fee.[24] He persuaded the Southern New England Telephone Company to install his pay phones, mainly in drug stores and hotels. The first outdoor phone booth was introduced in 1905.

Recognizing a market for personal calls, American Bell ran an 1894 print ad campaign that read: "Don't Travel—Telephone." By 1911, the phone company was sloganeering: "Telephone your happiness" and "The Telephone Brings Companionship." At this time, Bell president Theodore N. Vail articulated his vision for a universal phone system that reached from "every man's door to every other man's door."[25] By 1909, 25% of US homes, predominantly in the Northeast, Midwest, and California, had phone service. By 1941, the proportion had only grown to 40%.[26] High costs, shared party lines, and problematic equipment prevented subscriptions from growing. Only during the post–World War II era did phone use become nearly universal.

The telephone, paradoxically, facilitated both the development of low-density suburbs and the intensification of business districts with clusters of high-rise office buildings.[27] The telephone fostered a suburban way of life in which residents could communicate with scattered friends and relatives and conduct business transactions remotely. Phones allowed factories and warehouses to relocate to the periphery, while keeping them tethered to management located in the central city. Downtown offices no longer required an army of couriers to run through the city delivering messages. This dual phenomenon prefigured digital globalization, which has permitted instantaneous communication with any place in the world while propelling the concentration of power, wealth, and talent in a select number of global cities.

Long-distance phone service progressed more slowly than local calls. American Bell built the first long-distance phone lines, from Boston to Lowell in 1880 and to Providence in 1881. The company introduced the first phone service between Boston and New York three years later. In order to build a national long-distance telephone network linking the various local exchanges, American Bell created a subsidiary, AT&T, in 1885. (Because New York state laws were more permissive for corporate capitalization than those of Massachusetts, AT&T was based in New York. By 1899, AT&T absorbed the American Bell Company, becoming the parent of the Bell System of local franchises. This resulted in the Bell headquarters moving to New York and Bell Labs being located in New Jersey.) AT&T opened service between Boston and Washington, DC, Buffalo, and Pittsburgh by 1890. Phone calls to New York cost $2.00 for five minutes, and calls to Washington, DC cost $4.00. Long-distance lines reached Chicago in 1892. It took another 23 years to extend transcontinental phone lines all the way to San Francisco. AT&T advertised long-distance service with the slogan "Making a Neighborhood of a Nation,"

The Evolution of the Global Information Network 89

though, by 1920, only 3% of all the country's phone calls were long-distance. Early transcontinental calls were a real production. It took fourteen minutes and eight operators to convey the call through their exchanges linking Boston to San Francisco. By 1930, placing a transcontinental call was pared to 2.1 minutes; by the 1970s, direct-dialing made the call virtually instantaneous.[28]

AT&T initiated the first transatlantic commercial phone service, between New York and London in 1927, using radio wave transmission instead of an underwater cable. The first transatlantic phone calls cost $75 for three minutes. The first transpacific calls to Japan, transmitted by radio, started in 1934 at a cost of $39 for the first three minutes. As late as the 1980s, international calls were expensive. With the breakup of AT&T's monopoly at that time, both domestic long-distance and international rates dropped dramatically; the volume of overseas calls grew by six times during the decade. The reduced phone, telex, and fax rates facilitated the capacity of these technologies to coordinate a globalized economy and oversee international supply chains.[29]

A major improvement in transoceanic electronic communications was achieved in 1956, when AT&T laid the TAT-1 underwater cable between Newfoundland and Scotland. This technology provided the first high-quality transatlantic phone transmission, although its limited capacity could handle only eighty-nine simultaneous conversations between North America and Britain. Callers had to make an appointment with an operator to place an overseas call. The first direct-dialing, between New York and London, became possible in 1970.[30] AT&T made a major advance in cable technology in 1975, when it introduced fiber-optic wires, which used light waves capable of carrying vast amounts of information. It took another 13 years for fiber-optical cables, which had 1,000 times the capacity of the 1956 underwater copper cable, to be laid across the Atlantic Ocean. By the late 1990s, a fiber cable, as thick as a strand of hair, could carry all North America's long-distance communications. Even with the prodigious capacity of satellites, fiber is capable of carrying 90+% of all international telecommunications. It is invaluable for transmitting video and data, which require substantial bandwidth. High-speed fiber cable and the telecom satellite infrastructure have vastly expanded the scope of computer communication.[31]

Telecommunications made another advance with the launch in 1962 of the Telstar satellite, which facilitated instantaneous television broadcasts and telephone service. Like the first high-quality underwater cable, the first telecommunications satellite had a very limited capacity. It could transmit 240 phone conversations or two TV channels at a time.[32] Within a decade, satellites were being widely used to carry electronic communications around the world. Today, 400 geostationary satellites form a band around the earth 22,000 miles above its surface, allowing a massive amount of communication. As a result, the cost of making an international three-minute phone call between New York and London dropped by almost 95% between 1960 and 2005.[33]

An ancillary use of telephone service has been the fax (facsimile) machine. The fax machine was an analog forerunner of digital communications with its capacity to electronically transmit photocopies of documents and photos around the world. Inventors had been experimenting with different ways to copy and send graphic messages over telegraph wires since the late nineteenth century, but it was not until 1924 that scientists at AT&T devised a means of transmitting over telephone lines photographs that could be reproduced in

Table 3. Cost of sending messages through different communications media

Communication Type	Original Cost	Cost in 2023 Dollars
Half-ounce Letter (1843)	.19	$7.75
Half-ounce Letter (1851)	.03	$1.18
International Letter (Pre-1870)	.24	$5.53
International Letter (1870)	.06	$1.38
Domestic Airmail Letter (1926)	.10	$1.71
Domestic Airmail Letter (1928)	.05	.88
Telegram 10 words, Boston- Northeast City (1888)	.25	$7.94
Telegram 10 words, Boston-Midwest (1888)	.50	$15.89
Telegram 10 words, Boston-California (1888)	$1.00	$31.77
Telegram, 10 words, Boston-London (1888)	$2.50	$79.43
Annual Local Phone Service-Business (1889)	$120.00	$3,937.00
Annual Local Phone Service-Residence (1889)	$90.00	$3,149.00
Phone Call 5-minutes, Boston-New York (1890)	$2.00	$66.34
Phone Call 5-minutes, Boston-Chicago (1890)	$4.00	$132.68
Phone Call 3-minutes, US.-England (1927)	$75.00	$1,301.00
Phone Call 3-minutes, US-Japan (1934)	$39.00	$878.00

Source: Bureau of the Census, *Bicentennial Edition Historic Statistics of the United States: Colonial Times to 1970*; Richard R. John, *Spreading the News: The American Postal System from Franklin to Morse*; US CPI Inflation Calculator, www.in2013dollars.com.

newspapers. In succeeding years, various improvements were made until, in 1964, Xerox produced what was considered the first modern fax machine. By the late 1970s, use of compact, affordable fax machines became widespread. Since the emergence of the Internet along with computer image scanning in the late 1990s, the use of fax machines has diminished.

THE TRANSFORMATIONAL IMPACT OF THE INTERNET

The development of the telegraph, telephone, and wireless telecommunications enabled instantaneous communication, setting the stage for the apogee of information networks, the Internet. The Internet, as everyone knows, has put billions of users around the world in immediate contact with each other and with an unimaginably vast storehouse of information related to every conceivable subject. The Internet has accomplished this through the convergence of the computer with the wires of the telephone and the wireless radio waves used by mobile phones, radios, and television.

Enormous vacuum tube-operated computers with relatively small computing power—the ENIAC computer—were introduced in the 1940s. The adoption of transistors and semiconductors during the 1950s enabled computers to become smaller and more powerful. Co-founder of Intel Gordon Moore asserted, in 1965, that the ongoing miniaturization of the semiconductor would allow the number of components per integrated circuit to double every year, exponentially expanding the capacity of a computer. This rule of thumb, which was later adjusted to predict a doubling of capacity every two years, has been called Moore's Law. It still has efficacy, although computer scientists feel that it will not be valid much longer. The evolution of the silicon chip has been astonishing:

- when Moore proposed his law in 1965, 30 transistors could fit on a silicon chip;
- Intel's first commercial microprocessor, introduced in 1971, contained 3,500 transistors;
- Intel's Pentium 4, of the late 1990s, carried 42 million transistors;
- 2015 Core i7 chip used in Macs and Windows PCs had 1.4 billion transistors on a surface area of 160 square millimeters;
- 2023 Apple M1 Ultra had 114 billion transistors, while Micron's flash memory V-NAND chip had 5.3 trillion transistors.[34]

This geometric increase in computing power led to the development of IBM desktop computers in the late 1970s and Apple computers a few years later. The development of smart phones began in the 1990s, and, the iPhone, introduced in 2007, marked another major breakthrough.

The Internet developed from efforts to link computers electronically—another area where Boston-based innovators played a prominent part. Perhaps their greatest contribution was conceptualizing and creating a universal network for sharing information. In 1945, MIT dean and US military science research director Vannevar Bush, who, fourteen years earlier, had built the world's first analog electrical-mechanical computer—the "Differential Analyzer"—envisioned a personal machine he called a "Memex," which would store all a person's records, books, and communications in an easily retrievable format.[35] Bush's article inspired JCR Licklider to imagine an "Intergalactic Computer Network" that would link together all computers, allowing them to share information on a universally-accessible basis. Licklidder, who had been an MIT professor and a researcher at the firm of Bolt Beranek and Newman, formulated this theory during 1962–1963, when he was working on a temporary assignment at the Defense Department referred to as "Libraries of the Future."[36] Licklidder foresaw how enormous databases could share information the way libraries could. The effort to implement this vision began when the Advanced Research Projects Agency (ARPA) of the US Defense Department contracted with Bolt Beranek and Newman to develop a network linking 16 ARPA research sites around the country. Bolt Beranek and Newman was a West Cambridge technology consulting firm formed by three MIT professors. The Advanced Research Projects Agency Network (ARPANET), inaugurated in 1969, permitted researchers at Stanford University to send the first message to compatriots at UCLA. The message was supposed to read "LOGIN," but the computer crashed after typing just "LO."[37]

At Bolt Beranek and Newman, Ray Tomlinson devised the first person-to-person email in 1971. Tomlinson, who had taught at MIT, was researching software for transferring files from one computer to another. In order to send the file, he developed a protocol for an electronic mail ("email") address that utilized the "@" symbol located between the name of the message's recipient and the computer that person was using. The email address format developed by Tomlinson—name@host computer—is universally used today.[38] This was as significant as Alexander Graham Bell's invention of the telephone.

For years, emails were used primarily by researchers in the ARPANET. In 1989, the Cambridge-based Lotus Development Corporation (whose Lotus 1-2-3 became a "killer app" that offered spreadsheet, database, and graphic chart functionality for IBM PCs) released Lotus Notes email software for use by the general public. Quickly adopted by millions of users, Lotus Notes allowed messages to be opened by multiple computers simultaneously.[39] The email started as a substitute for phone calls and quickly became a substitute for "snail mail" and paper-based faxes. Paradoxically, while the Internet dramatically diminished first-class mail, e-commerce intensified the demand for the physical delivery of packages.

Another significant Cambridge-related Internet innovator has been Tim Berners-Lee, an MIT professor since 1994. While working previously as a computer scientist at CERN (European Organization for Nuclear Research) supercollider particle physics lab in Geneva, Switzerland, he devised (and named) the World Wide Web in 1989 as a means of facilitating the worldwide distribution of text, graphics, video, and sound. Just as Ray Tomlinson had stumbled upon electronic mail as a means of communicating between ARPANET computers, Berners-Lee developed the World Wide Web as a means of facilitating communications between researchers of the CERN's global research network. In 1990, he published the first website. In developing his web page, he introduced the essential Internet protocols:

- Uniform Resource Locator (URL)—the address for a web page;
- Hypertext Transfer Protocol (HTTP)—a tool used with the URL to allow Internet servers to communicate with each other and facilitate the exchange of information;
- Hypertext Markup Language (HTML)—the standard markup language for creating web pages.[40]

His software was designed to easily share and retrieve all information on any computer by attaching a unique address to the prefix http://www.___. When interviewed about his innovation, Berners-Lee admitted that there was no useful reason for him to have included "double slashes" in the web address.

As Berners-Lee stated in *Weaving the Web*, "By being able to reference anything with equal ease, a computer could represent associations between things that might seem unrelated but somehow did, in fact, share a relationship. A web of information would form."[41] If someone put information on the World Wide Web, anyone could find it. With this breakthrough, anyone in the world to utilize the Web, not just the scientists that worked at CERN. Tim Berners-Lee's achievement was world changing. According to Walter Isaacson, "more than most digital-age innovations, the conception of the Web was primarily by one person."[42]

In 1994, the World Wide Web started to achieve widespread public use, growing from 700 websites globally to 10,000 and multiplying by ten times the following year. The key breakthrough was produced by the development of the web browser MOSAIC (later absorbed by Netscape). The Web became not just a communication system, but an inexhaustible source of information.[43]

Tim Berners-Lee became concerned that his dream of a single universal web of shared information could be jeopardized. He feared that the Web "could splinter into factions—some commercial, some academic, some free, some not."[44] He wanted to establish an international organization that would create an orderly framework with standard interfaces so that the Web could grow in an unconstrained way, without requiring central management. Berners-Lee envisioned a body which would convene developers of servers and browsers to achieve consensus of how the Web would operate. CERN, which was focusing on construction of its Large Hadron Collider, dropped out of being a sponsor of the Consortium. Berners-Lee obtained strong support for creating the World Wide Web Consortium (W3C) from Michael Dertouzos, Director of the MIT Laboratory for Computer Science. In 1994, Berners-Lee moved from CERN to lead the new Consortium in Cambridge.[45] Under Berners-Lee's leadership, the World Wide Web Consortium has worked assiduously to promulgate protocols ensuring that the Web remains open to all and that specific actors—corporations, governments, academics, or individuals—do not fragment or privatize elements of the universal communications space. He has argued that "universality must exist across the spectrum of cost and intention. People and organizations have different motivations for putting things on the Web: for their benefit, commercial gain, the good of society, or whatever."[46] The World Wide Web has been an essential element in promoting universal use of the Internet.

By 1995, Berners-Lee recognized that the surge in Internet content was creating a logjam that drastically slowed service. He called on MIT faculty to invent a faster way to transmit Internet content. MIT Applied Mathematics Professor Tom Leighton responded with algorithms for routing and replicating Internet content over a worldwide network of distributed computer servers. With colleagues, Leighton moved to commercialize his content delivery network by establishing Akamai Technologies in 1999 in Cambridge's Kendall Square. This network increased the speed of the Internet dramatically, permitting the streaming of video that people take for granted today. Today, Akamai's distributed computing platform, the world's largest, allows the company to provide state-of-the-art cloud and cybersecurity services.[47]

One of Tim Berners-Lee's foremost projects at the World Wide Web Consortium was introducing the concept of the "Semantic Web" in 1999. After realizing his vision of person-to-person electronic communication through the World Wide Web, he postulated a second vision—creating a framework for computers and machines of every kind to analyze "all the data on the Web—the content, links, and transactions between people and computers." He maintained that great advances in human experience could result from machines communicating through the Web. The routine "mechanisms of trade, bureaucracy, and our daily lives will be handled by machines talking to machines leaving humans to provide the inspiration and intuition."[48] The "machine-understandable Web" concept has influenced the development of the Internet of Things and artificial intelligence (AI). In the intervening years, Tim Berners-Lee has continued working at the World Wide Web Consortium, MIT, and other academic institutions to maintain a highly adaptable and accessible global information network, passing up opportunities for fabulous wealth in the capitalist sector to do so.

Social media also experienced a major breakthrough in Cambridge. In 2004, Harvard student Mark Zuckerberg launched an online student directory for fellow students which quickly expanded to other colleges and opened to the general public as Facebook two years later. When Zuckerberg and his partners could not obtain funding from the Boston-based venture capital firm Battery Ventures, they moved their company to Silicon Valley, where they obtained financing from PayPal co-founder Peter Thiel and others. Zuckerberg's Harvard experience, like that of Microsoft founder Bill Gates, testified to the talent pool that is drawn to Boston, though not always retained here.

Although California's Silicon Valley is frequently regarded as the foremost center for Internet, software, and apps development, Greater Boston has continued to play a major role. Information technology companies headquartered in Greater Boston include:

- Dell EMC—data storage and information security specialist
- Analog Devices—semiconductor maker

- Teradyne—semiconductor testing company
- HubSpot—developer of inbound marketing software
- Nuance Communications—Siri/voice recognition software maker
- LogMeIn—maker of software for remote work and customer engagement.

Many of the country's leading tech companies have a significant R&D presence in the Boston area. They include tech communications conglomerate Cisco Systems; Google's Android mobile device research operation; Amazon's developers of Alexa, Amazon Web Services, Amazon Pharmacy, and Amazon Robotics. Microsoft's New England Research & Development (NERD) Center, IBM's largest software development operation, and Meta Platforms/Facebook R&D are located in Kendall Square. The presence of these companies indicates the attraction of Greater Boston as a technology innovation hub.

TELECOMMUNICATIONS AND GLOBALIZATION

The Internet revolution, which has been underway for more than thirty years, offers sweeping openness and versatility for communications. It has enabled an endless number of uses, from phone calls and videos to shopping and medical diagnosis, all drawing upon globalized connections. Internet-enabled communications have powerfully boosted the capitalist system. According to Peter Hall, the Internet has been "increasing rates of profits, accelerating internationalization, and engendering a new policy agenda on the part of governments, to foster capital accumulation at the expense of social redistribution."[49] During the COVID-19 pandemic, the Internet enabled business to carry on and workers to operate remotely while connecting all parts of the world. Internet communications have bolstered the advantages of cities. Advanced telecommunications infrastructure is most likely to be found in major cities, thus augmenting their capacities and influence.

Operating under the free market system, the early rollout of broadband Internet occurred where the greatest profits could be made—in densely populated metropolitan cores. Broadband and cloud computing has an overwhelmingly urban geography. In Peter Dicken's words, "the map of the Internet mirrors the network of global cities."[50] Fiber cables often piggyback on the established rights-of-way of railroad lines and highways and even run inside sewers. Such a competitive advantage has played a major role in Boston's ability to project its business and ideas across the globe. Boston and neighboring communities have leading-edge 5G digital infrastructure, which is almost universally available in the service areas of the major providers T-Mobile, Verizon, and AT&T. 5G service provides download speeds at least 10 times faster and theoretically up to 100 times faster than 4G service. The full potential of 5G will be realized as the infrastructure is built out. Besides easing viewing of films and other data-rich content, 5G can support "smart city" initiatives, the Internet of Things, autonomous vehicles, and other technologies that have yet to be invented.[51]

As of 2023, there were 5.6 billion global mobile phone users (66% of world population), 5.3 billion Internet users, and 4.95 billion social media users, out of a total world population of 8 billion people. According to the ITU, 88% of the world has access to 4G service. Robust 5G service, introduced in 2019, reached 1.2 billion users within three years, with the largest concentration of users in Europe (52%), the Americas (38%), and the Asia-Pacific region (16%). All major US carriers are constantly expanding 5G service. As of 2023, Facebook had almost 3 billion active global users, while YouTube had 2.5 billion, Instagram 2 billion, and TikTok 1.08 billion.[52]

The quantum leap in mobile telephone computing power and fiber and wireless connectivity have been decisive breakthroughs in democratizing Internet service around the world. They have made the cost of communicating negligible, ending the days of expensive long-distance phone calls. Inexpensive mobile phones have helped poor countries avoid the significant capital costs entailed by constructing land lines, while taking full advantage of the Internet (though poorer communities around the world still lack even 3G or 4G connectivity). It is difficult to predict exactly where telecommunications are headed in the future. Video-calling and conferencing platforms like Zoom will be enhanced, and holographic images will augment the video experience. As telecommunications become even more immediate and convenient, their impacts on cities and face-to-face interactions will continue to evolve.

CHAPTER 5

Jet Age Global Node

"Flows of high-value products and high-value people [through major airports] . . . include everything and everybody from sushi-grade tuna, biomeds, and smartphones to investment bankers, international corporate lawyers, and foreign tourists."

John K. Kasarda, "Aerotropolis"

Before World War II, international air travel hardly existed. If you wanted to travel to Europe, the Caribbean, or Asia, you sailed there on a ship. Europe—Southampton or Le Havre—was at least six or seven days away. The travels of Cardinal William O'Connell (1907–1944) shed a light on pre-Jet Age travel. Cardinal O'Connell was nicknamed "Gangplank Bill" by the Boston press for his annual winter sea voyages to the Caribbean and his vacation home in the Bahamas. He also traveled frequently to Europe, particularly for ecclesiastical business in Rome. His many sea journeys, departing from and returning to Boston, demonstrated how local citizens were likely to connect to the world beyond their shores.

Commercial air services started slowly, like the development of many new technologies. Logan Airport (originally called Jeffrey Field) opened in 1923 on landfill on the East Boston waterfront. It was first used for fledgling airmail and by the Massachusetts Air National Guard and the US Army Air Corps. The first regularly scheduled commercial flights were introduced by

Colonial Air Transport (a predecessor to American Airlines) in 1927, flying to New York. The first daily trips to New York were offered in the late 1930s. The World War II military buildup spurred the filling of an additional 1,800 acres of wetlands in East Boston and the construction of runways and terminals. This created a major airport right alongside the city's long-established seaport.

Scheduled transatlantic commercial flights started in 1946. Peace in Europe attracted business and vacation travelers who would have formerly traveled by ship. Boston, after New York, was the foremost American airport with transatlantic service, because of its proximity to Europe and the size of its travel market. American Airlines introduced one flight per week. The flight originated on Tuesday at New York's LaGuardia Airport, flew to Boston, refueled at Gander, Newfoundland, and arrived at Ireland's Shannon Airport at 10:10 a.m. on Wednesday. The flight would then proceed to London's Heathrow Airport. From London, one could fly via other airlines throughout Europe and beyond. The flying time to Shannon was fifteen hours and seventeen hours to London. Although the transatlantic flight was lengthy by today's standards, it was far faster than the ocean journey. The one-way fare to London was $366 ($5,737 in 2023 dollars), and round-trip (60-day limit) was $454 ($7,117 in 2023).[1]

Pan American Airways developed air routes to every continent except Australia and offered round-the-world service. In 1950, Pan Am operated two flights a week from Boston to Europe, stopping in Gander, Shannon, London, and Frankfurt, and taking about 19 hours. The second flight traveled beyond Frankfurt to Istanbul, Beirut/Damascus, Karachi, Delhi, Calcutta, Bangkok, and ended in Hong Kong (most Boston-based travelers disembarked at one of the European destinations). The flight departed Boston on Tuesday at 11:00 a.m. and arrived at Hong Kong Friday at 11:00 a.m. The Frankfurt round-trip fare was $615 ($7,800 in 2023) and the Hong Kong round-trip fare was $1,670 ($21,182 in 2023). Transatlantic Pan Am passengers flew in Lockheed Constellation planes, which provided the first pressurized cabins. This allowed the planes to fly above the "air sickness zone," around 12,500 feet, to above the clouds at 24,000 feet. These planes, which carried between 60 and 81 passengers, could fly 340 mph. Some planes provided sleeping berths for long-range trips. In 1951, the Super Constellation upgraded the passenger experience by introducing air conditioning, reclining seats, and extra toilets.

TWA also made flights out of Boston by the late 1940s on two different routes. One route traveled via a fuel stop at Santa Maria, Azores, to Lisbon on to Madrid, and Rome. The travel time to Lisbon was almost seventeen hours and twenty-four hours to Rome. The other route flew to Gander, Shannon Paris, Zurich, and Rome. During the 1950s, European national airlines, including Air France, BOAC (British Overseas Airways Company), Ireland's Aer Lingus, and Italy's Alitalia, offered propeller-driven plane flights from Boston to their respective countries.[2]

The speed of air travel doubled from 200–300 mph to 500–600 mph when the jet plane was introduced in 1958. The following year, Pan Am inaugurated the first Boeing 707 jet service to Europe out of Boston. There was no longer a need to stop in Gander or the Azores to refuel. The flight time to Shannon took only five-and-a-half hours, which still stands today. All airlines were soon flying jet planes to Europe. By 1964, between 25 and 30 long-haul international flights were departing Logan daily. The capacity of commercial airplanes and the flying range was virtually doubled by the Boeing 747, which Pan Am started flying out of Logan Airport to London Heathrow in 1970.[3] During this period, the Massachusetts Port Authority (Massport), which managed the seaport, took over management of the airport as well.

Jet airplanes revolutionized the process of traveling between Boston and distant cities. The Jet Age coincided with the proliferation of multinational corporations, as high-speed airplanes allowed businessmen to easily traverse the globe, making deals and managing far-flung operations. Local economic development officials and businesspeople maintained that a well-served Logan Airport was essential to the region's economy. With short travel times and declining costs, international tourism gradually became important. Another important Logan Airport function became serving as a gateway for immigrants. In fact, Massport proclaims that "Logan is Boston's Ellis Island."[4]

To service mushrooming travel growth, Logan Airport opened its first dedicated international terminal in 1961. Faced with a boom in foreign travel, Logan Airport thirteen years later replaced it with Terminal E. Between 1974 and 1997, the volume of international travelers tripled.[5] This increase occurred in tandem with commensurate growth of domestic passenger flights and cargo shipments. In the decades after World War II, Logan Airport expanded from 200 acres more than 2,300 acres, most of it on made land. It has six runways and four passenger terminals and employs approximately 16,000 people. Massport added capacity for international carriers in a new, vastly expanded terminal that opened in 2023. *Conde Nast Traveler* marveled at the new international terminal's design, saying it "is like taking a trip back in time to an era

Figure 4. Logan Airport International Terminal E expansion (2023). The sweeping roof's color is a unique "Boston Red," sourced by architect Luis Vidal specifically for this building, to connect with the red color in the city's red brick architecture, fall foliage, and Harvard's trademark crimson.—Courtesy of Massport.

when going to the airport held the promise of glamour and whimsy." Architect Luis Vidal explained that the stylish aesthetic is appropriate: "airports are the cathedrals of the 21st century, they serve as the main gateway of countries, requiring a bold presence to leave a positive and lasting impression on the traveler."[6]

Logan International Airport has been growing rapidly as a global gateway. Since 2022, there has been a resurgence of air travel with the waning of COVID-19. It has been driven by leisure and international travelers. Although business trips are not at 2018 levels, they have been increasing.[7]

In 2023, 40 million passengers used Logan, making it the #16 busiest airport in the country. It ranked #12 in the US for international passenger arrivals and departures in 2023, with 8.4 million passengers. New York's JFK International Airport ranked #1 for international passengers. As of April 2024, Logan International Airport was served by thirty-seven airlines connecting directly with over 50 international destinations and over 75 domestic destinations. According to a 2023 survey of the top 50 International Megahubs, Logan Airport ranks #45. London's Heathrow and New York's JFK rank #1 and #2 in the world.

The largest number of international passengers at Logan (FY2022)— 644,886—were traveling between Boston and London Heathrow. The other leading destinations, like Heathrow, are airports that are connecting hubs for major airlines. The majority of passengers are changing planes to fly to further destinations.

Much of the increased international travel at Logan Airport has been driven by opening new routes. Around 2010, local business leaders made the case to Governor Deval Patrick that attracting international airlines from beyond Europe would boost airport use as well as the regional economy. Governor Patrick directed Massport to offer incentives to any carrier that offered new service to Latin America, Africa, or Asia. Japan Air Lines introduced nonstop service to Tokyo in 2012. Copa Airlines started flying in 2013 to its Panama

Table 4. Leading international destinations for passengers flying to and from Logan Airport (October 2022–September 2023)

Airport	Passengers
London Heathrow	865,968
Paris de Gaulle	425,687
Dublin	390,163
Amsterdam	387,709
Reykjavik	295,814
Lisbon	251,946
Oranjestad, Aruba	247,091
Zurich	244,714
Toronto Pearson	243,376
Frankfurt	228,762
Rome Fiumicino	227,085
Dubai	215,120
Cancun	199,734
Munich	197,587
Doha, Qatar	172,434
Santo Domingo, DR	163,373
Istanbul	161,337
Madrid	159,781
Toronto Bishop	141,051
Santiago de los Caballeros, DR	132,381

Source: "Logan International Airport," Wikipedia, accessed April 6, 2024, https://en.wikipedia.org/wiki/Logan_International_Airport#cite_note-internationalreport-167.

City hub. The following year, Logan beat out other major US airports when Turkish Airlines decided to start service to Istanbul, offering a multitude of connections beyond. The same year, Emirates inaugurated flights to Dubai, the world's busiest hub for international flights. In 2016, Qatar Airways, with the sixth largest air cargo service in the world, started flights to Doha. In 2018, LATAM Brazil initiated service to its Sao Paulo hub, plugging Boston travelers into its extensive network linking 120 destinations across Latin America. Avianca started flying to Bogota in 2017. Korean Air, in a joint venture with Delta, started service from Seoul to Boston in 2019. Korean Air introduced service to Boston as much for shipping Massachusetts-produced high-tech products as for encouraging tourism.[8]

In 2015, El Al Israel Airlines introduced nonstop flights between Boston and Tel Aviv. The New England-Israel Business Council, in a 2016 economic impact study, touted the attractiveness of doing business in Boston compared with Silicon Valley or even New York, since it is closer to Tel Aviv and allows more efficient use of a businessperson's time. Boston has become an attractive El Al Israel gateway to the United States because of Israel's connections to innovation sector businesses in Boston. The New England-Israel Business Council has claimed that more than 200 Israeli-owned companies, primarily in the knowledge sector, operate in Massachusetts.[9]

With Delta almost doubling its Boston flights, the airline is developing Boston an intercontinental hub. Boston has not traditionally been a "hub" for airlines because of its peripheral US geographical location. But it is well-positioned to funnel air traffic from Europe and the Middle East into Delta's western hemisphere route system. Boston is becoming more appealing as an international hub because New York's major international airports, JFK and Newark, are at capacity. It should be noted that JetBlue, which has been flying to US and Caribbean destinations, has added London, Dublin, Edinburgh, Paris, Amsterdam as destinations.

Besides providing greatly expanded air passenger service, Logan Airport's freight service has also grown. Around the world, air freight increased five times between 1987 and 2017, while the cost declined dramatically. Air freight carries more than one-third of the trade value of US exports. For Boston, this includes seafood, flowers, semiconductors, medical and dental instruments, and centrifuges. Logan Airport, in 2023, handled 255,616 tons of air cargo and mail, making it the #32 busiest airport in the US in terms of cargo.[10] It is served by dedicated cargo airlines DHL, FedEx Express, and UPS Airlines, as well as many of the passenger airlines serving Logan. Logan serves the needs of the Boston region. It is not a major transfer point for cargo to other cities. Expansion of air cargo service at Logan is limited by its small operational footprint in East Boston. In light of Logan's spatial constraints, Manchester, New Hampshire's Airport and Hartford's Bradley International Airport have enjoyed a significant increase in air cargo since 2010.

One of the more noteworthy global business sectors utilizing Logan Airport is the seafood processing industry. Since the seventeenth century, Boston has been exporting seafood to the rest of the world. The "Sacred Cod," a five-foot wooden effigy memorializing the one of the state's first great export industries, has been hanging in the Massachusetts State House since colonial times. During the nineteenth century, fish exports dropped precipitously, but Boston still provided fish for the domestic market. The state modernized the harbor's fishing operation by building the Fish Pier in 1915. That year, 163 million pounds of fish were landed at the Fish Pier. The volume rose to 300 million in the 1930s. During the early 1960s, Boston's fish catch fell to 117 million pounds. By the twenty-first century, over-fishing and stringent federal regulation had shrunk the catch dramatically. In 2019, the total was at 15 million pounds, compared with New Bedford's 103 million pounds and Gloucester's 45 million pounds (the total fish landings of Massachusetts placed #2 to Alaska's top rank.)

In the 1970s, Massport considered demolishing the Fish Pier because of its deteriorating condition and the reduced amount of use its was receiving. But, because the state agency was committed to encouraging maritime uses on Boston Harbor, it rehabilitated the facility. This enabled the Fish Pier to become a seafood processing center, handling seafood caught or harvested in Massachusetts and elsewhere in the world. Today, virtually all the space in the Fish Pier is occupied by wholesale businesses filleting, freezing, and producing seafood products. Between the Fish Pier and other companies operating within a 1 ½-mile radius, there are 50 plus seafood businesses. This activity supports more than 6,400 jobs, including people employed in downstream logistics and in local retail sales operations. Total business revenue for the seafood processing companies totaled $916,748,000 in 2018. With the clustering of the varied functions creating valuable efficiencies, seafood processing is a big business. Boston is one of the country's four top processing hubs, along with Seattle, San Francisco, and Miami.[11]

Since the Massachusetts seafood processing sector depends upon importing and exporting fish, it requires close proximity to truck and air freight infrastructure. The seafood sector is clustered around Boston Harbor more because of nearby Logan Airport and interstate highways than because of fishing boats based in the port. Convenient multi-modal transportation is essential to the seafood processing industry because it is time-sensitive and highly competitive. As of 2017, 10% of all the fresh and frozen fish imported into the United States came through Logan Airport, most of it being processed and packaged here before transshipment elsewhere. A study by UMass-Dartmouth, *Navigating the Global Economy*, reported that "these processors are mostly processing fish that is brought in from overseas." Many are small niche businesses which "focus on high value-added products, such as smoked haddock, salmon bacon, and a wide range of other cured fishes." Some businesses concentrate on preparing sushi-grade fish for the Japanese market.[12]

THE IMPACT OF INTERNATIONAL TOURISM

Tourism is a major expression of globalization. It exposes the experience of a place to people from around the world. The world's ubiquitous air network has made tourism a common experience for hundreds of millions. Tourism has economic impacts, providing jobs and stimulating development and cultural initiatives. Increased international flights have boosted Boston to the rank of #9 US city for international visitation (2022), with New York being #1. *Condé Nast Traveler* proclaimed that Boston is "a city that's always on the move—and it encourages visitors to do the same."[13] Between 1991 and 2017, the number of international visitors in Boston grew from 475,000 to 1.7 million, out of a total of 23.5 million visitors. The number of local hotel rooms doubled from 12,800 to 25,000.[14]

For Chinese travelers, Boston was the #5 US destination before the COVID-19 pandemic and rising political strains, behind Los Angeles, New York, San Francisco, and Chicago. China was Boston's leading market for tourism, with 18.2% of all trips, ahead of visitors from the United Kingdom and Brazil. The introduction of nonstop flights on Hainan Airlines (2014) from Beijing and Shanghai and on Cathay Pacific (2016) from Hong Kong made Boston a convenient place for Chinese travelers to visit. Aggressive marketing by Massport, Massachusetts Office of Travel & Tourism, Greater Boston Convention & Visitors Bureau (now called Meet Boston), and private businesses played a significant role in attracting international tourism. Chinese visitors increased in Boston from 3,100 in 2007 to 119,000 in 2013 to 301,000 in 2017.

These visitors spent an average of $5,000 per visit, far more than those from other countries. They stayed on average 9.7 days in Boston-area hotels. Of $3.9 billion spent in Greater Boston by international visitors, $1.3 billion was spent by those from China, followed by India and the United Kingdom at $417 million and $297 million, respectively. Spending by overseas visitors is especially impactful, since they account for nearly 15% of total visitor spending while making up only 8% of overall visitors. The upgraded air service has also helped boost the number of Chinese students studying in Massachusetts universities from approximately 13,000 in 2013 to 23,000 in 2022.[15] The volume of Chinese tourists dropped dramatically during the COVID-19 lockdowns in China. Only by mid-2023 did the Chinese government permit group tourist travel from China to the US to resume. Boston's touristic appeal is based upon offering an engaging urban experience unattainable in most places in the US The city's dense, fine-grained, human scale has earned it the title of "America's Walking City." You can still walk the crooked streets, the former "cow paths" allegedly laid out for cows to be driven to the Boston Common in colonial times. Besides historic sites, the urban fabric affords visitors a panoply of restaurants, bars, shops, and cultural attractions. The modern architecture blends judiciously with historic landmarks. Boston's competitive advantage is that it is a "real city."

Tourism in Boston has grown tremendously as its urban charms have been discovered and enhanced. When visitors were surveyed in 1967, 8% said their primary interest was the "city" itself; by 1994, a majority of visitors declared the "city visit" to be the primary reason for visiting.[16] The 1960s was an era when most vacationers went to the beach or the mountains for a period of relaxation, not to cities for stimulation and excitement (American cities were in decay at this time). Boston's adroit blend of historic preservation with modern development draws travelers from far and wide.

Boston made important steps toward highlighting its historic landmarks when a journalist, in the 1950s, proposed creating a Freedom Trail physically connecting sixteen historic landmarks primarily related to the city's Colonial and Revolutionary Eras. To link the sites, stretching from the Boston Common to Bunker Hill, the city actually painted a 2.5-mile red line to lead visitors through the city. This was probably the world's first such heritage walking trail. The Freedom Trail was the foremost attraction for the twenty-one million people who visited Boston in 2022.[17] City government helped preserve the fabric of several neighborhoods when it established historic districts with architectural design control, including Beacon Hill (1955), Back Bay (1966) and the South End (1983). The North End, which is the country's largest Little Italy, is a compelling example of an authentic neighborhood with dozens of locally owned Italian restaurants, cafes, bakeries, and food stores. One of Boston's most important preservation projects was the creation of Faneuil Hall Marketplace/Quincy Market in 1976. This project turned languishing aging wholesale food structures into a vital festival marketplace that provided unmatched urban theater and an influential revitalization strategy that was emulated around the country.

The most popular attractions for international visitors tend to be MIT and Harvard because of Boston's sterling reputation for higher education and technological innovation. Other attractions popular with overseas visitors are New England Aquarium, the Museum of Science, the Museum of Fine Arts, and the Boston Symphony Orchestra. Ultimately, according to David O'Donnell, Vice President of the Greater Boston Convention and Visitor Bureau, international visitors are attracted by Boston's impression of cosmopolitanism.[18]

Boston's leading-edge hospitals form a niche travel market for medical patients from around the world. Because of Boston's reputation as an outstanding health care center, it draws affluent people with the resources to afford top-flight care. Thousands of patients from over 100 countries come to Boston hospitals every year for advanced medical treatments at Massachusetts General, Brigham & Women's, Boston Children's Hospital, Beth Israel Deaconess, Lahey Clinic, Tufts Medical Center, Spaulding Rehabilitation Hospital, Dana-Farber Cancer Institute, and Joslin Diabetes Center. Many of these hospitals have special programs servicing international patients The UK digital health care company Medbelle, which has ranked the leading medical cities in the world on metrics related to infrastructure, medical personnel, quality of care, and access, rates Boston the #2 medical tourism city in the world after Tokyo (#1).[19]

DOES BOSTON HAVE AN "AEROTROPOLIS"?

In 2010, the *Boston Globe's* editorial page editor Peter Canellos wrote an article lamenting how Boston had missed a great economic development opportunity by not building a second major airport in the 1990s. He titled his piece: "Aerotropolis: The Rise of a Vibrant New Kind of City—And How

Massachusetts Missed a Chance to Have One." Massport had considered converting the surplus Fort Devens Army base, on the I-495 outer beltway, into an airport with ample surrounding land to support large-scale spinoff development. But local opposition fearing noise, congestion, and the degradation of the quality of life became vocal. State government backed down.

Canellos reflected: "It was, in the eyes of some economists, a big mistake, the kind that separates the truly global metropolises from the boutique cities." He cited the book by John D. Kasarda and Greg Lindsay—*Aerotropolis: The Way We'll Live Next*—which has popularized the idea that airports with ample surrounding open space can become an "aerotropolis" or a "city of the 21st century." Cities are growing around runways in roughly the same way that earlier cities developed around waterways and railroad lines.[20] An "aerotropolis" combines a busy airport with surrounding business activities that connect its region to the global marketplace. With highways, aerotropolises located on the periphery of major cities make ideal warehouse and distribution centers.

Aerotropolis profiles cities around the world that have crafted economic development strategies organized around air transportation. Washington, DC's Dulles and Dallas-Fort Worth International Airport are prime examples of airports purposely sited far from urban centers to accommodate future growth. They have spun off office and warehouse parks and residential complexes housing businesspersons seeking easy air connections to the world. The "aerotropolis" concept has become trendy in strategizing the role of airports in shaping twenty-first-century business locations and promoting urban competitiveness. *Time* magazine named the "aerotropolis" "One of the Ten Ideas that Will Change the World." In 2013, *Future Cities* magazine named Kasarda among "The Top 100 City Innovators Worldwide."[21]

So popular has the concept become that Memphis has fashioned itself as "America's Aerotropolis"™ for being the FedEx hub and the world's busiest air cargo facility. Paris Charles De Gaulle has been dubbed "Aerotropolis Europe,"™ and "Asia's Aerotropolis"™ is Guangzhou, China. The Persian Gulf emirates of Dubai (Emirates Airlines), Abu Dhabi (Etihad Airways), and Qatar/Doha (Qatar Airways) have shaped their booming cities around airports and state-owned airlines connecting to destinations worldwide. Since 2014, Dubai has been the busiest airport in the world for international travelers, with 66.1 million in 2022. Doha and Abu Dhabi also have ranked in the twenty-five busiest international airports.[22] Other flourishing aerotropolises are located at Amsterdam's Schiphol Airport and South Korea's Incheon International Airport, which has been called the largest private real estate development in the world.

According to criteria developed by John Kasarda and associate Steven Appold, Logan Airport is not on the list of more than thirty-eight American aerotropolises, mainly because the criteria required a demonstrated commitment and policies for creating an "aerotropolis," something that Boston and Massport has not done.[23]

The *Globe's* Canellos bemoaned Logan's small size and lack of nearby developable property. Although the airport has relatively more air traffic on its cramped footprint than any other airport in the world, Canellos remarked that "Logan doesn't even compete—it simply doesn't have the space to be an airport city." Logan Airport, like Los Angeles International Airport, JFK and LaGuardia in New York, San Francisco, San Diego, and other airports in densely built areas, is lacking in developable land for complementary activities that generate the spinoff economic development. East Boston has little warehouse space and virtually no factories or corporate offices. It is primarily a densely built residential neighborhood. Neighboring Chelsea, Revere, and Winthrop are also heavily built-out communities. The one major opportunity for new development is the vacant 161-acre grounds of Suffolk Downs. The developers have not explicitly designed their plans to build upon opportunities presented by Logan Airport, though the project could take advantage of its proximity to the airport.[24]

Nevertheless, Boston could be considered to have an aerotropolis district. The reasoning would be that Boston's economic base is not related to warehouses and factories surrounding the airport. The aerotropolis for Logan Airport is the central city business districts. The driving distance between Boston's Financial District and the Seaport is less than three miles. One could argue that downtown Boston is an office park that corresponds to those that surround the Dallas-Fort Worth, O'Hare, Atlanta, and Amsterdam Airports. Kasarda maintains that the outer boundaries of the aerotropolis are set by "the connectivity time of aviation-linked businesses and businesspeople to the airport," which is usually twenty to thirty minutes. He believes that an aerotropolis "is largely nonspatially defined and often unobservable. It consists of firms and frequent air travelers who may be widely dispersed throughout a metropolitan region or clustered at a substantial distance from the airport."[25] For example, in New York, the JFK and Newark Airports have an effective aerotropolis corridor reaching to Lower Manhattan, and London's aerotropolis corridor can reach as far as Canary Wharf in East London from Heathrow Airport.

Obviously, the Boston and Cambridge business and higher education districts did not depend upon aviation to develop, as have office-commercial districts around the Chicago's O'Hare and Atlanta's Hartsfield-Jackson Airports. The booming innovation districts of the Seaport and Cambridge's Kendall Square have thrived in recent years partly because of the easy access to Logan Airport. Logan Airport ranked #2 for having private sector employees within a 5-mile radius, with 637,477 employees (New York's LaGuardia was #1).[26]

The link between the innovation economy and extensive airline service provided by Logan Airport helps explain Boston's rise to global city prominence. During the industrial heyday between 1900 and 1970, when the US economy emphasized domestic markets and the transportation system was dominated by railroads and, later, highways, Boston was in a relatively weak geographical and economic position. Located on the edge of the continent, Boston had difficulty competing on transportation costs with the centrally located Midwest. This trend was exacerbated after World War II, when markets swelled in the West and South. During the 1970s and 1980s, when the high-tech economy began to take off, expanded airplane service and electronic communications made geographically peripheral cities more competitive. These technologies provided an economic advantage for Boston and helped weave it into the network of global cities.

The construction of the Ted Williams Tunnel during the "Big Dig" project (opened to commercial traffic in 1995 and all motor vehicles in 2003) was regarded by Massport and the business community as a vital connector for unlocking the economic potential of Logan Airport. The Ted Williams Tunnel, which forms the final section of I-90, funnels motor traffic to the airport from eastern New England's highway network. Perhaps the foremost impact of the Ted Williams Tunnel has been opening up the slumbering Seaport District. This waterfront had been a hive of busy wharves and warehouses from the late nineteenth century until World War II. After the war, the harbor area fell into disuse, and a patchwork of discount parking lots appeared. The economic boom of the 1980s induced the first sprouts of modern development, with Fidelity Investments converting Commonwealth Pier into the World Trade Center (1986). Massport, which owned the ground lease, sponsored this facility to launch trade missions that would help regional manufacturers increase exports. Project co-developer John E. Drew explained that, "It [World Trade Center] was meant to bring international companies, Boston-based companies and national companies into one building and have them share some conference space and meeting space."[27]

By 2000, the $4.7 billion cleanup of Boston Harbor's fetid pollution, required by federal court order, was completed. This made the South Boston waterfront a more appealing place to be. The district received underground Silver Line transit service connecting to Logan Airport and South Station four years later. The stage was set for spillover from Boston's densely built financial district into a new corporate "aerotropolis" neighborhood of 1,000 underutilized acres. It has been a pattern for global cities to develop new business districts in areas that had become obsolete. In New York, the megadevelopment of Hudson Yards is built over railyards serving Penn Station. In Dublin, the Dockland Development Authority, set out to develop its decaying port district into "a world-class city quarter paragon of sustainable inner-city regeneration." The Docklands, which are located near Dublin Airport, has become the hub for multinational corporations seeking to take advantage of Ireland's lenient corporate tax regime.[28] And Boston's neglected port area, called the "Seaport" District, became the ideal place for a new globally oriented business and residential district.

THE GLOBAL CHARACTER OF THE SEAPORT DISTRICT

When people visit the Seaport, they often wonder: "Does this place look like Boston?" Its homogeneous glass buildings, most built during the 2000s, feel radically different from the varied architecture that reflect multilayered historical character in the city's other neighborhoods. From across the harbor at Logan Airport, the Seaport looks like a stubby office park. The squat skyline has been limited to a height of 250 feet, which is mandated by the Federal Aviation Administration to allow for safe aircraft landings and takeoffs. With such a constrained height limit—compared with the roughly 700 feet allowed in the adjacent financial district—developers have been maximizing square footage and creating boxy forms. Although the Boston Redevelopment Authority's (BRA) "public realm" design guidelines for the Seaport, issued in 1999, stated that "building tops should be shaped with attention to their view against the sky," that precept has been ignored. The BRA's "public realm" guidelines also endorsed "imagery of port . . . [that] should reinforce a new sense of place."²⁹ There is scant visible sense of connection to Boston's maritime heritage in the Seaport.

The appearance of many of the buildings is formulaic, their symbolism is that of a "global city," where the work of multinational free market capitalism is being done. The architecture fits Peter Canellos's observation that aerotropolis buildings have an "international," often "generic" character that looks like they could be "anywhere." He stated, of the globalized businesses, that "their aspirations are written in their architecture." The foremost element of "anywhere" architecture is the glass box, which seems ubiquitous in the Seaport. A district predominated by glass buildings can convey a sterile impression. Paul Goldberger, architectural critic for *The New Yorker*, asserts that single glass buildings can make beautiful aesthetic statements, but they are "less likely to make appealing street-scapes," which serve as "the mortar of civilizing cities."³⁰

The BRA's 1999 urban design guidelines for the Seaport declared that "large, undifferentiated expanses of curtain wall and mirrored glass should be avoided. Lively facades with a variety of transparency, shadow, shade and layering should be constructed." The guidelines added that "the sense of human scale in new construction should be emphasized through familiar block and building sizes volumes and shapes, modulated materials, detailed facades and storefront, and articulated entryways."³¹ It is apparent that these guidelines were ignored.

An opportunity existed to draw upon the design of the late-nineteenth-century brick warehouses of the adjoining Fort Point Channel Historic District and the maritime legacy of the harborfront. Henry N. Cobb complemented the historic Fort Point warehouses with his red brick Moakley Federal Court House (1998). The Fidelity/Drew Company development at the Seaport Hotel (1998), World Trade Center West (2000), and World Trade Center East (2002) also adopted a red brick palette. No attempts to work within this context followed, as glass boxes became the norm. The area's urban design fails to convey any sense of the *"genius loci"* of a seaport. Critics believe that the city's eagerness to promote the Seaport's development and the developers' desire to play it safe with a functional and marketable design produced this outcome.³²

Yet, there are some outstanding buildings in the Seaport. They include the Institute of Contemporary Art (ICA), which opened in 2006, and embraces its location on the waterfront. Encouraged by Mayor Menino, the ICA set out to create an architectural landmark. It was designed by the firm of Diller Scofidio+Renfro, who have designed New York's High Line, buildings in Hudson

Yards, and Los Angeles's Broad Museum. Diller Scofidio+Renfro created a glass-and-steel container for the ICA's contemporary art that incorporates outdoor wooden bleachers overlooking the Harborwalk and the rippling waters beyond. Cantilevered over the bleachers are light-infused galleries and a theater, which provide an immersive view of Boston Harbor. ICA director Jill Medvedow explained that the museum and its surrounding space needed to be welcoming to visitors: "We felt our new museum needed to be as much civic space as artistic space." *New York Times* architectural critic Nicolai Ouroussoff called the new ICA "the most important building to rise here in a generation."[33]

District Hall is another inviting place in the Seaport. When Mayor Menino christened the area an "Innovation District," he insisted that there should be a space where entrepreneurs could meet like-minded people and exchange ideas. What came out of that is District Hall, an 8,000-square-foot space available for small conferences, meetings, and casual networking in the public lounge. Hundreds of meetings and events take place there every year. District Hall calls itself "the world's first free-standing public innovation center."[34]

For an international convention center, the Boston Convention Center (2004) has an eye-catching facade. The design by noted architect Rafael Viñoly features a huge curving overhang that protects visitors and anchors the view from downtown. The convention center provides up-to-date amenities for conventioneers and business exhibitors. Many conventions serving Boston's innovation sectors have utilized the facility. The major design shortcoming is that the hulking superblock obliterates any sense of a walkable, urban fabric in the area. It is fortunate that the convention center is on the southern edge of the Seaport District.

The open space in the Seaport is a salutary feature of the area. The Harborwalk offers superb views of the downtown skyline, the East Boston waterfront, Logan Airport, and the harbor itself. The Fan Pier and WS Development's Seaport Square projects provide a one-third-mile-stretch of open space connecting the Harborwalk to Summer Street and the convention center. The WS Development's Harbor Way promenade has been designed by James Corner Field Operations, landscape architect for New York's vaunted High Line. The open space includes pop-up stores, a farmers' market, and space for outdoor performances.

A feature of global city districts is attracting international capital. Multinational real estate brokerage firms JLL and Newmark Knight Frank, which seek to identify good opportunities for global investment, target just such places as the Seaport. JLL reports that Boston attracts the greatest volume of international real estate investment of sixteen designated international "innovator" cities it has identified. Such cities tend to attract more real estate investment relative to their size than other categories of global cities.[35] The Seaport District has become a next-best technology center to Cambridge's Kendall Square. In terms of international investment, WS Development, for example, has attracted financing from the Canadian Public Sector Pension Investment Board to construct two buildings it is leasing to Amazon. The development firm Tishman obtained financing from two Chinese insurance firms for the office building on Pier 4 that has been leased to the Boston Consulting Group.[36]

The Seaport's pricey condos and apartments (with a sprinkling of municipally mandated "affordable" units) are intended to appeal to affluent buyers from around the world, some of whom are seeking a *pied-à-terre* in a fashionable city. A marketing video for the Seaport's St. Regis Residences, which is available in Mandarin and Cantonese, opens with a map showing the condos' location directly across the harbor from Logan Airport. After this initial selling point, St. Regis's pitch about "Location" is titled: "Enrichment. All About You." Privilege is on offer. There is no mention on the video of the rest of the city's cultural attractions, history, higher education, or innovation industries. The appeal of luxury properties in Boston to international investors is also evident in the video for the Four Seasons Private Residences at One Dalton Street, which opens with the words: "Boston is an international city where elegance meets intelligence and innovation thrives." The video proclaims: "Boston, with over fifty daily nonstop international flights, is now more accessible than ever before."[37]

The annual Knight Frank *Wealth Report* pitches Boston to the top "one percent" as a target for real estate investments with a strong upside. With the United States being considered #2 to Switzerland as a major country tax haven and secrecy jurisdiction, Boston has been attracting its share of overseas investment in high-end residential real estate. A 2018 report published by the Institute for Policy Studies researched the ownership of condos at a dozen luxury properties in the Seaport and downtown Boston. The condo buildings in question had 1,805 units with an average condominium price of approximately $3 million. Limited liability companies (LLCs) or trusts, which conceal the identity of the owners, owned more than 35% of these units. The report found that the more expensive the condo, the more likely it was to be owned by an LLC. Of the 1,805 luxury units, 64% did not claim a residential property tax exemption, indicating that the owners were not using their units as their primary residence. A large number of condos were purchased with cash by shell corporations and international buyers. It is difficult to tell exactly who owns the luxury condos, but researchers have identified investors from such countries as China, Taiwan, Kuwait, and Saudi Arabia in addition to those from Greater Boston and other parts of the US.[38]

In addition to social inequality issues posed by the Seaport development, there is another major challenge: sea level rise. A report prepared by the World Bank and OECD asserts that Boston is the #8 most threatened coastal city in the world in terms of the potential overall cost of flood damage. Other cities at the greatest risk of flooding are Guangzhou, China (#1), Miami (#2), New York (#3), and New Orleans (#4).[39] This threat has increased in recent years, as storms in the Northeast have become heavier and more frequent. Warmer weather brings heavier rains, which contribute to sea level rise and larger storm surges. The Seaport District, which is built on wetlands, is the most vulnerable part of Boston. City government has required projects in the Seaport to locate electrical and HVAC equipment above ground level and erect flood barriers. The City of Boston, which is considered a global leader because of its Climate Ready Boston planning process, is also proposing various buffers along the harbor's edge to keep the tides at bay. Whatever steps are taken, climate change-induced sea level rise and increasingly intense storms will continue to threaten the Seaport. This message is driven home by the 2023 documentary film, "Inundation District." Directors David Abel and Ted Blanc point out how scientists estimate that Boston should expect tides to rise by four to seven feet by 2100. *Globe* columnist Yvonne Abraham, writing about the Seaport in the wake of the extreme weather of Hurricane Ida (2021), fulminated: "Here's a brand-new futuristic neighborhood that seems to have been built without nearly enough regard for the future. And not to pick on the place, but it makes a metaphor for our whole messed up planet."[40]

REACTION TO THE SEAPORT

The Seaport has received mixed reviews. The dissatisfaction evoked by the sterile design and social exclusiveness of the Seaport has been conspicuous. The Seaport has the highest household income of any of Boston's neighborhoods, at $133,000. This exemplifies the gentrification that accompanies globalization. The Seaport's lack of demographic diversity is demonstrated by the fact that African Americans represent only 3% of the population. The *Boston Globe's* Spotlight Team, which published a series about changing race relations in Boston in 2017, described the sense of exclusion conveyed by the Seaport District to people of color. Reporter Andrew Ryan wrote: "The Seaport's whiteness is not the result of overt prejudice, they say, but rather a symptom that indicates Boston has not addressed systemic issues involving race. Billions of dollars in public investment offered leverage to push harder for inclusion, but some believe government officials squandered that chance to enrich all Bostonians, including black residents." Since then, many have been forthright in their criticism of the Seaport. Former Acting Mayor Kim Janey stated: "When it comes to the Seaport, so many things went wrong. More than $20 billion created the Seaport and yet, we have a neighborhood that does not have equity or inclusion in its foundation—in terms of who built it, who lives there now, and the businesses that exist there." Penn Loh, of Tufts University's Department of Urban and Environmental Policy and Planning, explained his disappointment in the Seaport: "A lot of cities like Boston that consider themselves global cities are competing for the global 1 percent. Boston could lose its soul as a place for regular, working people of all colors."

Even *Globe* restaurant critic Devra First had a negative opinion of the Seaport: "So how can Boston preserve and build on its unique local restaurant scene? . . . With the Seaport, there was the chance to develop something filled with personality, reflective of the city's diversity, history, culture, and fishing industry. Instead, we have glossy, expensive waterfront dining, which may have its own appeal, but many properties would fit into any American city."[41] Many restaurants that have opened in the Seaport are upscale national restaurant chains, which include Del Frisco's, Morton's, Ocean Prime, and Mastro's. The reason for their presence is that pricey new construction requires steep rents, and the only restaurants that can afford them are national chains charging high prices. Unique local mom-and-pops are priced out.

Of approximately, 4,500 rental units built or planned in the Seaport, 450 are "income-restricted" or "affordable," while, of 1,427 condos, only 58 units are "affordable" (5%). The Seaport's units have been skewed to singles, couples, and small families, with only 4% of rentals and 5% of condos having three or more bedrooms. State Senator Lydia Edwards has asserted: "A lot of the units are too small. You make a bunch of one-bedrooms, studios. You definitely are telling families you are not welcome here, whatever color, whatever income." Average rentals for one-bedroom apartments in the Seaport were $4,261, while the citywide average was $2,873.[42]

In all fairness, many people living, working, doing business, and visiting in the Seaport may provide a more positive perspective. Upwardly mobile, mainly younger, singles and couples fill the area's condos and rental units. On weekends in good weather, thousands of visitors stroll through the Seaport, particularly on the Harborwalk, which is a treasured amenity. Seating in small plazas and green spaces is available. As the area gets built out, it makes a more lively and attractive impression. Observers believe that the Seaport is emerging as Boston's second high-end shopping district, behind the Newbury Street-Prudential Center-Copley Place area. They argue that a "world-class city" like Boston should be able to support two top-of-the-line retail areas. Koushik Koganti, owner of the Madras Dosa Company reflected this point of view when he said that a few years ago people considered Boston a "dull city" that was just "historic." According to Koganti, "the whole vibe changed" with the development of the Seaport.[43] A lot of people like the modernist Seaport because it makes Boston seem like an up-to-date city.

Still, the Seaport District is becoming a cautionary tale of urban planning for other neighborhoods. In North Allston, neighbors are concerned about how Harvard is developing 150 acres it controls. Anthony D'Isidoro, president of the Allston Civic Association, said, "They talked about Beacon Park [Harvard's developable property in Allston] being the next Seaport District. If it's going to turn out like the Seaport, we don't want any of that."[44] Seaport critics worry about the impacts of creating another built-from-scratch upscale neighborhood near Logan Airport (three miles away) at Suffolk Downs in East Boston and Revere. The defunct racetrack is a 161-acre tabula rasa located between two Blue Line transit stations. Developer HYM Investment Group has proposed a master plan that mixes commercial office space, biotech labs, retail and entertainment, and hotel. The HYM Investment Group plan features a prodigious 10,000 housing units, which include rental apartments, condos, senior units, and single-family town homes. Nine hundred thirty units would be "income-restricted."[45] The bulk of the Suffolk Downs market-rate housing units would accommodate a largely upper-middle-class population, some of whom might be attracted by the proximity of Logan Airport's aviation links. The developer is also providing additional open space and public amenities. Located near Belle Isle Marsh and the coastline, the project plans to provide state-of-the-art stormwater runoff and sea level rise protection. In many ways, the Suffolk Downs project parallels the Seaport in scope. It will be interesting to see what lessons the developers have taken away from the development of the Seaport.

CHAPTER 6

How Greater Boston Global Supply Chains Operate

"Current scientific and global health challenges are too complex for any one player in the healthcare ecosystem to solve alone."

Pfizer, Inc.

When COVID-19 swept through the United States in March of 2020, the hitherto obscure notion of "global supply chains" became apparent to Americans. Many were astonished that we were so heavily reliant on China for providing medical face masks, ventilators, and essential medicines. Covid-related shutdowns in Asia disrupted supply chains, delaying deliveries of, not only medical supplies, but consumer goods like electronics and bicycles. The breakdown in the supply chain for semiconductors had far-reaching disruptive impacts on the manufacturing of automobiles, computers, and medical devices. It has been reported that 51,000 global companies had suppliers in China during the early months of the pandemic, with another five million companies relying on products provided by the affected global companies.[1]

During the pandemic, inflationary prices and shortages of every kind of product were blamed on unreliable supply chains. The Federal Reserve Bank of San Francisco has estimated that supply chain disruptions were the cause of 60% of US inflation in 2021 and 2022.[2] While realizing that we consume a surfeit of products made in other countries, Americans seldom paid close attention to the complex global supply chains that produce and convey them to our doorsteps. It has been a concern primarily to businesspeople who manage the supply chains. Virtually every manufacturing industry around the world is involved with extensive supply chains, in an effort to reduce labor costs and optimize the return on investment.[3] Since the onset of COVID-19, the public better understands how globalization operates through worldwide supply chains and how those supply chains can have significant vulnerabilities. That awareness has been hastening efforts to reshore supply chains. The Biden administration launched an initiative to bring back components of global supply chains that are strategically important to this country. These supply chains range from those related to semiconductors and biopharmaceuticals to other advanced technologies.

It is important to understand that companies cannot make much without obtaining materials from outside their local area. This has been a long-held lesson in Boston, which has maintained a place in global supply chains since it emerged as the leading seaport in British North America in colonial era. As New England became an industrial power in the nineteenth century, Boston traded for products across the world, some of which it used to fuel local industries. Cotton from the South and wool from England, South America, and Australia sustained textile manufacturers. Shoe manufacturing, one of the region's foundational industries, imported animal hides from Argentina, Australia, India, and the Near East. The port received more animal skins and hides than any city in the world, so much that, after tanning hides for New England shoe manufacturers, merchants exported leather to England, Russia, and other countries.[4]

Today, the leather business is mostly gone, but the footwear business has maintained a presence. New Balance, Reebok (owned by Galaxy Universal), Converse (Nike), Timberland (VF Corporation), Saucony, Stride Rite, Keds, and Sperry Top-Sider (all owned by Wolverine World Wide), and Puma have American corporate headquarters in Greater Boston, managing supply chains that reach to Asia. New Balance has its world headquarters in Brighton, where it manages its supply chain as well as overall administration, design, marketing, and distribution functions. New Balance is unusual for US athletic shoe companies in that it manufactures 25% of shoes for the domestic market in the States. This validates its "Made in America" pledge. New Balance obtains the remainder of its shoes from a company-owned factory the United Kingdom and from contractors in China, Vietnam, and Indonesia. (Other leading athletic shoe companies, including Nike, have most all their shoes made in

Asia to keep labor costs low.) New Balance has factories in Methuen, MA, Lawrence, MA, and Skowhegan, Norway, and Norridgewock, ME. Two-thirds of the American-made shoes are assembled from uppers and soles sourced from East Asia. The other third uses soles sourced from East Asia. New Balance makes the uppers in New England from raw materials imported from Asia. New Balance believes that New England factories provide the company enhanced oversight of its manufacturing process and the capacity for quick fulfillment for United States-based orders.[5]

The use of global supply chains, like those for athletic shoes, expanded during the 1980s and 1990s, when computers, instantaneous digital telecommunications, and container ships and air freight took advantage of low-cost labor around the world. Companies realized they could build supply chains on the cheap, using offshore firms rather than having to invest in factories and equipment domestically, thus replacing plants in the United States. Elaborate supply chains materialized. Companies moved basic materials from their country of origin to countries where they were turned into components, then sent to another country where they were assembled and packaged, often with additional steps in the process along the way. The great majority of tech products purchased in America are manufactured in China, Hong Kong, Taiwan, South Korea, and other East Asian countries. When COVID-19 disrupted various links in supply chains, their fragility became manifest. A *Guardian* article explained that "this logistical model is the engine of breakneck capitalism . . . The tightly calibrated infrastructure is designed for perpetual motion. Once one link breaks or stalls, the impact on today's just-in-time supply chains can be felt immediately."[6]

Managing supply chains is a complex undertaking with many actors. Harvard Business School Professor Michael Porter, in *The Competitive Advantage* (1985), proposed the term "value chain" to explain how lead firms, usually located in developed countries, maintain control of the "core nodes of value creation" while outsourcing lesser-value functions to branch operations and third-party businesses. Value chains are likely to entail such relationships among firms as licensing arrangements, joint ventures, research collaborations, and long-term strategic partnerships. Manufacturers do not need to dedicate limited capital to owning factories anymore. This frees up companies to focus on management aspects of their business and contract out everything else.[7] Thomas Friedman, in his best-selling *The World Is Flat* (2005), explains how global supply chains can leverage the optimal value from each participant in the supply chain: "The best companies outsource to win, not to shrink. They outsource to innovate faster and more cheaply in order to grow larger, gain market share, and hire more and different specialists—not to save money by firing more people."[8] When these benefits are evident, the lead firms take advantage of far-flung value chains. In most instances, these businesses undertake the research and development in-house and manage the manufacturing and distribution processes, much of which can be outsourced. Some of the value-added also comes from patent attorneys, logistics contractors, and marketing firms. Since "value chains" and "supply chains" are overlapping terms, "supply chains" will be mainly used in this book, as it is more commonly understood.

LIFE SCIENCES GLOBAL SUPPLY CHAINS

An advantageous way to understand the operation of supply chains would be to trace how they are used in life sciences, one of the most significant global economic sectors in Greater Boston. Encompassing biotechnology, pharmaceuticals, and medical devices and supplies, the life sciences use global supply chains that may not be immediately obvious. These companies do not ship goods in enormous quantities. The essential function of the Greater Boston biopharmaceutical industry is research and development that is taking place in collaboration with the region's academic community. In addition to R&D, much corporate management is located in the region, overseeing the development of products from their conception through sourcing materials, manufacturing, marketing, distribution, and consumer support. Some biopharma manufacturing takes place in the region, though much of it is outsourced to other places, domestically and abroad.

A good case to start with is Vertex Pharmaceuticals, one of Boston's leading biotech companies. Founded in Cambridge in 1989, the company has specialized in developing drugs that treat chronic life-threatening conditions. Its foremost drug has been a treatment for cystic fibrosis, which has allowed patients to effectively manage what had been a debilitating lung disease. In 2023, the Federal Food and Drug Administration (FDA) approved the company's sickle cell disease drug, co-developed with CRISPR Therapeutics. Called Casvegy, it is the first US treatment to utilize the groundbreaking gene-editing tool CRISPR-Cas9. Vertex has also been developing a non-opioid pain killer and a diabetes medicine.[9]

Vertex Pharmaceuticals consolidated its Boston area administrative and R&D operations, in 2014, in a new building in Boston's Seaport District. The company also maintains R&D facilities in Watertown and Providence, as well as in San Diego and Oxford, England. Like many biotech companies, Vertex relies upon third parties to manufacture drugs and conduct preclinical work and clinical trials. The company's 2019 annual report to the US Securities & Exchange Commission provides a broad overview of its supply chain operations:

> Our supply chain for sourcing raw materials and manufacturing drug product ready for distribution is a multi-step international endeavor. Third-party contract manufacturers, including some in China, perform different parts of our manufacturing process. Contract manufacturers may supply us with raw materials, convert these raw materials into drug substance, or convert the drug substance into final dosage form. Third parties are used for packaging, warehousing and distribution of products. Establishing and managing this global supply chain requires a significant financial commitment and the creation and maintenance of numerous third-party contractual relationships.[10]

Vertex's development since the 1990s provides some valuable insights into how cutting-edge biotech companies operate global supply chains. When Vertex was ready to manufacture a hepatitis C medication in 2011, the company contracted out the process. John Condon, the manufacturing operations manager explained: "We were not going to build a manufacturing plant. We would leverage the external world."[11] In contrast with Big Pharma companies like Merck, which own almost all of its manufacturing facilities, including the railcars for carrying raw ingredients, it did not make economic sense for Vertex, with a nascent product line, to own a full-scale manufacturing plant. For producing its cystic fibrosis drug, Condon developed a twenty-first-century supply chain that contracted with two Chinese firms to manufacture the five active pharmaceutical ingredients (API) that constitute it. Vertex recognized that Shanghai region companies charged low costs and had the technical capacity to produce ingredients that required a complex preparation process. Vertex also viewed Shanghai contractors as a means of increasing its overall presence in the rapidly growing Chinese pharmaceutical market. After the production of the five active ingredients in China, they were flown to northern England, where an Indian-owned company had built a facility for synthesizing the basic ingredients. Next, the ingredients were flown to Portugal, where another drug manufacturer had a reactor that mixed the compound with a polymer to keep it from crystallizing. This turned the drug molecules into dry powder. The powder was then shipped across the Atlantic to Cincinnati to be mixed with other chemical agents to become tablets. For the final step, the tablets were shipped to a packaging company in Illinois to be placed in blister packs and boxes before distribution to hospitals and pharmacies.[12] One might wonder at the challenges of ensuring quality control in such a complex production process. In a move that could simplify supply chain issues, Vertex built an advanced pill-making facility in the South Boston Seaport in 2016. Five years later, it opened a 256,000 square-foot research and manufacturing facility for genetic and cellular therapies in the Seaport's Innovation Square.

American dependence upon extended global supply chains and drugs manufactured overseas became a concern during the COVID-19 pandemic. The Biden administration published a review of critical supply chain vulnerabilities, *Building Resilient Supply Chains, Revitalizing American Manufacturing, and Fostering Board-Base Growth* (2021). The study identified four supply chain areas that have the most serious strategic importance: semiconductors, large capacity batteries, critical minerals, and pharmaceuticals and active pharmaceutical ingredients (API). The White House report stated that "shortages of critical generic drugs and APIs have plagued the United States for years. . . . 87 percent of generic API facilities are located overseas which has helped reduce costs by trillions of dollars in the past decade but has left the US health care system vulnerable to shortages of essential medicines."[13]

Studies undertaken by Boston University professor Rena Conti and MITs Ernst R. Berndt have determined that "the base ingredients required for the manufacturing of these prescription drugs are overwhelmingly and increasingly manufactured in non-domestic locations, specifically India and China. The manufacturing of finished prescription drugs for the American market is more equally split between domestic and foreign locations but is increasingly foreign as well." Based on data provided by the USFDA, the vast majority (almost 90%) of active pharmaceutical ingredients (API), biologically active but not readily consumable ingredients, are manufactured in foreign countries. About 60% of final dosage forms, which include tablets, capsule, and ointments, are also manufactured overseas.[14] The largest pharmaceutical US concentrations making final dosage forms are in New Jersey, New York, Philadelphia, Baltimore, and New England. United States-based API facilities are distributed more evenly across the country, with many located in the Midwest.

Under current FDA policy, the labeling of prescription drugs sold in the US does not disclose the name or location of the actual API or finished dosage form (FDF) subcontractor (although the labeling typically discloses the name and contact information for the company marketing the drug). Contract manufacturing relationships among API and FDF companies remain hidden from public view. FDA disclosure rules essentially provide a de facto endorsement of this practice by allowing such information to remain confidential.[15]

BOSTON BIOPHARMAS DEVELOP COVID-19 VACCINES

The COVID-19 pandemic has trained a spotlight on Greater Boston's biopharma sector and its supply chains. The region's biopharma companies have played a major role in the development of a COVID-19 vaccine. These companies include Moderna, Pfizer/BioNTech, and Johnson & Johnson working with the Beth Israel Deaconess Medical Center. The global real estate firm Newmark Knight Frank declared: "With more than 100 local companies working on various treatments and vaccines for the virus and 17.3% of active COVID-19-related National Institutes of Health (NIH) funding going to Massachusetts-based institutions, this market is at the forefront of the fight against the coronavirus. . . . Expect a greater emphasis on life sciences as a result of COVID-19, which will undoubtedly benefit this region, seen as one of the pre-eminent life science clusters in the world."[16]

Moderna

One of the COVID-19 vaccine leaders has been Moderna, the small, heavily capitalized biotech company headquartered in Cambridge's Kendall Square. Moderna burst into public consciousness for pioneering use of a messenger RNA (mRNA) vaccine for the COVID-19 virus. The mRNA inserts part of the virus's RNA genetic code into human cells, which produces a piece of the virus that triggers an immune response molecule that relays genetic instructions to generate antibodies for COVID-19. Messenger RNA therapeutics treats the root genetic trigger of a disease rather than suppressing its symptoms. Unlike other vaccines, mRNA vaccines do not contain the virus itself. The mRNA technology was primed for application when Moderna obtained the virus sequence online. CEO Stéphane Bancel boasted that it took Moderna researchers only ten minutes to apply the mRNA methodology to the virus and only another two days to demonstrate that it worked.[17]

The US Biomedical Advanced Research and Development Authority (BARDA) / Operation Warp Speed awarded nearly $1 billion for Moderna's vaccine development and almost $10 billion to produce 566 million vaccine doses. Moderna has sought to keep its operations Massachusetts-oriented as much as possible. When the company decided it wanted a dedicated in-house manufacturing plant to complement its Cambridge R&D facilities, it opened one in nearby Norwood. Moderna's Norwood facility has been designed to provide "fully integrated end-to-end capability from production of critical raw materials (e.g., plasmid), mRNA, formulated LNP [liquid nanoparticle] drug product, sterile filling, and labeling and packing." This facility was originally intended to produce small batches of personalized cancer treatments but shifted gears to mass-producing the COVID-19 vaccine. Since the onset of COVID-19, Moderna has doubled the size of its manufacturing facility. A preponderance of its vaccines has been produced in the Norwood plant. Because of the importance of having a manufacturing facility near Moderna's Cambridge labs, CEO Stéphane Bancel has said: "If we didn't have Norwood, we would be dead in the water."[18]

With the worldwide demand for billions of vaccine doses, Moderna formed a partnership with the multinational Swiss vaccine producer Lonza Group to do additional vaccine manufacturing at its plants in Portsmouth, NH and Visp, Switzerland. Moderna also made deals with Sanofi to manufacture millions of doses at the company's Ridgefield, NJ, plant, with National Resilience to make the vaccine near Toronto, with Rovi in Madrid, and with Recipharm in Monts, France. A Moderna subcontractor is the German company Corden Pharma, which makes lipids at a facility in Boulder, CO. Moderna, like many biotech companies, has used unnamed third parties for other specialized manufacturing activities.[19]

After Moderna's basic vaccine was manufactured in Norwood, it was shipped to the Catalent plant located in Bloomington, IN, for the final stage of filling and finishing the vaccine. Catalent is considered the leading global provider of advanced drug delivery. It uses fully automated packaging facilities to provide vial filling, packaging, labeling, storage, and distribution services. Moderna also forged a partnership with Waltham-based Thermo Fisher Scientific, which has provided raw materials for the vaccine and also filled, labeled, and packaged the COVID-19 vaccine at its Greenville, NC, plant. Moderna has been a global ambassador for Greater Boston's life sciences innovation sector. The vaccine has been approved for use in more than eighty countries around the world.[20]

Moderna believes that the key to its success has been its uniquely qualified workforce. When asked how Moderna was able to rapidly recruit a workforce capable of developing and manufacturing its revolutionary vaccine treatment, Chairman Noubar Afeyan responded: "I don't know where else you can do that. You might be able to do that in little pockets here and there. But Boston, Massachusetts is, I would argue, the only place where this could have been developed."[21] Going forward, Afeyan is betting on future growth driven by his R&D talent and their pioneering use of mRNA treatments for a whole range of medical issues. As of May 2024, Moderna received FDA approval for its second mRNA vaccine, this one to treat respiratory syncytial virus in older adults.

Pfizer and BioNTech

Pharmaceutical giant Pfizer was the first company to develop a COVID-19 vaccine for the United States. The Pfizer vaccine was developed by BioNTech, a German drug maker (whose North American R&D base is located in Cambridge, where it specializes in cancer treatments). BioNTech and Pfizer started working together in 2018 on an mRNA vaccine for influenza. Building on this experience, the companies developed a COVID-19 vaccine using mRNA to deliver genetic instructions to cells to elicit an immune response, similarly to Moderna's. Messenger RNA vaccines have been at the forefront of COVID-19 treatments because they have been easier to test and deliver than traditional viral-based vaccines. The collaboration leverages Pfizer's expertise in vaccine R&D, regulatory capabilities, and its global manufacturing and distribution network.

Pfizer's Andover, MA, campus has been used for manufacturing the COVID-19 vaccine. The state-of-the-art manufacturing facility, which opened in 2019, manufactures biotherapeutics and vaccines. In Pfizer's vaccine supply chain, its St. Louis plant produces the active pharmaceutical ingredients (API), Andover synthesizes these ingredients into the actual vaccine, and a Kalamazoo, MI, facility is responsible for handling the formulation and filling of vials for administering the vaccine. With an enormous global demand for the vaccine that Pfizer cannot fulfill entirely on its own, the company contracted with both Novartis and Sanofi to utilize their vaccine-making capacity as well.[22]

In addition to producing its COVID-19 vaccine in the Boston area, Pfizer maintains the global headquarters for its Center for Therapeutic Innovation in Kendall Square. Pfizer has located this research facility, employing 1,000 staffers, in space leased from MIT. The aim is to be located in a major academic/entrepreneurial cluster. The Cambridge lab has been pursuing medical breakthroughs in rare diseases, inflammation and immunology, and internal medicine, drawing upon genetics, molecule technologies, and computational sciences.[23] Pfizer, which was founded as a chemical company in New York City in 1849 and continues to be headquartered there, has long maintained its main R&D facility in Groton, CT.

In a positive sign for the biotech industry in Cambridge-Boston, Pfizer has been recrafting its core mission and identity in the wake of its work on the COVID-19 vaccine. Pfizer's CEO Albert Bourla has announced: "After 171 years, we arrive at a new era. A time of extraordinary focus on science and dedication to patients. Pfizer is no longer in the business of just treating diseases—we're curing and preventing them." Pfizer is refocusing on the life sciences and the potential of mRNA in particular. It has been selling off some of its lines of conventional pharmaceuticals. The Cambridge-Boston biopharma cluster promises to play an important role in these efforts [24]

Beth Israel Deaconess Medical Center and Johnson & Johnson

The third COVID-19 vaccine to be approved in the United State has been produced by multinational pharmaceutical Johnson & Johnson. The original vaccine was developed at the Center for Virology and Vaccine Research at Boston's Beth Israel Deaconess Medical Center. The story of this partnership is illustrative. On January 10, 2020, the Beth Israel Center for Virology and Vaccine Research was holding its annual retreat at Boston's Museum of Science. One of the topics for discussion was the cases of a mysterious pneumonia that were being reported out of Wuhan, China. One of the scientists suggested that the laboratory should consider researching a potential vaccine, since the disease might be comparable to SARS, which had appeared in China in 2002. That night, one of the lead researchers discovered an Internet post by Yong-Zhen Zhang, a professor at Shanghai's Fudan University and a leader of the consortium studying the new disease, which contained the entire genetic sequence of the new coronavirus. Professor Zhang declared: "Please feel free to download, share, use, and analyze this data." Led by the lab's director Dr. Dan Barouch, the Beth Israel Deaconess research team dove into analyzing the genomic sequence and, over the weekend, decided that they might be able to develop a vaccine to treat it. Dr. Barouch, whom the *New York Times* called "one of the world's leading vaccine-makers," had been researching vaccines for twenty years. One of his early projects was a vaccine for HIV, which he was able to reengineer to treat the Zika virus in 2016. He believed that, by building on earlier vaccine research, they could develop a vaccine for the new coronavirus. In contrast with rival COVID-19 vaccine makers who used the untried method of mRNA, Pfizer and Moderna, the Beth Israel researchers used the traditional vaccine-making approach of injecting humans with a dead or weakened virus, triggering the immune system to generate antibodies as if the vaccine were the full-fledged virus.[25]

While the Beth Israel team in Boston experimented with a vaccine designed to stimulate antibodies protecting against COVID-19, Dr. Barouch established a partnership with Janssen Vaccines & Prevention, B.V. (since renamed Johnson & Johnson Innovative Medicine), a Dutch-based pharmaceutical research division of Johnson & Johnson. Janssen had worked with Beth Israel on the Zika vaccine, developing a formula for producing the vaccine in huge quantities. Janssen operates a facility in Leiden, Netherlands that has been specifically designed to launch new vaccines. Johnson & Johnson funded the research and clinical trials with an infusion of $1 billion from the US BARDA. In February of 2021, Johnson & Johnson received the go-ahead from the FDA to initiate distribution of its vaccine. Because of lower efficacy rates than the mRNA vaccines and rare but serious blood clotting side effects, the J&J vaccine experienced minimal use in the US. It has been used more extensively in developing countries because of its single-shot design and easy storage requirements, features the mRNA vaccines lacked.

J&J contracted with Emergent BioSolutions as a contract manufacturer to produce vaccines at a plant in Baltimore; but, after Emergent BioSolutions spoiled fifteen million doses of the vaccine, J&J took over management of the Baltimore plant. The company also contracted with Catalent, in Indiana, to fill the vaccine vials. Corning Glass, in upstate New York, manufactured hundreds of millions of non-breakable glass vials to hold the vaccines. To supplement its in-house manufacturing capacity, J&J engaged with Merck, which abandoned efforts to develop its own COVID-19 vaccine, to dramatically increase its vaccine supply. A North Carolina Merck plant manufactured the vaccine, while a Maryland facility filled and distributed the vials.

In the Boston area, J&J undertakes broad-based research at its Cambridge Innovation Center, which is a tenant of the Cambridge Innovation Center in Kendall Square (other J&J Regional Innovation Centers are located in San Francisco, London, and Shanghai). Each Innovation Center combines R&D with venture capital investment and the expertise necessary for producing and marketing new medical treatments. The J&J Innovation Center staff seeks to build relationships with startup companies, universities, and research institutes that are developing early-stage innovations for immunology, cancer, digital healthcare, neuroscience, medical devices, cardiovascular and metabolism, and infectious diseases.

Vulnerabilities and Opportunities for Biotech Supply Chains

Although the R&D side of the biopharmaceutical industry in Greater Boston is strong, there are concerns that the region does not have a stronger presence in the manufacturing of drugs. According to the Massachusetts Biotechnology Council (MassBio), Massachusetts ranks #9 among states for biopharma manufacturing, with 10,493 jobs. California ranks #1 with 47,141 jobs. New Jersey, North Carolina, and New York also rank well ahead of Massachusetts.[26]

Most of the drugs developed in Massachusetts are manufactured in other states and countries. One factor is the presence of long-standing pharmaceutical manufacturing clusters in New Jersey, Philadelphia, New York, and North Carolina. They pre-date Greater Boston's involvement in the biopharma field. The location of pharmaceutical factories in foreign countries stems from a couple factors. First, many Massachusetts biopharma firms are owned by large multinationals that have production facilities outside the US. Second, medical treatments tend to have worldwide markets, so it can be useful, if not necessary, to have manufacturing facilities in countries that are markets for pharmaceuticals.

Developing the biopharma manufacturing sector would strengthen the Greater Boston's position in the global supply chain. Workers without advanced scientific education could find employment in the biotech field. The MassBio argues that the state needs to make biotech manufacturing a priority because its R&D sector, which is exceedingly dependent upon federal grants and venture capital for startups, is vulnerable to funding fluctuations. With concerns about supply chain vulnerabilities highlighted by the COVID-19 pandemic, expanding local production capabilities could help solve US supply chain problems. The MassBio *State of Possible 2025 Report* explains that, with medical treatments becoming more customized for patients, manufacturing drugs will have to follow suit. MassBio urges that "Massachusetts should look to take advantage of its R&D leadership to push forward with manufacturing capacity and expertise."[27]

McKinsey & Company maintains that biomanufacturing could grow dramatically in Massachusetts, as companies with R&D operations seek to ramp up manufacturing in convenient locations. The consulting firm estimates that the state has the potential to add $6–8 billion in GDP and 30,000–80,000 jobs through biomanufacturing. Since 2015, almost $2 billion has already been invested in new or expanded local biomanufacturing facilities by private companies and such academic centers as the Massachusetts Biomanufacturing Center at UMass Lowell, the Massachusetts Accelerator for Biomanufacturing at UMass-Dartmouth, and Worcester Polytechnic Institute. MassBio argues that, as medical and therapeutic technologies grow dramatically over the next decade, new manufacturing facilities will be needed. It would be efficient to open them near the innovators already working in Massachusetts. The coming trend in biopharma is "continuous manufacturing," where pharmaceutical ingredients would be moved nonstop through the same facility, in contrast with the current mode of "batch manufacturing," which entails transporting, testing, and re-feeding materials from one process to the next. "Continuous manufacturing" could dramatically condense global supply chains, respond more nimbly to market changes, and create economic synergy with the R&D laboratories that already exist here.[28]

Facilities for manufacturing biopharma treatments are most likely to be located in communities outside the Cambridge-Boston core with lower real estate prices. These communities also offer less costly housing and shorter commutes for workers. We have already seen how COVID-19 vaccine pioneer Moderna and Pfizer have factories making vaccines in Norwood and Andover, respectively. While Moderna's factory is a highly specialized facility, Pfizer's campus employs 1,200+ people working in eight state-of-the-art buildings capable of manufacturing multiple products at the same time. Other Big Pharma companies have manufacturing facilities in Boston suburbs. Bristol-Myers Squibb maintains a manufacturing facility in Devens, west of Boston. The 700,000 square-foot facility manufactures biologic medicines for such conditions as rheumatoid arthritis and cancer. A new 244,000 square-foot facility makes cell therapy treatments, with an initial focus on a lymphoma treatment. In 2019, Sanofi (Sanofi bought Genzyme in 2011 and dropped the name Genzyme entirely in 2022) opened a 100,000 square-foot fully digital facility in Framingham that its CEO proclaimed the "holy grail" of biopharmaceutical manufacturing plants. Sanofi's plant has received the Facility of the Year Award in the Facility of the Future category from the International Society for Pharmaceutical Engineering. Overall, 1,500 employees work both in production and R&D in Framingham.[29]

As COVID-19 has underscored the need for securing biopharma supply chains, local manufacturing initiatives have been increasing. Thermo Fisher Scientific, a scientific instrument company which is the most valuable publicly traded company in the state, has opened a $180 million contract manufacturing facility in Plainville for gene therapies developed by other companies. This plant is making gene therapies for Duchenne muscular dystrophy, sickle cell disease, multiple myeloma, Parkinson's disease, deafness, and central nervous system diseases.[30]

CRISPR Therapeutics, a pioneering gene-editing company focused on developing gene-based medicines for serious diseases, opened a new cell therapy manufacturing facility in Framingham in 2021 to produce clinical supplies and commercial products. Approximately 100 employees work there. CRISPR Therapeutics, which has moved its main R&D lab from Kendall Square to South Boston, was co-founded by 2020 Nobel Prize for Chemistry laureates Jennifer Doudna and Emmanuelle Charpentier. CRISPR Therapeutics is collaborating with Vertex on treatments for sickle cell disease, beta thalassemias, Duchenne Muscular Dystrophy, and Myotonic Dystrophy Type 1 (DM1). While the gene-editing process continues to advance, CRISPR Therapeutics is involved in a long-running patent battle with Feng Zhang and the Broad Institute. An April 2022 US patent decision ruled that Feng Zhang and the Broad Institute were the first to successfully use CRISPR to work in cells of organisms and that they own the patent for CRISPR gene editing instead of the lab of Doudna and Charpentier. Nevertheless, knowledgeable observers believe that the patent battle will continue for a long time.[31]

At Devens, on the I-495 beltway, King Street Properties is developing a $500 million contract biomanufacturing facility. Its goal is to serve small- and medium-sized companies, who are in the process of developing new drugs and are not able to own their own facility.[32] Contract manufacturing facilities are becoming a growing option for pharmaceutical companies, as witnessed during the production of COVID-19 vaccine. They can dramatically speed up to the production of emerging drugs.

Even universities and teaching hospitals are getting into the biomanufacturing business. Dana-Farber Cancer Institute, in 2018, opened a 30,000 square-foot facility for cell manufacturing. It was immediately oversubscribed, as it is the only state-of-the-art biomanufacturing facility serving academic researchers in New England. Subsequently, Harvard University, MIT, Dana Farber, Massachusetts General Hospital, Beth Israel Deaconess Hospital, Brigham & Women's Hospital, and Boston Children's Hospital committed to developing a new collaborative nonprofit $50 million facility for biomanufacturing. It is called Landmark Bio and is located in Watertown.[33]

The COVID-19 pandemic has increased awareness of the global supply chain of the life sciences. Massachusetts received a significant influx of investment in the biotech industry and lab space in the wake of the pandemic. One of the benefits is building up a manufacturing base that can capitalize on the pioneering R&D being undertaken here.

CHAPTER 7

How the Cambridge-Boston Life Sciences Ecosystem Works

"The next great revolution which we're in right now, and whether it's coronavirus vaccines or gene editing, it's paving the way, is the biotech revolution in which molecules are going to be the new microchips."

Walter Isaacson, *The Code Breaker*

Cambridge set itself on course to becoming a global center of biotechnology in 1976, when Harvard University proposed building a laboratory for researching recombinant DNA (molecules of DNA from two different species that are inserted into a host organism to produce new genetic combinations). The National Institutes of Health had just published regulations intended to make federally funded labs safe by mandating sealed chambers with state-of-the-art containment and ventilation, the use of protective clothing, and other steps. Even with these safety measures, Cambridge Mayor Alfred Velluci and members of the City Council were alarmed by Harvard's proposal. Mayor Velluci wanted a 100% guarantee that the research would entail no risks. Following a raucous public hearing, Velluci proposed a two-year moratorium on building the lab while the risks could be studied. Because of the urgency expressed by Harvard biologists, the moratorium was reduced to three months. A citizen advisory committee held over 100 hours of public hearings before coming up with a biosafety research ordinance that was the first such municipal law in the country. At first, it appeared that the Cambridge regulations might be so stringent that they would inhibit genetic research. It produced the opposite. Since the city's DNA research regulations made residents feel they were safe, educational institutions and for-profit companies could proceed doing research with a level of confidence.[1]

Biogen and Genzyme became private sector pioneers in Cambridge. Founded by Harvard's Walter Gilbert, MIT's Phillip Sharp, and European scientists in 1978, Biogen opened its first research laboratory in Geneva, Switzerland, because of uncertainty about operating in the United States. By 1982, Gilbert and Sharp moved Biogen to Cambridge because of the proximity to Harvard and MIT, a seemingly workable local biosafety code, and the availability of vacant land in Kendall Square. These ingredients worked not just for Biogen, but eventually for a slew of biotech research organizations. The involvement of Walter Gilbert and Phillip Sharp demonstrated the key role played by preeminent geneticists in forming the Cambridge biotech cluster. Gilbert won the 1980 Nobel prize for Chemistry for his work on DNA sequencing, while Sharp won the 1993 Nobel Prize for Physiology for his discovery of "split genes." (Phillip Sharp also co-founded Cambridge-based Alnylam Pharmaceuticals.) The development of Biogen and later biotech companies was no sure thing because there was for a longtime ambivalence in academia about the legitimacy of developing for-profit companies out of university-based academic research.

Biogen evolved into one of the leading biotech companies. After its early years of R&D, the company now makes drugs to treat relatively rare conditions such as multiple sclerosis, leukemia, and hemophilia. Biogen is well known for the controversial Alzheimer's treatment, Aduhelm, which the FDA approved in 2021. Because of a problematic rollout of the drug and resistance from insurers to cover the cost of treatments, Biogen sidelined Aduhelm. Yet, the company has been able to come up with another Alzheimer's drug called Leqembi, which has been found to be more efficacious. The FDA granted accelerated approval for Leqembi in 2023.

Biogen maintains its headquarters in Cambridge's Kendall Square, occupying multiple buildings for administrative and research functions. After residing in Cambridge since the 1980s, Biogen moved its headquarters to an office park in Weston (it still houses business functions there), just off Route 128. A year later, the company returned to Kendall Square because of the desire to be close to the R&D operations of the area's world-class biotech ecosystem. The primary sites for manufacturing Biogen's drugs, including the Alzheimer's treatments, are located in the Research Triangle of North Carolina and Solothurn, Switzerland.

Genzyme, established in Cambridge in 1981, grew into one of the leading biotech companies in the world. It specialized in developing medicines for rare genetic disorders, rare blood disorders, multiple sclerosis, cancer, and autoimmune diseases. Although Genzyme had offices, manufacturing plants, and genetic-testing labs around the world, it maintained its main administrative and R&D functions in Greater Boston. Early on, when Genzyme needed a manufacturing facility, it considered locating it in the New Jersey-Philadelphia pharmaceuticals cluster. But Genzyme decided to build a manufacturing center near its home base to help create a Greater Boston biotech ecosystem. In 1996, Genzyme built its flagship manufacturing plant, one of the largest cell culture-making facilities in the world, on the banks of the Charles River in Allston (since vacated).

In 2011, Genzyme was acquired by Sanofi for more than $20 billion. The operation was known as Sanofi Genzyme until 2022, when the Genzyme name was dropped and the company became known simply as Sanofi. This acquisition marked a major move by France's largest multinational pharmaceutical company to enter the biotechnology field. Since then, Sanofi and other pharmaceutical companies have been scooping up promising small biotech firms to get a leg up on innovative medical treatments. Conventionally, pharmaceutical companies make drugs with a chemical basis, while biotechnology treatments utilize living organisms. This can entail harnessing cellular and biomolecular processes, including gene therapy, tissue regeneration, and developing recombinant therapeutic proteins. The Genzyme division, with its breakthroughs in treating rare diseases, has proven to be a boon for Sanofi, which had been experiencing a decline in revenues from its traditional pharmaceuticals.

Sanofi has continued its Genzyme-originated operations in Greater Boston. Long located in Kendall Square, the company has relocated much of its Greater Boston administrative and R&D operations to two large buildings one mile away in Cambridge Crossing. This centralizes 2,700 Sanofi R&D and administrative employees from locations scattered across Cambridge and Boston suburbs. Meanwhile, Sanofi moved the biotech manufacturing operation to an award-winning facility in Framingham.

In addition to these vanguard companies, a key factor in the evolution of Kendall Square as a global biotech hub has been the mapping of the human genome (1990–2003), much of which was accomplished at MIT and Harvard laboratories. Knowledge of the makeup of the human genome has enabled scientists to unlock secrets of life. This unlocking process is only in relatively early stages, with genome-related companies multiplying in the area. The Whitehead Institute for Biomedical Research (1982), an MIT nonprofit spinoff, through its Center for Genome Research, was the single largest contributor to the Human Genome Project. It contributed one-third of the human genome sequence, which was assembled by an international consortium of sixteen laboratories. Whitehead produced more than one billion base pairs or DNA letters that have gone toward assembling a "book of life." The Whitehead Genome Research Center director was Eric Lander, who later became director of affiliated Broad Institute (co-founded by MIT and Harvard). It was spun off from the Whitehead Institute in 2004 to spearhead human genome research to develop applications of molecular medicine. Los Angeles businessman Eli Broad and his wife Edythe contributed more than $1 billion to the Broad Institute after considering funding biomedical research at California state universities. Eli Broad and his wife decided that they would donate their bequest to the Cambridge research institution because "the science is more important than the geography. There is no place in America, or elsewhere in the world, we believe, that has the combined scientific quality and leadership that's here in Cambridge."[2]

HOW THE LIFE SCIENCES CLUSTER FUNCTIONS

The Cambridge-Boston life sciences hub is a premier example of a global knowledge economy cluster. It demonstrates how innovation is driven, not only by top-flight research universities and creative entrepreneurs, but also by risk-taking financiers, appropriately designed research space, specialized scientific and technological services, and experienced lawyers, accountants, and management consultants. A competitive innovation cluster is usually located in a metropolitan area with high-quality air transportation and information infrastructure, ample housing opportunities, and an appealing quality of life. With a combination of these elements, capital, talent, and business services, cities are poised to play a significant role in the global economy. Urbanist Peter Hall has explained that the "milieux of innovation—places like Silicon Valley, but also older urban places like Munich, Paris, and Boston—continue to command the crucial productive chains; they are the powerhouses of the contemporary capitalist economy."[3]

The Cambridge-Boston life sciences cluster has been centered in Kendall Square because of close proximity to MIT and the initial availability of cheap land. From the late nineteenth century through World War II, Kendall Square was a district of assorted factories making boilers, soap, ink, organs, rubber hoses, and caskets. By the 1950s, the aging factories had become uncompetitive and either moved to new quarters in the suburbs or across the country or simply went out of business. During the 1960s, Cambridge embarked on an urban renewal clearance plan for the area, which became the site of the National Aeronautics & Space Administration's (NASA) Electronics Research Center. Unfortunately, President Nixon closed that operation in 1970. Kendall Square found itself with a lot of vacant land. Over the long term, the vacant land turned into an asset that allowed up-and-coming technology and biotech companies to find low-cost space near MIT. The real estate has turned into the priciest lab and office space in the country. The innovation vibe that has been created by scores of established and startup companies has gained worldwide attention. Philip Sharp explained: "'There is so much interaction and sharing of people back and forth between companies.... And the pressure to actually do something new, to really move the needle, is very high.... Just to step out and say "I gotta do something new or I can't justify my existence" is really quite, quite prominent in Cambridge.'"[4]

Big pharma players like Pfizer, Sanofi, and Bristol Meyers Squibb, joined by such information technology behemoths as Google, Facebook, Apple, and Microsoft, want to get in on the innovation action created over the years by academic-related startups. These megabucks firms have been driving up real estate prices. Since the biotech market is so active and Kendall Square lab rates are so high, biotech startups have had to seek out other locations, leaving Kendall Square to the blue-chip companies. Alternative sites for biotech companies are located in Boston's Seaport District, for established players like Vertex and Foundation Medicine; Cambridge Crossing; the Alewife area in West Cambridge; Kenmore Square/Fenway, near the Longwood Medical Area; Watertown's Arsenal Yards; and such I-95/Route 128 suburban communities as Waltham, Lexington, and Burlington. Future opportunities for life sciences development are projected for the Harvard University Enterprise Research Campus in Allston and the former Suffolk Downs site in East Boston and Revere. Though a benefit for individual communities, there are concerns that this spread of R&D firms may sap some of the face-to-face idea exchanges that have fueled the Kendall Square ecosystem.

Another concern about the life sciences in Boston is the prevalence of remote work in the wake of the COVID-19 pandemic. Experienced hands tend to argue that the biotech field operates in tighter geographic clusters than other technology sectors. Biotech researchers and entrepreneurs want to be located near universities undertaking cutting-edge research. MIT itself has had the greatest impact on biotech innovation. According to a Kauffman Foundation study *Entrepreneurial Impact: The Role of MIT*, MIT alumni, as of 2009, founded 26,000 active technology companies overall, employing about 3.3 million people and generating annual world sales of $2 trillion. This economic activity produced the equivalent of the eleventh largest economy in the world. Massachusetts firms ranked access to MIT and other universities ahead of low business costs, in contrast with other states, where the cost of doing business ranks as the foremost factor. MIT has been distinguished by its entrepreneurial culture since its founding in 1861. MIT stood alone for decades in actively encouraging faculty members to translate their research findings, in tandem with business, into publicly available innovations. Historian Merritt Roe Smith contends that MIT "stood at the center of a fundamental shift from craft to professional training in America. Though apparent only to the most astute observers, this shift played a pivotal role in the emergence of the United States as a leading industrial nation and world power." This culture gives the Cambridge-Boston area a competitive advantage in innovation that other regions envy.[5]

The capability of today's MIT and the Kendall Square life sciences ecosystem to generate new businesses and discoveries is demonstrated by legendary MIT chemical engineering professor Robert Langer, whose patents have been licensed by at least 400 companies. Professor Langer has served as a founder, director, or scientific advisor for forty-three new businesses since joining the MIT faculty in 1978. Perhaps his most notable entrepreneurial venture has been to help found Moderna, the pioneer in messenger RNA (mRNA) that developed a world-leading COVID-19 vaccine. Although Langer's is an extreme example of entrepreneurship, many local academic researchers have established companies for carrying out state-of-the-art research and development.[6]

Much of the innovation in life sciences is dependent upon star researchers in molecular biology and genetic engineering. As a study of the development of the biotech industry by sociologist Lynne G. Zucker, economist Michael Darby, social psychologist Marilyn B. Brewer demonstrated, scientific research stars who publish papers about major discoveries play a more important role in the industry's development than venture capital or government funding.[7] They tend to be more necessary to start-ups than to mature businesses. Cambridge's scientific stars attract the best talent from around the world. Whitehead Institute for Biomedical Research Director Ruth Lehmann has described how superstars doing basic scientific research drive medical innovation: "My most important role is to make sure that we get the most brilliant minds, empower them, and then make them centers so that they spread what they find and make the interactions. It's a hub-and-spoke model with clinical and biotech interactions."[8]

Because of the cutting-edge nature of biotech research, scientists rely on face-to-face information exchanges with colleagues working at universities and other companies. Biotech research can be highly tentative, compared with other innovation sectors. It can take as much as 10 to 15 years to bring biomedical treatments to market, compared with three years for typical computer hardware innovations. MIT historian of science Robin Scheffler explains: "Unlike the hardware and computing industries the path to becoming a molecular biologist continued to rely heavily on academic training, and the particular ethos of pure science that it imbued to molecular biologists." Because of the riskiness of working in the biotech business, researchers like to be located near university laboratories and other biotech companies so they can find employment if their for-profit endeavors falter.

According to Scheffler, life sciences clusters tend to be "stickier" than information technology and conventional manufacturing sectors because they require costly biosafe research facilities and state-of-the art equipment that discourage moving. It would be a complicated task to relocate complex and fragile cell lines and bacteria to far-flung spots.[9] Biotech companies estimate that at least 50% of their research work has to be done in a lab (the remainder can be done remotely), while conventional office-oriented companies can do most of their work remotely if they so desire. This is the reason that so many biotech labs are being built in Boston while traditional offices are going vacant. Economist Enrico Moretti explains, in *The New Geography of Jobs*, why contemporary innovation ecosystems are anchored to specific places: "it makes it harder to delocalize innovation than traditional manufacturing. ... a biotech lab is harder to export, because you would have to move not just one company but an entire ecosystem." Moretti observes that "the self-reinforcing nature of clusters means that once a cluster has started, it keeps attracting companies and workers. First-movers benefit from this lock-in effect, and early advantages become magnified over time."[10]

A critical factor driving the Cambridge-Boston biotech cluster and innovation industries in general has been federal funding for scientific and technological research. Since World War II, the federal government has been pumping billions of dollars in research funding into MIT and other Massachusetts institutions, much of it related either to military or healthcare purposes. This research funding was set in motion by MIT Engineering School Dean Vannevar Bush, who served as President Roosevelt's chief military science advisor in his role as Director of the US Office of Scientific Research and Development during the war. In this role, he oversaw the Manhattan Project and the development of radar and the country's air defense network. With his background as an academic researcher, a founder of the Raytheon Company, and government science coordinator, Bush understood how powerful collaboration between university researchers, private sector corporations, and government funding could be in advancing technology. Walter Isaacson has argued that the Vannevar Bush was the person most responsible for fusing together "into an iron triangle: the military-industrial-academic complex." MIT President Jerome Wiesner maintained: "No American has had greater influence in the growth of science and technology than Vannevar Bush."[11] Bush made sure that his Cambridge academic base received significant resources to support technological research. During the Cold War, copious funding flowed to such MIT-associated military and space research laboratories in the region as Lincoln Laboratory, MITRE Corporation, and Draper Laboratory.

The flow of federal funding for scientific research has also benefited the pharmaceuticals, biotech, and medical devices and supplies clusters in the Cambridge-Boston area, creating one of the world's foremost life sciences ecosystems. The region's major research hospitals have been prime recipients of federal research funding. As of 2021, Cambridge and Boston had five of the top eight teaching hospitals receiving funding from the NIH—#1 Massachusetts General, #2 Brigham & Women's, #4 Boston Children's Hospital, #8 Dana-Farber Cancer Institute, and #9 Beth Israel Deaconess Medical Center. Other local research hospitals receiving NIH funding included #13 Boston Medical Center, #17 McLean Hospital, #14 Massachusetts Eye and Ear, and #28 Tufts Medical Center. Overall, 2022 NIH grants to Massachusetts institutions totaled over $3.2 billion, ranking behind only California and New York. The Mass General Brigham system attracted $2.3 billion in research funding in FY 2022 alone, the most of any hospital system in the country. This system has spun off more than 130 health, biotech and medical device companies. Between 2007 and 2022, Mass General Brigham was awarded more than 10,000 patents for lifechanging technology and treatments. Built on cutting-edge research, the hospitals offer patients access to more than 2,700 ongoing clinical trials, accelerating the adoption of new treatments and therapies around the world.[12]

As of 2024, there were 116,937 biopharma jobs (up from approximately 60,000 in 2016) in Massachusetts, not including people working in hospitals. Laboratory space has tripled since 2011, from 18.4 million to 62 million square feet (2022), with an additional 14 to 17 million square feet (also including

Table 5. Largest biopharma employers in Massachusetts

Rank	Company	Employees
1	Takeda	6,214
2	Moderna	4,400
3	Sanofi	4,326
4	Vertex	3,400
5	Pfizer	2,800
6	Novartis	2,600
7	Bristol Myers Squibb	2,460
8	Alnylam	2,076
9	AstraZeneca/Alexion	1,900
10	Biogen	1,654
11	Abbvie	1,542
12	Foundation Medicine	1,100
13	EMD	1.086
14	Merck	944
15	Sarepta	721
16	Gingko Bioworks	700
17	GlaxoSmithKline	667
18	Alkermes	574
19	Novo Nordisk	450
20	Amgen	430

Source: Massachusetts Biotechnology Council, *MassBio 2024 Industry Snapshot*.[14]

"good practice" biotech manufacturing space) in the pipeline for completion by 2025. Labs in Massachusetts had 2,010 drug candidates in R&D, representing 15.2% of the US, drug pipeline and 6.4% of the global pipeline. In addition to universities and hospitals, there are more than 250 companies doing business within a couple miles of Kendall Square alone. Eighteen of the top 20 global drug companies and all 10 of the top medical device companies have a presence in the area.[13]

Greater Boston's prodigious scientific innovation reputation is affirmed in a study by Startup Genome, a global innovation research think tank. It ranks Boston #4 worldwide as an ecosystem for life science startup companies. The Startup Genome report takes into account metrics for research, grant funding, venture capital, talent, knowledge, infrastructure, and government policy. In innovation sub-sectors, Boston is one of the world's foremost centers, not only for biotechnology, but also for climate tech (renewable energy and energy efficiency), 3-D printing, and robotics. A highly skilled workforce is enabled by a Massachusetts labor pool that ranks #1 for workers with college degrees, at 44.7% (compared with the US proportion which is 33.1%.)[15] The World Intellectual Property Organization *Global Innovation Index 2018* ranks Boston #7 in the world for patents and scientific papers related to medicine.[16]

The model for successful contemporary biotech R&D relies upon a mix of large and small companies and research institutions working on a variety of health issues. The stand-alone, vertically integrated corporations like AT&T and its New Jersey-based Bell Labs and Big Pharma companies like Johnson & Johnson, Merck, and Pfizer used to do much of their R&D in-house. In recent years, the innovation model has shifted to become more extended and collaborative. Industry clusters have emerged as the preferred model for innovation. Thomas Friedman, in his bestseller *The World Is Flat*, has explained: "The best companies are the best collaborators. In the flat world, more and more business will be done through collaborations within and between companies, for a very simple reason: The next layers of value creation—whether in technology, marketing, biomedicine, or manufacturing—are becoming so complex that no single firm or department is going to be able to master it alone."[17] Thus, Cambridge-Boston life science R&D labs prove ideal partners for the big multinationals.

Yossi Sheffi, Director of the MIT Center for Transportation and Logistics, maintains that "a cluster may be an optimal balance between the complexity, bureaucracy, lock-in with internal suppliers, unionization, and slow decision-making that hamper innovation in large enterprises, and the lack of scale and reach that holds back smaller firms." The interaction of independent players in a cluster helps avoid the "groupthink" that can occur in an individual company. Harvard Business School's Michael Porter has summarized the message: "A cluster allows each member to benefit *as if* it had greater scale or *as if* it had joined with others formally—without requiring it to sacrifice its flexibility."[18]

The life sciences cluster is a magnet for small, entrepreneurial companies, who want to take advantage of proximity to other companies and universities. The biotech cluster's shared culture, customs, and laws promote a tacit exchange of knowledge and project collaboration among researchers and entrepreneurs. Yossi Sheffi cites the different levels of achievement between innovation cultures in Cambridge, MA, and Cambridge, UK. The Massachusetts city's ecosystem encourages risk-taking and does not tend to excessively penalize those who fail at an endeavor. Falling short in the English university town, on the other hand, tends to make it difficult for a researcher to obtain support for further projects. It is notable that UK economic development officials and entrepreneurs are seeking to emulate the Kendall Square namesake in creating a comprehensive innovation ecosystem and building shared biotech lab space.[19]

In an innovation economy, the constant search for new products, new ideas, and increasing returns has magnified the importance of being in the locations where innovation, learning, and execution is easier. Peter Hall explains the dynamic of innovation development: "like all creative activities, they depended on interaction, on networking, on a certain amount of buzz and fizz, which was more likely to be found in such places than anywhere else." Robert Krim and Alan Earls, who authored a historical study of Boston's innovation culture, *Boston Made*, explain that the phenomenon of "bump and connect" has provided the secret sauce that animates the Kendall Square innovation cluster. Frequent personal interactions make possible strong entrepreneurship, close-knit local networks, and hefty local funding.[20]

A recent Brookings Institution study explains that innovation and economic development are self-reinforcing, leading to rich cities becoming more successful and leaving less innovative cities farther behind: "With more innovation there is more investment, which attracts more knowledge workers and more firms, enabling more resources to be invested, which leads to even more innovation. When a region possesses an initial economic advantage, agglomeration effects can result in increasing innovation and investment in a positive cycle that ensures that favored regions and districts within them become even more innovative and attractive, intellectually and physically." Harvard economist Edward L. Glaeser conceptualizes the cluster phenomenon as "agglomeration economies, [which] are the benefits that come when firms and people locate near one another together in cities and industrial clusters." His research demonstrates that workers in large metropolitan areas are 50% more productive than workers in smaller metropolitan areas, whether they are in high-earning professional positions or low-wage service jobs.[21]

Major pharmaceutical and healthcare corporations have been flocking to the Greater Boston life sciences cluster for collaborative opportunities. The Japanese-based firm Takeda has moved its US headquarters from suburban Chicago to Kendall Square. Takeda's R&D facility, located in the former Sanofi Genzyme building, emphasizes research on cancer, rare diseases, gastrointestinal, and vaccines. Bristol-Myers Squibb has R&D facilities at Cambridge Crossing working on cancer resistance and immune-related and fibrotic diseases.

The Dutch-owned Philips Corporation has sold off its lighting and television businesses and is concentrating on healthcare technology. In recent years, it has acquired over 14 healthcare companies, with half of them in North America. Philips is pursuing innovations that provide telehealth to patients in their homes and apply data science and artificial intelligence in radiology, ultrasound, and minimally invasive surgical technologies. In 2008, Philips moved its North American headquarters from New York to Andover, MA. In recent years, Philips moved its headquarters and R&D operations to Cambridge and is now located in a spanking-new building at Cambridge Crossing near Kendall Square in 2022. Philips Research Americas has proclaimed that "it has relocated to the Boston/Cambridge hotspot, to strategically leverage the innovation ecosystem in the Boston/New York/Washington corridor with its many leading players in pharma, biotech, and healthcare, as well as some of the most renowned academic institutions."[22] Recognizing the salience of the Cambridge-Boston life sciences ecosystem, the federal government's new Advanced Research Projects Agency for Health (ARPA-H) has established one of its three centers in Cambridge—the main office is in Washington, DC and a third office is in Dallas. Cambridge hosts the agency's "investor catalyst" hub, which partners with researchers, entrepreneurs, and financiers to bridge the gap between basic research and the market availability of new technologies and medicines. ARPA-H seeks to accelerate breakthroughs for treating difficult-to-cure diseases such as cancer and Alzheimer's. The agency is modeled on the Defense Department's research division, the Defense Advanced Research Projects Agency, which was responsible for developing the Internet, among other technological advances. Agency staff are working out of leased space at the Cambridge Innovation Center. It is anticipated that ARPA-H initiatives should provide a sizable boost to the region's life sciences cluster.[23]

LIFE SCIENCES ECOSYSTEM SUPPORTING PLAYERS

An essential part of Greater Boston's life sciences ecosystem is the financing and professional business services that support it. Any successful innovation cluster requires these elements. The region's financial institutions and professional services are built upon traditions and networks that have developed over many decades, long before the current information technologies were in place. Many of the most successful global cities, from New York and London to Amsterdam and Hong Kong, have been part of financial and professional service networks for long spans.

Boston's most important advantage is the amount of venture capital invested in local life sciences enterprises. Between 2019 and 2021, the Boston area received $61.8 billion in venture capital. The venture capital raised by Massachusetts life sciences firms alone ballooned from $4.8 billion in pre-COVID-19 2018 to $8 billion in 2020 to $13.66 billion in 2021. This figure amounted to 36% of all biopharma venture investment in the United States. Because of Boston's high level of venture capital investment, urbanists Richard Florida and Ian Hathaway have ranked Boston as one of six "Superstar Global Startup Hubs" with San Francisco, New York, London, Beijing, and Los Angeles, a group that accounts for more than half of all venture capital investment worldwide.[24] Venture capital and innovation startups are necessary collaborators. Seed capital is not important for big, established corporations, while it is essential for entrepreneurs with new ideas.

Boston is the birthplace of the world's first venture capital investment firm. In 1946, MIT President Karl Compton, Boston Federal Reserve Bank President Ralph Flanders, and Harvard Business School's Georges Doriot founded the American Research and Development Corporation (ARDC) to finance promising startup enterprises that conventional bankers would not touch. They recognized that companies developing advanced technologies with long-term growth potential desperately needed strategic investments to get off the ground. Over the years, venture capital investment matured, and, today Boston is one of its foremost centers, particularly for the life sciences.

Some of the leading local venture capital firms include Atlas Venture, Bain Capital Life Sciences, Flagship Pioneering, F-Prime Capital (Fidelity), Polaris Partners, RA Capital Management, Third Rock Ventures, the Rockefeller family's Venrock Management, and 5AM Capital. Most of these venture investment firms are located either in Cambridge or Boston's Back Bay. It should be noted that Greater Boston healthcare companies also obtain funding from venture capital firms located outside the area. Venture firms raise hundreds of millions, sometimes billions, of dollars from institutional and independent investors. Besides supplying investment funds, they assist in developing successful corporations. This may include participation on the board of directors. Because of such hands-on involvement in business management, it has been important for biotech startups obtaining venture capital to be located in the Cambridge-Boston area. There is no evidence that this has changed significantly with the increased remote work caused by the pandemic.[25]

Even major biopharma multinationals like Johnson & Johnson (JLABS), AstraZeneca (Boston BioHub), Pfizer (Pfizer Ventures), and Takeda have venture capital divisions operating in Greater Boston, scouting out investment opportunities in emerging academic and private sector research. The most active corporate incubator in Boston is Johnson & Johnson. This site is one of eight JLABS incubators and three affiliated sites around the world. JLABS have more than a couple hundred investments. Their no-strings-attached model provides the lab space and support to help entrepreneurs develop their research.[26]

One of the most active venture capital firms has been Flagship Pioneering. Located in Kendall Square, it assembles scientific experts to conceive of valuable medical breakthroughs, then recruits first-rate talent, and develops strategies for pursuing those breakthroughs. Flagship Pioneering employs about seventy PhD scientists working on different problems. They file hundreds of patents, the most promising of which the firm then entrusts to a startup company to bring the patent to the marketplace. The venture firm has the goal of forming six to eight companies a year, not just investing in them. For companies that prove commercial potential, Flagship Pioneering helps attract financing from outside investors, forges partnerships, and helps businesses grow into public companies. Twenty of Flagship's growth companies have completed initial public offerings (IPOs) since 2013. Flagship's most notable growth company has been Moderna. In 2018, Moderna became the largest IPO in history, raising $600 million, implying an overall valuation of $7.5 billion. When Moderna broke through with an effective mRNA COVID-19 vaccine in 2021, its market valuation soared to $200 billion in August 2021 at the peak of speculative fever. By March, 2025, its value had decreased to $29.7 billion, affected by the waning of vaccine sales and challenges in developing new medical products.[27] Such are the vagaries of the marketplace in a capitalist innovation-oriented economy, despite the contribution to humankind made by Moderna's COVID vaccine. In any case, Flagship Pioneering, led by CEO Noubar Afeyan, has been one of the most profitable biotech VC funds, powered by Moderna. Flagship is betting that some of its other investments may successfully ride the wave of biotech breakthroughs in mRNA treatments, gene editing, and artificial intelligence.

Successful VC firms do not tend to be passive investors in biotech startups. Often they are active participants in launching and managing these companies. Like Flagship Pioneering, Third Rock Ventures has sought to get in on the ground floor work with biotech startups. Professional staff at these firms work with scientific researchers and experienced advisors to develop a vision and strategy for the new company. The VC firm launches the company with the necessary financial and personnel resources, ensuring that an experienced management team is in place to oversee the regulation, production, and distribution of the drugs. Cutting-edge companies that Third Rock Ventures has launched include Foundation Medicine and Voyager Therapeutics.

Even major hospitals have created their own venture funds. Mass General Brigham Innovation has invested in emerging diagnostics, medical devices, research tools, medical software, therapeutics and vaccines.[28] This fund has licensed technologies developed at Mass General Hospital, Brigham & Women's Hospital, Mass Eye & Ear, and McLean Hospital to more than seventy private companies, ranging from behemoths like Merck, Bayer, and Novartis to more specialized local firms like Athena Diagnostics, Correlagen Diagnostics, and Mersana Therapeutics.[29]

Some private investors become impatient with the long timeline that is typical for converting academic research into market-ready medical treatments. In 2024, investors seeded Arena Bioworks with $500 million to both fund the research stage and the transition to commercial drug development. Arena

Bioworks, which is located in Kendall Square, near but not affiliated with MIT, is blurring the line between the discovery process and the business of creating companies. The for-profit research institute seeks to avoid the complicated process of obtaining grants from the NIH and other academically oriented sources by providing research funds from private resources. Arena Bioworks has lured research scientists with salaries that are greater than those offered at universities, which tend to rely on federal grants. Arena scientists are seeking to develop next-generation technologies, including gene editing, machine learning, and tackling cancers, brain diseases, immune system disorders, and maladies tied to aging. Investors at Arena Bioworks are betting that, by speeding up the research and development process, the company can bring valuable innovations to market much more quickly and, thus, earn substantial profits on inherently risky early-stage investments.[30]

Another variation on venture capital deployment is MassChallenge, which calls itself an "accelerator." This is an enterprise that takes a startup to a level where it can grow into a thriving business. Their biotech startup candidates need to have a viable medical product that has been validated by a pre-clinical model to be eligible for the funding and management expertise that can "accelerate" them into clinical trials and scaled manufacturing. MassChallenge, which also manages accelerator programs in Providence, Texas, Israel, Mexico, and Switzerland, provides selected early-stage innovation startups a four-month program offering hands-on support from highly accomplished corporate partners, coworking space in the Seaport, and cash awards. MassChallenge HealthTech is a health-oriented program that works with later-stage startups in which startups are paired with an established business or institution to launch their product. Between 2009 and 2021, MassChallenge Boston accelerated 2,900 startups, which raised $8.6 billion in funding, earned $3.6 billion in revenues, and created 186,000+ jobs.[31]

An indispensable source of seed capital for startups, before they become established enough to attract venture capital funding, is "angel" investors. Often "angels" are high-net-worth individuals who invest personal funds in startups. Many participate in networks of similar investors who share information while making individual investment decisions. Leading Greater Boston "angel" networks investing in life sciences and healthcare startups include Boston Harbor Angels, Boynton Angels, Hub Angels, Mass Medical Angels, Walnut Ventures, and Harvard Business School Alumni Association of Boston.

Table 6. Institutions supporting the Greater Boston life sciences ecosystem

Factor	Local Examples
Universities	MIT, Harvard, Northeastern, Boston University
Research Institutions	Whitehead Institute, Broad Institute
Hospitals	Mass General Hospital, Beth Israel Deaconess Medical Center, Tufts Medical Center, Dana-Farber Cancer Institute
Venture Capital Firms	Flagship Pioneering, Polaris Partners, RA Capital Management, F-Prime Capital Partners, Bain Capital Life Sciences
Real Estate Firms	Alexandria, King Street Properties, IQHQ
Startup Incubators & Accelerators	Cambridge Innovation Center, MassChallenge
Legal Firms	Wolf Greenfield, McDermott Will & Emery
Specialized Scientific Services	Charles River Labs, Addgene
Government Agencies	Massachusetts Life Sciences Center
Trade Associations	MassBio

Source: Author's research

An essential complement to Boston's venture capital firms are entities that provide workspace and networking opportunities for startup entrepreneurs. The Cambridge Innovation Center (CIC), established in 1999 by two MIT grads, provides flexible shared office space in Kendall Square and Boston's Financial District. The shared work and meeting space is available at reasonable monthly rates to startups. Without affordable shared workspace, the pipeline of startups could dry up and fatally damage the innovation ecosystem in Kendall Square. Tenants range from single-person startups up to discreet endeavors of tech giants. When Google set up its Boston headquarters in 2005, its first employee, working at the CIC, was Android co-founder Rich Miner. Intel has an "innovation unit" and Johnson & Johnson has its Boston Innovation Center in the CIC to take advantage of proximity to emerging entrepreneurs. Over 10,000 companies have circulated through CIC, often moving on to larger spaces to accommodate their growing business. Currently about 20% of the businesses using the CIC are dedicated to the life sciences.[32]

The CIC does not provide financing or management advice to startups, but it does provide robust programs to promote networking and information-sharing through its Venture Café, which meets most Thursday evenings. The

CIC also operates LabCentral, which has provided shared wet labs for up to 200 biotech startups, and MassRobotics, which offers work and office space in the Seaport for robotics and automation companies.

The CIC provides a compelling example of how to spread innovation and knowledge around the world. It manages over one million square feet of shared workspace, wet labs and event space in Boston, Cambridge, Philadelphia, Providence, St. Louis, Rotterdam, Tokyo, Berlin, and Warsaw. Each of these shared workspaces carries the name "CIC" followed by the name of the city in question. This displays the potency of the Cambridge brand as a center of innovation. Tim Rowe maintains that there are about fifty major innovation cities around the world, and his long-term goal is to open branches of the CIC in all of them. The CIC also influences the global spread of innovation-spurring practices by hosting in Cambridge government representatives from France, Japan, Chile, South Korea, and other countries seeking to identify opportunities for technological development, recruit talent, and promote

Figure 5. Venture Café, Cambridge Innovation Center. Tech researchers and entrepreneurs network and swap ideas at the weekly Venture Café meetups, exemplifying the process of "bump and connect" that helps promote innovation.—Courtesy of Courtesy of Venture Café Global Institute, Cambridge Innovation Center.

their own country's entrepreneurs. Nineteen South Korean companies maintain a presence at the CIC. These CIC activities exemplify the global reach that Boston and Cambridge have in the sphere of technological innovation.[33]

Greater Boston has a number of law firms serving the life sciences sector. One of the foremost of these law firms is Wolf Greenfield. Ninety percent of the firm's 150 legal professionals have an educational background in science or engineering. Some of them were hired directly from scientific grad schools and then sent to law school by Wolf Greenfield. The law firm has complementary divisions for chemical & materials technologies and pharmaceuticals. Their clients include such recognized biotech companies such as Biogen, Takeda, Moderna Therapeutics, and Ginkgo Bioworks. Wolf Greenfield also represents MIT, Harvard Medical School, Boston Children's Hospital, and Dana-Farber Cancer Institute.[34] Most of the leading Boston law firms, including Goodwin, McDermott Will & Emery, Ropes & Gray, and Nutter, have specialists in intellectual property.

The area has several real estate development firms specializing in scientific labs and offices. Alexandria Real Estate, one of the biggest developers of life science space, has concentrated its holdings in Cambridge/Boston, followed by San Francisco, San Diego, and New York.[35] Alexandria has constructed purpose-built lab structures in Kendall Square, the Seaport District-South Boston, the Fenway, and Watertown. To promote the businesses that it would lease space to, the company operates a venture capital arm, Alexandria Venture Investments.[36] The firm uses a converted industrial building in Kendall Square to provide selected startups office and lab space, access to seed capital, collaborative opportunities with other researchers, and professional management support.

King Street Properties, another large life sciences real estate firm, owns biotech lab buildings in Lexington, the Alewife area of Cambridge, and Waltham.[37] Another significant biotech facility developer is BioMed Realty, a Blackstone-owned company. In the Boston/Cambridge area, it manages nineteen properties dedicated to life sciences and tech companies. The California-based IQHQ real estate firm has become a partner with Meredith Management in building the second phase of the Fenway Center on air rights over the Massachusetts Turnpike. The intention is to provide lab space near the Longwood Medical Area.[38] Another life science real estate development firm, Breakthrough Properties, is also focused on development in Boston. Formed in 2019 by the global real estate company Tishman Speyer and life sciences investors Bellco Capital, Breakthrough Properties is developing the first phase of Harvard's Enterprise Research Campus in Allston. With the explosion of lab space construction since the advent of COVID-19, Greater Boston appears to have a glut. While this may be a problem for real estate investors, the plethora of lab space may spur further biotech development by providing ample, reasonably priced lab space for researchers and entrepreneurs. If researchers and entrepreneurs, from the area to other states and countries, want to participate in the Greater Boston life sciences cluster, appropriate facilities are readily available.

Greater Boston's life sciences cluster also benefits from companies that provide specialized scientific services. One of the foremost is Charles River Labs. Headquartered in Wilmington, it has eighty facilities located in twenty countries, performing laboratory work for multinational corporations and small emerging biotech firms. Charles River Labs has Massachusetts facilities in Woburn, Shrewsbury, and Worcester. Charles River Labs' 14,700+ employees currently serve 30% of the world contract lab market, working on 85% of FDA-approved drugs in 2018.[39]

Another biotech asset is Watertown-based Addgene, a global nonprofit plasmid repository. Operating like a library of genetic material, Addgene conserves and sends plasmids to research biologists around the world. Since its founding in 2004 by MIT graduates Melina Fan, a fourth generation Chinese-Bostonian, and Chinese immigrant Benjie Chan, Addgene's repository comprises 141,000+ plasmids, deposited by 6,000+ nonprofit labs around world. When scientists—a dozen Nobel Prize winners have donated research plasmids to Addgene—publish papers related to the genome, they send the plasmids identified in their research to Addgene. According to a study published by the Immigrant Learning Center, founders Fan and Chan "think Addgene could only be launched in Boston because of plethora of biotech and presence of international researchers."[40]

The Commonwealth of Massachusetts has played a strong role in supporting the life sciences ecosystem. In 2008, Governor Deval Patrick established the Massachusetts Life Sciences Initiative, promising $1 billion over a decade to further the development of the biotech industry with grants, loans, R&D tax credits (in addition to federal tax credits), and workforce training. Governors Charlie Baker and Maura Healey added hundreds of millions more in funding. The initiative is administered through the Massachusetts Life Sciences Center (MLSC), a state-chartered economic development agency.[41]

Trade organizations, particularly the Massachusetts Biotechnology Council (MassBio), also play a significant role in promoting the state's biotech cluster. Founded in 1985, MassBio is the oldest biotechnology trade association in the world and has 1,300+ members. MassBio organizes conferences and many sorts of information exchange and advocates for biotechnology interests across the state. Boston frequently hosts the annual BIO International Convention, which is considered the foremost global biotech trade meeting. The 2023 BIO International Convention, held at the Boston Convention Center, attracted more than 18,000 attendees from around the world.[42] Events like the BIO International Convention reinforce Boston's reputation as the world's leading center of life sciences innovation and attract all types of talent to work in the area.

GREATER BOSTON'S FUTURE AS A GLOBAL LIFE SCIENCES HUB

One has to wonder whether the Greater Boston life sciences cluster could end up being vulnerable to the fate of the minicomputer industry, which thrived here during the 1970s and 1980s before collapsing. The minicomputer sector drove the "Massachusetts Miracle," but ultimately failed when it did not recognize the rise of personal computers as a threat. The Digital Equipment Corporation's founder Ken Olsen long considered them a "toy" and prohibited using the term "personal computer" at his company. By the early 1990s, Digital was working on a range of products for enabling the Internet, but the company never effectively capitalized on them. Massachusetts ended up losing out to the Silicon Valley in computer development. By the early 1990s, Prime Computer, Data General, Wang, and a host of smaller tech companies had to close shop. In 1998, Compaq absorbed Digital.

AnnaLee Saxenian, who received her PhD from MIT and has taught at University of California-Berkeley, had a ringside seat for the action on both coasts. Her influential book *Regional Advantage: Culture and Competition in Silicon Valley and Route 128* concluded that "by the end of the 1980s Route 128 had ceded its position as the locus of computer innovation to the West Coast."[43] Saxenian attributed this collapse to the self-contained, vertically integrated business model of the Massachusetts companies, which made it difficult to share information and adapt to changing markets. Silicon Valley proved more adaptable and flexible because its companies were less hierarchical and more open to cross-pollination. Silicon Valley encouraged the exchange of information and job-hopping, while Greater Boston did not. During the 1980s, Boston venture capital firms focused on tech hardware and avoided software, which Silicon Valley picked up on to achieve tech dominance. Boston and Route 128 focused more on corporate applications, while Silicon Valley had the field to itself for consumer applications, later, social media, and, now, artificial intelligence. Silicon Valley has become known for its culture of "breaking things," exerting far-reaching social control through its social media algorithms and amassing enormous amounts of wealth and political power.

Since the 1990s, Greater Boston's information technology and biotech practitioners have taken the lessons of Silicon Valley to heart. They have promoted information-sharing and sought to break down corporate silos. The region's innovation sectors are thriving, even as competitors on the West Coast, Europe, and China also grow. Greater Boston's strengths have been highlighted by the research undertaken to combat COVID-19. There is much to suggest that Greater Boston should remain a major global life sciences hub for the foreseeable future. The life sciences ecosystem, organized around an outstanding array of research universities and medical centers, is robust and diversified. Researchers are working on a broad range of path-breaking treatments for cancer, Alzheimer's, transmittable diseases, rare diseases, and immune diseases. Genomic editing and other forms of personalized medical treatments are just emerging as methods for radically improving the health of large populations. The successful development of COVID-19 vaccines has boosted the visibility and prestige of the region's research capacities, attracting additional global research talent, entrepreneurship, and investment. The deployment of data science and artificial intelligence for medical treatment promises revolutionary advances. Greater Boston's bets on life science innovation are spread widely. Some research may hit dead ends, but other efforts could open up untold opportunities. Boston's innovation culture is more academically oriented and less controversial than its West Coast rival.

The bedrock of Boston's life sciences ecosystem is its talent base. The region's universities attract the superstar researchers who provide the vision and secure the resources and the students who form the skilled research workforce. Although corporate management, particularly in the multinational biopharma sector, and financing sources may be scattered across the world, a concentration of qualified R&D workers determines success. Startup Genome and other innovation city rankings maintain this is Boston's greatest strength.

Boston's scientific community has even been ahead of the curve in cultivating female talent. Startup Genome has observed that "the Boston ecosystem is particularly welcoming to women, with several local ecosystem standouts headed by female leaders. . . . Around 10% of startups here are founded by women, which compares favorably to a national average of 3% of VC dollars going to female founders." Less to the area's credit, only .5% of overall venture capital in Massachusetts goes to Black entrepreneurs.[44]

One threat to Cambridge-Boston's life sciences ecosystem is the disruptive impact of remote and hybrid working that has arisen in reaction to the COVID-19 pandemic. In sectors where in-person work is not necessary, some employers are allowing entirely remote work. The life sciences, which entail hands-on research, require more in-person work. Apparently, this imperative could redound to the local cluster's benefit.[45] The biggest thing that could go wrong for Greater Boston's life sciences cluster as the region's flagship innovation sector would be a situation in which some dramatic overarching change to the field occurred that Boston's entire ecosystem could not adjust to, as when its minicomputer cluster collapsed in the 1980s. For the foreseeable future, this is unlikely because Boston's life sciences are extraordinarily diverse. The proverbial eggs of R&D are distributed in myriad baskets.

FURTHER GREATER BOSTON INNOVATION CLUSTERS

Besides life sciences, Greater Boston has several other innovation clusters that are internationally competitive. They include robotics, 3-D printing, climate/clean tech, financial technology/fintech (see discussion in Chapter 3), and the red-hot field of artificial intelligence (AI). The combined importance of the innovation sectors to the Massachusetts economy is undeniable. The state has the country's highest proportion of workers in innovation economy jobs at 41.4% (2021), with other leading states being New York (35.3%), California (30.8%), and Texas (30.7%).[46] This section provides capsule descriptions of each cluster.

Robotics

One of Boston's leading innovation sectors is robotics. Robots, which often act autonomously and interactively, form a foundational technology base that can be applied for a wide range of uses, including manufacturing processes, health care (hospital patient care), logistics (transportation and inventory management), unmanned defense systems (drones), and household tasks (vacuum cleaners and security systems). Robots are "Things" interacting in the Internet of Things. As AI becomes more sophisticated, the functioning of robotics will expand in unimagined ways.

There are over 400 Massachusetts companies making and using robotics. The importance of the robotics cluster is demonstrated by the fact that Massachusetts ranks #2 only to California in receiving early-stage R&D funding from the federal Small Business Innovation Research & Small Business Technology Transfer Programs (SBIR/SBTT). Between 2017 and 2021, California ranked #1 with 162 awards, Massachusetts was #2 with 111 awards, and Pennsylvania was #3 with 66 awards. With these R&D awards, Massachusetts manufacturers have developed 90% of military mobile ground robotics devices.[47]

The Greater Boston robotics cluster includes businesses from small start-ups to major corporations. Bedford-based iRobot has been one of the most influential robotics companies in Massachusetts. The pioneering firm has helped spawn the dynamic robotics ecosystem, as its former employees have created at least fifteen spinoff companies over the last two decades. The companies have been developing products different from the Roomba vacuum cleaner and other consumer products manufactured by iRobot. These products include industrial and military robots. IRobot has been such a standout in the robotics field that Amazon, in 2022, tried to purchase it; but the lack of European Union regulatory approval scotched the deal. Despite this, Amazon has been active in the Greater Boston robotics industry. Amazon Robotics has grown since the purchase of North Reading-based Kiva Systems in 2012. This enterprise invents and manufactures robots for Amazon's heavily automated warehouses. Since buying up Kiva Systems, Amazon Robotics has manufactured over 750,000 mobile robots operating in over 300 fulfillment centers worldwide. In addition to the North Reading headquarters, the e-commerce company has a manufacturing plant in Westborough. The Proteus robot, which is designed to have an expressive "face" and make noises of approval when completing tasks, carries bins of packages through the warehouse to trucks on loading bays.[48]

A trail-blazing direction is being taken by Hyundai-owned Boston Dynamics (the company that developed "Pluto," the robot dog, and "Atlas," the humanoid robot), which opened its AI Institute in Kendall Square in 2022. Situated to draw on synergy with MIT and other cutting-edge businesses, the

Boston Dynamics AI Institute is focusing on how AI/machine learning and robotics can be integrated to make machines that can contribute to human safety, care for the elderly and disabled, and enhance industrial productivity.[49]

Greater Boston's robotics ecosystem has many other players. In the Seaport District, MassRobotics Innovation Center has provided shared workspace for more than 100 robotics startups, helping them raise $350 million in venture capital. The facility offers a mechanical lab for startups, with hand and power tools, an industrial innovation lab with industrial robot arms and conveyor belts, a human-robot interaction lab with humanoids and collaborative robot arms, and an electronics lab with 3-D printers. High-level robotics R&D is taking place at Draper Laboratory, MIT Lincoln Laboratory, MITRE, Woods Hole Oceanographic Institution, and UMass Lowell NERVE Center. Eighteen Massachusetts universities operate thirty-five robotics R&D programs. One of the most noteworthy is Worcester Polytechnic Institute (WPI), which started the first undergraduate robotics engineering program in the country. WPI has over 400 undergrads and 300 MS and PhD students studying robotics. Such programs help develop a deep talent pipeline and spur entrepreneurship.[50]

3-D Printing

Just as robotics is a foundational technology of what is being called "advanced manufacturing," so is 3-D printing, or "additive manufacturing." A 3-D printer uses laser beams to fuse together metallic powders, plastics, or liquids to create almost any sort of machined item. The printers translate digital designs, which can be guided by artificial intelligence, into material objects. For manufacturers, 3-D printing is a boon for customizing products and avoiding unwieldy supply chains. The technology, which until recently has been a niche process for making design prototypes and custom medical devices like implants and prosthetics, has finally achieved the potential to undertake complex mass production processes. The Biden administration had programs betting on 3-D printing, robotics, and other forms of technological innovation to drive the resurgence of manufacturing in America.

Greater Boston is at the center of these developments. According to the *Boston Globe*, the region "has emerged as perhaps the most important 3-D printing cluster in the world." Professors and students from local universities, especially MIT, have played a pivotal role in developing the technology. One of the leading 3-D printing businesses is VulcanForms, which was founded by

MIT professor John Hart and former student Martin Feldman. It is considered a "unicorn" company (with a valuation of over one billion dollars) whose 3-D printers deliver higher quality products at greater speed and lower cost than anything yet available. Instead of using one or two lasers to fabricate a product, as has been the practice, a VulcanForms printer at Devens uses 150 computer-guided lasers to assemble the metallic powders. For some metal parts, their 3-D printers can reduce materials costs 90% and energy use 50%. They can make knee and hip implants, computer-cooling devices, semiconductors, and small missile engines. The Devens plant has 20 enormous 3-D printers, which are 20 feet high and weigh 30 tons. Hart and Feldman believe that theirs is the "most productive metal additive manufacturing plant in the world." Their ambitious business strategy calls for manufacturing customized parts at their plants for corporate customers instead of selling 3-D printers to other companies to make their own components.[51]

There are several other local "unicorns" developing 3-D printers for large-scale production. Desktop Metal, of Burlington, was bought out by Nano Dimension in 2024. Prior to being acquired, Desktop Metal sold its 3-D printing systems to more than 6,000 industrial customers. Waltham's MarkForged, which is also being acquired by Nano Dimension, makes 3-D printers to fit the needs of customers in aerospace, automotive, manufacturing, medical technology, and energy. Formlabs, of Somerville, is the world's leading maker of 3-D printers employing polymer resins and nylon-based materials to make an endless array of plastic objects. Formlabs has sold more than 100,000 printers. The company's customers include Ford, Gillette, New Balance, Hasbro, Louisville Slugger, and Harvard University.[52]

Climate Tech

Massachusetts has been carving out an impressive niche working on technological solutions to the climate crisis, a sector referred to as climate tech or clean tech. Startup Genome ranks Boston #5 globally for its climate tech ecosystem, with its greatest strengths being in "performance," "knowledge," and "talent."[53] Massachusetts has one of the country's first two commercial-scale offshore wind farms, with New York's Long Island. Vineyard Wind I, operational in 2024, has 62 wind turbines producing 800 megawatts of electricity in the open ocean 15 miles south of Martha's Vineyard. The project has the capacity to provide power to 400,000 homes and businesses. This wind energy project has been constructed out of the New Bedford Marine Commerce Terminal, which is the first purpose-built US offshore wind port. The Vineyard Wind II project, which also will produce 800 MW of electric power, received financing in 2024. Two larger wind energy projects—Commonwealth Wind and SouthCoast Wind Energy—have been permitted but have not proceeded because of rising costs due to inflation. Depending on further negotiations, they could still be built. The Massachusetts wind energy projects are creating a great deal of expertise, which is influencing projects elsewhere in the country.

There is a great deal of climate tech R&D taking place around Boston, with MIT being at the epicenter. MIT's The Engine is an incubator and a venture capital funder for extremely challenging, potentially transformative innovations in life sciences, human health, fusion energy, and advanced materials that may be years away from realization. Recognizing the need for a more comprehensive approach to advance "tough tech" startups, MIT's The Engine provides them lab space with specialized equipment, business services, technological expertise, and venture capital.[54]

One of The Engine's most significant spinoffs is Commonwealth Fusion Systems, which is seeking to make fusion energy feasible. Fusion energy is thought to be the holy grail of energy production because it would be able to release enormous amounts of energy, comparable to that produced by the sun and stars. Commonwealth Fusion Systems, which originated with research at MIT's Plasma Science and Fusion Center, is building the world's first fusion reactor at Devens with more than $2 billion in funding, some of which came from The Engine. The company expects to have its experimental plant in operation by 2025 and a commercial fusion reactor operating in Virginia by the early 2030s.

MIT-based scientists are pursuing another previously-unattainable source of energy—namely geothermal energy, which exists six to twelve miles beneath the earth's surface. Until now, techniques used to extract fossil fuels have been inadequate to drill deep enough to capture thermal energy. Quaise, a startup nurtured by MIT's Plasma Science and Fusion Center and The Engine, has pioneered a technique of using a gyrotron, a large machine used for industrial heating and curing processes, to blast electromagnetic waves through rock and reach the earth's thermal energy. Quaise is moving forward with its efforts to demonstrate the efficacy of this technology.

Another offshoot from The Engine is Somerville-base Form Energy. It has developed iron-air batteries which can store electrical power for exponentially longer periods than lithium-ion batteries and at one-tenth of the price.

These high-capacity batteries are effective at storing energy from wind and solar power facilities for many days, making those energy sources reliable on a year-round basis.

General Electric has located the headquarters of its $30 billion stand-alone energy business, GE Vernova, in Kendall Square to take advantage of the place's innovation synergies. GE has been one of the world's leading manufacturers of power production technology since Thomas Edison built the world's first electrical generating plant in New York in 1882. With approximately 54,000 wind turbines and 7,000 gas turbines, GE Vernova's technology helps generate approximately 30% of the world's electrical supply. The company's mission is to play a meaningful role in the energy transition.

There are many more early-stage climate tech startups in the Boston area, many of whom can be found at Somerville's Greentown Labs. Greentown Labs (2011) is considered to be the largest climate tech incubator in the world, something which Prince William recognized when he visited there in 2022 as part of his Earthshot Awards event. The incubator has coworking space, a machine shop and labs for electronics, prototyping, and wet lab research. Greentown Labs has hosted over 450 startups, who have attracted more than $1.5 billion in investment. The Northeast Clean Energy Council, a climate tech trade association, is one of the tenants at the Greentown Labs. Surveying the development of the climate tech sector and the spread of its discoveries around the world, Dennis Whyte, director of MIT's Plasma Science and Fusion Center, has remarked that "Massachusetts has a really good chance of being the hub of this thing."[55]

Artificial Intelligence (AI)

Artificial intelligence (AI) is a paramount topic for technology and society these days. With the 2022 release of ChatGPT by OpenAI, San Francisco and the Silicon Valley have emerged as the hottest spot for AI development. Boston ranks among the six leading US cities for early-stage generative AI R&D.[56] Governor Healey has created an AI Task Force to plot a strategy for developing the field in this state. The state has allocated $100 million to create an "Applied AI Hub," comparable to state efforts to support biotechnology and advanced manufacturing.[57]

The leading local player for AI, yet again, is MIT. Lay persons may be surprised that MIT has been working on AI applications for decades. The university established its Artificial Intelligence Laboratory back in 1959. Over the years, the MIT AI Lab pioneered methods for machine learning, enabling machines to autonomously learn from data and experiences to undertake a variety of complex tasks. The MIT AI Lab produced breakthroughs in image-guided surgery, natural-language-based Web access, touch screen interfaces, and behavior-based robots used for planetary exploration and military reconnaissance. The AI Lab merged with MIT's Laboratory for Computer Science (1963) in 2003 to form the Computer Science & Artificial Intelligence Laboratory (CSAIL). CSAIL is headquartered in the Frank Gehry-designed Stata Center. With 1,000 faculty, postdoc researchers, and graduate and undergraduate students, it is the largest lab at MIT. Researchers from the AI Lab and CSAIL developed the first time-shared computers, the first mobile robots (including the Boston Dynamics "robot dog"), the first computer vision systems, and even Dropbox.

In recognition of the meteoric pace of computing and AI development, MIT established the Schwartzman College of Computing in 2019 to coordinate MIT's various departments and research centers involved with AI,

Figure 6. Ray and Maria Stata Center (2004), MIT. The Stata Center was designed by superstar architect Frank Gehry in his Deconstructionist style to symbolize and facilitate the interactive and creative spirit entailed in technological innovation.—Courtesy of WikiCommons, posted by Tony Webster.

including CSAIL, MIT Quest for Intelligence, and MIT-IBM Watson AI Lab. MIT, with its Schwarzman College of Computing, intends to play a leading role in ensuring that the applications of AI affect human beings responsibly and that the creation of Frankenstein monsters is avoided. At the core of the Schwarzman College mission is teaching, research, and engagement framework on the Social and Ethical Responsibilities of Computing (SERC). Such a perspective is being incorporated into the teaching and research of every MIT department and program.[58]

Other local universities have well-resourced, influential AI initiatives. Harvard's Kempner Institute for the Study of Natural and Artificial Intelligence (2021) has received initial funding of $500 million from Harvard alumni Mark Zuckerberg (Facebook/Meta Platforms, founder & CEO), and his wife Dr. Priscilla Chan. Two other robust AI programs at local universities are Boston University's AI Research Initiative at the Hariri Institute for Computing and Computational Science & Engineering and Northeastern's Institute for Experiential AI. These programs and similar ones at other universities around the state are training a highly skilled AI talent pool. The Future of Life Institute (2015) is a Cambridge-based think tank founded by academics and entrepreneurs seeking to reduce global catastrophic risks facing humanity, including risks from AI. It has played a convening role in discussions about ethics and AI. In spring, 2023, the Future of Life Institute published a letter signed by dozens of leading developers of AI and computing entitled "Pause Giant AI Experiments: An Open Letter." With the release of ChatGPT, the signatories called for a pause in developing AI in order to create a framework for ensuring the safety of further AI iterations. The letter warned of out-of-control disinformation, the loss of millions of jobs, and a loss of human control over the impacts of AI technology.

CHAPTER 8

The First Waves of Migrants Reshape Boston Society

"Migration is encoded in the DNA of cities."
German Marshall Fund of the United States,
"Cities Managing Migration" Report

One of the elemental features of globalization is migration. The flow of people joins the flows of traded goods, investments, and information in creating the global economy and society. The movement of people seeking to work and settle in a foreign country is the most consequential form of migration. It reshapes international labor markets as well as national and local cultures. Other significant forms of the international movement of people include business and leisure travelers and international university students.[1]

In the United States, the percentage of foreign-born people has fluctuated enormously. From the late nineteenth century until the 1920s, approximately 14% of the population was foreign-born. Due to immigration restriction laws, that number dropped to a historic low of 13% in 1970. After the loosening of immigration laws in the 1960s, the percentage of foreign-born people returned to almost 14%. Today, other countries also have significant numbers of immigrants. Almost all of the top twenty-five cities for immigration are located in the United States, Canada, Western Europe, Australia, and the Arabian Peninsula. These are prosperous places where there is plenty of work for both high-skilled and less-skilled workers. Global cities in East Asia tend not to be destinations for foreigners since countries like China, South Korea, and India have large domestic populations migrating internally to fill the demand for workers. Of the top 25 urban immigration destinations, metropolitan Boston ranks #25 in the world and #9 in the United States, with 684,165 people born in foreign countries. This represents 18.8% of metropolitan Boston's population.[2]

Given native-born Americans' relatively low birth rates, immigrants and their children today generate almost all of the prime-age population growth in the United States. Diminishing native demographic growth is a similar phenomenon in the advanced economies of Europe and Japan, where workforces are shrinking and people from outside the country are needed to support local populations. Two types of immigrants have been pursuing work opportunities in developed countries. First are the well-educated and entrepreneurial, who are attracted to innovation and education hubs like Boston. Major metropolitan areas are home to the majority of skilled foreign talent in any given country. The second, larger group of immigrants comprises less-skilled workers who hold lower-paid service jobs such as hotel, food service, and maintenance workers, groundskeepers, construction workers, and home health aides. This bifurcated workforce exists in all global cities in the developed world as well as megacities of the less developed world. Immigrants do not simply add to the workforce. Through their acculturation, they transform the local society.

Table 7: US percent foreign-born, 2016, 25 largest metropolitan areas

1.	Miami	40.5%
2.	Los Angeles	33.6%
3.	San Francisco	30.9%
4.	New York	29.3%
5.	San Diego	24.1%
6.	Houston	23.5%
7.	Washington, DC	23.0%
8.	Riverside, CA	21.5%
9.	Boston	18.8%
10.	Dallas	18.2%

Source: Luc Shuster and Peter Ciurczak, *Boston's Booming . . . But for Whom?: Building Shared Prosperity in a Time of Growth.*

IRISH IMMIGRANTS MAP OUT PATTERNS OF ADAPTATION

The roots of immigration in Boston and its relationship with globalization are deep and instructive. The immigration experience has involved: 1) the forces that drove people to leave their homelands for America; 2) the routes that immigrants took to reach Boston; 3) how the immigrants were received and how they joined the labor force; and 4) how their efforts to acculturate reshaped the Greater Boston community. These issues are relevant to understanding the impact of immigration in global cities from the nineteenth century to the twenty-first. Early immigrants established patterns of sociocultural adaptation that remain germane today.

Boston's development as a major seaport created the conditions for becoming an important immigrant gateway to America. The port served as an entry point throughout the colonial era. Merchants, sailors, travelers, and migrants of various sorts came through Boston, leavening the cosmopolitan quality of the place.

The Irish abruptly fractured this demographic when they migrated by the thousands to Boston during the calamitous Potato Famine of 1845–1850. There had always been Irish-born residents in Boston, but many were Protestants who assimilated easily with their co-religionists. Those fleeing the Potato Famine were predominantly poor Catholics, who were squeezed out of Ireland by skyrocketing demographic growth and landlords forcing impoverished tenants off the land. Half the rural Irish populace, who were at-will tenants or laborers, subsisted on the readily raised staple crop of potatoes. When a fungal blight struck the potato crop in 1845, it led to the death by starvation and disease of over one million and the emigration of two million more.

The majority of unfortunates sailed to North America. The ships tended to be rundown hulks, on which the fares could be as low as three pounds. Some immigrants traveled directly to Boston, while others disembarked in Halifax or Quebec and made their way south by coastal ships or overland. Either way, payment for the trip left them virtually penniless by the time they arrived.[3] Many died of disease en route on what were called "coffin ships." Boston was the closest American port to Ireland, and it ended up being the city with the largest proportion of Irish immigrants. In 1850, of 136,881 Boston residents, 35,000 (25%) were Irish born. Between 1820 and 1880, 90% of Boston's immigrants were Irish.[4] Like subsequent immigrant groups, the Irish multiplied

The First Waves of Migrants Reshape Boston Society 167

their numbers through "chain migration," the process through which relatives and friends immigrated to join their clan's trailblazers.

For the capital of Yankeedom, this was a traumatic social upheaval. Overnight, Bostonians saw parts of their orderly, prosperous city turn into squalid slums. The size of the Irish population was enormous, poor, and not easily assimilable. In their home country, the Catholics had long been treated as a subordinate people or "race" (not based on skin color, but by being considered an inferior people to the Anglo-Saxon or Nordic "races") by the Protestant English. Founded by English Puritans, Boston and New England were the most homogeneous places in the United States up until the 1840s. The city was probably less tolerant of ethnic newcomers than any major US city. Irish Catholics carried a religious stigma to Massachusetts. Despite the fact that Catholicism became officially tolerated in the Massachusetts Constitution of 1780, hidebound Protestants scorned Catholics and harassed them during the 1820s and 1830s. This culminated with the burning of the Ursuline Convent in Charlestown in 1834. In the wake of the famine migration, nativist politics reigned supreme in Massachusetts. Yankee workers feared competition from the new arrivals. Protestants feared that Catholics would be loyal to the absolutist supranational Pope instead of to American democracy. Historian Michael Rawson summed up the prevailing social animosity: "Anglo-Saxon natives considered the Irish to be an inferior race and a non-white people."[5]

In the 1854 state elections, the newly formed "Know-Nothing" Party (called that because they disavowed any knowledge of nativist bias when queried about their political intentions) swept every constitutional office, the entire State Senate, and every seat but four in the House of Representatives. The state legislature disbanded all Catholic militias and confiscated their weapons, made the reading of the Protestant King James Bible compulsory in public schools, deprived the clergy of the ownership of property, and launched surprise inspections of "certain practices" in schools and convents.[6] Within a couple years, the "American Party" faded away, primarily because politics was refocusing on the national crisis over slavery. Nevertheless, anti-Catholic bias persisted.

Among Irish Catholics, there was a different mindset. The Irish regarded the Protestant Reformation, in the words of historian Oscar Handlin, author of the classic *Boston's Immigrants*, as "the root of all Irish misery."[7] Centuries of economic and political oppression rooted in religious bias had embittered

Irish Catholics. Unfortunately for them, they landed in the most staunchly Protestant city in America. Irish opposition to the local power structure and mores found political expression in the Democratic Party, which has maintained the allegiance of the majority of Irish Catholics in Massachusetts ever since. The Democratic Party, as it evolved in the 1830s under Presidents Andrew Jackson and Martin Van Buren, welcomed the Irish immigrants to become part of its pro-slavery coalition of southern planters and northern workingmen. During the 1840s and 1850s, the Irish Catholic Democrats tended to oppose the Yankee Whig and subsequent Republican reform policies, which included abolition.[8]

Xenophobic treatment of immigrants as "outsiders" has been a constant theme in American society. Descendants of the Anglo-Saxon settlers debated how or even whether the newcomers could be "real Americans." The Irish participation in the Union Army during the Civil War, when they turned away from the slaveholding South, helped them establish their patriotic bona fides. From then on, politics became their leading pathway for assimilation, to the point that Irish Democrats dominated in Boston for almost a century. Their machine-oriented, patronage politics clashed with the values of disinterested public service and clean government of Yankee Republicans.

The most significant impact that Irish immigration made on Boston was fracturing the region's social homogeneity and creating a template for a pluralistic community. Their churches, parochial schools, and social welfare organizations paralleled the institutions of the long-established society. In the words of historian John Stack, "the Irish worked to establish as complete a society within a society as possible." They established a pattern for asserting ethnic identity that was followed by other immigrant groups. Oscar Handlin explained that "the concern with status created by the presence of the Irish immigrants and their offspring affected every group in the city. No man now could think of his place in society simply in terms of occupation or income level. It was necessary also to consider ethnic affiliation."[9] This extended to the American-born, who self-consciously categorized themselves as descendants of Anglo-Saxons, with Oliver Wendell Holmes christening the city's traditional elite as "Brahmins" to signify their elevated status.

The rise of the Irish alarmed Protestant Yankees, who used the state legislature to circumscribe the authority of Boston's municipal government and the power of the Irish.[10] The divisions were so great that Boston became handicapped in addressing economic and social problems for decades. Some of the fiercest clashes took place during the tenures of Mayors John "Honey Fitz" Fitzgerald and James Michael Curley, both of whom rose to power by appealing to Irish tribalism. John Gunther, in his magisterial *Inside U.S.A.* (1947), wrote that Curley was "the undisputed champion of the local Irish, and his basic source of power was his identification with all the resentments closely cherished by the Irish underpossessed."[11] The ethnic conflict remained contentious in Boston until the post–World War II era, when economic prosperity vaulted the Irish and other European immigrants into the assimilated middle class. John F. Kennedy's election as the country's first Roman Catholic President marked a symbolic milestone that recognized the full citizenship of Irish Americans and other non-Protestant European ethnics in American society.

A significant Irish achievement was making Roman Catholicism respectable in New England. Just as the Potato Famine was driving Irish immigrants to Boston in 1846, the Catholic diocese received its first ethnic Irish bishop, the Most Reverend John Bernard Fitzpatrick. Though born in Boston and educated at Boston Latin School, his parents hailed from Ireland. Bishop Fitzpatrick's tenure was absorbed in settling the impoverished refugees in Boston and helping them confront anti-Catholic bias. During the height of "Know-Nothing" power, Bishop Fitzpatrick advised members of his flock to confidently exercise their electoral franchise. He encouraged Irish immigrants to become naturalized citizens and adopt American customs. During his bishopric, he recruited many of his clergy from Ireland. This marked the point where, in the words of historian James O'Toole, "Boston Catholicism meant Irish Catholicism. So dominant were the Irish in the Boston church that they almost ceased to exist as a separate group. When they spoke of 'ethnics,' they meant someone else, not themselves."[12] To this day, Massachusetts is the most Catholic state in the country after Rhode Island—and it remains the most Irish. Not only did the Irish establish Roman Catholicism as the leading institutional support for European immigrants who belonged to that denomination, they modeled informal habits of acculturation. When Italians first arrived in the North End, they absorbed a lot about street life and politics from the Irish who were living there.[13]

With such anti-immigrant sentiment, one wonders how the United States admitted such numbers of Irish immigrants in the first place. The basic answer is that the nation was seeking to occupy the continent and build out an infrastructure of transportation, utilities, and industries and needed as many able-bodied workers as possible. Since most Irishmen had lived subsistent agrarian existences, they lacked urban skills needed for business or industry. Most of the men worked as unskilled day laborers, doing heavy lifting on the docks and in warehouses. They did the grunt work on public works, laying railroads and streets and creating new land by filling the shoreline to build neighborhoods like the Back Bay and South Boston. Young women might get positions as servants in middle- and upper-class households. One avenue for acquiring skills and advancement was in the building trades, as construction was booming in Boston. Operating boarding houses and saloons offered opportunities for entrepreneurship. Gradually, Irish workers moved to textile and shoe mill towns, where they accepted lower pay for entry-level jobs than natives. In the expanding industrial economy, subsequent generations of Irish obtained more stable and better-paying employment, which provided opportunities to enter the middle class. Much of Boston's success as a manufacturing city between the Civil War and the 1920s was due to the labor force that the Irish and other immigrants provided for the industrial sector.[14]

ITALIANS RECREATE THEIR VILLAGES IN BOSTON

A second wave of European immigrants swelled Boston's population and that of other American cities between 1880s and 1920. The most prominent groups were Southern Italians and East European Jews. The Southern Italians hailed from the region stretching south from Naples and into Sicily. Drought, poor harvests, and onerous taxes exacerbated rural poverty. Catastrophic earthquakes and volcanic eruptions at Mt. Vesuvius and Mt. Etna killed thousands. Military conscription for the national Italian army also induced peasant men to emigrate. Between 1880 and 1920, 4.2 million Italians immigrated to the United States. Taking advantage of regular steamship service, migrants traveled from Naples, Palermo, and smaller ports to New York, Boston, Philadelphia, and New Orleans.[15]

Like their Irish predecessors, Italians settled where their ships landed—just off the docks, in Boston's North End. The Irish were relocating from their original stronghold in the North End to Dorchester, Charlestown, South Boston, and suburban communities. Jews also were moving out from their blocks on Salem Street. By 1895, there were 7,700 Italians living in the North End, comprising 27% of its population. Over the ensuing 25 years, the Italian presence in the neighborhood swelled, reaching 38,800 residents and 90% of its population. The North End, comprising a mere 100 acres, was one of the country's most densely inhabited areas. Italians also settled in the adjacent West End, which had a more heterogeneous ethnic mix. Overall, the Italian population in Boston grew from 2% to 16% of the city's total between 1900 and 1920.[16] This was the population peak, as immigration was severely reduced after passage of the restrictive National Origins Act of 1924. The North End exemplified the concentrated ethnic neighborhoods that sprang up in Boston and most American cities. Many migrants settled where living was cheapest, usually in the least desirable urban areas.

Groups of families and friends emigrated together and usually settled in same urban neighborhood. This enabled poor immigrants to adjust socially and find an economic foothold. Each clan clustered on certain streets. For example, those from the province of Avellino lived on Sheafe Street and on North Square, the Abruzzese lived around Endicott and North Margin Streets, and the Sicilians lived along North and Commercial Streets. Remarkably, 82% of marriages taking place at the North End Italian parishes of St. Leonard's

Figure 7. San Rocco Procession, North End, 1971. Some of the characteristic community celebrations of Italians in the North End have been the religious feasts and processions dedicated to patron saints from Italy, in this case St. Rocco.—Courtesy of photographer Spencer Grant.

and Sacred Heart between 1873 and 1929 were between people hailing from same province. Many of the first generation would not leave the confines of the North End unless their job required them to. Some even said that they were "going to America" when they ventured out of the neighborhood.[17]

The two most important factors for Italians in adapting to their new home were jobs and home ownership. Like the Irish immigrants, the Italians started as day laborers, digging subways, grading streets, and laying sewers. As late as World War I, 40% of Italians were "pick and shovel men." Others found employment on the waterfront. The first entrepreneurs were fruit and produce vendors. At first, women took care of their households, though this often entailed taking in boarders to augment the family's income. By the 1920s, many women entered the garment trades.[18] After getting a job, no matter how low-paid, the chief goal for Italian families was to own a home, which, in the North End, meant an apartment. Since it had been virtually impossible for them to afford home ownership in Italy, it became a gleaming prize. Owning a home was of primary importance to Italians in establishing themselves, even more so than job mobility, education for them or their children, or political power.[19]

Italians had considerable difficulty adapting to American society. Their language and folkways seemed alien. Their attachment to family and their native lands caused Americans to suspect their commitment to their new country. More than other immigrant groups, Italians remained very connected to their homeland, as many traveled back and forth to Italy. According to historian Stephen Puleo, about 40% of first-generation immigrants were reverse migrants or "birds of passage." The Irish resented Italians because they were slow to gain citizenship (only 25% in 1909) and lacked interest in voting. The Italian version of Catholicism seemed strange. It focused on celebrating feasts of unfamiliar saints and engaging in folk religion practices, in contrast with the Irish hierarchy's emphasis on moralism and a ritualistic liturgy.[20]

Nativists went further in expressing bias. Many expressly considered Southern Italians, as opposed to their Northern counterparts, to be an "inferior race" (echoes of the Irish experience in the 1840s and 1850s), though they were legally treated as "white." The country's foremost anti-immigration organization, the Immigration Restriction League, was founded by members of the Brahmin elite in Boston in 1894, partly in reaction to the arrival of large numbers of Southern Italians. They raised the alarm over the threat to American society from the illiterate, impoverished migrants pouring into the country from Southern and Eastern Europe. This organization advocated for Congress's *Dillingham Commission Report* of 1911, which laid the groundwork for the restrictive immigration legislation of the 1920s. The report painted a picture of Italians that had long-term influence: "The proportion of more serious crimes of homicide, blackmail, and robbery, as well as the least serious offenses is greater among the foreign-born. The disproportion in this regard is due principally to the prevalence of homicides and other crimes of personal violence among Italians."[21]

The reputation of Italians, stigmatized as violence-prone, was tarnished further by murderous anarchist attacks in the years after World War I. The trial and execution of Saco and Vanzetti for murders and robbery at a South Braintree shoe factory became an international *cause célèbre*. Though many believed that the evidence was inconclusive, the authorities took a hard line with the Italian anarchists. Even more damaging to the reputation of Italians was the rise of violent gangsterism related to bootlegging during Prohibition. For decades, Italians were associated with the Mafia in the popular mind.

For each immigrant group, the question of integration into American society arises—how did the group establish a place in American society? During the first half of the twentieth century, the model, constructed by natives, had ethnic groups conforming to Anglo-American culture. By the 1960s and 1970s, this model was being questioned and a different one was presented, which maintained that different nationalities form a multicultural society that allows them to retain elements of a distinct ethnic cultural identity while being American. Over the years, the question of assimilation has been vigorously debated, and variations of multiculturalism have been essayed.[22]

The experience of Boston's Italian Americans has demonstrated different ways that acculturation can play out. The scale and homogeneity of the North End's immigrant population encouraged the development of a strong ethnic identity, though one that became hybrid "Italian American." Such an ethnic culture provided a framework for collective and individual action. This has been a proven immigrant strategy that allows for gradual integration into mainstream society. They obtain access to urban social and economic networks, while retaining their religious, social, and culinary customs. The adaptation pathways for males of the second generation became bifurcated. William Foote Whyte, in his sociological classic *Street Corner Society: The Social Structure of an Italian Slum* (1943), posited that the neighborhood had

"College Boys" and "Corner Boys," ranging in age from 18 to 30 years old. The "College Boys" made their way into the American middle class through public schools and learning opportunities presented by settlement houses; many of them actually went on to college. Like other ethnic groups, Italians were able to take advantage of college funding from the GI Bill and Federal Housing Administration (FHA) and Veterans Administration (VA) mortgages. They became professionals, educators, and businessmen. They moved onto outlying neighborhoods like East Boston and suburbs like Revere and Saugus. The "Corner Boys," in the words of North End native and Boston University historian James Pasto, became part of the local "racket subculture [which] was based on organized criminal activity around numbers, off-track gambling, loan sharking, and prostitution." He went on to call some parts of the Corner sub-cultural life "problematic and harmful . . . a pathway that exposed them to violence, jail, and downward or stagnant mobility."[23]

A third way of "Americanization" emerged with a post–World War II influx of immigrants that resulted in a "segmented assimilation," in which the new immigrants maintained an identity distinct from both the American middle-class and their own co-ethnics from prior migrations. Many of the postwar Italian immigrants of the 1960s, 1970s, and 1980s did not get entirely absorbed into the distinctive Italian American culture that had been developing for generations. The new immigrants were bringing with them different experiences of the home country and tended to be better educated and more entrepreneurially minded. This gave them an advantage in grappling with the forces of gentrification at work in the North End. They often maintained older businesses or opened restaurants and other venues to cater to gentrifiers, who wanted to live in an "Italian neighborhood." Their new businesses traded upon Italian sophistication and authenticity, appealing to a fascinated non-Italian population. The number and varieties of North End Italian restaurants, cafes, and bakeries grew from 24 in 1970 to 88 in 2016. This version of the Italian North End represented a new stage of global diasporic connections. James Pasto has explained how this process helped shift Italian American identity away from its older image of "Mafia and meatballs." He asserted that "the North End as Little Italy thus condenses multiple entities: the Italian nation and ethnicity, food, history, migration" into "part of Boston's 'diversity capital' with which it can market itself against other global urban centers."[24]

EAST EUROPEAN JEWS ESTABLISH THEIR COMMUNITY

Jews had a different experience of migration and acculturation, though there were structural similarities. The first Jews to migrate in any number to Boston came from German lands in the 1840s and 1850s. Their number grew from a few hundred in 1850 to around 3,000 by 1875. They settled in the Lower South End, south of Boston Common. They formed their first permanent synagogue in 1843 and erected their first synagogue building nine years later. Those Jewish families who became prosperous moved to the Upper South End, Roxbury, and Brookline.[25]

The Jewish community started growing rapidly in the 1880s, when Jews from Russian territories started immigrating in large numbers to Boston. Increasingly repressive Russian policies restricted where they could live, what work they could do, and what property they could own. These immiserating handicaps were compounded by violent pogroms launched against them, the worst taking place in 1881–1882 and 1903–1906. Just as acute suffering motivated the flight to America of Irish and Italians, so it did for Russian Jews, who were living in the so-called Pale of Settlement in parts of today's Poland, Ukraine, Belarus, and Lithuania. Some Russian Jews reached Boston directly by steamship from Hamburg, Bremen, or Liverpool, while others transited through New York's Ellis Island, then by train to Boston. Because of discrimination in Eastern Europe, Jews were more likely than other ethnic groups to settle permanently in the United States.

Eastern European Jewish immigrants first settled in the North End, which was starting to attract Italians as well. Between 1880 and 1895, the North End Jewish community grew from a few hundred to 6,000. Similar population growth took place in the adjacent West End, which was a step up from the jam-packed North End. As late as 1926, 75% of the West End was Jewish. Their numbers declined to 20% over the following decade. They were replaced by second-generation Italians moving from the North End.[26] At that time, there was also a large Jewish population in Chelsea and significant numbers in the industrial cities of Malden, Cambridge, Lynn, and Brockton. During the 1910s, second-generation Jews started moving from the North, West, and South Ends en masse to Roxbury, Dorchester, and Mattapan. By 1930, 77,000 Jews (half of the Greater Boston Jewish population) lived in these neighborhoods, concentrating along Blue Hill Avenue. During the 1920s, middle-class Jews started settling in large numbers in Brookline, Newton, and Allston-Brighton.[27]

Occupationally, Russian Jews followed the economic path established by German/Central European Jews. They worked in the textile business and garment-making, having acquired skills in the needle trades in Eastern Europe. They ran tailor shops, dry goods stores, and salvage collection operations. By the twentieth century, young unmarried women worked in clothing sweatshops. Many men worked as peddlers and salesmen. Others opened businesses catering to their communities with kosher butcher shops and neighborhood retail stores. When they got into industry, it tended to be in skilled positions in textiles and shoemaking. William Braverman explained the ability of Jews to thrive in Boston's economy: "Coming from urban settings and used to living in a capitalistic economy, they were able to adjust to Boston with less trauma than the Irish or Italians who in their homelands had almost all been agricultural workers." Another attribute Jews brought from Europe was esteem for education.[28]

The ability of Jews to adjust to American society was based on a two-pronged approach. They sought to be economically self-sustaining, while maintaining a strong communal identity to validate themselves in the midst of the Christian majority. From the 1840s on, they cultivated a strong sense of community rooted in synagogues. Besides nourishing spiritual life, synagogues extended support to widows, orphans, and others in their community needing help. They created an elaborate network of support that helped thousands of Russian Jews adjust to life in Boston. Social organizations provided health care, temporary housing, employment bureaus, English language training, sewing circles, and recreational and cultural activities. These charitable activities matured into the Combined Jewish Philanthropies, Beth Israel Hospital, the Young Men's Hebrew Association, and a host of other social and charitable organizations. Philanthropic activities were supported by the successful endeavors of Jewish businessmen. Synagogues and social service organizations promoted the idea that Jews had to adapt to the ways of their new country and become committed to their role as citizens.[29]

This sentiment was important to combat prejudice Jews encountered. Historian Thomas O'Connor wrote that, when Russian Jews arrived in Boston around 1900, "they had to contend with the same inbred and hostile Anglo-Saxon Protestant environment that had confronted the Irish a half century earlier . . . but also with the Irish themselves, who were just moving into control of the political apparatus of the city, and who were not prepared at all to share that power with any other groups—and certainly not with the Jews."[30] Like the Irish and Italians, Jews were considered a different "race," because of their different religious and cultural heritage. It was questioned whether they could be assimilable into American society. These views hemmed Jews in their own community and enterprises.

A darker brand of antisemitism emerged nationally during the 1920s, when anti-immigrant attitudes reached a high point and restrictive immigrant laws were enacted. These were aimed at excluding Eastern European Jews and Italians in particular. Jews ran the gauntlet of racial judgment, with acceptance alternating with antisemitism. Karen Brodkin described their status prior to World War II as "almost white." Jews were excluded from living in certain neighborhoods (enforced through restrictive property covenants) and from being members of private clubs, including country clubs. Jews were limited in their ability to study at prestigious WASP colleges, a campaign spearheaded by opaque admissions criteria introduced by President A. Lawrence Lowell at Harvard during the 1920s. They had difficulty obtaining positions in the professions. There were spates of physical harassment against Jews in Boston by Irish toughs, especially during stressful economic times of the 1930s, when the Detroit-based priest Father Charles Coughlin railed against Jewish bankers and Bolshevists. One of the most egregious examples of antisemitic and anti-immigrant attitudes was America's refusal to admit into the country all but a handful of European Jews seeking refuge from Nazi persecution during World War II.

During the post–World War II economic expansion, antisemitism receded and Jews, like other European ethnic groups, were able to enter into the American middle-class mainstream. Jews utilized FHA and VA mortgages and college funding from the GI Bill. They took full advantage of the postwar explosion of higher education in which college enrollments increased by five times between 1940 and 1970. Their presence in the professions was evident in the increase from being 1% of Boston's doctors before the war to being 16% in the postwar generation.[31] Jews as well as Catholics became fully accepted as "whites" in American society. Meanwhile Black people who were migrating from the South to cities in the North were becoming the prime target for racial prejudice. The worlds of big business, high finance, entertainment, and academia opened to Jews in Boston and around the country. Jewish academic and economic achievement raised their social status. Antisemitism seemed to be in remission, until recent years when it has been resurgent in American society.

CONSTRAINTS ON CHINESE IMMIGRANTS

By the 1910s, Boston also had significant numbers of immigrants from Poland, Lithuania, Greece, French Canada, the Canadian Maritimes, Syria/Lebanon, Armenia, the West Indies, and the Portuguese Azores and Cape Verde. These groups tended to cluster in the South End, South Boston, Cambridge, and surrounding communities that offered factory jobs. Members of each immigrant group had their challenges in establishing themselves in Boston.

One immigrant group that had a particularly difficult path was the Chinese. The Chinese, fleeing the scarcity of land, famines, and the violence of imperially instigated wars, had originally been lured across the Pacific from the Pearl River Delta to join the California Gold Rush. They ended up becoming the cheapest, most biddable source of labor. They did much of the hard work of building the transcontinental railroad across the Sierra Nevadas in the 1860s. Motivated by fear of losing jobs to the Chinese, working-class whites attacked them. Drawing upon deep reservoirs of racial bias, Americans considered the Asian newcomers to be a "yellow peril." These feelings led, first, to a Congressional ban in 1875 on Chinese women immigrating for "immoral" purposes, which was used to ban almost all Chinese women. The Chinese Exclusion Act of 1882 prohibited the entry of all Chinese male laborers, becoming the only such law to forbid a specific national group from entering the country. It should be noted that Chinese merchants, educators, and college students were allowed into the US; some Chinese migrated illegally through Canada.

The Chinese arrived in Massachusetts in the 1870s, fleeing the violent racial attacks they suffered in the West. They were recruited as strike breakers by a shoe factory in North Adams. They moved on from there to Boston to work on construction projects. By 1900, there were approximately 1,000 Chinese living in a tight little neighborhood in South Cove, south of downtown. Of these, 99% were male. This Chinatown became the third largest in the United States, after San Francisco and New York. From the beginning, Chinatown had restaurants that served both Chinese immigrants and adventurous Bostonians.

While Chinatown today is celebrated for its cultural heritage, for a long time it was a virtual ghetto. Chinese were considered as a different and lesser

The First Waves of Migrants Reshape Boston Society   179

Figure 8. Chinatown, ca. 1950. The restaurants in Chinatown reflected how ethnic eateries introduced the cultures of immigrants' countries to Bostonians.—Courtesy of author's collection.

race. For years, they were the most disdained and low-paid of immigrant groups. To overcome, this disadvantage, they relied on mutual aid to find work for newcomers. This included opening laundries and eating places, efforts coordinated by the Chinese Consolidated Benevolent Association (The organization survives today and is the neighborhood's largest real estate developer and landowner).

During World War II, the situation for Chinese immigrants began to improve as the US sought to support its Republic of China ally. The federal government repealed the Chinese Exclusion Act of 1882 and permitted a small quota of Chinese to immigrate. The US admitted Chinese college students to prepare to rebuild their country after the war. By 1952, 140 students were studying at Massachusetts colleges, including at Harvard and MIT. Because of the Communist takeover, many students stayed in Boston and became involved in academia, engineering, and scientific research. From the 1950s through the 1970s, Chinese immigrants to the Boston area came only from Hong Kong and Taiwan. During the 1980s, immigrants from mainland China made up the largest number of Asian immigrants settling in Boston. There were two streams of immigrants, one of students and college graduates and another of working people. By 2000, 62.3% of Chinese immigrants had college degree.[32]

College-educated Chinese Americans settled in such communities as Cambridge, Newton, and Brookline and, in more recent years, have been residing all across the metropolitan area. Working-class migrants tended to live in Chinatown, which was being hemmed in by urban renewal, highway construction, and gentrification. During the 1960s, the land area of Chinatown was reduced by half, while the population grew by 25%. In the following decade the population doubled, with a growing flow from Southeast Asia. Many Chinese Americans moved to such towns as Quincy and Malden.[33] Like suburban Italians, who like to visit their old neighborhood in the North End, Chinese return to Chinatown regularly for shopping, dining, and cultural opportunities. It is important to note that Chinese Americans have dramatically improved their socioeconomic standing in recent decades. In 2017, they earned $79,435, while US-born whites earned $91,977. They emerged through a strong work ethic, education, and high economic achievement to become a respected ethnic group, a "model minority," even though sometimes they are still considered "foreign" and are subject to anti-Asian hate crime.[34]

Like other immigrant groups, Chinese established themselves in Greater Boston society with the help of community-based organizations. The Chinese American Civic Association developed in 1967 to oppose the construction of the Massachusetts Turnpike extension, the expansion of Tufts-New England Medical Center, and the development of the Combat Zone, which was the only area zoned for strip clubs in the city. The organization broadened its mission and changed its name to the Asian American Civic Association to address the needs of post-Vietnam War immigrants from Vietnam, Laos, and Cambodia, who were moving into Chinatown. The Asian American Civic Association became a significant player in advocating for Asian American interests and providing a broad range of educational, social, and cultural services. Another important Chinatown organization has been the Asian Community Development Corporation (CDC). It was established in 1987 to develop affordable housing and promote business opportunities. The Asian CDC has developed several hundred subsidized units in several projects in the Chinatown area. It also has operated a first-time homebuyer financing program. The Asian CDC also provides cultural and recreational programs for young people. Activist Michael Liu has explained that ethnic communities like residents of

Chinatown have leveraged influence and built social capital by challenging exploitive moves made against them. Liu has written that ethnic neighborhoods "offer alternative ways of negotiating the US landscape and daily life. By exposing cities to diverse perspectives and cultures, moreover, they support a more vital civic life and a more profound understanding among people."[35] This is the pattern of social adjustment that was undertaken by earlier ethnic groups and has served as a model for later immigrant groups.

THE 1920S RESTRICTION OF IMMIGRATION

Immigration dried up during the 1920s, as nativists set out curtail the incursion of newcomers from Southern and Eastern Europe. Starting during World War I, Congress passed legislation constraining immigration, culminating in the National Origins Act of 1924. A bill in 1917 imposed a literacy test on immigrants, and a 1921 bill established national quotas for immigrants, which the 1924 bill made more restrictive. The bill expressly mentioned that its goal was to achieve "national homogeneity." It limited the annual number of arrivals from a country to no more than 2% of their number in the United States as of 1890. This date was deliberately chosen because large numbers of Italians, Jews, and Eastern Europeans were just starting to arrive at that time. The 1924 Act banned almost all Asians and Africans. It favored Northwestern Europeans, though even their immigration was restricted because the total number of immigrants per year was limited to 165,000, down from the one million that entered the country in 1914. The law had a pronounced effect on Italian immigration. Between 1900 and 1914, an average of 210,000 Italians per year immigrated to the US. Under the 1924 quota, only 3,854 Italians were admitted. The overall percentage of foreign-born people living in Boston declined from a peak of 36% in 1910 to 30% in 1930 to 24% in 1940 to a low point of 13% in 1970.[36] Potential employers were not inconvenienced by the reduced flow of workers because New England mills were entering decline and fewer workers were needed. Construction methods were becoming more mechanized, so fewer "pick and shovel men" were being hired. The Depression of the 1930s reduced the need for additional workers to virtually zero. There was meager overseas immigration until the US reform legislation of 1965. Nonetheless, Boston and other northern cities did experience an influx of migrants during these years.

BLACK MIGRATION AND SOCIAL TRANSFORMATION IN BOSTON

It might seem incongruous to include African Americans in a chapter on immigration, but their experience as migrants—forced in the colonial era and voluntary later—provides an instructive perspective on the experience of outsiders seeking to carve out a place in the Boston community. Boston had a Black population virtually from its founding, but it always made up a small proportion of the community. The first Black people, who were enslaved, started arriving in town in 1638. Between 1755 and 1764, 2.2% of the Massachusetts colony's population was made up of enslaved people.[37] After the adoption of the Massachusetts State Constitution in 1780 and a judicial ruling outlawing slavery three years later, the state became the first state to prohibit slavery outright. In 1800, there were 1,174 Black people (4.7% of population) living in Boston, rising to 2,261 (1.3%) by 1860.

Until the Civil War, free Black people lived mainly on the North Slope of Beacon Hill. They played a significant role in making Boston a seedbed for abolition and civil rights. Their activism led Massachusetts to become the first state to prohibit the de jure segregation of public schools, in 1855, as well as being the first state to pass a racial civil rights protection law, in 1865. This story is interpreted by the Black Heritage Trail/Boston African American National Historic Site, located on Beacon Hill. During the ensuing decades, grass-roots activism spearheaded by journalist William Monroe Trotter placed Boston "at the center of radical African American politics" and "pushed Massachusetts's racial politics further Left than the rest of the country," according to historian Kerri K. Greenidge.[38] It should be noted that living in Boston during the post–World War II era shaped the careers of Martin Luther King and Malcolm X.

The First Great Migration of Black people from the South started during World War I, spurred by racial repression and the demands of northern factories for industrial workers. Boston's Black population grew from 13,564 (2.0%) in 1910 to 23,679 (3.1%) in 1940. Boston had the lowest proportion of Black residents of any major city in the country, while having the highest percentage of locally born Black people and the highest percentage of "foreign-born" (viz. West Indies) Black people.[39] Between 1940 and 1970—the Second Great Migration—African Americans from the Jim Crow South came to Boston in unprecedented numbers. The majority were poor and working-class Black people escaping the socioeconomic shackles of the South, while a smaller group were drawn to Boston from around the country for college and career

The First Waves of Migrants Reshape Boston Society 183

opportunities. Between 1950 and 1990, the Black population increased from 40,057 (5.0%) to 146,945 (23.8%) in 1990. In 2020, the Black (Non-Hispanic) population was 148,780 (22.0%). The foreign-born share of Black people in Boston from the Caribbean and Africa increased from 21% to 37% between 1990 and 2016.[40] (Table 8) The Black migration played a determinative role in the development of Boston and its transition to more of a multicultural community.

Table 8. Black (non-Hispanic) population in Boston, 1800–2020

Year	Black Population	% of Total Population
1800	1,174	4.7%
1830	1,875	3.1%
1860	2,261	1.3%
1910	13,564	2.0%
1940	23, 679	3.1%
1950	40,057	5.0%
1960	63,165	9.1%
1970	104,707	15.8%
1980	126,229	21.7%
1990	146,945	23.8%
2000	140,305	23.8%
2010	138,073	22.4%
2020	148,780	22.0%

Source: Campbell Gibson and Kay Jung, *Historical Census Statistics on Population Total by Race, 1790–1990, and by Hispanic Origin, 1970–1990, for Large Cities and Other Urban Places in the United States*, Population Division, Working Paper No. 76; Boston Indicators, *Changing Faces of Greater Boston*.

Black Americans were subject to discrimination that foreign immigrants did not face. They were effectively limited to living in certain neighborhoods such as Roxbury and the South End, in the early and mid-twentieth century, and parts of Dorchester, Jamaica Plain, and Mattapan starting in the 1960s. Government housing policies served to contain them in these neighborhoods. Starting in the 1930s, FHA mortgage financing guidelines maintained that Black and white people should not live in the same neighborhoods. The FHA's notorious "redlining" policy stipulated that mortgages should not be granted to houses in declining neighborhoods, where Black people tended to live. FHA maps rated the housing quality in cities under four categories, with the areas depicted in "red" being ineligible for its mortgages. Starting in the 1930s, Roxbury and the South End were "redlined" because their aging housing stocks were considered "substandard." Without the ability to obtain low-cost federal mortgages in older urban neighborhoods, as suburban residents could, Black families were unable to purchase homes where they were living. They were forced to rent. This prevented them from building equity and accumulating wealth that could be passed on generationally, as whites could do in the suburbs. The consequences of this phenomenon have been described in a 2015 Boston Federal Reserve Bank study, which reported that the median net worth of Black families in Boston was at eight dollars. This shocking statistic is due mainly to the lack of wealth equity gained from home ownership.[41]

When Black people were able to buy homes in their neighborhoods, their houses often lost value because of their inability to obtain adequate financing for home improvements. This intensified the downward spiral of housing conditions in redlined neighborhoods. Another misfortune occurred as they moved into white neighborhoods such as Mattapan—it was called "blockbusting." Unscrupulous realtors stirred panic among white homeowners that a "Negro Invasion" would destroy the quality of the neighborhood and the value of their home. This practice panicked whites to sell houses at low prices, which would be resold to Black people at inflated prices.[42] Today, even as discriminatory housing policies have been ruled illegal, Black people often find themselves limited to living in certain neighborhoods and find it uncomfortable being pioneers in predominantly white areas.

Black people also suffered discrimination in job opportunities and general hostility from whites threatened by the growing Black presence. Stuck in deteriorating neighborhoods, Black children were forced to attend outdated, subpar neighborhood schools. In the 1960s, Black people in Boston were inspired by the civil rights movement taking place to desegregate the South. Emulating southern activists, they protested in myriad ways the de facto segregation in Boston that was confining Black children in inferior schools. They utilized churches and community organizations to carry forward their cause. Starting in 1963, activists mounted petitions and demonstrations calling for the improvement of the quality and provision of an equitable distribution of resources to schools in Black neighborhoods.[43] When these efforts failed to move the all-white Boston School Committee, they took the issue to the courts. Their efforts ultimately resulted is a 1974 decision from Federal Judge

Arthur Garrity that Boston had unconstitutionally segregated its schools and that Black students had to be bused to white neighborhood schools.

The targeted neighborhoods were South Boston and Charlestown, Irish working-class bastions. The federal court mandate rankled the residents of these neighborhoods who believed that they were being forced to carry the burden of desegregation, while better-off white neighborhoods and suburbs were evading any responsibility. The backlash from whites during the busing crisis was notorious. Whites angrily resisted busing Black students to schools in their neighborhoods. Passions were intensified by a clumsy implementation of the federal court-ordered busing plans. Over forty riots and attacks on bused students took place over a two-year period. In 1975, racial animosity spilled onto South Boston's Carson Beach when six out-of-town Black salesmen stopped by the beach to enjoy the afternoon. A mob of white youths chased them off the beach, with one of the salesmen having to be taken to the hospital with injuries. A couple weeks later, 700 Black protesters responded by returning to the beach to hold a picnic and demonstrate that they had as much right to use the beach as anyone else. The situation escalated as 1,500 whites harassed the Black protesters, heaving racist insults and physical projectiles. Eight hundred police were needed to quell the riot. A comparable beach race riot took place two summers later.[44] The damage to race relations from these events lasted for years, harming Boston's reputation. Boston Celtic Hall of Famer and civil rights activist Bill Russell declared: "I had never been in a city more involved with finding new ways to dismiss, ignore, or look down on other people."[45]

There is a sense that South Boston has become far more accommodating to racial minorities in recent years. Black residents, as well as Latinos, Middle Easterners, and Asians, enjoy Carson Beach along with whites. The South Boston neighborhood has become more integrated (as well as becoming gentrified by educated young people). The Mary Ellen McCormack public housing project, which was virtually all white between its opening in 1938 and the late 1980s, became well integrated by 2004. In 1989, the McCormack project had 915 white households and 50 minority households, including ten that were Black. A court decision forced integration, and fifteen years later, the complex had become 39% Latino, 26% white, 19% Black, 14% Asian, and 1% Native American. Black residents claimed that they felt at ease living in the South Boston housing project.[46] As Boston has become more multicultural, Black people have achieved a more comfortable place in the community.

Black professionals in groups like Boston While Black and the Black Economic Council of Massachusetts, joining such established organizations as the NAACP and the Urban League, have made a concerted effort to assert themselves by growing their network and navigating the local halls of power.

In Boston, as well as throughout American history, the multicultural experiment has been difficult to pull off. There are always those who feel threatened by those different from themselves. When socioeconomic conditions turn sour, people want a scapegoat. Yet, Black residents modeled a way that migrants from other countries and other marginalized people can challenge discrimination and organize their themselves to participate effectively in the Boston community. This subject will be pursued further in the following chapter, describing the acculturation of immigrants arriving in Boston after the 1965 federal immigration reforms.

CHAPTER 9

Post-1965 Immigration Becomes Truly Global

"Cities are good for immigrants and immigrants are good for cities."

Edward Glaeser, *Triumph of the City*

The demographic makeup of Boston has changed dramatically in recent years, as migrants from Asia, Latin America, the Caribbean, and Africa have been arriving in large numbers. The mix has moved from being primarily European to global in its reach. Migrants have taken different routes to Greater Boston, settled in neighborhoods with ethnic counterparts, and formed social and political organizations in becoming incorporated into the community. Each group has made a distinct impact on the social life of Boston.

This wave of immigration has been enabled by historic immigration reforms enacted in the 1960s. After World War II and the development of a dynamic economy, pressure to restrict immigration diminished. In 1965, President Lyndon B. Johnson signed an Immigration Act which replaced the national origins quotas with a preference system designed to reunite families of US citizens and legal permanent residents, attract professional and skilled migrants, and admit refugees to the United States. The Immigration Act of 1965, passed during the same period as groundbreaking domestic civil rights legislation, marked a major turning point in US immigration policy. This legislation declared that all ethnic groups were be considered equal in being admitted to America, paralleling the demise of legal racial discrimination in the country. This legislation marked a new way of thinking about America. Starting in the 1960s, the phrase "nation of immigrants" has been widely used to epitomize this country.[1]

Originally, the total immigration cap was set at 290,000 per year. Since then, further legislation has allowed more people from a wide range of countries into the United States. Under these reforms, all immigrants legally admitted into United States are granted Lawful Permanent Resident status and are given a green-colored document called a "green card" that attests to their status. This document allows a non-citizen immigrant to live legally and permanently in the country. After five years, a Lawful Permanent Resident can apply for citizenship. As of 2022, there were an estimated 12.9 million green card holders living in the United States.[2] Another venue for immigrants to enter the country is the H-1B temporary work visa, which was introduced in 1990. It admits each year a specified number of people to assume high-skilled jobs for which there is a scarcity of workers. They must have specialized knowledge and a bachelor's degree or equivalent work experience. The duration of their stay is three years, extendable to six years with a fresh application. The number of H-1B visas is limited. In 2023, 266,000 new H-1B visas were issued. The Refugee Act of 1980 allows a fixed number of refugees and asylum-seekers escaping dangers related to civil discord in their home countries to enter the US each year. In 2016, the US government accepted 85,000 people under its refugee resettlement program; by 2020, President Trump had reduced the number to 18,000, while increasing the red tape. In 2023, the Biden administration admitted 60,000 refugees.[3]

In the 1960s, few could have anticipated how much immigration reforms would change the country's demographics. The majority of immigrants to both Boston and America since then have come from Asia, Latin America, and the Caribbean rather than Europe, as was the case before the 1960s. By 2010, 80% of Boston's and 75% of the metropolitan area's immigrant population came from these regions.[4] In some countries—Vietnam and Cambodia—war was a primary factor behind emigration. In other countries—Haiti and El Salvador—a combination of political upheaval, natural disasters, and persistent poverty drove migrants to the US. Many of these immigrants have been as much victims of globalization and its effects on their vulnerable economies as they have been victims of repressive regimes. In places like Puerto Rico (a US Commonwealth), the Dominican Republic, Cape Verde, Colombia, and

Brazil, the agricultural sector foundered in the wake of increased competition, and industrial jobs did not grow fast enough to make up the difference. Puerto Ricans first moved to Massachusetts for seasonal agricultural jobs, then transitioned into textile manufacturing, where Dominicans and Colombians also found employment. The economic model of global capitalism imposed by national governments, the International Monetary Fund (IMF), the World Bank, and various international free trade agreements caused plant closings and extensive unemployment. Foreign investment allowed large corporations to capture markets from small farmers. Migrants representing a mix of the poor and upward-strivers have been seeking better economic opportunities. Chain migration, with family and neighbors traveling to join the first-movers, has intensified the flow of migrants.[5]

The recent immigration experience is far different from that of the nineteenth and early twentieth centuries. No longer do migrants suffer lengthy sea voyages living in noisome steerage. The luckier ones take a plane flight to America. The less fortunate take a circuitous, harrowing journey, often on foot, though Central America and Mexico. Once in the States, inexpensive transportation makes it easy to move around. "Secondary migration" of foreign people who first settled in New York or Miami and want to settle in more opportune circumstances has led them to Boston and other New England destinations.[6] Air travel facilitates returns to the homeland. Mobile phones and the Internet help immigrants carry on connections with family and business opportunities, contributing to the sense of living in a "global village." Telecommunications technologies help foster a sense of ethnic identity, which, ironically, can make it easier to function in American society. The coherence of the ethnic diasporas is supplemented by the flow of monetary remittances back to home countries. The World Bank estimated that $719 billion was sent from the US and other developed nations to immigrant homelands in 2020, up dramatically from $414 billion only 11 years earlier. The World Bank asserts that this money flow reduces global inequality.[7]

Immigration has played a major role in replenishing the labor force and driving economic growth in Greater Boston. As of 2021, approximately 29% of the city of Boston's population was made up of foreign-born people (the peak foreign-born population was 36.3% in 1910 and the low point was 13% in 1970). The Boston metropolitan area's population was 19% foreign-born. Between 1990 and 2017, new immigrants totaling 479,810 were responsible for 90% of net population growth in the region.[8]

Boston's new immigrant population hails from many countries. This contrasts with cities in the Southwest and West, where the predominant groups are from Mexico and Central America. The most prominent foreign-born groups in Greater Boston are the following:

- China 9.9%
- Dominican Republic 9.4%
- India 6.9%
- Brazil 6.7%
- Haiti 5.9%
- El Salvador 4.1 %
- Jamaica 3.7%
- Vietnam 3.2%
- Guatemala 2.7%
- Cape Verde 2.7%
- Colombia 2.3%.[9]

Foreign-born people are scattered across Boston and the metropolitan area, with the well-educated tending to live in suburbs and the working class in older industrial cities. It is noteworthy that the latter often settle in neighborhoods that had been inhabited by earlier immigrant groups. Dorchester is the largest Boston neighborhood for foreign-born. It has substantial numbers of Dominicans, Haitians (third largest US Haitian community after Miami and New York), Vietnamese, and Cape Verdeans. East Boston is a Latino bastion, comprising 54% of its population. The neighborhood has large numbers of Salvadorans and Colombians. Puerto Ricans, who live in several neighborhoods, comprise 28% of all Latinos in Boston. The growing Chinese population, with a longtime base around Chinatown, has moved into other city neighborhoods and suburbs. Because of gentrification and the high cost of housing in Boston, the proportion of foreign-born in the city has decreased slightly, with immigrants settling in lower-cost outlying communities. Some of their largest communities are in the inner ring suburbs of Quincy and Malden. Cambridge is home to Portuguese, Haitians, Salvadorans, and Guatemalans. One of the largest concentrations of Brazilians in the United States lives in Framingham. Large numbers of Dominicans and Puerto Ricans have settled in Lawrence, while the largest number of Cambodians in the US live in Lowell. Brockton has attracted Haitians, Cape Verdeans (the largest such community in the US), and migrants from other African countries. Skilled migrants from China, India, Korea, and other countries, especially those working in the technology sector, live in such suburbs as Lexington, Waltham, and Newton.[10]

Table 9. Percentage of foreign-born in selected Boston suburbs, 2020

Town/City	Foreign-Born%, 2020	Largest Ethnic Groups
State	14	China, Dominican Rep., Brazil, Portugal, India, Haiti
Boston	28	China, Dominican Rep., Haiti
Belmont	26	China, Korea, India
Brookline	31	China, India, Israel
Cambridge	29	China, India, Korea
Chelsea	47	El Salvador, Honduras, Guatemala
Everett	43	Brazil, El Salvador, Haiti
Framingham	32	Brazil, India, China
Lexington	32	China, India, Korea
Lynn	36	Dominican Rep., Guatemala, El Salvador
Malden	42	China, Brazil, Haiti
Marlborough	27	Brazil, Guatemala, India
Newton	23	China, India, Russia
Quincy	35	China, Vietnam, India
Randolph	37	Haiti, Vietnam, Dominican Rep.
Revere	41	El Salvador, Colombia, Brazil
Sharon	22	Ukraine, China, Egypt
Somerville	21	El Salvador, Brazil, Portugal
Waltham	25	Guatemala, China, India
Watertown	25	India, China, Brazil

Source: "Foreign-Born Population in Boston Area Communities," *Global Boston: A Portal to the Region's Immigrant Past and Present*, Boston College, Department of History.

Post-1965 immigrants have had different experiences finding work from immigrants of the nineteenth and early twentieth centuries. The Immigration Act of 1965 carved out preferences for people with technical skills needed in the workforce. Well-educated immigrants have found work in medicine, technology, and entrepreneurial activities. Some migrants initially came to the US to attend college or graduate school, while others came on temporary H-1B visas. In 2022, 43% of adult immigrants in Massachusetts had a bachelor degree, with 24% having a graduate degree. Twenty-five percent of the founders of biotech companies in Massachusetts are foreign-born. New England biotech companies with at least one foreign-born founder produced over $7.6 billion in sales and employed over 4,000 workers in 2006.[11]

Counterbalancing these highly skilled workers in the "hourglass" or "bimodal" occupational structure are a larger proportion of immigrants who are fleeing from depressed, mainly agrarian communities. These less-resourced immigrants have taken service jobs as custodians, landscapers, home care and day care workers, cleaners, restaurant workers, nail salon workers, and security guards. Taken together, immigrants play a vital role in Boston's economy. Between 1980 and 2010, immigrants accounted for 89% of the growth of the labor force.[12]

Table 10. Percentage of immigrant workers in Massachusetts, by occupation, 2019

Occupation	Percentage
Taxi Drivers	65.4%
Maids & House Cleaners	62.9%
Life Scientists	53.4%
Painters & Paperhangers	42%
STEM Workers	37%
Health Care Aides	36.2%
Software Developers	35%
Nurses	15.6%

Source: American Immigration Council, "Immigrants in Massachusetts."

FINDING A PLACE IN THE COMMUNITY

Recent immigrants have established themselves in the same ways as their predecessors. They have taken advantage of small-scale entrepreneurial opportunities, opening food-related and property maintenance businesses in particular. Vietnamese people have made a specialty of operating nail salons. Brazilians have done well in cleaning, construction, and landscape work.[13] Churches have been a first-resort institution that fosters spiritual lives and a purposeful sense of community. Catholic parishes previously served as acculturation institutions for the Irish, Italians, Poles, Lithuanians, and French Canadians.[14] By the late twentieth century, these parishes were losing members, but the inflow of migrants from Puerto Rico, the Dominican Republic, Haiti, Vietnam, Korea, and Brazil revived a number of them. The parishes and the Catholic Archdiocese as a whole had to change to accommodate the immigrants' different religious practices and social needs. Mainline Protestant denominations, including Episcopalians, have revived dying congregations by reaching out to new immigrants with inclusion initiatives. Evangelical churches, many of which are governed by congregation members, can be more flexible in accommodating the spiritual and material needs of immigrants. Evangelical churches have sprung up to serve Latinos, Chinese, Koreans, and Brazilians.

Acculturation of new immigrants is a thorny process. Contemporary immigrants are vulnerable to discrimination and geographical segregation. Immigrants from Asia, Latin America, and Africa, especially if they are working class, have been prey to nativist hostility. While Americans of European stock are generally regarded as being "white," immigrants from these other continents can get caught up in "non-white" racial categorization, whether on US Census forms or in informal casual personal interchanges. The "black-white" cleavage still pertains in American society. The complications of racial identity are evident with Latinos, who can fall into "white" and "Black" categories. Dark-skinned natives of Cuba or the Dominican Republic could get treated as "Black," while light-skinned Latinos of European descent might be considered "white." Even though people from Latin American countries prefer to be identified by their nation of origin, they can easily get lumped together under the "Latino" or "Hispanic" label. Depending upon their social class and education, Asians may be determined to be "near-white."[15]

When migrants from a particular country are new to a community, natives may resent those who they perceive as competitors for jobs and threats to their social standing. Marilynn Johnson has reported in detail on nativist reactions to the arrival of Vietnam and Cambodians during the 1980s. When Asian newcomers moved into formerly all-white areas of Dorchester, East Boston, Revere, Chelsea, Quincy, and Lynn, they were physically harassed and their homes were vandalized. There were several murders. The fear of job competition from people willing to work for lower wages combined with residual animosity from the Vietnam War fueled the attacks. Resentment that government agencies were providing assistance to the immigrants exacerbated tensions further. A *Boston Globe* headline from 1986 summed up the situation: "Tattered Dreams: Once in America, Some Asians Find Bigotry, Violence."[16]

Members of the victims' communities were able to organize and demand accountability for the perpetrators. In some instances, their efforts were successful, but not in others. In any event, these struggles impelled the new immigrant groups to form advocacy and social organizations that helped solidify their presence in the greater community. Activists pressed for civil rights protections, intercultural programs, job placement, bilingual services, and English as a Second Language (ESL) education. In more recent years, immigrant rights organizations, both local and national, have arisen in response to the intensification of anti-immigration politics. Immigrant advocacy initiatives joined a broad range of community-based organizations and community development corporations (CDCs) that have sprung up in Greater Boston since the late 1960s. Black civil rights activists played a major role in creating the model for CDCs which assumed the function of neighborhood planning and development from municipal agencies. These organizations have helped form an effective pluralistic model of community development. They can ease migrant integration in the country, enhance ethnic solidarity, and help combat the sense of marginalization.

A notable Puerto Rican CDC is Inquilinos Boricuas en Acción (IBA)/ Puerto Rican Tenants in Action, which has grown since its founding in 1968 to become one of the largest such CDCs in the US IBA originated when neighbors living in the South End protested a proposed Boston Redevelopment Authority urban renewal plan that would have demolished a large part of their neighborhood. The IBA convinced the BRA to designate it the developer of the site. The organization ended up building Villa Victoria with 435 units of subsidized housing, a community center, and retail shops. Subsequently, the IBA has built and managed several hundred additional housing units and provided a range of social services and cultural programs. Other Latino community-based organizations have grown up in Cambridge, Lawrence, and other communities.

Boston's community organizations have produced political leaders who have accrued power and advanced progressive political objectives. South End State Representative Mel King made a breakthrough when he ran for mayor in 1983. He put together a "rainbow coalition" (one year before Jesse Jackson employed the concept in his presidential campaign) of Blacks, Latinos, Asians, other marginalized residents, and progressive white reformers. King lost by a wide margin to City Councilor Ray Flynn, but his campaign made an impact. Mayor Flynn adopted a strong pro-neighborhood agenda that welcomed participation from all ethnic groups in decision-making. His administration made significant appointments of Blacks, Latinos, and Asians to city jobs. Ray Flynn's successors Tom Menino and Marty Walsh also provided political and material support for neighborhood needs and appointed many people of color to municipal positions.

The 2000 US Census reported that Boston had become a majority-minority city. Politics began to reflect the new reality. In 2003, Felix D. Arroyo, who is Puerto Rican, became the first elected Latino city councilor. Two years later, Sam Yoon, who is Korean, was elected city councilor. The influence of Haitians became evident with the election of Marie St. Fleur and Linda Dorcena Forry to the state legislature. Forry's state senate district even includes the Irish bastion of South Boston. Cape Verdean-descendant Attorney Andrea Cabral became Sherriff of Suffolk County in 2004 and Massachusetts Secretary of Public Safety eight years later. The most significant political milestone has been the election of Michelle Wu as mayor of Boston in 2021. Wu, who was born of Taiwanese parents (her predecessor Martin Walsh was the son of Irish immigrants), was the first Chinese American to be elected to the City Council, in 2013. As a progressive Democrat, Wu campaigned on issues related to providing greater equity for minorities. The Congresswoman for most of Boston, Cambridge, Somerville, and several surrounding communities is Ayanna Pressley, a Black woman who served as city councilor. It is worth noting that political power has been accruing to women in recent years, as Maura Healey was elected Governor, Kim Driscoll became Lieutenant Governor, and Andrea Campbell became Attorney General in 2020. State Senator Karen Spilka became Senate President, while Congresswoman Katherine Clark, of Revere, serves as Minority House Whip and the third-ranking Democrat.

It has taken several decades, but the Irish and Italian male-dominated ethnic politics that long prevailed is being superseded by new migrant groups who have been moving into Boston since the 1960s. Contemporary politics in Boston is progressive, as the city's marginalized minorities are prioritizing their issues related to equity and inclusion. This follows the example of boosting marginalized ethnic groups employed by Irish Mayors John "Honey Fitz" Fitzgerald and James Michael Curley a century ago.

Recent activities of community-based organizations in Boston illustrate an important feature of global cities. Global cities are both command centers for the capitalist economy and workplaces for significant concentrations of less-resourced service workers. According to geographers Marie Price and Lisa Benton-Short, the presence of "large numbers of foreign-born and ethnically distinct people" makes "cities become the places where global differences are both celebrated and/or contested."[17] In Boston, as in other global cities, issues of socioeconomic inequality are exposed, debated, and addressed with various levels of success. It is easier for people with less privilege to have an impact on politics at the local than at the national level. This happens through participation in elections and in community activism, advocating for improvements to local living conditions, wage levels, and educational opportunities.

THE IMPACT OF INTERNATIONAL COLLEGE STUDENTS

A different feature of global migration in Boston is the impact that international students have on Boston's regional economy and culture. These students enrich the education of all who attend the area's colleges and universities. They also have a demonstrable economic impact, as they serve as exports of the local knowledge economy. During the 2022–2023 academic year, Massachusetts enrolled 79,751 students from foreign countries. The state ranked third in the country, behind California and New York. The only US cities with larger college student enrollments are New York and Los Angeles.

The Massachusetts universities with the largest enrollments of international students (2023) are:

- Northeastern (20,637 foreign students)
- Boston University (13,281)
- Harvard (7,236)
- MIT (5,290)
- UMass-Amherst (4,893).

Other local universities with significant numbers of foreign matriculants include Brandeis, Tufts, and UMass-Boston. The bulk of international students in Massachusetts come from China (29.1%) followed by India (28.1%), South Korea (3.4%), Canada (3.2%), and Vietnam (2.0%). International students, although they make up only 9% of the Massachusetts college student body, have an economic impact of $1.8 billion and generate over 24,000 jobs.[18]

Boston University provides an example of how global exchanges work at a university. Willis Wang, Vice President for Global Programs, has stated that "BU's worldwide footprint is a central focus of the University's mission and long-term vision." BU launched the country's first overseas academic exchange program in the late nineteenth century. Besides its international students, who represent 130+ countries, there are more than 1,250 foreign nationals representing 80+ countries who teach, research, or work in administration at BU. The university operates 70+ teaching, research, and service programs in over 20 cities in more than 15 countries.[19]

Students and potential employers lament the fact that international students are prohibited by immigration laws from staying on in the States and working long term. Their best hope for remaining in this country is to obtain a "green card" and a job offer entailing specialized work skills. There is a good argument for the United States to allow, at least, graduate students to remain in the country to work since it has effectively subsidized their education. Despite the loss of potential workers, Boston still benefits from the international students who study here. When they return to their home countries, they are likely to maintain contacts made in Boston related to their business and professional pursuits. They are important ambassadors for spreading Boston's reputation as a globally open city.

IMMIGRATION AND URBAN REDEVELOPMENT

Perhaps the most important impact of immigrants on Greater Boston since the reforms of 1965 has been the repopulation of aging cities and towns suffering from deindustrialization. With diminishing work opportunities, local businesses closed and residents left town. Factories and warehouses became vacant and communities appeared derelict. Real estate values stagnated. The resulting cheaper cost of living in the old industrial cities made them a magnet for working-class immigrants.

Boston is a good example of how migrants can revitalize a declining city. Without these immigrants, Boston would be a smaller, less vibrant place. The US Census Bureau has estimated that if, between 2000 and 2006, there had been no net new immigrants settling in metropolitan Boston, the area would have 101,000 fewer people. The process of immigrants making up for the loss of existing population has been continuing. In 2022, for example, it was estimated that 49,000 Massachusetts residents left the state, while 34,5000 international migrants came into the state.[20] Overall, Latinos (both foreign- and US-born) have accounted for 92% of Boston's population growth since 1980. They have made up 24% of births and 31% of children. Ten percent of the business owners in Boston are Latinos.[21]

Without newcomers, neighborhoods would be hollowed out. With them, East Boston is a teeming neighborhood full of Latinos, Chinatown has a vital population of Chinese and Southeast Asians, Fields Corner is a flourishing center of Vietnamese culture, Dorchester, Hyde Park, and Roslindale have vital communities of Cape Verdeans, Haitians, and West Indians. Communities throughout Greater Boston, especially traditional industrial towns like Chelsea, Lynn, Malden, Quincy, and Brockton, have large foreign-born populations. Chelsea and Lynn lost 38% and 20% of their populations respectively between 1940 and 1980. Chelsea rebounded by 2020, growing from 25,431 to 40,787 people, the most residents in its history. This growth was driven by the in-migration of Latinos, who grew from 14% to 62% of the city's population. Lynn's story has been similar. After dropping from 103,230 in 1930 to 78,471 in 1980, its population rebounded to 101,253 today. Most of this growth has been driven by Latinos, who grew from 3% to 32% of the population.[22]

Perhaps the foremost Massachusetts example of immigrants remaking a city has been in Lawrence. Because of postwar deindustrialization, the city's population dropped from 80,936 in 1950 to a low of 63,175 in 1980. During these years, the imposing Merrimack River mills became vacant shells, storefronts emptied out, and poverty and crime increased. Since then, the population has rebounded to 89,143. This is directly due to migration of Latinos, especially Dominicans and Puerto Ricans. Many of them had been living in New York City. They recognized that Lawrence was a safer community with a much lower cost of living. It allowed migrants to find a place in the smaller city and open their own businesses. Latinos now make up 77.1% of the population. It has not been a smooth transition. In 1984, Lawrence experienced a calamitous riot between Latino newcomers and local whites. Commercial buildings were burned, and hundreds were arrested. In subsequent years, there was more arson, drug-dealing, and gang violence. The public school system was in disarray, with some of the state's lowest test scores, skyrocketing truancy, and administrative corruption. In 2011, the state took the schools into receivership and improved the system dramatically. Dan Rivera, of Dominican parentage, enjoyed a successful run as mayor of Lawrence between 2013 and 2021, facilitating economic development and community progress.

Lawrence's location on the northern edge of Greater Boston has boosted the regional economy, since many Lawrence residents find jobs outside their home city. In a sense, Lawrence is a working-class bedroom community and no longer a major employment center. Even though deindustrialized cities like Lawrence still endure economic hardship and above-average crime rates, immigrants have boosted local tax revenues, revived local business, enhanced local cultural and civic life, and improved social mobility prospects for their families. These contributions to urban redevelopment tend to be overlooked, as credit has often been given to the "creative class" and hip gentrifiers.[23]

The need for immigration persists. In recent years, Massachusetts has experienced a net decline of US-born workers. The retirement of baby boomers is intensifying the need to attract and develop new workers. Economists and many business leaders argue that encouraging immigration can fill many job openings.[24]

THE IMMIGRATION DEBATE

The issue of immigration has become a prism for viewing globalization and its repercussions. Fears of injurious economic and cultural impacts from immigrants have animated populist politics in the US and Europe. The major target of anti-immigrant antipathy is undocumented/"illegal" immigrants. The number of undocumented immigrants in Massachusetts has been estimated to be about 153,000 (2023). About 10,000 are entrepreneurs with small businesses.[25] These migrants tend to cluster in restaurants and food services, construction, and waste management, in jobs that American-born people are reluctant to take. Undocumented workers often were migrants who entered the country on tourist visas and over-stayed them, working and living below the radar of immigration officials. In recent decades, there has been a national crackdown on this mode of migration. Recent undocumented migrants have followed a more perilous path, either being smuggled in or otherwise slipping into the country unobserved. Many undocumented migrants fleeing violence and repression in Haiti and Central America have reached Boston. Since they work "under the table," these immigrants can easily be exploited and paid less than the minimum wage. Nevertheless, many businesses that benefit from employing immigrant workers and trade associations have supported increasing legal migration as well as legalizing the status of undocumented migrants working in the country.

There has been antagonism toward immigrants from American-born workers who feel their economic position is being undercut. Rural and deindustrialized factory towns that have suffered economic stagnation and social breakdown due to deindustrialization are often the communities most opposed to immigration. Even when there are demonstrable overall economic advantages of immigration, it can be difficult for people to support it in the face of individual job and wage loss and increasing social inequality.[26] American-born persons may look down upon migrants from other societies. Their customs are different and their presence in large numbers can seem unnerving. The newcomers are often from a different social class, with habits unattuned to US society. They may not speak English. These cultural differences and the resulting tensions exacerbate the difficulties for newcomers to integrate into American society. The United Kingdom (with Brexit), Hungary, France, Italy, the Netherlands, and Australia have all experienced comparable misgivings over the influx of immigrants. Japan, China, and South Africa have had similar concerns. Many countries have policies that deliberately exclude most immigrants. In the United States, there has been a rising strain of nativism. As American society is becoming more pluralistic, with immigrants from Asia, Africa, and Latin America and the continuing rise of Black Americans, whites are becoming more aware of being just one racial group in an increasingly diverse country. This sense has been fueling increasing white hostility toward immigrants and minorities in general. Those feeling most threatened by immigration, often in more rural states, are calling for draconian curbs on immigration. The twenty-first-century social context is entirely different, but the sentiments are not unlike the sentiments that many Anglo-Saxon Yankees had toward immigrants from Eastern and Southern Europe during the late nineteenth and early twentieth centuries.

In the meantime, the benefits of immigrants tend to get overlooked. First, there are the contributions of the educated, legally admitted immigrants, who come from all over the world. This theme has come up throughout this book. Economic research points to international diversity being invaluable for a dynamic knowledge economy. Despite anti-immigrant sentiment, highly educated and entrepreneurial foreign-born people are eager to participate in the United States economy. The US offers comparatively high rewards to people of talent. This country has the scale to absorb them into the economy and offers a vibrant entrepreneurial environment.[27] Another factor is that current immigrants are more likely to know English than those of the early twentieth century, given that English is now the universal language of business and research. Sustained by these advantages, foreign-born make up 50% of all doctorates and 33% of engineers in the US labor force, while comprising only 14% of the total population. They make up nearly 20% of US inventors and are twice as likely to start a business and file a patent than American-born peers. The majority of these patents are concentrated in life sciences and information technology, which are leading sectors in Greater Boston. A 2018 study found that the Boston area had 569 startup businesses with at least one foreign-born founder.[28]

AnnaLee Saxenian, who has written insightfully about innovation in Greater Boston and Silicon Valley, argues that foreign-born innovators "have made America richer, not poorer. Far from stealing jobs, immigrant entrepreneurs have created them in large numbers, both in the United States and overseas."[29] The McKinsey Global Institute contends that cities acting as gateways for migrants generate "significant economic output and high-quality jobs, and it helps a city accumulate knowledge, skills, and talent, with positive spillover effects on its broader economy." One estimate claims that documented foreign-born workers, both educated and less-resourced, contribute about $2 trillion, or 10%, of annual GDP, while undocumented immigrants contribute an estimated 2.6%.[30]

Less-educated workers also make positive contributions to the local economy. The Boston Foundation's report *Boston's Booming . . . But for Whom?* provides a clear-eyed analysis of the role these immigrants play in this community. It argues that they tend to be strivers, since, hailing from poor countries, they are prepared to make sacrifices and work long hours to take advantage of America's opportunities. Research shows that immigrants buy into the notion of the American Dream. They have more traditional views on family structure than native-born and lower rates of out-of-wedlock births. They commit less crime—1.6% of immigrant males aged 18–39 are in prison compared with 3.3% of native-born men. To successfully adapt to US society, a majority of immigrants seek to live the cultural values of hard work, honesty, and social cooperation.[31]

The country's 500 most dynamic counties tend to attract immigrants and embrace diversity, while 2,600 counties that are less prosperous do not attract immigrants and are more likely to voice anti-immigrant opinions. Greater Boston is in the pro-immigration camp with its diverse population, enterprising multicultural urban society, and "blue state" politics. The New American

Economy organization's Cities Index, which analyzes the integration of immigrants in American cities, gives Boston's "government leadership" and "community and legal support" five out of five points for providing a supportive atmosphere. The Cities Index, however, gave Boston only two points for "job opportunities" and "livability" (high cost of housing).[32] These metrics indicate areas where more work needs to be done. Like the general evolution of cities, the immigration process has been messy and beset by setbacks.

Competitive cities pursue immigration policies that help them better navigate a globalized world. Welcoming highly educated immigrant researchers and entrepreneurs is a proven strategy. Toronto has become the third largest hub for tech workers in North America, after Silicon Valley and New York, thanks to liberal Canadian immigration laws that attract highly educated workers.[33] Canadian laws are more inviting for less-resourced service workers as well. The Canadian government believes that optimizing human capital is an assured way of securing economic success. Boston and the state of Massachusetts understand the value of receiving more legally admitted immigrants, but federal policies remain restrictive. Despite political gridlock in Washington, Boston can develop the human capital of immigrants who are already here through education, job training, and support for housing and health. The payoff for creating such pathways for mobility could be considerable.[34]

CHAPTER 10
Fashioning a Global City Image

"A regional identity that is magnetic, sticky, and globally resonant is essential for a metro area to remain competitive. . . . Those that succeed in building a recognized identity . . . find that not only does opportunity come to them, but that the world starts to tell their story for them."

Brookings Institution, *The 10 Traits of Globally Fluent Metro Areas*

An essential quality of "global" or "world" cities is having a reputation that expresses their consequential achievements and style of life. The reputations of New York, London, Paris, Rome, and Tokyo obviously put them in this class. There are many more cities contending to fit the bill; but reputations are constantly shifting, often reflecting realities in a city's experience, but sometimes not.

A city's image is often projected through calculated public relations and marketing and through images represented in popular culture. Ambitious cities launch projects that upgrade their economic and social life and attract international attention. Such projects range from hosting Olympic Games to building state-of-the art airports to undertaking iconic projects like Bilbao's Frank Gehry-designed Guggenheim Museum. In the case of a mid-tier global city like Boston, it is worth exploring how its reputation has evolved. How much does Boston project Mayor Kevin White's 1980 proclamation of it being a "world-class city"?

Boston is not that large. As of the 2020 Census, it ranked as the #24 largest US city and the #11 largest metro area. For a medium-sized metropolitan area, Boston punches above its weight. Its global reputation rests on its influence in the realms of higher education, healthcare, technological innovation, sports, and popular culture. It is known for its singular, somewhat self-satisfied way of conducting business. The city has a tradition of seeking to portray itself as a significant place in the world. Like most cities, Boston has tried to accentuate the positive and the exceptional.

A short trip through Boston's history reveals the city's evolving reputation. When the Puritans settled Boston in 1630, Massachusetts Bay Colony Governor John Winthrop claimed that their Protestant Dissenter community would be "as a city upon a hill, the eyes of all people are upon us." Winthrop's vision was so compelling that 21,000 migrants flooded through Boston and across New England over the following decade, forming the region's breeding stock for the next two centuries.[1] The Puritans created a culture that prized self-government and exacting moral values. This culture heavily influenced the development of much of the northern United States, spreading with settlers across Upper New York State, the northern parts of Ohio, Indiana, Illinois, and Iowa, the eastern Dakotas, Michigan, Wisconsin, and Minnesota. Nineteenth-century Yankees settled and made their imprint on such cities as Buffalo, Cleveland, Chicago, St. Paul, Denver, San Francisco, Seattle, and Portland. With this heritage, Boston has been recognized as a political and intellectual lodestar for the "blue states" of America.[2]

Perhaps the foremost legacy was education, as reading was critical to understanding the Bible and encountering the word of God. The Puritans established Boston Latin School as America's first public school (1635) and Harvard College (1636) as a place to train ministers. These institutions incubated a culture of learning and inquiry that forms the foundation of the region's current-day knowledge economy preeminence.

As a port, Boston flourished in the Atlantic trade. It was the leading city in British North America for more than a century. Its role as a port eventually led to disputes with the London government about taxation and the regulation of trade, which morphed into the independence movement of the Thirteen Colonies. The Boston Massacre (1770), Boston Tea Party (1773), and the Battles of Lexington, Concord, and Bunker Hill (1775) triggered the American

Revolution. The city became known as the "Cradle of Liberty," creating an image that forms its primary tourist appeal to this day. After the Revolution, Boston grew as a mercantile port, standing second only to New York through the nineteenth century. During this period, it traded with China, Russia and the Baltic, the Mediterranean, India, Latin America, and other corners of the globe.

As the new nation sought to establish a distinctive national culture that reflected its democratic yearnings, Boston took the lead as the "Athens of America." Starting in the 1830s, Ralph Waldo Emerson, Henry David Thoreau, and Margaret Fuller spearheaded Transcendentalism, America's first home-grown intellectual movement. Their writings and those of Nathaniel Hawthorne, Henry Wadsworth Longfellow, Louisa May Alcott, and others made Boston the country's literary epicenter. Bostonians undertook a range of reform movements which included women's rights, penal reform, universal education, and the abolition of slavery. Boston's status as a leading intellectual, political, and economic center was wittily expressed by Dr. Oliver Wendell Holmes, who wrote that the "Boston State-House is the hub of the solar system."[3] Wags opined that, even better, the city should be known as "The Hub of the Universe," a title inscribed in the pavement in front of the former Filene's Department Store (today a Primark). The "Hub" is still a favorite moniker in Boston, as much for self-mockery as for its pithiness.

After the Civil War, Boston lost ground in size and economic dominance to New York and other US cities. Nevertheless, between 1860 and 1910, Boston's population grew by 265%, from 177,840 to 670,585 people (partly through annexation of surrounding communities). As late as 1910, it ranked as the country's #5 largest city. It remained wealthy and an influential center of thought with its renowned universities, hospitals, and cultural institutions. Late nineteenth-century Back Bay, with the Museum of Fine Arts, Boston Public Library, Natural History Museum, Massachusetts Institute of Technology, and Harvard Medical School, was where "Boston first established itself as one of the centers of world culture in the arts and sciences," according to urbanist Lewis Mumford. Just as Transcendentalism had reshaped American thought, so did the late nineteenth- and early twentieth-century Pragmatism of William James and fellow Boston thinkers. British philosopher Alfred North Whitehead, who held an endowed chair in philosophy at Harvard in the 1920s, declared Boston to be the "capital of learning of the Western world."[4]

Yet, between the 1920s and 1960s, Boston fell into a "Long Stagnation," as the region's industrial mills became uncompetitive. The corrupt political regime of Mayor James Michael Curley was at loggerheads with the conservative Yankee Republican business community. In the late 1940s, political reporter John Gunther wrote that "much of Boston seems physically ragged, dilapidated, and in a way, deserted." Essayist Elizabeth Hardwick pilloried Boston for its "dying downtown shopping section" and "feckless, ugly, municipal neglect."[5] Despite its cultural importance, Boston's economic and political torpor made it seem like a tired, provincial town stuck in the past. It was no "world-class city."

In the 1960s, Boston began a turnaround that became branded as the "New Boston." The linchpin was the Government Center Urban Renewal project, which replaced the shabby Scollay Square skid row. The centerpiece was the Brutalist concrete Boston City Hall (1968). Though its design has been scorned by many, it was considered a high point of urban revitalization in America at the time. The avant-garde architecture represented an about-face from a stifling past toward a dynamic future. *Washington Post* architecture critic Wolf Von Eckhart called it "a great work of architecture . . . that proclaims the majesty of government by the people."[6] At the 1976 Bicentennial, the American Institute of Architects named City Hall the eighth greatest achievement in American architecture. Regardless of the criticism of the design of City Hall and its yawning plaza, its symbolism gave the private sector confidence to build high-rise office towers in the adjacent financial district. The construction of the Prudential Center (1965) spurred the a "high spine" of office and residential towers in the Back Bay. Boston's skyline was expressing the city's reemergence as a vital place.

The New England Aquarium (1969) opened on the waterfront, initiating a transformation along the harbor. The nearby Christopher Columbus Waterfront Park (1976) was one of the first urban harborfront parks built in this country. Boston's signature revitalization achievement of the 1970s was the rehabilitation of Faneuil Hall-Quincy Market (1976) into the first US urban festival marketplace. It was the country's most influential historic preservation project. The urban buzz was not just about architecture, it accompanied multifarious civic and cultural events, many of them inaugurated under the auspices of Mayor Kevin White, who was a master at using them to boost the city's reputation. The Fourth of July Boston Pops Concert on the Esplanade, first held in 1974, has attracted hundreds of thousands of spectators ever since and has been broadcast on national television. Boston invented the idea of First Night, celebrating it initially on New Year's Eve, December 31, 1975. The

1976 Tall Ships Parade across the harbor established another local tradition. Dozens of festivals, parades, and outdoor concerts brought people together to physically experience a vital sense of community, contributing to the city's appeal. Syndicated journalist Neal Peirce wrote that Boston "has suddenly become one of the two or three most livable and exciting cities of America. For one who once lived in the closed old Boston, and now returns to the new Boston, the experience is a continual wonder."[7]

The energy unleashed by 1960s efforts to revitalize Boston was reflected in an initiative to hold a Boston World's Fair in 1976 to celebrate the US Bicentennial. Civic leaders conceived the idea after witnessing the urban redevelopment catalyzed by the 1962 Seattle and the 1967 Montreal World's Fairs. Shortly before his death in 1963, President John F. Kennedy wrote to the Bureau of International Expositions requesting that it designate Boston the site of an International Bicentennial Exposition. The Boston Redevelopment Authority and the Greater Boston Chamber of Commerce led the way. Their goal was nothing less than inventing a futuristic environmentally sustainable model for urban redevelopment on Boston Harbor. After the fair ended, the fairgrounds would be repurposed for permanent habitation and recreational use. It would include housing for 45,000 residents, a new transit line, and more than 350 acres of open space and public amenities on the mainland and Harbor Islands. The signature Expo Boston '76 structure would be an enormous climate-controlled geodesic dome. Many of the other structures would be built on floating platforms in the harbor.

The leader of the planning efforts for the BRA was architect Jan Wampler, who conceived Expo Boston '76 as a laboratory for "an all out attack" on the urgent problems of density and inequality in US cities." A BRA report stated: "By exploiting the positive potential of the environment for creative recreation, integration of daily activities and social communication the new community can demonstrate how cities of the future can be more healthy, and enjoyable places in which to live." The visionary architect, who subsequently taught many years at MIT, compared his ambitions with NASA's space exploration: "Like the Moon effort, only much more realistic."[8] Expo Boston '76 was intended to certify Boston as a globally important city by a demonstrating a cutting-edge urban design that was environmentally responsible.

Boston's World's Fair proposal competed with World's Fair bids from Philadelphia and Washington, DC for designation by the federal American Revolution Bicentennial Commission. Intense opposition to the Expo Boston'76 plan emerged in South Boston, which abutted the proposed fair site. Led by School Committeewoman Louise Day Hicks, opponents voiced concerns about environmental damage to their neighborhood and concern about who might inhabit the thousands of housing units left by the fair. In 1969, the Boston City Council voted 8–0 against the Expo Boston '76 bid, refusing to provide any funding for the project. The American Revolution Bicentennial Commission ultimately recommended to President Nixon that none of the three city bids should be selected and that the Bicentennial festivities should be dispersed throughout the country. Late 1960s political discord and government budget constraints worked against holding an extravagant World's Fair. Local leadership was not game for such a grandiose project. Yet, Boston eventually realized certain features of the Expo plan, including building UMass-Boston on Columbia Point, cleaning up the harbor, conserving the Boston Harbor Islands for recreational uses, and constructing the southern extension of the Red Line.[9]

Technological innovation was becoming part of Boston's brand at this time. During the 1950s and 1960s, business parks sprang up along the region's new suburban beltway Route 128 (later I-95/I-93), earning the corridor the

Figure 9. Rendering of proposed Boston Expo '76, prepared by architect Jan Wampler. The futuristic world's fair would have covered the Columbia Point harborfront and spread onto the Harbor Islands.—Courtesy of Jan Wempler.

nickname "America's Technology Highway," even as the central city suffered blight and abandonment. Research labs and businesses spun off from MIT were driving metropolitan Boston's newfound image. During the 1980s and the minicomputer boom led by Digital Equipment Corporation, the state earned the sobriquet "Massachusetts Miracle." Running on the state's rebirth, Governor Michael Dukakis earned the Democratic presidential nomination in 1988 (losing to the Republican George H.W. Bush in the election). Boston's reputation as a metropolitan area at the cutting edge of technological innovation and entrepreneurship, while remaining a city steeped in history and culture, positioned it well in the "global city" sweepstakes. Urbanist Stephen V. Ward summed up Boston's newfound status: "If it is valid to speak of a formula for the post-industrial city, Boston stumbled across it first."[10]

Boston's reputation as an economically competitive metropolitan area has been affirmed by the high ratings it has received in benchmarking studies of global cities, as described earlier in this book. The authoritative *Global Urban Competitiveness Report* (2020–2021), published by UN-Habitat and Chinese Academy of Social Sciences, ranked Boston #14 for overall economic competitiveness and #6 for technological innovation. Other metrics-based studies have given Boston comparable marks for R&D, talent, finance, and global connectedness. Although Boston is not in the top tier of global cities, with New York, London, Tokyo, and the like, it does project a global reputation through myriad global city rankings prepared by social scientists and business consultants.

When Boston was named runner-up to Vienna for the 2020 Lee Kuan Yew World City Prize, its global status was further confirmed. Every two years, the Republic of Singapore awards this prize to world cities that display foresight, good governance, and innovation in tackling urban challenges. The award is considered to be the "Nobel Prize" for urban development. The World City Prize recognized Boston for model initiatives related to sea level rise, improving housing affordability, laying out the Rose Kennedy Greenway, and fostering civic participation, which the prize jury found to be evident in developing the Imagine Boston 2030 Master Plan.[11] Yet, the award slipped by in Boston almost without notice. The *Boston Globe* never reported on it. This indifference seems to reflect a lurking regional suspicion of hype.

Athletic teams tend to serve as proxies for North American urban brands. Cities define themselves by whether they are considered a "major league city" or not. A championship team is a potent metaphor for a city intent on "winning." Since 2002, the New England Patriots have won six Super Bowls, the Boston Red Sox have won four World Series, the Boston Celtics have won two championships, and the Boston Bruins have won a Stanley Cup. This feat has been matched by no other North American city. The Duck Boat parades that course through the teeming crowds celebrating sports championships bring together hundreds of thousands who want to feel connected with Boston. Boston's professional sports teams play a more important role in shaping a regional identity than almost anything else. Fenway Park, home of the Red Sox, is a bona fide tourist attraction. Boston also draws attention for the Boston Marathon, the world's oldest annual marathon and a truly global athletic event. Marathon Monday (third Monday in April), a.k.a. Patriot's Day, is Boston's great civic holiday, when the region celebrates itself. The 2013 terrorist bombing at the marathon finish line seemed so outrageous because it struck at the heart of Boston's identity. For rowers, the Head of the Charles, held in late October, is regarded as the largest rowing event in the world. Physical attendance at these events reaffirms Boston's abiding sense of tradition and identity.

City reputations are revealed in urban rivalries. Cities often define themselves in opposition to other cities—London-Paris, Toronto-Montreal, Los Angeles-San Francisco, and Boston-New York. Boston and New York were evenly matched rival ports in colonial British America. During the nineteenth century, New York surpassed Boston dramatically, rising to national and world preeminence. To New Yorkers, it might appear a one-sided rivalry because the metropolitan area of their Northeast competitor is only one-quarter their size and Boston's economic clout is much less. New York blows the mind with its massive scale and matchless energy. In comparison, Boston reflects a manageable, history-steeped urbanity most notable for higher education and intellectual expertise. It resembles mid-sized European capitals like Dublin, Edinburgh, or Copenhagen. The Hub-Big Apple duel is primarily conducted by sports teams, most famously by the Boston Red Sox and the New York Yankees. Since the two cities are geographically proximate, their citizens cannot help but keep track of each other's circumstances. For Bostonians, this rivalry elevates their self-identity and aspirations.

Despite Boston's achievements in urban revitalization and technological innovation, it has earned an image in popular culture for being a hard-nosed

East Coast place beset by discontent and conflict. The city is remembered for ethnic clashes between Yankees, Irish, Italians, Jews, Black Americans, Chinese, and Latinos. From the Depression into the 1970s, Boston was considered one of the country's most blighted cities. Suburban flight caused the city's population to drop from 801,444 in 1950 to 562,994 in 1980. Italian and Irish gangsters, typified by the notorious James "Whitey" Bulger, waged a grim reign of violence. The dramatic low point was the busing crisis of the 1970s, when whites opposed to court-ordered school desegregation slung rocks and racial slurs at Black students being bused into South Boston and Charlestown. This story has been best told by J. Anthony Lukas's Pulitzer-Prize-winning book *Common Ground: A Turbulent Decade in the Lives of Three American Families* (1986). The racial hostility of the era was encapsulated in the Pulitzer Prize-winning photograph referred to as "The Soiling of Old Glory" (1976), taken by Stanley Forman of the *Boston Herald American*. It shows a young white protester trying to impale Black attorney Ted Landsmark with the pole of an American flag in City Hall Plaza.[12] Even though racial tensions have eased as Boston has become a minority-majority city (partly because of an influx of Latinos and Asians), the city still carries a racist burden, complicating desires to project the image of a liberal bastion.

It is worth noting how popular culture has fixated on the dark side of Boston. Films such as *Good Will Hunting* (1997), *Mystic River* (2003), *Gone, Baby, Gone* (2007), *The Town* (2010), *The Fighter* (2010), and *Manchester-by-the-Sea* (2016) served up working-class tragedy. *Mystic River* and *Gone, Baby, Gone* were based on novels by Boston's Dennis Lehane, master of *noir*. The violent career of South Boston mobster Whitey Bulger provided fodder for books and movies, including Martin Scorsese's *The Departed* (2006). The film of *The Friends of Eddie Coyle* (1973), about the travails of a small-time hood, was based on a novel by George V. Higgins, whose entire *oeuvre* limned the seamy side of the city. *The Boston Strangler* (1968) told the story of then 1960s serial killer of young women. In *The Verdict* (1982), Paul Newman portrayed a down-and-out alcoholic attorney trying to make a comeback. Sinister events in more recent years have also been treated in films. Two were made about the 2013 Boston Marathon bombing—*Patriots Day* (2016) and *Stronger* (2017). Academy Award-winning *Spotlight* (2016) told the story of the *Boston Globe*'s efforts to reveal the pedophile crimes perpetrated by Roman Catholic priests and the cover-up by the Boston Archdiocese. Sometimes a more genial side of Boston has been portrayed, as in the television show *Cheers*, about the neighborhood bar "where everybody knows your name." Oddly enough, the bleak films and books about Boston have used a gritty, lived-in, urban attitude to complicate its reputation and project a sense of authenticity. These cultural markers emphasize Boston's distinctive, sometimes parochial identity and a provide a counterweight to its brand as a highly educated, cosmopolitan place.

GOING FOR THE GOLD: THE BOSTON 2024 SUMMER OLYMPICS

In 2015, Boston took a big step toward achieving international distinction. The US Olympic Committee selected Boston as the US candidate to become the site for the 2024 Summer Olympics. Boston won the bid over Los Angeles (by one-half vote), San Francisco, and Washington, DC. Given that the US had not hosted a Summer Olympics since 1996 in Atlanta, there was a sense that Boston had the inside track with the International Olympic Committee (IOC) to beat out Paris, Rome, Budapest, Toronto, and Hamburg. Boston's Summer Olympics nomination was an honor that seemed to confirm that it had come of age as a "world-class city."

The proposal made by the Boston 2024 Partnership (a coalition of local business leaders) that won the approval of the US Olympic Committee (USOC) highlighted these characteristics: "The identity of Boston is one of forward progress, a living legacy of innovation that defines and motivates our city to drive forward, to discover, to create, to inspire and to be inspired by big ideas from every corner of the globe." The document described Boston's attributes as a host site:

> Boston is a geographically compact city with diverse historic and contemporary assets. The city boasts an unrivaled waterfront and America's cleanest urban harbor, a network of celebrated park spaces and public recreation venues, a history of independence and historic architecture. Boston is also home to distinguished academic and medical institutions, a hub of innovation and invention, and a vibrant, expansive economy.

The bid made a point of emphasizing the connection between the Olympics and Boston's innovation culture: "We will open the doors of many of our prestigious colleges and universities within the Greater Boston area, including

Harvard and MIT, so that our guests from around the world can experience firsthand the thought leadership, breakthroughs and innovation taking place within our classrooms, lecture halls and labs each day."[13] This is how Boston presented itself and, apparently, how the USOC wanted to perceive the city. Boston's proposal pitched the city as being compact and walkable, already having in place many of the venues that would be needed for the Games, including Fenway Park, TD Garden, Gillette Stadium, and numerous college athletics facilities.

Hosting the 2024 Summer Olympics would bestow the Olympic aura on Boston. Mayor Marty Walsh claimed that "this selection is in recognition of our city's talent, diversity, and global leadership." *Boston Globe* sports columnist Dan Shaughnessy believed that Boston edged out its US competitors because of its exceptional sports culture, opining that "Boston is the American sports city of the 21st century.... I think the USOC saw this. And fell hard for Boston." Nevertheless, he worried that it might be "a bad idea and could strangle us financially and logistically for decades." A judicious *Globe* editorial titled "Let the Olympic Dialogue Begin" declared that the USOC designation "is great news, and a credit to Boston 2024. But Boston is, and will remain, a world-class city whether it chooses to bid for the Olympics or not."[14]

The "Olympic dialogue" did begin. There was a split in the community about the merits of hosting the 2024 Summer Olympics. Many felt flattered and wanted Boston to show itself off to the world. Others, represented by the No Boston Olympics Committee, argued that the Olympic Games usually run way over budget and leave the host city and its sponsors holding the bag. Olympic cities like Montreal (1976) and Athens (1992) took financial hits from which it took years to recover. A public opinion survey about the Olympics taken after the USOC site designation found that 51% of respondents favored the Olympics bid, while 33% opposed it. As the details of the Boston 2024 Partnership proposal became better known, doubts were voiced about the availability and costs of building the 30-odd sports venues. That winter, Boston endured four blizzards in four weeks. "Snowmageddon" smashed all-time snowfall records and closed down the MBTA for several days. The regional transit system was supposed to be one of Boston's major Olympic selling points, but the blizzards revealed myriad defects. Within a month, polls flipped with 46% opposing and 44% supporting the Olympic bid. The polls never measured a plurality of support again.[15]

The No Boston Olympics Committee, according to the book written by skeptics Chris Dempsey and Andrew Zimbalist, meticulously countered the four primary arguments for hosting the Summer Games:

1. This bid will avoid the mistakes of past hosts—Cities underestimate costs to win bids. Any cost overruns are borne by the host city. The IOC does nothing to help cover construction or operating costs. A good number of the Olympic facilities, including the temporary Olympic Stadium, the velodrome, and other specialized venues, will become white elephants.
2. Olympics are a good planning exercise for the city's future—Cities tend to accommodate the desires of the IOC for venues and infrastructure plans before taking into account the needs of the community. This subverts responsible city planning.
3. The Olympics will be a "catalyst" for needed infrastructure, particularly transportation. The problematic state of the MBTA, which continues today, should be addressed without having to accommodate the temporary needs of the Olympic Games.
4. Games will put the host city on map—There is no scholarly evidence that hosting the Olympics leads to long-term increases in tourism, trade, and foreign investment. In any case, Boston is already "on the map.[16]

The 2024 Olympics proponents proposed a balanced budget that would be funded by private investment, without state and local taxes (They did not release their original Olympics bid to the public until two weeks after the USOC decided to choose Boston as the US Olympics candidate and never provided a more detailed implementation budget.). The No Olympics Boston Committee counteracted the proponents with far more detailed and persuasive estimates based upon the experiences of prior Games. Their numbers maintained that the Boston Olympics would earn between $3 billion and $5 billion in revenues while the true costs would range between $10 billion and $20 billion. They pointed out how the 2012 London Olympics went $10 billion over the original estimates. The Boston 2024 Partners scenario, which had originally promised there would "not be a penny of public funding," relied upon $4.5 billion in private investment, the sources for which were never identified, and $5 billion of publicly funded infrastructure, funding for which was not secured.[17]

By July 2015, Mayor Walsh was confronted with having to sign a commitment to the USOC that Boston would cover cost overruns. He realized he could not do it. Governor Charlie Baker refused to offer the USOC an unqualified endorsement of state support. A poll indicated that 42% of respondents statewide supported the Olympic bid, while 50% opposed it.[18] Before the USOC could pull Boston's designation and select a better-prepared, more supportive Los Angeles as its replacement, Mayor Walsh officially withdrew the Boston bid.

Many were relieved, but some were disappointed. Boston University political scientist Thomas Whalen summed up one school of thought, calling Boston a "parochial backwater." He blamed the organizers for being "completely incompetent" and lamented that "the time of big dreams, big accomplishments is over. 'Think small,' that's the mantra for Massachusetts. Limit your dreams."[19]

In retrospect, Boston was prescient about the fiascos associated with hosting the Olympic Games. Massive cost overruns were evident at the corruption-soaked, $50 billion 2014 Sochi Winter Games (which were immediately followed by the illegitimate Russian occupation of Crimea and parts of the Donbas). The COVID-19-delayed Tokyo 2020/2021 Summer Games were held without spectators. The original budget was supposed to be $7.4 billion, but a conservative estimate of the final bill doubled that, with infrastructure projects adding $10 billion. The cost overruns are being covered by Japanese taxpayers.[20] Bidding to host the Games has dried up. There were only two finalists for the 2022 Winter Games—Beijing and Almaty, the capital of Kazakhstan. The bidding process has become so shunned that the IOC awarded the 2032 Summer Olympics to Brisbane, Australia, without any competition, simply negotiating the deal behind the scenes. The *Globe's* Kevin Cullen asserted that "watching the Olympics in China [2022 Winter Games] has only reinforced how lucky Boston was to avoid the boondoggle that would have been hosting the games, not to mention the ignominy of hosting the utterly amoral IOC."[21] With the embarrassing deterioration of MBTA transit service, Boston is lucky that it did not secure the Olympics bid.

Although Boston Olympic Games proponents put an overly optimistic spin on their proposal, one should be wary of judging them as purely elitist business persons seeking to make a buck. The leaders of the Boston 2024 Partnership, including Suffolk Construction CEO John Fish, Patriots owner Robert Kraft, Bain Capital's Steve Pagliuca, and Bentley University President Gloria Larson, had long-term involvement with a wide array of civic projects. The 2024 Partnership took its best shot, and the USOC bought it, because

Figure 10. Rendering of the Stadium for the proposed 2024 Boston Summer Olympics. This rendering, provided in the Olympics bid submitted by Boston 2024 Partnership, depicted the proposed stadium to be located at Widett Circle, near South Boston.

of Boston's impressive urban revitalization track record. The proposal was designed to win USOC and IOC approval while appearing feasible to the local authorities and citizenry. It was an impossible balancing act that could only work if some government entity, like those in London, Tokyo, and Beijing, was prepared to cover cost overruns for the prestige of hosting the Olympics. Boston did the sensible thing and passed on the Games once the real costs were fully understood. Maybe the true test of a "global city" is that it knows its own mind and does not pursue chimerical branding quests in which the benefits would not justify the costs.

MARKETING A GLOBAL IMAGE

Boston has tended to pursue international recognition with ambivalence. Although the city has been successful in economic and educational achievements befitting a world city, it has been relatively low key in marketing efforts and urban planning rhetoric. It is not a booster city. In fact, not many American cities have been very explicit about becoming "global cities," as places like Singapore, Seoul, or Dubai have been. A major reason American cities have not trumpeted their "global" reputations is that they have been more attuned to jockeying in the domestic race of economic performance.

In the early 1990s, Boston admitted that it had failed to effectively trumpet the story of the "Massachusetts Miracle." Local leaders assumed they did not need to. A recession convinced them it was time to get the message out that Boston had a "combination of Old World charm and a go-for-it attitude" in a purposeful business marketing campaign. In a print ad published in 1992–1993, municipal government showed historic Beacon Hill backed by high-rise corporate towers with the label: "Boston: A Tradition of Innovation," also incorporating the message in Japanese and Mandarin characters.[22] By the 2010s, Boston became more confident in expressing its global status. The Greater Boston Chamber of Commerce unveiled a short promotional video on its website titled "Boston: Global City" (2016). Business and civic leaders extolled Boston's connections across the world in health care, academia, business, and innovation. Northeastern University President Joseph Aoun proclaimed "We are impacting and being impacted by the whole world. We are the Athens of Higher Education. Everybody comes to us, and we send our students all over the world—and that is unique."[23]

A useful vehicle for cities to project a self-image and ambitions is in their master plans. The City of Boston, in its recent master plan *Imagine Boston 2030: A Plan for the Future of Boston* (2017), is modest in setting goals for achieving "global" status. The plan's single meaningful statement about being a "global leader" relates to its work in addressing climate change.[24] This approach differs from master plans goals for many of the world's megahubs, which are more likely to emphasize global standing as essential for their competitiveness. In London's 2011 plan, Mayor Boris Johnson asserted that "London must retain and build upon its world city status as one of the three business centres of global reach [presumably, New York and Tokyo were the other two]."[25] The cities that are most ambitious about harnessing their "global city" identity to propel long-range development are in East Asia. Tokyo's 1986 comprehensive plan stated that its primary goal was to be the foremost "world city." The 2016 Tokyo plan indicated that one of its "Four Challenges" was to improve its Global Power City Index ranking in the Mori Memorial Foundation annual report from #3 to #1 between 2016 and 2020, surpassing London (#1) and New York (#2).[26] Booming Seoul issued a report *Can Seoul Become a World City?* (2003), which affirmed its ambition to be an international center in a "network of corporations, work forces, resources and finance." Seoul's

2030 Plan cited the goal of being one of the top five global cities.[27] Cities in the Gulf States are also focused on global prominence. The *Dubai 2040* Master Plan boasts that its "main goal it to make Dubai the best city in the world to live in from a leisure and working perspective" (even if this pertains only for citizens and First World expats, not low-skilled migrant workers from developing countries).[28]

Municipal vainglory aside, Boston has discovered that it can be a popular international tourist destination, with China being a major market. Tourism marketing by Meet Boston (changed its name from Greater Boston Convention & Visitors Bureau in 2022), the Massachusetts Office of Travel & Tourism, and private groups tout the traditional historic and cultural attractions, colleges and universities, the walkable cityscape, restaurants, top-flight hotels, convention facilities, and the ease of traveling to and within the region. These are the features of many global cities, but Boston blends them in an inimitable way that conveys a singular sense of place. The walkable urban fabric, which is uncommon in the United States, is laced with buildings from every era of the region's history. It stretches beyond the urban core into such surrounding cities and suburbs as Cambridge, Brookline, and Quincy.

Though not an overwhelming megacity like New York, Tokyo, Mexico City, or Beijing, Boston promotes itself as a "real city" that provides a stimulating urban experience. Boston's signature attraction is the Freedom Trail, which connects sixteen historic landmarks related primarily to the city's Colonial and Revolutionary Eras. Walking the streets of the Freedom Trail sets a historical tone for experiencing Boston. During the 250th anniversary celebration of the American Revolution in 2020–2026, the sights connected to the Boston Massacre, the Boston Tea Party, Paul Rever's Ride, the Battles of Lexington and Concord, Bunker Hill, and the British evacuation of Boston in 1776 resonate internationally.

Before the modernistic renewal of the 1960s, immersion in history seemed to be a drawback. It weighed the city down. In recent years, heritage has become more entertaining—costumed interpreters recount the bloody details of the Boston Massacre or the drama of Paul Revere's Ride. Ghosts and Gravestones Tours reconnoiter the Granary and the King's Chapel Burying Grounds. The picturesque historic neighborhoods of Beacon Hill, Back Bay, the South End, and the North End's Little Italy enrich the visitor experience. For iconic sights, travelers check out globally renowned Harvard and MIT. So numerous are tourists at Harvard that the Harvard Coop has filled the main floor of the academic bookstore with sweatshirts and souvenirs, catering to out-of-town visitors.

To spotlight the city's rich variety of outlying multicultural neighborhoods, the City of Boston and Meet Boston launched a promotional campaign called "All Inclusive Boston" in 2021. Instead of trotting out familiar destinations like Fenway Park and Faneuil Hall, the partnership conjured a celebration of Roxbury, Dorchester, Chinatown, East Boston, and Jamaica Plain and the Black, Latino, and Asian American artists, storeowners, and restaurateurs who live and work there. The campaign was designed to alert visitors and business recruiters to a wider, more intriguing array of experiences in the city as well as boosting the morale and entrepreneurship of citizens who may have felt overlooked.[29]

A promising effort is being made to highlight Boston's technological breakthroughs. To make innovation more noticeable in the cityscape, historian Robert Krim and *Boston Globe* columnist Scott Kirsner have been developing an Innovation Trail that takes visitors to sites in Boston and Cambridge, where the telephone, anesthesia, Polaroid instant camera, genome mapping, Moderna's COVID-19 vaccine, and many other inventions have been devised. The MIT Museum, in Kendall Square, and the Massachusetts General Hospital Museum of Medical History and Innovation are among the visitable locations.[30]

These efforts to interpret Boston's heritage of innovation are suggestive of a more comprehensive Greater Boston brand. At present, Boston has no established overarching initiative touting its culture of innovation. Individual universities, research centers, cultural institutions, trade associations, sports teams, and businesses undertake specialized marketing initiatives. They tend to utilize their own networks to reach international partners and audiences. One endeavor that took an all-embracing marketing approach was HubWeek, a week-long "creative festival" that was held to celebrate and build upon Boston's innovation economy. Organized by a consortium of the Boston Globe, Harvard, MIT, and Massachusetts General Hospital, HubWeek convened a bevy of thought-provoking practitioners between 2015 and 2019. During COVID-19, the project was suspended. The Boston Globe mustered a comparable lineup of urban, tech, and business thought leaders for virtual Globe Summits in 2023 and 2024. The Boston Globe has also started producing virtual "Weeks" on Sustainability, Tech, Health & Biotech, and Health Equity with expert panelists.[31] Lacking the buzz and opportunities to "bump and connect" that an in-person event can provide, it is uncertain how impactful the virtual Globe Summit is on the city's brand beyond the area. Nevertheless, these efforts reinforce the city's innovation culture and spur initiatives that make tangible improvements in the community. By making headway on such issues as workforce development, affordable housing, an upgrading the MBTA, Boston can bolster its status as a "global city," reinforcing its reputation as an innovator, in public policy as well as in technology and health care.

CHAPTER 11

Inequality and Global Cities

"If there is a silver lining to the pandemic perhaps it is the clarity with which inequalities have been laid bare and the opportunity that affords us to take decisive action for positive change."

Cambridge Community Foundation, *Equity and Innovation Cities*

On September 30, 2011, a group of protesters set up an Occupy Wall Street camp on the Rose Kennedy Greenway, opposite the Federal Reserve Bank of Boston. It was a follow-on to the initial protest launched near the actual Wall Street, in New York's Zuccotti Park, two weeks earlier. The Occupy Boston tent city lasted ten weeks, longer than any other American city. At its peak, the camp had about 100 tents. The denizens were an assemblage of populist idealists, anti-corporate crusaders, and unemployed and homeless persons. Thousands of sympathizers filtered through the camp and participated in various marches that took place that fall.

The Occupy movement was a response to the economic pain inflicted by the Great Recession of 2008. It was a leftist counterpart to the right-wing anti-tax Tea Party. Occupy sympathizers targeted the globalized financial industry, which had triggered the recession and was subsequently bailed out at taxpayer expense while resisting more stringent governmental regulation. Citizens with stagnant wages, poor job prospects, and debilitating debt were feeling alienated. A *Boston Globe* editorial opined that Occupy Boston represented a movement "about creating an economy that's fair and raises all boats equally."[1]

The enduring meme emanating from these protests, imprinted on banners and badges, was: "We are the 99%." The clarion call asserted that the preponderance of wealth and power in the world is now held by the richest 1% of the population. The remaining 99%, no matter how affluent, cannot match the privilege and influence of the top percentile. Data compiled by the Federal Reserve Bank in 2019 estimated that the threshold for net worth of the top #1 is $11,099,166. To rank among the top #1 in annual income, a household would have to earn at least $531,020 annually.[2]

The Occupy message resonated around the world. Protest marches occurred in over 900 cities, on every continent and in hundreds of American cities. Global demonstrations on October 15 coincided with a Paris meeting about the debt crisis attended by finance ministers and central bankers from the Group of 20 nations. Thousands marched peacefully in London, Paris, Hong Kong, Sao Paulo, and Auckland. In Rome, the protest turned violent, and seventy were arrested after clashing with police. The common message was that inequality was a global problem caused by a hegemonic and reckless financial sector. In Boston, hundreds of labor leaders and workers, representing the Greater Boston Labor Council (AFL-CIO) and its 154 local unions, Community Labor United, Brotherhood of Electrical Workers, and Boston Teachers Union, marched with the Occupy protesters.[3]

What distinguished Occupy Boston was the basic respect for the protest's right of free expression, exemplified by Mayor Thomas Menino and the Police Department's relative hands-off treatment. According to municipal ordinance, camping out overnight in public space is prohibited. But the mayor took a light touch with the protest and allowed the protesters to camp out. During the camp's duration, police officers mingled amiably with protesters. With winter and below-freezing temperatures closing in, Mayor Menino ordered the camp to be closed on December 10. The police, without riot gear, first asked the protesters to disband. The forty-six who would not leave were arrested. The *Boston Globe's* Brian McGrory remarked that "Boston now stands apart from any place else in terms of the Occupy movement. The tent city here was allowed to stand longer. Police developed relationships that were stronger. And when the end came, at 5:00 a.m. yesterday, it was far quieter." The main reason for Mayor Menino's restraint was his sympathy with the basic concerns about inequality. The day following the breakup of the protesters' camp, the mayor spoke at the police headquarters, where he stated that "They [the protesters] shined a much-needed light, still needed, on the growing economic inequality in this country." His main frustration was that Occupy Boston failed to articulate specific policy demands. He remarked: "If they had leadership and an issue, they could have been the most powerful group in America."[4]

Veteran Boston community organizer Mel King agreed with Menino's perspective. He was worried that protesters had become more focused on the logistics of inhabiting the Greenway than on clearly defining a couple issues that the public could act get behind. He said the protesters had achieved powerful "leverage," but they had not used it. Occupy demonstrators in Boston, New York, and elsewhere did not present well-defined set of demands because they wanted decision-making to reflect group consensus, which was nearly impossible to achieve with so many disparate political and personal perspectives.

Globe columnist Yvonne Abraham took a somewhat more positive perspective. She asserted: "In a few short months they've shifted the terms of the debate, holding banks, big corporations, and the politicians who do their bidding up to scrutiny. They've made it impossible to ignore huge income disparities in this country."[5] Others thought that the Occupy movement largely dissipated after the tent camps were removed. There seemed to be little immediate follow-up action under the Occupy banner. But, over the ensuing years, movements percolated for the $15 minimum wage, Black Lives Matter, universal national health insurance, and initiatives to make the super-rich pay their fair share of taxes. Journalist Michael Levitin declared that "The movement itself has mostly disappeared. But 10 years later, its legacy is everywhere."[6]

GLOBAL FREE MARKET CAPITALISM AND INEQUALITY

Inequality has always been with us. What is different now, as "inequality" has become a catch-all for significant social and economic disparities in power, opportunities, and resources? People use the term to connote class and racial differences, as well as occasions and structures of discrimination. The concept is used to describe disparities within communities and national societies. "Inequality" is an elemental issue in a global knowledge economy that privileges those endowed with "knowledge."

Urbanists tend to regard "inequality" as a feature of globalization. In Saskia Sassen's book *The Global City*, she observed that the "concentration of major growth sectors in global cities" has been accompanied by "the polarized occupational structure of these sectors." These cities have been experiencing the growth of a bifurcated workforce with large numbers of high-income and low-income workers. Sassen posited that the "high-income stratum" was situated in the business services, finance, and innovation sectors, while the "low-income stratum" held the jobs providing services to the general community.[7] Since then, the wealth gap has grown progressively more extreme.

Inequality is not only a feature of life within cities and their neighborhoods, it also characterizes the disparity of economic performance between superstar cities like Boston and cities and regions that have been less successful in adjusting to the global knowledge economy. Such former New England industrial cities include Pittsfield, Springfield, Fall River, Rumford, ME, and Berlin, NH. In these cities and towns, investment has diminished, poverty has increased, and economic dynamism and civic capacity have atrophied.

The ruptures in the socioeconomic fabric of communities pushed millions of middle- and working-class families into more vulnerable circumstances. People with access to capital have prospered, while wage earners saw their incomes stagnate. A select number of cities, including Boston, have benefited tremendously from globalization by undertaking the high valued-added research and management functions for far-flung global supply chains and innovation operations. The inequalities that have accompanied globalization were not inevitable outcomes of more rapid and efficient communications and transportation. Inequality was intensified by the policies of free market capitalism, viz. neoliberalism, of Ronald Reagan and Margaret Thatcher that intentionally prioritized rewards for investors in the globalized—and financialized—economy. During the 1980s, the American and British governments, along with others, promoted an ideology of unfettered business, limited government, low taxes, reduced tariffs, and marginalized labor unions. They encouraged the accumulation of capital at the expense of social redistribution. Economic performance would be optimized by adhering to the laws of supply and demand and allowing individual choices and arrangements to drive economic decisions. Free market capitalism became a bedrock ideology of international economics and a driver of globalization.

As emerging economies around the world sought models for modernization, bodies like the IMF and the World Bank proselytized for reducing taxes, regulation, and government spending, while providing tax incentives for businesses. These trends intensified after the collapse of the Soviet Union and the end of the Cold War, which demonstrated to many the shortcomings of a Marxist statist economy and the superiority of the free market economy. During these years, emerging economies in China, South Korea, Vietnam, India, and the Gulf States experienced significant growth, while less developed economies in Africa, Latin America, and elsewhere increased their GDP's. The benefits were shared by hundreds of millions, even though these countries, too, experienced rising income inequality benefiting a small, fabulously wealthy business elite. At the same time, manufacturing cities in North America, Western Europe, and other industrialized places lost many well-paying jobs. When the Great Recession rippled around the world in 2008, it spurred misgivings about the instability of global capitalism. The supply chain breakdowns that became widespread with the onset of COVID-19 and the inflation that they sparked further undermined confidence in global free trade.

The results of free market policies are evident in national income data. They demonstrate how the distribution of wealth has changed in this country. Between 1945 and 1973, the share of national income for the wealthiest 1% fell from 12.5% to 9%. From that point until 2015, the wealthiest 1%'s income share rose to more than 22%. Slow economic growth during this period produced stagnation for low- and medium-income households. According to economist Thomas Piketty, in *Capital in the Twenty-First Century*, between 1980s and 2014, the top 10% acquired 75% of national income growth, with the top 1% alone receiving 60% of the increase. The result is that three of the wealthiest people in the United States—Jeff Bezos, Bill Gates, and Warren Buffett—own as much wealth as the bottom half of the US population combined.[8] In the table below, data demonstrate the current distribution of wealth in America by economic tier.

Table 11. Shares of US income by economic tier, 2010

Economic Tier	Population (Approx.)	Share Total Labor Income	Share Total Capital Ownership	Share Combined Income & Capital
Top 1%	3.09 million	12%	35%	20%
Next 9%	27.81 million	23%	35%	30%
Middle 40%	123.6 million	40%	25%	30%
Bottom 50%	154.5 million	25%	5%	20%

Source: Thomas Piketty, *Capital in the Twenty-First Century*.

The full-blown adoption of free market capitalism principles failed to generate the promised growth. The aggregate global growth rate was 1.4% in the 1980s and 1.1% in the 1990s, compared with 3.5% in the 1960s and 2.4% in the 1970s. This failure was obscured by the dazzling success of leading global cities. It could be argued that the extraordinary shift in wealth to the richest cohorts has stemmed from redistribution of wealth from the mass of society upward—through privatization, financialization, and preferential government treatment through tax structures, subsidies, and business-friendly regulations. A RAND Corporation study found that between 1975 and 2018, $47 trillion was distributed upward from the lower 90% of Americans to the top 10%. It should be noted that, since the onset of COVID-19 and a massive infusion of government investment in the US economy, wealth inequality declined somewhat, including for Black and Latino people, although inequality remains high by any measure.[9]

The top 1% has achieved its commanding wealth through capital accumulation. The preponderance of wealth is shaped by favorable policies governing taxation rates on investments, laws governing inheritance and gift-giving, savings and investment practices, and the workings of real estate and financial markets. The Trump tax cuts, enacted in 2017, reduced the effective tax rate on the richest 400 American families to 23%, below the 24.4% rate paid by the bottom half of households. The upper-middle class, which comprises the next 9%, makes a substantial share of its total income from payment for work. Members of this group are entrepreneurs, college and hospital executives, and high-end lawyers, doctors, and business consultants. Their income is based upon skills that usually require an advanced degree. They benefit from meritocratic work standards and institutions. This group also owns significant capital assets. The middle 40% earns the preponderance of its income from salaries and small business profits. For the middle class, home ownership amounts to between 50% and 75% of their capital wealth. The income of the bottom 50% mainly derives from wages. Their small amount of capital accumulation is mainly tied to home ownership. Most of the American public has difficulty grasping the scale of great wealth and the power that the top 1% has accrued.[10] This is a major reason why Congressionally-enacted tax policy has been so accommodating to the interests of the wealthiest at the expense of the rest. The wealth gap continues to widen because it is self-perpetuating. It is not difficult for families to pass on the wealth they have accumulated to the next generation. Meanwhile, the advance of great fortunes produces ever more distortive social outcomes.

WHO GETS WHAT IN BOSTON

Examining wealth distribution in Boston brings this issue and its consequences into sharper relief. The Boston Foundation and its Boston Indicators project has been tracking regional socioeconomic indicators since 2000. In 2015, Boston Indicators published a study focusing on the issue of inequality—*Shape of the City: Making Boston America's Upwardly Mobile City*. Its 2018 report *Boston's Booming... But for Whom?: Building Shared Prosperity in a Time of Growth* followed up, spotlighting the policies for alleviating the conditions of working and middle-class persons who are being left behind in the knowledge economy.

The Boston story parallels that of other global cities around the country and the developed world. The 2018 Boston Indicators report had Boston ranked #7 (more recent data from 2021 ranked Boston #8) in the United States for income inequality. The inequality index, also called the Gini index, is created by measuring the ratio between the income of the 95th percentile of the population and the 20th percentile. These metrics originated in a study by the Brookings Institution, which chose them for their ability to illustrate the income gap between people near the top rung and near the bottom. In Boston, the 95th percentile earned $261,973 while the 20th percentile earned $17,734 (2016), producing a ratio of 14.8. Between 1979 and 2017, the 95th percentile in Massachusetts experienced inflation-adjusted wage increases of 52%. People in the middle percentiles witnessed an increase of 25%, and those in the bottom 10th percentile saw increases of only 7%.[11]

The inequality gap in Boston is comparatively large because the city has so many people with well-paying work in health care, higher education, the innovation sectors, and professions servicing businesses and institutions. The city's lower-income cohorts represent service workers (where the job growth is greatest) in restaurants, hotels, shops, entertainment, building maintenance, security, construction, and delivery services. The lower-income level also includes the large number of students who live in the city. Another way to understand inequality in Boston is to track the change in the number of low-, middle-, and high-income households in the city between 1990 and 2014. During this period, Boston grew by a total of 88,000 households. Low-income households grew by 30,000, high-income households increased by 43,000, and middle-income households shrunk by 15,000. The growth in high-income households reflected the boom in financial services, health care and information technology as well as the ability of these people to afford the spiraling housing prices.[12]

The high rate of inequality has broad-based negative consequences. The *Boston's Booming* study observes: "As more income goes to those at the very top, less is available to be distributed to workers and families throughout the economy. As inequality increases, the rungs of the ladder become further apart, making it harder for people to advance upward."[13] This trend has been occurring across the country. The gentrification that takes place in urban neighborhoods as well as high-cost suburbs is a spatial manifestation of economic inequality and social exclusion.

Yet, there is a positive dimension to Boston's inequality because its economy creates work opportunities for lower-income workers. There is an advantageous spinoff from innovation work, as it creates five spinoff jobs for every innovation job. Spinoff workers include custodians, sales clerks, and restaurant servers, as well as doctors, lawyers, and teachers. This employment multiplier effect is three times greater than the manufacturing sector, which has a spinoff effect of about 1.7 jobs. Accompanying this effect, innovation also provides a human capital "externality," meaning that interacting with highly educated professionals makes workers as a whole more productive.[14]

Boston's lower-income workers do have opportunities for economic mobility. Boston has the #2 mobility rate among the country's 100 largest commuting zones. Boston Indicators maintains that the region has a "growing economic pie that positions us well to provide greater economic opportunity to a broad swath of our residents and workers." The top ten cities for mobility are located on the two coasts, while the bottom ten are all in the South. For Black mobility, Boston ranks #1, while ranking #4 for white mobility and #10 for Hispanic mobility. Black male mobility is still relatively low in Boston, though it is higher than in other American cities. One reason is that Massachusetts incarcerates Black males at the second lowest rate in the country. Educational reform, adequate school funding, and universal health care also strengthen the economic stability of lower-income people.[15]

As we have seen on a national level, the gap in "total net worth" (including home values, savings, investments, and retirement accounts, minus debts) is the biggest factor in creating inequality. Wealth inequality is greater than income inequality because wealth can be passed between generations, and it has a compounding effect. A 2015 study by the Federal Reserve Bank of Boston demonstrated the enormous wealth gap between racial groups in the following metropolitan Boston data.

Table 12. Income, assets, and new worth of Boston racial/ethnic groups

	Median Family Income	Median Assets	Median Net Worth
White	$90,000	$256,500	$247,500
US Black	$41,200	$700	$8
Caribbean Black	$55,000	$12,000	$12,000
Puerto Rican	$25,000	$3,020	$3,020
Dominican	$37,000	$1,724	$0
Other Hispanic	$65,000	$15,000	$2,700
Asian	$96,000	N/A	N/A

Source: Ana Patricia Muñoz, et al., *The Color of Wealth in Boston*.[16]

What is most startling is the $8 net worth (net worth equals the value of assets minus debts) for US-born Black families and the $0 net worth for Dominican families. How can this be? The answer provided by the Federal Reserve Bank of Boston is that many Black families tend to carry substantial debt and do not own homes. Another reason for the net worth disparity is the fact that there is a larger proportion of non-whites than whites in younger cohorts. They tend to have lower educational attainment and have not had as much of an opportunity to purchase a home and accumulate wealth. The most important reason for the racial net worth disparity is the unequal opportunities to accumulate assets over the generations. The Federal Reserve Bank study ascribes this to the legacy of slavery and Jim Crow segregation, racially restrictive property covenants, redlining, and the racially discriminatory allotment of FHA loans and GI Bill benefits. The Federal Reserve Bank study concludes that, since there will be a significant increase of non-white population in the coming years, "the financial well-being of communities of color is central to ensuring the inclusive long-term growth and prosperity of the Boston MSA. Unless net worth outcomes in communities of color improve, the aggregate magnitude of the wealth disparity will increase. This is a first-order public policy problem requiring immediate attention."[17]

A further instance of economic inequality relates to women and their pay gap with males. Even though Massachusetts has some of the strongest equal pay laws in the country, women still only earn an average of $0.81 on their earnings compared to $1.00 for men. Minority women fare worse. Black women earn $0.57 and Latina women earn $0.51. This amounts to the average woman earning $13,000 less per year than the average man, a rate that ranks at 17 out of 50 states for gender pay equity.[18] A major factor affecting the pay discrepancy is that women tend to work in jobs that are less valued than those filled by males. For example, women predominate in the lower-paying jobs of social workers, elementary and middle school teachers, home health aides, day care workers, and cleaners. Even women in higher-paying and executive positions are paid less than their male counterparts. According to Harvard economist Claudia Goldin, who has won the Nobel Prize in Economics for her work related to women's inequality in the American economy, a salient cause of unequal pay for college-educated women can be attributed to their not matching men in work continuity and hours worked because they are more likely to take time out for family care and other household responsibilities over the course of their career.[19] With more flexible post-pandemic workplaces, it is likely that this impediment to closing the gender pay gap will diminish.

In spite of the fact, that women have lagged men in executive leadership positions and the innovation sectors in general employment, women have been making advances. At the 100 largest public companies in Massachusetts, 21.9% (2023) of the executive officers were women. Interestingly, in the biotechnology sector, women make up 52% of the overall workforce and 46% of executive management teams.[20] The situation shows gradual improvement in women's participation and leadership in the knowledge-based economic sectors, yet there is still much room for improvement, especially for women in lower-income jobs.

In Greater Boston, the economic burdens of inequality are intensified by the region's high housing costs, which rank #13 in the nation, with $793,400 (second quarter, 2024) for the price of the median existing single-family house. San Jose was #1 with an astonishing $1.75 million for a single-family home. With a challenging market for home ownership, 30% of Black families in Greater Boston own their own homes, while the overall level of home ownership is 64%. One advantage Boston does have is its deep stock of subsidized affordable housing. Boston's Suffolk County is #1 in the country for the percentage of affordable units for low-income residents. The county has 61 affordable units for every 100 low-income residents; 48 are federally assisted and 13 are "naturally affordable." Rival coastal cities follow. Manhattan has 52 affordable units per 100 low-income residents; Washington, DC has 47 units; the United States average is 45 units; and San Francisco has 41 units. By accommodating working people with income-restricted affordable housing, Boston's inequality gap is less negative. San Francisco, for example, has a lower rate of inequality, but that is because it has a much lower percentage of low-income residents than Boston, primarily because it does not offer as much affordable housing.[21] Nevertheless, Greater Boston still needs to build significantly more housing units, both market-rate and affordable. It is a question, not only of social justice, but of the region's economic competitiveness.

Globalizing trends exacerbating the problem of unaffordable housing are present in Boston. Wealthy international investors have been buying up real estate in prosperous cities like Boston. Their purchases, usually for cash, drive up the overall cost of housing for everyone. A measure of the amount of global (and national) investment flowing into the local housing market, as it is doing around the world, is the activity of LLCs, which are investment vehicles designed to maintain the anonymity of their owners. corporate investors, institutional investors, or speculators. These are entities purchasing residential property with profit, not shelter, as a primary goal. One study found that 35% of condos in such luxury properties as Millennium Tower, Ritz Carlton Residences, and the Mandarin Oriental were owned by LLCs; and 64% of these units did not claim the City's residential property tax exemption, implying that the unit is not occupied by the owner the majority of the year. At least 80% of units in Millennium Tower, the Mandarin Oriental, and One Dalton do not claim the residential exemption. Newer condo buildings at One Dalton and in the Seaport and the Fenway have comparable levels of LLC investment. An example of the activity of LLCs in the single-family market is evident in Lexington, where forty-three of sixty-eight teardowns being replaced by larger, multi-million-dollar houses were owned by LLCs. In the Oak Hill neighborhood of Newton, twenty-eight out of forty-three teardowns were financed by LLCs. Comparable LLC activity has taken place in such upscale suburbs as Brookline and Wellesley.[22]

A study by the Metropolitan Area Planning Council has found that, between 2004 and 2018, 21% of single-family homes in Greater Boston were purchased by investors. In 2018, investors were responsible for 30% of two-family home purchases and 50% of three-family purchases. The ability to buy the homes with cash has given investors a large advantage over homeowners requiring a mortgage. These investments have ended up inflating home prices. Corporate investors, institutional investors, and speculators, which are making these investments, have profit-making as their purpose, not providing housing for people who live and work in the community. The Greater Boston submarkets that investors have been targeting are the high-value suburbs west of the city and apartment buildings and three-deckers in the urban core.[23]

UBS, the Swiss-based bank, publishes the *UBS Global Real Estate Bubble Index*, which ranks twenty-five global cities on how speculative their housing markets are. It warns investors about runaway "bubble" markets. Boston ranked 19 out of 25 for likelihood of a housing bubble. Boston was one of five US cities, including, New York, Los Angeles, San Francisco, and Miami, on the index. All five US cities were classified as "overvalued." Nine cities, led by Frankfurt, Toronto, and Hong Kong, were labeled most vulnerable to a "bubble risk." UBS attributes the "bubble risk" to "strong investment from abroad," as well as to restrictive local land use controls that curb new home construction. It is noteworthy that even a global financial institution like UBS has warned about the "downside" from the rise in housing prices caused by investment-driven purchases: "They nudge low- and middle-income earners out of the market, increasing the gap between rich and poor." Another significant indicator of Boston's status as a target for foreign investment is it being identified by the US Treasury Department as one of nine real estate markets attractive for money laundering. Other money-laundering targets include New York, Miami, Los Angeles, San Francisco, and Hawaii.[24]

ADDRESSING THE HARMFUL EFFECTS OF INEQUALITY

The damaging effects of inequality are evident, not only in the lives of affected individual and their communities, but also in the broader culture we live in. Socioeconomic inequality is contributing to the social fragmentation and the resentment that is driving politics both here and abroad. The alienation that people who have been "left behind" feel is widespread. Their concerns need to be addressed on multiple fronts, in affordable housing, education, workforce training, and health care. The Boston area is recognizing this imperative. The Boston Foundation, the region's largest grant-making organization, has stated that its over-riding priority "is to close the gap on this region's greatest

Inequality and Global Cities 233

disparities . . . The systemic and structural inequities that drive disparities cannot be dismantled without extraordinary perseverance and collaboration among visionary and courageous partners." Under the leadership of president and CEO Lee Pelton, The Boston Foundation is targeting its research, advocacy, and grant funding initiatives toward the following goals:

- closing the Racial Wealth Gap by increasing homeownership in communities of color;
- building social stability and individual and collective wealth through more equitable housing, business, and creative systems;
- promoting equitable early education and health care ecosystems for children and the adults who care for them;
- ensuring that residents have a continuum of education and career support;
- equipping community organizations, social service agencies, and supporting partners to provide crucial leadership and support for marginalized communities.[25]

The Boston Foundation social equity agenda covers issues that are being addressed by a broad array of government and private institutions in Boston and Massachusetts as a whole. A leading area of concern is providing education that better prepares people to participate in the innovation-oriented economy. This investment in human capital entails more effective education in STEM (science, technology, engineering, and mathematics), digital skills, analytical problem-solving, and critical thinking. Such education needs to be offered at the K-12 level as well as in college and as continuing education for those in the workforce. One of the major shortcomings of the knowledge economy until now has been the fact that many technology innovations have been designed by and for those with advanced education. If technology training is widely disseminated, it will make the entire workforce more productive. Contending that this is the "Human Capital Century," Enrico Moretti argues that the single most important economic development policy that can be undertaken is investing in education, as "the return is much higher than investing in roads, bridges, or rail."[26]

The Massachusetts Business Roundtable, a group of leading business executives, recognizes that adopting "effective talent development strategies" is a "top priority" for their companies. The Roundtable has estimated that, by 2030, 30,000–40,000 Massachusetts incumbent workers will need up-skilling.[27] Important players in such an educational transformation are community colleges, which help extend access to the knowledge economy and facilitate continuing career education. Beefing up technology offerings, expanding partnerships with local businesses, and increasing graduation rates can have a real impact on growing the region's talent base. Boston-based Roxbury and Bunker Hill Community Colleges offer associate degree and certificate programs in such fields as biotechnology / biomanufacturing, health care technology, information systems technology, web technologies, and cybersecurity. Roxbury Community College operates a Center for Smart Building Technology, which trains students to retrofit buildings for energy efficiency. To attract, working-age students, the Commonwealth of Massachusetts has instituted the MassReconnect program, which offers free tuition, fees, and textbooks in any community college program to anyone twenty-five or older who does not have at least an associate degree.[28]

Another critical social equity issue is the sky-high cost of housing. State government, under Governor Maura Healey, is undertaking a number of policies designed to spur the development of affordable housing, particularly in suburban communities that have resisted building multifamily units that would serve lower-income families. The City of Boston, under progressive Mayor Michelle Wu, and many surrounding cities and towns are promoting development of affordable units (see the concluding chapter for detailed descriptions of these initiatives). Besides these efforts, communities are improving the quality of life for residents by upgrading community facilities, expanding recreational space and bike and walking infrastructure, and providing social outreach services.

Despite the efforts of Massachusetts and the City of Boston to narrow the inequality gap, state and local initiatives are unable to tackle many of the forces that exacerbate inequality. Former US Treasury Secretary Larry Summers has stated "that global integration won't work if it means local disintegration. The essence of the solution has to be strengthening our systems of social insurance and preparation of people for a world that's going to change more rapidly."[29] Summers's comments represent a Neo-Keynesian perspective that national policies are needed to close the income gap, raise living standards, and create suitable work opportunities across the social spectrum.

The US government steered away from such policies in adopting the "supply-side" program of President Reagan cutting taxes to, supposedly, incentivize business to make transformative investments. Since the 1950s,

US corporate taxes have fallen from 5% of GDP to 2% today.[30] The burden of taxation shifted from corporations onto the lower-middle class and middle class. The movement to reduce taxes has hamstrung the US government's ability to close the widening gap of inequality with initiatives benefiting those who have been left behind by global economic and technological change. The federal government has the capacity to adopt fiscal policies to reduce inequality, but proponents of free market libertarianism have stymied such government intervention. Summers, Joseph Stiglitz, Thomas Piketty, and other Neo-Keynesian economists have been arguing that the United States, which usually ranks near the bottom of advanced societies in social protection programs, needs to increase the share of after-tax income for the lower 90% of society.[31]

For years, left-of-center policymakers, economists, and politicians have been making the case for enhanced social protection programs, but only with the need to provide COVID-19 pandemic relief were meaningful measures taken. In the first months of 2020, Congress passed an economic rescue package that pumped $2.2 trillion into the economy. The most important features of the legislation were extended unemployment benefits for those kept out of work due to the pandemic as well as stimulus checks for income-eligible families and individuals. Small businesses received loans and tax credits to continue paying employees who had been idled by COVID-19. President Biden's American Rescue Plan (2021) added another $1.9 trillion in economic and social support, including an expanded one-year child tax credit that decreased the child poverty rate from 9.6% to 5.2% (when the tax credit expired in 2022, the child poverty rate rose to 12.4%).[32] Government programs spurred economic growth and reduced the unemployment rate to 4.1% (December, 2024). This federal spending made some of the most consequential improvements on equity issues in decades.

Under the Biden administration, cities received unprecedented support for the development of their civil infrastructures and innovation economies. The Infrastructure Jobs & Investment Act of 2021 provided $1.2 trillion over a ten-year period for road and bridge construction and repair; upgrading railroads, public transit, airports, ports, water infrastructure, the power grid, and rural broadband. The Inflation Reduction Act of 2022 committed $369 billion to renewable energy and energy efficiency. These climate investments are projected to reduce carbon emissions by 40% from their 2005 level by 2030. This is the most ambitious climate change legislation enacted by the

US government. These commitments to an upgraded infrastructure bolster employment opportunities and enhance economic productivity

There have been encouraging developments for manufacturing. After decades of neglect, postindustrial cities across the country are receiving federal support for unprecedented investments in advanced manufacturing, research and development, and clean energy. In tandem with $280 billion in funding from the CHIPS and Science Act (2022), the semiconductor industry invested almost $640 billion (2024) in at least 22 states. The climate action initiatives of the Inflation Reduction Act are spurring the development of state-of-the-art factories making electric cars and batteries, thus increasing levels of high-wage employment. The federal Build Back Better Regional Challenge dedicated $1 billion to shape advanced manufacturing ecosystems, emulating the innovation hubs of Boston, San Francisco, Austin, and Seattle. The program awarded between $25 and $65 million each to industrial sectors in 21 cities, intending to spread the benefits of innovation beyond the usual "superstar" metros. Detroit is boosting its electrical vehicle sector. New Orleans is developing a specialty in hydrogen energy. St. Louis is creating an Advanced Manufacturing Innovation Center to support the defense-oriented aerospace sector. The overall picture for manufacturing jobs, which require specialized skills and pay ample wages, is bright. Employing almost 13 million workers (2022), the manufacturing sector is larger than it has been since 2008. It has been trending in a positive direction for the first time since the late 1970s.[33]

The Biden administration viewed these investments to reduce inequality and promote the growth of the innovation economy as "modern supply-side economics." In contrast with the free market libertarian tax cuts for large corporations and the wealthy, the Biden strategy sought to spur development by investing in less competitive communities, small entrepreneurs, and workers.

US Treasury Secretary Janet Yellen argued that "inequality in income, race, and geography is keeping millions of potential workers, researchers, and entrepreneurs from contributing fully to growth and innovation." This approach incentivizes economic production by investing in research and development, public infrastructure, and upgrading workforce education and training. Secretary Yellen said that "these focus areas are all aimed at increasing economic growth and addressing longer-term structural problems, particularly inequality."[34].

The issue of inequality has become more germane than in decades. According to Richard Florida, in *The New Urban Crisis* (2017), income inequality triggered by globalization has become the most serious problem facing cities around the world. He calls this "winner-take-all-urbanism."[35] Thomas Piketty has surmised that "it is hard to imagine an economy and society that can continue functioning indefinitely with such extreme divergence between social groups."[36] This implies the alienation of millions, whose economic fortunes have become more precarious. In the United States (and in other countries) citizens need to feel there is an element of fairness in the economic system—without it, there is no "American Dream."

The divergence in wealth is most on display in superstar global cities, where great wealth is juxtaposed with the largest concentrations of less-resourced populations, often people of color. Even while human society is making great technological and economic breakthroughs, large swathes of society are experiencing straitened prospects. This causes people to lose faith in the Information Age economy, institutions, and politics and open themselves to polarizing demagogic rhetoric. The divisions over the economic impacts of the global knowledge-based economy are occurring both within flourishing metropolitan areas and between those places and those that believe they have been left behind. The issues of inequality need to be addressed in global cities like Boston, where inequalities are most evident, but also where the requisite human and material resources and cultures of innovation are most available to promote equity. Without meaningful efforts to reduce socioeconomic inequality and the sense of vulnerability and alienation that it engenders, society could devolve into dysfunction.

CHAPTER 12

Global Cities in an Age of Disruption

"The [COVID-19] crisis has fueled a number of trends already creating tremendous strain on cities, from growing fiscal pressure and economic inequality to the effects of increasing deglobalization and environmental disruption."

A. T. Kearney, *2020 Global Cities Report*

Boston's evolution as a global city is uncertain. The global economy and political order that have endured in recent decades have entered a period of disruption. The global ties facilitated by telecommunications, transportation, and trade have made the world unprecedentedly interconnected. This is a planet where problems in one place can have adverse impacts anywhere else.

The rapid spread of COVID-19 demonstrated this reality. The disease, which originated in China, spread across the world within weeks, circulated by intercontinental airplane flights. Boston, ironically, played a major role in circulating the disease, when a conference of the biotech firm Biogen for 175 executives from around the world in February 2020 became a "superspreader" event that led to more than 300,000 cases globally. The disease has sickened over 770 million and killed more than seven million (as of April 2024), depressing economic activity and shutting down travel and tourism for a long period.[1] The breakdown of global supply chains reflected the vulnerability of global trade relations, particularly with China. Yet, there has been a remarkable upside from COVID-19: the rapid development of effective vaccines for inoculating populations around the world. The vaccines of Moderna, Pfizer, and Beth Israel Deaconess Medical Center/Johnson & Johnson were either researched or manufactured in Greater Boston, solidifying the region's international reputation as a center for medicine and innovation. The spread of vaccines facilitated the reopening of economies around the world. The COVID-19 experience has been instructive about how adroit public health measures and cutting-edge science can ameliorate contagious disease impacts. It remains to be seen how well these lessons have been learned for dealing with future diseases.

Other ominous disruptions are political in nature—Russia's attack on Ukraine, Middle East tensions around the Israeli-Palestinian conflict, and friction between the US and China over Taiwan and the broader global power struggle. The Russian invasion of Ukraine exemplifies how the standing rules-based world order is being upended. The post–Cold War era of America setting and enforcing the rules is over. There are fears that this war may presage further military conflicts of aggression and possibly even nuclear war. As international political tensions increase, trade relations are fractured and economies become destabilized. This is particularly true with the rupturing of trade between Russia and Europe and between the United States and China.

Another consequence of the Russian invasion is an increase in military spending. The Russia-Ukraine War has been a boon for Raytheon Technologies, the world's second largest defense and aerospace contractor. Although Raytheon moved its headquarters to Washington, DC, in 2022, the company has committed to maintaining R&D and production facilities in Massachusetts to take advantage of the state's experienced workforce and its advanced technology ecosystem. The United States has supplied Raytheon's Stinger missiles, Javelin anti-tank missiles, and NASAMS short-range air defense systems to Ukraine. In recent years, Raytheon has also made major arms deals, which include Patriot missiles, with such countries as Saudi Arabia, Egypt, Israel, United Arab Emirates, South Korea, Romania, and Taiwan (China has sanctioned Raytheon).[2]

In addition to outright wars, countries are being plagued by all manner of political division and turmoil. Institutions of democracy and the rule of law are under assault in the West, including in the United States, and the developing world.

The most worrisome long-term threat to human society is climate change. It has been looming in recent years—now extreme weather events are demonstrating the harmful effects from carbon emissions that scientists have been predicting. The projections for Boston give a sense of how much disruption may be wreaked by climate change. The average summer temperature in Boston in the years before 2010 was 69 degrees. According to the City of Boston's *Climate Ready Boston* report, the average summer temperature could rise as high as 76 degrees by 2050 and 84 degrees by 2100. This would mean that Boston's summer by 2050 would be as hot as Washington, DC, and the 2100 temperature would be hotter than Birmingham, AL, today. During the period between 1971 and 2000, there were an average of 11 days per year over 90 degrees. The number could climb to 40 days by 2030 and 90 by 2070. Sea level rise and the concurrent flooding is becoming an increasing threat. During the twentieth century, the sea level at Boston rose about nine inches. Between 2000 and 2030, the sea level is projected to rise another eight inches; by 2050, it could be 1.5 feet higher and three feet higher by 2070. This is driven by a combination of the melting of ice and the expansion of water as it warms.[3] Damage from flooding along the coastline could easily reach into the billions of dollars with the attendant disruption of life in seaside communities. The changes brought about by the atmosphere's warming also include more extreme precipitation, increased mortality from summer heat, and disruptive shifts in habitats of flora and fauna that could diminish food supplies. The injurious impacts are likely to intensify, and patterns of global exchange and migration are bound to be affected, including increased flows of climate migration.[4]

Economic and environmental disruptions call for state-of-the-art responses. Boston has been a leader in climate planning, adopting ambitious goals for reducing carbon emissions and creating a more resilient community. The city reduced its carbon emissions by 21% between 2005 and 2019. The goal is to reduce emissions by 50% from the 2005 baseline by 2030 and achieve 100% emissions reduction by 2050. In her vision of Boston's Green New Deal, Mayor Michelle Wu has declared more ambitious aspirations for the city of achieving 100% carbon neutrality by 2040 and 100% renewable power by 2030.[5]

The Commonwealth of Massachusetts has been playing a parallel role by securing renewable energy supplies and mandating energy efficiency standards. With California, it has been a leading state in replacing fossil fuels with renewable energy sources. A 2021 carbon emissions law requires that the state reduce its emissions by at least 50% of 1990 levels by 2030, 75%

below those levels by 2040, and achieve "net zero" emissions by 2050. The bill established a goal of building 4,000 megawatts of offshore wind facilities by 2027, with an additional 1,600 megawatts in subsequent years. In early 2024, Vineyard Wind I, with Long Island's South Fork Wind, became the nation's first offshore wind farms. Vineyard Wind I will produce up to 800 megawatts of electricity. Two wind energy projects, to be operated by Commonwealth Wind and SouthCoast Wind Energy, which are projected to produce 3,600 megawatts, are in limbo due to inflation's impact on construction costs. State government has also established benchmarks for adopting electric vehicles, charging stations, heat pumps, and new solar technologies. The state authorized municipalities to adopt a new building code which promotes new construction that does not use fossil fuels. Such sustainable energy initiatives have the potential to spur entrepreneurship and a wide range of economic opportunities that can energize the city and the region.[6]

With these efforts, Boston has been assuming a leadership role recognized globally. The city belongs to the C40 Cities Climate Leadership Group, which represents ninety-six leading metropolitan areas around the world. Boston has served on the C40 steering committee with London, Paris, Seoul, Mexico City, and Tokyo. The group's members played an important advocacy role in the development of the Paris Climate Accord of 2015 and the Glasgow Climate Pact of 2021.[7] The city's plans for managing sea level rise, urban greening, reducing heat impacts, and zero emissions buildings have been seen as international models.

Another area of disruption is driven by the rise of artificial intelligence (AI). AI has been referred to as the Fourth Industrial Revolution. It builds upon the Third Industrial Revolution, which introduced digital technology. Artificial intelligence utilizes algorithms, big data, data mining, and networked computing architectures in the "cloud." Artificial intelligence is facilitating development of the Internet of Things, wearable Internet connections, driverless vehicles, the connected house, and robotics-provided services. The AI-driven economy will have the capacity to transform entire companies, industrial sectors, and societies. It is predicted that AI will advance at a faster pace than the development of computer chips, according to Moore's Law, which posits that computer capacity doubles every 18–24 months. Since the release of ChatGPT, tech companies are barreling ahead in developing AI applications. The impact of AI on the workforce could be damaging. A Goldman Sachs report has predicted that 25% of work in the United States at risk of being automated. White collar professionals will be at risk of losing their jobs to AI to a similar degree that blue collar workers were put out of work by automation a generation or two earlier. Economist Richard Baldwin warns that "every great transformation creates triumphs for those who can seize the opportunities and tragedies for those who can't. . . . Explosive economic changes have, in the past, led to explosive social upheaval."[8]

The Boston area will have to grapple with these transformational changes with the rest of the world. There are many local companies and researchers, working on AI, big data, and machine learning, though San Francisco/Silicon Valley and New York have a leg up on the AI R&D race. One of the early in researchers on AI, working in the field since the 1960s, is Boston's Ray Kurzweil, who serves as Google's "Principal Researcher and AI visionary." His books *The Singularity is Near* (2005) and *The Singularity of Nearer: When We Merge with AI* (2024) have predicted that advances in AI will match human intelligence by 2029. He contends that the development of ChatGPT proves the validity of his predictions. His concept of "singularity" maintains that human intellects will merge with artificial intelligence by 2045. This will have the potential for brains to be augmented with millions of times more computational power by directly accessing all knowledge in the cloud simply by thinking a question.[9] MIT and its Schwarzman College of Computing intends to play a leading role in ensuring that the applications of AI affect human beings responsibly and that the creation of Frankenstein monsters is avoided. Other local universities, including Harvard, Northeastern, and Boston University, are involved with their own research efforts related to socially ethical applications of AI.

The negative shocks from pandemics, climate change, wars, and AI and the loss of control they portend are intensified by global connectivity. The hyperlinked connections between cities, countries, institutions, and businesses can spur conflict as much as useful interchange. The flows of markets, information, ideas, and people can be utilized for injurious purposes, whether weaponizing digital communications, propelling mass migration, promoting terrorism and transnational traffic in illegal drugs and weapons, investing across borders to control strategic assets, or flooding competing markets with cheap goods.

People who feel as if they are losing control over their lives are turning inward to isolationism and nationalism, which are on this rise in the US and elsewhere. Yet, global connections cannot be easily severed. It is folly to think that a nation, particularly the economic, military, and technological hegemon, can "go it alone" in a highly interconnected world.

BOSTON'S FUTURE AS A GLOBAL CITY

With all these disruptive forces at play, it will be up to global cities to prove their mettle and provide leadership for addressing these challenges. Though national governments have the preponderance of power, they are not nimble or especially creative at local problem-solving. When they do assume a role in domestic policy, it often is picking up on ideas tested in cities. They, as urbanist Bruce Katz points out, are "networks of corporate, civic, public institutions, and leaders. And therefore they tend to be hyper-pragmatic and hyper-focused on problem- solving in innovative and inclusive ways."[10] Ultimately, the development and exchange of ideas and products are the *raison d'etre* of cities.

To understand Boston's capacities for addressing the challenges facing global cities, we should recognize that the knowledge economy, in which Boston's innovation sectors thrive, should continue to drive the global economy. Solutions for ecological, health, and political-economic disruptions are being developed here. The biggest vulnerability to the innovation sectors, especially the globally preeminent life sciences, is that, for some reason, they lose their competitive edge and the region's overall economy falls into severe decline. Boston relies heavily on the creativity of its innovation sectors; beyond them, it lacks the economic diversity of some rival cities.

Besides having to working assiduously to maintain its technological advantages, Greater Boston must address problematic trends threatening its livability. The high cost of housing, which is second only to San Francisco and the Silicon Valley, and the high cost of doing business are constraining post-pandemic economic growth. A 2023 CNBC report on the business climate of the states ranked Massachusetts #49 for the cost of doing business and #47 for the cost of living (The overall Massachusetts score was #15, abetted by #1 ranking for technology and innovation and #3 for education and access to capital). High costs and remote working trends are discouraging workers from migrating here and incentivizing people to leave Massachusetts for less expensive states. Between April 2020 and July 2022, Massachusetts lost a net 110,000 people, after growing by 7.4% during the 2010s.[11]

In addition to the negative influence of its high cost structure, Boston has a workforce shortage caused by an aging population and immigration restrictions. Northeastern University economist Alan Clayton Matthews has warned that growth in the New England economy is likely to be handicapped by a shortfall in the labor force. He projects that Massachusetts is likely to add no more that 20,000 net new jobs between 2022 and 2030, even with continued development of the state's cutting-edge innovation sectors. The current labor force already is insufficient to fill existing job openings. The only thing that is keeping the labor force from contracting substantially is international inmigration. Matthews points out that, except for a period around 1900 when New England was the country's most industrialized region, it has always relied upon immigrants to help provide a sufficient workforce. This makes strategic national immigration reform imperative.

Professor Matthews has added a warning related to Massachusetts' longtime edge in maintaining an educated workforce. He argues that the state, which has led the country in educational attainment and, consequently, technological innovation for decades, is likely to lose that advantage in the coming years as other regions increase their proportion of college graduates to reach the level of Massachusetts.[12]

The most important factor in attracting and maintaining a skilled workforce, whether recent college graduates or mid-career talent, is having an adequate and affordable housing stock. It is widely acknowledged that the housing shortfall is Greater Boston's Achilles heel. Thousands of younger workers are leaving the state because of the unaffordable housing market. As previously noted, Greater Boston ranks #13 in the nation, with $793,400 (second quarter, 2024) for the price of the median existing single-family house. Boston ranks #4 for one-bedroom rental rates at $2,810 per month, following New York, San Francisco, and Jersey City. The main reason is the severe lack of available apartments. Boston's apartments have a vacancy rate of 0.49%, with a 6% vacancy rate being considered a healthy vacancy rate. State government and the Citizens Housing & Planning Association estimate that 200,000 additional housing units need to be built between 2020 and 2030 to alleviate the pressure on housing costs. Governor Maura Healey's 2024 Affordable Homes Act is projected to create more than 40,000 new for low-income and middle-income households. In addition, the $5.16 billion bill is intended to preserve or rehabilitate approximately 25,000 homes, including a large number of public housing units.[13]

The City of Boston has done more than its share in constructing housing of all kinds. Recent Mayors Tom Menino and Marty Walsh and current Mayor Michelle Wu have supported ambitious housing initiatives. Between 2011 and 2020, 36,000 total units were built or permitted in the city, with 7,346 units being income-restricted/affordable. The city has been making solid progress in meeting its goal of 69,000 new units by 2030, which was established in the *Housing Boston 2030 Plan* (2014).[14] Other communities that have also built substantial numbers of new housing units are the metropolitan core cities of Cambridge, Watertown, Waltham, Malden, Quincy, and Somerville.

The real shortfall in building needed housing units is in suburban communities where single-family homes predominate. Many suburbs have resisted the development of multifamily housing units. State government regarded this as a problem when it enacted Governor Charlie Baker's Housing Choice legislation in 2021. The law eased requirements for zone changes that allow multifamily and affordable housing. Legislation also required communities in the Massachusetts Bay Transit Authority service area to zone at least one district for multifamily housing, located within a one-half-mile radius of subway, commuter rail, and ferry stations.[15] It is important that a variety of housing units should be built. Units for families are desperately needed, since the majority of new units are studios and one-bedroom units designed for individuals or couples. There are expectations that the MBTA Communities Act should spur housing development, though the complex process of rezoning and development is likely to be drawn-out and there will be difficulties in meeting the projected need for 200,000 new units by 2030.

In addition to housing, the state must resolve the public transit crisis at the MBTA. As of December 2024, weekday ridership on buses was at 80% of December 2019 levels, while subway ridership was at 55% and commuter rail ridership was at 80%.[16] A major reason for diminished ridership is lack of public confidence in reliability and safety. Because of safety concerns cited by the Federal Transit Administration and the need to repair deficient trackage and signals, service slowdowns were imposed all too frequently. These slowdowns are taking place because of inadequate long-term maintenance. This is a shame because there are few American cities that can match Boston's subway-streetcar, bus, and commuter rail infrastructure for geographic coverage. Prior to COVID-19, it was one of the top five most used transit systems in the country. If the public lacks confidence in public transportation and the MBTA does not operate to meet post-Covid needs, one of Boston's significant comparative advantages would be lost and economic development would be stymied. This is another challenge Governor Healey is saddled with. It requires a significant infusion of fresh managerial talent and vision, which seems to be occurring under the leadership of MBTA General Manager and CEO Phillip Eng. The biggest need is a stream of billions of dollars of capital to remedy the maintenance shortcomings that have accumulated over decades and to put in place improvements, such as electrification of the commuter rail lines, that will support Greater Boston's development as a global innovation hub going forward. So far, such funding has yet to be secured.

A cause for the decline in MBTA ridership is the high vacancy rate of downtown office buildings. Fewer people are working in downtowns across the country because of remote working. At best, many offices are full only three days a week. Workers are reluctant to return to a five-day office schedule. As of January 2024, downtown offices had a vacancy rate of 15.7%.[17] Besides the reduced number of office workers, downtown retail has also suffered. Because of the dearth of downtown workers, many small businesses and eating places have closed and property values and attendant real estate taxes are falling. Reviving downtown is a significant challenge, which is essential for achieving this and any city's future viability. While Boston's resulting fiscal situation is not as dire as New York's with its massive supply of aging office buildings, the erosion of the downtown office market, poses a critical threat.

Mayor Wu's administration issued a planning study *Revive and Reimagine: A Strategy to Revitalize Boston's Downtown* (2022), which recommended diversifying the central business district from being mainly an office area to incorporating new housing, including family units, and adding cultural, recreational, and retail activity. Like other cities grappling with the same problems, Boston's strategy calls for improving the livability of downtown to attract residents and encourage more social interaction.[18]

These are specific policy areas that need to be addressed. The overarching theme that ties them together is focusing on the development of human capital through life-long education and efforts to promote social equity. All this contributes to optimizing the talents of the community. Augmenting the region's human capital is a particularly important need, given the shortage of workers that is looming for Massachusetts. By focusing on this issue, Boston will be better positioned to be a leader in addressing dislocations related to socioeconomic inequality, public health, climate change, and artificial intelligence.

As we consider Boston's likelihood to surmount the challenges, it is worth reflecting back on Mayor Kevin White's proclamation about Boston being a "world-class city." Since the 1980s, Boston has strengthened its claim to be "world-class" with its outstanding higher education, medical care, technological innovation, and talented workforce. It has the intellectual openness, a legacy of policy reform, human talent, and fiscal resources that other cities would envy. The community respects science, the rule of law, and human rights. The challenges that Boston and other cities are facing are being taken seriously here.

Despite the globally impactful work done here, Boston cannot be complacent. The competition between cities around the world is intense, and global threats are pervasive. To continue playing the influential role of a "global city," Boston must stay ahead of the curve, not only in producing technological innovations and economic wealth, but in improving social equity.

Notes

PREFACE

1. The World Bank, "Exports of Goods and Services (% of GDP)," accessed July 21, 2022, https://data.worldbank.org/indicator/NE.EXP.GNFS.ZS. According to the US Commerce Department, only 1 percent of US companies export and only 0.5 percent export to more than one country. Bruce Katz, Jennifer Bradley, *The Metropolitan Revolution: How Cities and Metros Are Fixing Our Broken Politics and Fragile Economy*, (Washington, DC: Brookings Institution Press, 2013), 149.

INTRODUCTION

1. Saskia Sassen, "Researching the Globalizations of the Global," *The Oxford Handbook of Global Studies*, eds. Mark Juergensmeyer, Saskia Sassen, Manfred B. Steiger (New York: Oxford University Press, 2019), 75.
2. Peter Hall, "Megacities, World Cities and Global Cities," in *Megacities: Exploring a Sustainable Future*, eds. Steef Buijs, Wendy Tan, Devisari Tunas, (Rotterdam: nai010 Publishers, 2013), 35–36.
3. "The Income Ranking of Metros Has Changed Little since 1980," US Department of Commerce, September 6, 2023, https://www.commerce.gov/news/blog/2023/09/income-ranking-metros-has-changed-little-1980.
4. Marie Price and Lisa Benton-Short, "Immigrants and World Cities: From the Hyper-Diverse to the Bypassed," *GeoJournal*, (June, 2007), 103–17, https://www.researchgate.net/publication/226194863_Immigrants_and_world_cities_From_the_hyper-diverse_to_the_bypassed.
5. Cleveland Amory, *The Proper Bostonians* (New York: E.P. Dutton & Co., Inc., 1947), 23.
6. Stephen V. Ward, *Selling Places: The Marketing and Promotion of Towns and Cities, 1850–2000* (New York: Routledge, 1998), 234.

CHAPTER 1

1. Charles E. Claffey, "Celebration of Cities Opens," *Boston Globe*, September 23, 1980, https://bostonglobe.newspapers.com/image/428652146/.
2. "A Great Dirty City," *Boston Globe*, September 16, 1980, https://bostonglobe.newspapers.com/image/428514991/.

3. Robert A. Jordan, "There's Another Side of the City That Visitors Don't See," *Boston Globe*, September 30, 1980, https://bostonglobe.newspapers.com/image/428669844/.
4. "School Workers Plan Protest," *Boston Globe*, September 18, 1980, https://bostonglobe.newspapers.com/image/428515165/.
5. Ada Louise Huxtable, "A Conference on Great Cities," *New York Times*, October 10, 1980, https://www.nytimes.com/1980/10/12/archives/architecture-view-a-conference-on-great-cities.html.
6. David Arnold, "The Visitors' Many Views," *Boston Globe*, September 27, 1980, https://bostonglobe.newspapers.com/image/428658500/.
7. Marc Levinson, *Outside the Box: How Globalization Changed from Moving Stuff to Spreading Ideas* (Princeton, NJ: Princeton University Press, 2020), 3–7.
8. John Friedmann, "The World City Hypothesis," *Development and Change*, Vol. 17 (1986), 69–83.
9. Saskia Sassen explained the rise of this triad of financial centers: "Briefly, in the 1980s Tokyo emerged as the main center for the export of capital; London as the main center for the processing of capital, largely through its vast international banking network linking London to most countries in the world and through the Euromarkets; and New York as the main receiver of capital, the center for investment decisions and for the production of innovations that can maximize profitability." Saskia Sassen, *The Global City: New York, London, Tokyo*, 2nd ed., (Princeton, NJ: Princeton University Press, 2001), 333. Jennifer Robinson argues that "all cities are ordinary," while still being autonomous, dynamic, and creative. Jennifer Robinson, *Ordinary Cities: Between Modernity and Development* (New York: Routledge, 2006), 1–2.
10. For a discussion of different definitions that have been provided for these "global" and "world" cities, see Saskia Sassen, "The Global City: Introducing a Concept," *Brown Journal of World Affairs*, Winter-Spring, 2005, 27–43, https://www.columbia.edu/~sjs2/PDFs/globalcity.introconcept.2005.pdf; Greg Clark, *Global Cities: A Short History* (Washington, DC: Brookings Institution Press, 2016), 139; Michele Acuto, Chapter 2: "The Idea(s)," *How to Build a Global City: Recognizing the Symbolic Power of a Global Urban Imagination* (Ithaca, NY: Cornell University Press, 2022), 17–33.
11. Greg Clark uses four criteria for the formation of global cities: 1) they foster innovation and achieve influence; 2) lead the discovery of new markets, routes, products, or service; 3) support trade and specialization in traded sectors; 4) they attract and retain entrepreneurial diverse populations. Clark, *Global Cities*, 139.
12. Jesus Leal Trujillo and Joseph Parilla, *Redefining Global Cities: The Seven Types of Global Metro Economies* (Washington, DC: Brookings Institution Global Cities Initiative, 2016), 29, https://www.brookings.edu/experts/; Robert D. Atkinson, Mark Muro, with Jacob Whiton, *The Case for Growth Centers: How to Spread Tech Innovation across America* (Washington, DC: Brookings Institution and Information Technology and Innovation Foundation, 2019), 5, https://www.brookings.edu/wp

-content/uploads/2019/12/full-report-growth-centers_pdf_brookingsmetro-bass
center-itif.pdf.
13. Enrico Moretti, *The New Geography of Jobs* (Boston: Houghton Mifflin Harcourt, 2012), 215, 15, 55.
14. Jonathan Gruber & Simon Johnson, *Jump-Starting America: How Breakthrough Science Can Revive Economic Growth and the American Dream* (New York: Public Affairs, 2019), 139; "The Income Ranking of Metros Has Changed Little since 1980," US Department of Commerce, September 6, 2023, https://www.commerce.gov/news/blog/2023/09/income-ranking-metros-has-changed-little-1980.
15. JLL and The Business of Cities, *The Universe of City Indices 2017: Decoding City Performance* (2017), 8, https://www.jll.co.uk/en/trends-and-insights/research/decoding-city-performance.
16. Manuel Castells, *The Rise of the Network Society, 2nd ed.* (Malden, MA: Wiley-Blackwell, 2000), 442.
17. Globalization and World Cities Research Network, "The World According to GaWC 2018," https://www.lboro.ac.uk/microsites/geography/gawc/world2018t.html; Peter J. Taylor, *World City Network: A Global Urban Analysis* (New York: Routledge, 2004).
18. DHL, *DHL Global Connectedness Index 2016: The State of Globalization in an Age of Ambiguity* (2016), back cover, https://www.dhl.com/content/dam/dhl/global/core/documents/pdf/glo-core-gci-2016-full-study.pdf.
19. National Travel & Tourism Office, "Overseas Visitation Estimates for U.S. States, Cities, and Census Regions: 2015," (2015), https://travel.trade.gov/outreachpages/download_data_table/2015_States_and_Cities.pdf; "U.S. States Hosting the Most International Students in the Academic Year, 2022/23," Statista, https://www.statista.com/statistics/237703/us-states-hosting-the-most-international-students/; The Institute of International Education, *Open Door Report 2023*, https://opendoorsdata.org/fact_sheets/state-fact-sheets/.
20. Trujillo and Parilla, *Redefining Global Cities*, 30–31.
21. JLL, with The Business of Cities, *Universe of City Indices 2018: World Cities: Mapping the Pathways to Success* (2018), 4, 10–23, 31, https://www.us.jll.com/en/trends-and-insights/research/world-cities-mapping-the-pathways-to-success.
22. Ni Pengfei, Marco Kamiya, Guo Jing, Zhang Yi, etc., *Global Urban Competitiveness Report: Global Urban Value Chain: Insight into Human Civilization over Time and Space (2020–2021)*, UN Habitat and Chinese Academy of Social Sciences, National Academy of Economic Strategy (2021), https://unhabitat.org/sites/default/files/2021/11/1_report_on_competitiveness_of_cities_worldwide2020-2021.pdf; Chinese Academy of Social Sciences and UN-Habitat, Ni Pengfei, Marco Kamiya, Wang Haibo, et al., *The Global Urban Competitiveness Report, 2017–2018 (Short Version)*, 4, https://unhabitat.org/wp-content/uploads/2017/11/GUCR2017-2018-Short-Version.pdf. For the 17 United Nations Sustainable Development Goals, see United Nations Sustainable Development Goals, UN Department of Economic and Social Affairs: Sustainable Development, accessed August 19, 2022, https://sdgs.un.org/goals.

23. World Intellectual Property Organization, INSEAD, Cornell SC Johnson College of Business, and PwCStrategy, *The Global Innovation Index 2022* (2022), 62, https://www.wipo.int/global_innovation_index/en/2022/.
24. Deloitte, *Global Cities, Global Talent: London's Rising Soft Power* (2016), 4, https://www2.deloitte.com/content/dam/Deloitte/uk/Documents/Growth/deloitte-uk-global-cities-global-talent-2016.pdf.
25. This data comes from the US Census Bureau's American Community Survey. "Leading Metropolitan Areas with the Highest Percentage of College Graduates in the United States in 2019," Statista, accessed November 25, 2022, https://www.statista.com/statistics/432859/us-metro-areas-with-the-highest-percentage-of-college-graduates/; Edward L. Glaeser, "Reinventing Boston, 1640–2003," NBER Working Paper 10166, December, 2003, 5, http://www.nber.org/papers/w10166.
26. Richard Florida, "The Post-Pandemic Geography of the U.S. Tech Economy," *Bloomberg*, March 8, 2022; https://www.bloomberg.com/news/articles/2022-03-09/where-venture-capital-and-tech-jobs-are-growing; Startup Genome, *Global Startup Ecosystem Report 2023*, July, 2023, https://startupgenome.com/report/gser2023.
27. "New Foreign Direct Investment in the United States, 2021," Bureau of Economic Analysis, July 6, 2022, https://www.bea.gov/sites/default/files/2022-07/fdi0722_1.pdf.
28. Z/Yen Partners with China Development Institute, *The Global Financial Centres Index 35* (March, 2024), https://www.longfinance.net/media/documents/GFCI_35_Report_2024.03.21_v1.0.pdf.
29. IESE Business School, University of Navarra, *IESE Cities in Motion Index* (2022), 29, https://media.iese.edu/research/pdfs/ST-0633-E.pdf.
30. Richard Florida, *The New Urban Crisis: How Our Cities Are Increasing Inequality, Deepening Segregation, and Failing the Middle Class-and What We Can Do About It* (New York: Basic Books, 2017), 3.
31. Knight Frank, *Wealth Report: The Global Perspective on Prime Property and Investment* (2021), 33, https://content.knightfrank.com/research/83/documents/en/the-wealth-report-2021-7865.pdf.
32. National Association of Realtors, "Change in Median Sales Price of Existing Single-Family Homes for Metropolitan Areas 2nd Quarter" 2024, https://www.nar.realtor/research-and-statistics/housing-statistics/metropolitan-median-area-prices-and-affordability.
33. Resonance, *World's Best Cities: A Ranking of Global Place Equity 2024* (2024), 7, 29, 56, https://www.worldsbestcities.com/rankings/worlds-best-cities/.
34. Boston Consulting Group, *Cities of Choice: Are People Happy Where They Live?* (2023), 17, https://www.bcg.com/press/7march2023-bcg-report-reveals-most-desirable-cities-live-in.

CHAPTER 2

1. The concept of globalization, in the sense of worldwide trade came into use during the Age of Exploration. At this time, the word "global," from the Latin *globus* for "ball" or "sphere," came into use it English. The term "global" conveyed the sense

of a new, expansive world. "Global," *Oxford English Dictionary*, accessed April 13, 2024, https://www.oed.com/dictionary/global_adj?tl=true&tab=meaning_and_use.
2. Edwin G. Burrows and Mike Wallace, *Gotham: A History of New York City to 1898* (New York: Oxford University Press, 1999), 119.
3. Burrows and Wallace, *Gotham*, 120.
4. Tristram Hunt, *Cities of Empire: The British Colonies and the Creation of the Urban World* (New York: Metropolitan Books, 2014), 35.
5. Samuel Eliot Morison, *The Maritime History of Massachusetts, 1783-1860* (Boston: Northeastern University Press, 1979), 14–15.
6. Margaret Ellen Newell, "The Birth of New England in the Atlantic Economy: From Its Beginnings to 1770," *Engines of Enterprise: An Economic History of New England*, ed. Peter Temin (Cambridge, MA: Harvard University Press, 2000), 15.
7. Mark Peterson, *The City-State of Boston: The Rise and Fall of an Atlantic Power, 1630-1865* (Princeton, NJ: Princeton University Press, 2019), 5, 20, 22, 88.
8. Burrows and Wallace, *Gotham*, 121.
9. Burrows and Wallace, *Gotham*, 112.
10. Burrows and Wallace, *Gotham*, 36.
11. Edward S. Cooke, Jr., *Inventing Boston: Design, Production, and Consumption, 1680-1720* (New Haven, CT: Yale University Press, 2019), 179.
12. Burrows and Wallace, *Gotham*, 122.
13. Burrows and Wallace, *Gotham*, xviii.
14. Salem was a competitor with Boston during the colonial era and after independence. The Embargo of 1807 and the War of 1812, which closed American ports, severely damaged their economies. Salem never recovered, and Boston absorbed many of Salem's merchants and ships. Salem's commercial status in the US was demonstrated by the fact it ranked #7 in population (7,921 population) in 1790, #8 in 1800, #9 in 1810, and #10 as late as 1820.
15. Workers of the Writers' Program of the Work Projects Administration in the State of Massachusetts, *Boston Looks Seaward, The Story of the Port, 1630-1940* (Boston: Boston Port Authority, 1941), 97; Brian Donahue, "Remaking Boston, Remaking Massachusetts," eds. Anthony N. Penna and Conrad Edick Wright, *Remaking Boston: An Environmental History of the City and Its Surroundings* (Pittsburgh: University of Pittsburgh Press, 2009), 111; Jenny Rose, *Between Boston and Bombay: Cultural and Commercial Encounters of Yankees and Parsi, 1771-1865* (New York: Palgrave Macmillan, 2019), 239.
16. Robert G. Albion, William A. Baker, Benjamin W. Larabee, *New England and the Sea* (Mystic, CT: Mystic Seaport Museum, 1972), 110, 182. The trajectory of ice harvesting in Maine is illustrative of its growth—30,000 tons were harvested by hand from Maine lakes in 1860, and 30 million tons were of the harvested with machinery by 1890. Writers' Program, *Boston Looks Seaward*, 96.
17. Albion, Baker, Larabee, *New England and the Sea*, 113.
18. Albion, Baker, Larabee, *New England and the Sea*, 101, 113, 116–18.
19. W. H. Bunting, *Portrait of a Port: Boston, 1852-1914* (Cambridge, MA: Belknap Press of Harvard University Press, 1971), 4; Dael A. Norwood, *Trading Freedom:*

How Trade with China Defined Early America (Chicago: University of Chicago Press, 2022), 61. Britain forced China to accept the importation of opium during the Opium War (1839–1842). The war received US support from John Quincy Adams, who was serving as a Congressman at the time, when he argued that China should be forced to open its ports to opium because all nations should allow free trade. Norwood, *Trading Freedom*, 83.
20. Bunting, *Portrait of a Port*, 101.
21. Bunting, *Portrait of a Port*, 101.
22. Lawrence Dame, *New England Comes Back* (New York: Random House, 1940), 85.
23. Anthony Sammarco, "S.S. Pierce: A Boston Tradition," presentation Boston Athenaeum, Sept. 24, 2015, https://vimeo.com/140696028; S.S. Pierce, *Annals of a Corner Grocery: 80th Birthday of S.S. Pierce Co., 1831–1911* (Boston, 1911), 13, 28.
24. Sammarco, "S.S. Pierce," 112.
25. Albion, *Rise of New York Port*, 126–27.
26. America's third busiest port, Philadelphia, decidedly trailed New York and Boston during the 1821–1860 period, with 7.5% of the nation's imports, 8.3% of its exports, and 4.4% of its immigrants. Albion, *Rise of New York Port*, 389.
27. Albion, *Rise of New York Port*, 241.
28. Albion, *Rise of New York Port*, 358.
29. Steamships during the nineteenth century dramatically shortened travel times and reduced transportation costs. For example, the cost of shipping wheat between the United States and Great Britain dropped by 87.5% between 1820 and 1896. Between 1815 and 1914, global trade increased by 30 times. Marc Levinson, *Outside the Box: How Globalization Changed from Moving Stuff to Spreading Ideas* (Princeton, NJ: Princeton University Press, 2020), 29, 32.
30. Writers' Program, *Boston Looks Seaward*, 147.
31. Glaeser, Edward L. "Reinventing Boston, 1640–2003," NBER Working Paper 10166, December, 2003, 40, http://www.nber.org/papers/w10166.
32. Bunting, *Portrait of a Port*, 13.
33. Writers' Program, *Boston Looks Seaward*, 170.
34. Albion, Baker, and Larabee, *New England and the Sea*, 164.
35. Boston Landmarks Commission, *The Fort Point Channel Landmark District Study Report* (Boston: Boston Landmarks Commission, 2008), 10, 58.
36. Charles Morrow Wilson, *Empire in Green and Gold: The Story of the American Banana Trade* (New York: Henry Holt, 1947), 23.
37. Marcelo Bucheli, "United Fruit in Latin America," *Banana Wars*, 96; "Andrew Preston," United Fruit Historical Society, accessed February 16, 2021, https://www.unitedfruit.org/preston.htm; also see Mark Moberg and Steve Striffler, "Introduction," *Banana Wars: Power, Production, and History in the Americas* (Durham, NC: Duke University Press, 2003), 10.
38. Stephen Puleo, *Dark Tide: The Great Boston Molasses Flood of 1919* (Boston Beacon Press, 2003), 48–49; Writers' Program, *Boston Looks Seaward*, 56.
39. Puleo, *Dark Tide*, 45–47.

40. Writers' Program, *Boston Looks Seaward*, 198.
41. Winfield M. Thompson, "Leathers from Many Lands Sold in Boston," *Boston Globe*, May 8, 1904, https://bostonglobe.newspapers.com/newspage/431005380/.
42. Bunting, *Portrait of a Port*, 17; Dame, *New England Comes, Back*, 45; James Aloisi, *Massport at 60: Shaping the Future since 1956* (Boston: Massport, 2017), 14.
43. Writers' Program, *Boston Looks Seaward*, 192, 227–28, 259, 289; Seymour E. Harris, *The Economics of New England: A Case Study of an Older Area* (Cambridge, MA: Harvard University Press, 1952), 264; Aloisi, *Massport at 60*, 50–51.
44. Writers' Program, *Boston Looks Seaward*, 195.
45. Aloisi, *Massport at 60*, 8; "Massport Continues to See Business Grow at Flynn Cruiseport in 2023, Looks Ahead to Busy 2024 Season," Massport, December 22, 2023, https://www.massport.com/media/newsroom/massport-continues-see-business-grow-flynn-cruiseport-2023-looks-ahead-busy-2024.
46. Writers' Program, *Boston Looks Seaward*, 293.
47. "Top U.S. Ports, 2023," Logistics Management, accessed August 21, 2023, https://www.logisticsmgmt.com/article/top_30_u.s._ports_trade_tensions_determine_where_cargo_goes_next; "Port of Boston Monthly Container and Cruise Passenger Summary," Massport, December, 2023, https://www.massport.com/sites/default/files/2024-01/Dec-2023-TEU-Volume.pdf; "Boston, MA Profile," OEC-Observatory of Economic Complexity, accessed June 22, 2022, https://oec.world/en/profile/subnational_usa_port/boston-ma-40.
48. World Institute for Strategic Economic Research, "WISERTrade: Port HS Database, Boston, MA," 2017, http://www.wisertrade.org/home/portal/index.jsp; Marc Levinson, *Outside the Box: How Globalization Changed from Moving Stuff to Spreading Ideas* (Princeton, NJ: Princeton University Press, 2020), 143.
49. David Grayson Allen, *Investment Management in Boston: A History*, (Amherst, MA: University of Massachusetts Press, 2015), 40; Peter Temin, "The Industrialization of New England," in *Engines of Enterprise*, 122.
50. Joshua Rosenbloom, "The Challenges of Economic Maturity: New England, 1880–1940," in *Engines of Enterprise*, 160.
51. David Koistinen, "Business and Regional Economic Decline: The Political Economy of Deindustrialization in Twentieth-Century New England," *Business and Economic History On-Line*, Vol. 12, 2014, 4–5, https://thebhc.org/sites/default/files/koistinen2.pdf.
52. Dame, *New England Comes Back*, x.

CHAPTER 3

1. Z/Yen Partners with China Development Institute, *The Global Financial Centres Index 33* (March, 2023), https://www.longfinance.net/media/documents/GFCI_33_Report_2023.03.23_v1.1.pdf. Boston was ranked at #22 in the rapidly-shifting index in 2024, though its combined financial metrics did not decline from 2023. The metrics of its closely-grouped rivals increased, with the difference between the #9

position and #22 being miniscule. Z/Yen Partners with China Development Institute, *The Global Financial Centres Index 35* (March, 2024), https://www.longfinance.net/media/documents/GFCI_35_Report_2024.03.21_v1.0.pdf.
2. Z/Yen Partners, *Global Financial Centres Index*, 38–40.
3. Joshua L. Rosenbloom, "The Challenges of Economic Maturity: New England, 1880–1949," in *Engines of Enterprise: An Economic History of New England*, ed. Peter Temin (Cambridge, MA: MIT Press, 2001), 188–89.
4. Arthur M. Johnson and Barry E. Supple, *Boston Capitalists and Western Railroads: A Study in the Nineteenth-Century Railroad Investment Process* (Cambridge, MA: Harvard University Press, 1967), 81.
5. J.M. Forbes & Co. LLP, accessed May 14, 2020, https://www.jmforbes.com/history.
6. Johnson and Supple, *Boston Capitalists and Western Railroads*, 99.
7. "F.L. Ames's Sudden Death," *New York Times*, September 14, 1893, https://timesmachine.nytimes.com/timesmachine/1893/09/14/issue.html.
8. Coolidge was manager of the Amoskeag Mill in Manchester, NH. He served on boards of prominent Boston banks and invested in the East India maritime trade before becoming involved with the Atchison, Topeka, and Santa Fe Railway. A prolific investor, Coolidge even played a role is organizing the United Fruit Company; and his son Thomas, Jr., served as its president.
9. *Northern Pacific Railroad Company, Charter, Organization, and Proceedings* (Boston: A. Mudge & Son, 1865), 21–22; Sean Fraga, "'An Outlet to the Western Sea': Puget Sound Terraqueous Mobility, and Northern Pacific's Pursuit of Trade with Asia, 1864–1892," *The Western Historical Quarterly*, Vol. 51, Winter, 2020, https://academic.oup.com/whq/article/51/4/439/5912184.
10. Vincent P. Carosso, *Investment Banking in America: A History* (Cambridge, MA: Harvard University Press, 1970), 26, 233; Noam Maggor, *Brahmin Capitalism: Frontiers of Wealth and Populism in America's First Gilded Age* (Cambridge, MA: Harvard University Press, 2017), 234.
11. Carosso, *Investment Banking in America*, 415–16.
12. Carosso, *Investment Banking in America*, 415–16.
13. Richard R. John, *Network Nation: Inventing American Telecommunications* (Cambridge, MA: Harvard University Press, 2010), 311.
14. Carosso, *Investment Banking in America*, 87.
15. Carosso, *Investment Banking in America*, 230.
16. Carosso, *Investment Banking in America*, 42, 93.
17. Carosso, *Investment Banking in America*, 318–19.
18. Allen, *Investment Management in Boston*, 77, 79. "The Emergence of the Family Office," KMPG, accessed March 1, 2022, https://home.kpmg/xx/en/home/insights/2019/11/the-emergence-of-the-family-office.html.
19. Allen, Investment Management in Boston, 78–79; Ward Just, "About Boston," *Twenty-One: Selected Stories* (Boston: Houghton Mifflin, 1990), 256.
20. Allen, *Investment Management in Boston*, 57.

21. Allen, *Investment Management in Boston*, 153, 192.
22. Allen, *Investment Management in Boston*, 260.
23. "Fidelity by the Numbers: Asset Management," Fidelity, December 31, 2023, https://www.fidelity.com/about-fidelity/our-company/asset-management.
24. "State Street Reports Fourth Quarter and Full-Year 2023 Financial Results," January 19, 2024, State Street, accessed April 3, 2024, https://investors.statestreet.com/files/doc_financials/2023/q4/STT-4Q23-Earnings-Press-Release-vFinal.pdf; Jon Chesto, "State Street Still a 'Consolidator' as It Regains Top Spot," *Boston Globe*, December 8, 2021, https://www.bostonglobe.com/2021/12/08/business/state-street-remains-consolidator-it-regains-top-spot-its-industry/; "Leading Fund Managers Worldwide in 2024, by Assets under Management," Statista, accessed April 3, 2024, https://www.statista.com/statistics/255864/top-global-fund-groups-worldwide-by-assets/; Allen, *Investment Management in Boston*, 240–41.
25. Allen, *Investment Management in Boston*, 187.
26. Jane Jacobs, *Cities and the Wealth of Nations: Principles of Economic Life* (New York: Random House, 1984), 228–29.
27. Allen, *Investment Management in Boston*, 212.
28. Nalin Patel, "Global VC Ecosystem Rankings," *PitchBook*, October 10, 2023, https://pitchbook.com/news/reports/q4-2023-pitchbook-analyst-note-global-vc-ecosystem-rankings; Richard Florida and Ian Hathaway, "The Rise of the Global Startup City," The Center for American Entrepreneurship, 2018, https://startupsusa.org/global-startup-cities/, 18.
29. Allen, *Investment Management in Boston*, 283; Troy Segal, "Understanding Private Equity (PE)," Investopedia, February 9, 2024, https://www.investopedia.com/articles/financial-careers/09/private-equity.asp.
30. Bain Capital, accessed May 5, 2023, https://www.baincapital.com/about-us.
31. "Boston Private Equity Firms," Cobble Hill Group, 2021, accessed March 1, 2022, https://www.cobblehillgroup.com/boston-private-equity-firms.html.
32. Allen, *Investment Management in Boston*, 305, 307.
33. Z/Yen Partners with China Development Institute, *The Global Financial Centres Index 33* (2023), 36, https://www.longfinance.net/media/documents/GFCI_33_Report_2023.03.23_v1.1.pdf; Massachusetts Technology Park Corporation, *Now, Next, and Beyond: Analysis of the FinTech Ecosystem in the Commonwealth of Massachusetts*, October, 2020, 1, https://fintechsandbox.org/sites/default/files/EY-Massachusetts-FinTech-Ecosystem-Assessment-October-2020.pdf; "Global Fintech Ranking: Top 25 + 10 Runners-up," Startup Genome, 2022, https://startupgenome.com/article/global-fintech-ranking-top-25-plus-10-runners-up.
34. Massachusetts Technology Park Corporation, *Now, Next, and Beyond*, 1; Mass. Fintech Hub, 2022, accessed July 6, 2023, https://massfintechhub.com/discover/success-stories/mass-fintech-hub-recap-look-ahead-2023/.
35. "Largest Fintech Companies in Massachusetts," *Boston Business Journal*, September 15, 2022, https://www.bizjournals.com/boston/subscriber-only/2022/09/15/largest

-fintech-companies-in-massachusetts.html; Justine Hoffer, "32 Boston Fintech Companies Shaking up Finance," Built in Boston, March 13, 2023, https://www.builtinboston.com/2016/09/08/boston-fintech-companies-you-should-know.
36. Mass. Fintech Hub, 2022, accessed July 6, 2023, https://massfintechhub.com/discover/success-stories/mass-fintech-hub-recap-look-ahead-2023/.
37. DCU Fintech Innovation Center, accessed July 7, 2023, https://dcufintech.org/, "FinTech," MassChallenge, accessed July 7, 2023, https://masschallenge.org/programs-fintech/; FinTech Sandbox, accessed July 7, 2023, https://fintechsandbox.org.
38. Allen, *Investment Management in Massachusetts*, 280.
39. "In Investing, It's the Prudent Bostonian," *Business Week*, June 6, 1959, 56–57.
40. Allen, *Investment Management in Massachusetts*, 151, 337.
41. Jon Chesto, "A Longstanding Pillar of Boston's Economy, Finance Is Fading Ever Faster since Covid," *Boston Globe*, November, 21, 2022, https://www.bostonglobe.com/2022/11/21/business/longstanding-pillar-bostons-economy-finance-is-fading-even-faster-since-covid/.

CHAPTER 4

1. Winifred Gallagher, *How the Post Office Created America* (New York: Penguin Press, 2016), 18–19.
2. Wayne E. Fuller, *The American Mail: Enlarger of the Common Life* (Chicago: University of Chicago Press, 1972), 23; Gallagher, *How the Post Office Created America*, 9, 11–16.
3. Within two years, seven-eighths of mail items were newspapers. Gallagher, *How the Post Office Created America*, 38–40.
4. Gallagher, *How the Post Office Created America*, 83, 87. Mail from the East to the West Coast, which entailed a long sea voyage, cost more.
5. Stamps allowed mail to be prepaid. Prior to the issuance of stamps, most letters were sent postage due because of the high cost of mailing. Recipients would refuse to pay for mail when it did not contain a message they were interested in receiving.
6. Richard R. John, *Spreading the News: The American Postal System from Franklin to Morse* (Cambridge, MA: Harvard University Press, 1995), 157.
7. Fuller, *The American Mail*, 159. In 1828, the United States had an average of 74 post offices for every 100,000 inhabitants, compared with 17 post offices per 100,000 in Great Britain and four post offices per 100,000 in France. John, *Spreading the News*, 5, 51.
8. Fuller, *The American Mail*, 193.
9. Menahem Blondheim, *News over the Wires: The Telegraph and the Flow of Public Information in America, 1844–1897* (Cambridge, MA: Harvard University Press, 1994), 28.
10. In 1846, Congress voted to subsidize American steamship lines to deliver transatlantic mail. The Collins Line initiated steamship service between New York and

Southampton, England, and Bremen, Germany. John, *Spreading the News*, 53; Fuller, *American Mail*, 196.
11. "History," Universal Postal Union, accessed January 14, 2021, https://www.upu.int/en/Universal-Postal-Union/About-UPU/History; Fuller, *American Mail*, 213, 227; Gallagher, *How the Post Office Created America*, 174.
12. Gallagher, *How the Post Office Created America*, 226.
13. The basic transpacific letter rate was 20 cents, while the basic transatlantic rate was 30 cents.
14. Daniel Walker Howe, *What Hath God Wrought: The Transformation of America, 1815–1848* (New York: Oxford University Press, 2007), 691–94.
15. Blondheim, *News over the Wires*, 75–95.
16. Blondheim, *News over the Wires*, 71–73, 114–17.
17. Tom Standage, *The Victorian Internet: The Remarkable Story of the Telegraph and the Nineteenth-Century's Online Pioneers*, 2nd ed. (New York: Bloomsbury, 2013), 58, 80.
18. Quoted in Howe, *What Hath God Wrought*, 696–97.
19. Bureau of the Census, *Bicentennial Edition Historic Statistics of the United States: Colonial Times to 1970* (Washington, DC: US Department of Commerce, 1975), 790–91. The table of telegram charges identifies the rates from New York to other cities. Boston had the same rate structure of New York. Richard R. John, *Network Nation: Inventing American Telecommunications* (Cambridge, MA: Harvard University Press, 2010), 2–3.
20. Peter Hall and Paschal Preston, *The Carrier Wave: New Information Technology and the Geography of Innovation, 1846–2003* (London: Unwin Hyman, 1988), 137.
21. Hall and Preston, *The Carrier Wave*, 48–49.
22. Sidney H. Aronson, "Bell's Electrical Toy: What's the Use? The Sociology of Early Telephone Usage," ed. Ithiel de Sola Pool, *The Social Impact of the Telephone* (Cambridge, MA: MIT Press, 1977), 22.
23. New England Telephone and Telegraph Company, *The Telephone: A Description of the Bell System with Some Facts Concerning the So-Called Independent Movement* (Boston: New England Telephone and Telegraph Company, 1906), 29, 37; John, *Network Nation*, 218.
24. New England Telephone & Telegraph Company, *Boston Division, Official List of Subscribers* (Boston: New England Telephone & Telegraph Company, July 1, 1890), 15.
25. John, *Network Nation*, 290–91, 306–8, 340; Jimmy Stamp, "The Pay Phone's Journey from Patent to Urban Relic," *Smithsonian Magazine*, September 18, 2014, https://www.smithsonianmag.com/history/first-and-last-pay-phone-180952727/.
26. Claude S. Fischer, *America Calling: A Social History of the Telephone to 1940* (Berkeley, CA: University of California Press, 1994), 195, 229, 255.
27. Jean Gottmann, "Megalopolis and Antipolis: The Telephone and the Structure of the City," ed. Pool, *The Social Impact of the Telephone*, 316; J. Alan Moyer, "Urban

Growth and the Development of the Telephone: Some Relationships at the Turn of the Century," Pool, ed., *The Social Impact of the Telephone*, 342–69.
28. New England Telephone, *Boston Division, Official List of Subscribers*, 20; U.S. CPI Inflation Calculator, www.in2013dollars.com; John, *Network Nation*, 11; Ronald Abler, "The Telephone and the Evolution of the American Metropolitan System," Pool, ed., *Social Impact of the Telephone*, 319.
29. Marc Levinson, *Outside the Box: How Globalization Changed from Moving Stuff to Spreading Ideas* (Princeton, NJ: Princeton University Press, 2020), 80.
30. Frances Cairncross, *The Death of Distance: How the Communications Revolution Is Changing Our Lives* (Boston: Harvard Business School Press, 1997), 5.
31. Arthur C. Clarke, *How the World Was One: Beyond the Global Village* (New York: Bantam Books, 1992), 273; Peter Dicken, *Global Shift: Mapping the Changing Contours of the World Economy*, 7th ed. (New York: The Guilford Press, 2015), 88.
32. Dicken, *Global Shift*, 88.
33. "Chapter 3: Making the Most of Globalisation," *OECD Economic Outlook, Preliminary Edition, 2007*, accessed July 21, 2021, https://www.oecd.org/economy/outlook/38628438.pdf.
34. Dicken, *Global Shift*, 81; "How Many Transistors in a Computer Chip," DRex, April 25, 2023, https://www.icdrex.com/how-many-transistors-in-a-computer-chip/.
35. Vannevar Bush, "As We May Think," *Atlantic Monthly*, July, 1945, 101–8.
36. J. C. R. Licklidder, *Libraries of the Future* (Cambridge, MA: MIT Press, 1964).
37. Walter Isaacson, *The Innovators: How a Group of Hackers, Geniuses, and Geeks Created the Digital Revolution* (New York: Simon & Shuster, 2014), 256.
38. Isaacson, *The Innovators*, 384.
39. The first spreadsheet usable by personal computers was VisiCalc ("visible calculator"), which was developed by Dan Bricklin and Bob Frankston in Cambridge in 1979. Walter Isaacson, in *The Innovators*, has called Bricklin "the most influential pioneer" in the field of applications software. VisiCalc became the "killer" app for Apple II. Isaacson, 354.
40. Isaacson, *The Innovators*, 411.
41. Tim Berners-Lee with Mark Fischetti, *Weaving the Web: The Original Design and Ultimate Destiny of the World Wide Web by Its Inventor* (San Francisco: Harper, 1999), 4.
42. Isaacson, *The Innovators*, 412.
43. Isaacson, *The Innovators*, 446.
44. Berners-Lee with Fischetti, *Weaving the Web*, 76.
45. France's National Institute for Research in Computer Science and Control became the European administrator for the World Wide Web Consortium.
46. Berners-Lee, *Weaving the Web*, 164–65.
47. "Akamai—About Us," Akamai, accessed August 12, 2023, https://www.akamai.com/company.
48. Berners-Lee, *Weaving the Web*, 157–58.

49. Peter Hall, *Cities of Tomorrow: An Intellectual History of Urban Planning and Design in the Twentieth Century*, 4th ed., (Cambridge, MA: Basil Blackwell, 2014), 445.
50. Dicken, *Global Shift*, 96.
51. "The Wired Guide to 5G," *Wired*, December 31, 2022, https://www.wired.com/story/wired-guide-5g/. This article provides links to maps that depict the extent of 5G, 4G, and 3G coverage throughout the entire service areas of the three major carriers, including Greater Boston.
52. "Digital around the World," *Datareportal*, accessed October 23, 2023, https://datareportal.com/reports/digital-2023-october-global-statshot; "Measuring Digital Development: Facts and Figures, 2022," *International Telecommunication Union*, accessed October 23, 2023; https://www.itu.int/itu-d/reports/statistics/2022/11/24/ff22-mobile-network-coverage/; "Key Internet Statistics to Know in 2023 (Including Mobile)," *Broadband Search*, accessed October 23, 2023, https://www.broadbandsearch.net/blog/internet-statistics.

CHAPTER 5

1. *US Inflation Calculator*, accessed August 26, 2023, https://www.usinflationcalculator.com/.
2. Transatlantic Service, American Airlines System, February 19, 1946, Airline Table Images, https://www.timetableimages.com/ttimages/aa-a046.htm; Pan American World Airways System Timetable, April 1, 1950, Airlines Table Images, https://www.timetableimages.com/ttimages/pa/pa50/pa50.pdf; Trans World Airways Timetable, April 1, 1948, Airline Table Images, https://www.timetableimages.com/ttimages/complete/tw48.htm.
3. James Aloisi, *Massport at 60: Shaping the Future since 1956* (Boston: Massport, 2017), 39–46. *US Inflation Calculator*, accessed August 26, 2023, https://www.usinflationcalculator.com/.
4. Massachusetts Marketing Partnership meeting minutes, September 19, 2022, https://www.visitma.com/wp-content/uploads/2022/12/Meeting-Minutes-from-the-9.19.22-MMP-Board-Meeting.pdf.
5. David Brush, "Logan 2000: A World Class Upgrade for the 21st Century," *ITE Journal*, Institution of Transportation Engineers, June 1997, http://findarticles.com/p/articles/mi_qa3734/is_199706/ai_n8764688/.
6. Jessica Puckett, "Boston's New Airport Terminal Design Brings Some Jet Age Glamor Back to Flying," *Conde Nast Traveler*, December 5, 2023, https://www.cntraveler.com/story/boston-logan-new-airport-terminal-design.
7. "North American Airport Traffic Report 2022," Airports Council International, accessed October 23, 2023, https://airportscouncil.org/intelligence/north-american-airport-traffic-reports/; "Boston-Logan International Airport Monthly Airport Traffic Summary—December, 2023," Massport, https://www.massport.com/sites/default/files/2024-01/avstats-airport-traffic-summary-dec23.pdf; "Logan Airport

International Nonstop Destinations," Massport, accessed April 6, 2024, https://www.massport.com/logan-airport/flights/airlines/nonstop-international-destinations/; OAG, *Megahubs 2023* (2023), https://www.oag.com/megahub-airports-2023#top-50-global.

8. "Going Global: Boston's International Flight Expansion," Massport, March 5, 2014, https://www.massport.com/massport/media/newsroom/going-global-bostons-international-flight-expansion/.

9. Matt Lebovic, "First Nonstop Boston-TLV Route Launched by El Al," *The Times of Israel*, June 29, 2015; David Goodtree, *The Massachusetts-Israel Economic Impact Study, 2016 Edition: The Boston-Israel Power Partnership*, (Boston: New England-Israel Business Council, 2016), http://neibc2.wpengine.com/wp-content/uploads/2016/07/The-Massachusetts-Israel-Economic-Impact-Study-1.pdf.

10. "Boston-Logan International Airport Monthly Airport Traffic Summary—December, 2023," Massport, https://www.massport.com/sites/default/files/2024-01/avstats-airport-traffic-summary-dec23.pdf; "Top50 Global Freight," Transport Topics, accessed April 6, 2024, https://www.ttnews.com/globalfreight/airports/2023.

11. Martin Associates, *Economic Impact of the Port of Boston* (Boston: Massport, 2019), 20, 25, 28.

12. Aloisi, *Massport at 60*, 53, 222; Martin Associates, *Economic Impact*, 20; Hanna Krueger, "The Last of the Seafaring Life at the Boston Fish Pier," *Boston Globe*, February 15, 2020, https://www.bostonglobe.com/2020/02/15/metro/sunrise-sundown-bostons-fish-pier/; Public Policy Center, UMass-Dartmouth, *Navigating the Global Economy: A Comprehensive Analysis of the Massachusetts Maritime Economy* (North Dartmouth, MA: University of Massachusetts-Dartmouth, 2017), 17–18.

13. "Overseas Visitors to U.S. Cities-MSAs," International Trade Administration, (2022), https://www.trade.gov/data-visualization/us-states-cities-visited-overseas-travelers; Rachel Chang, "The 9 Most Visited Cities in the United States," *Condé Nast Traveler*, December 19, 2023, https://www.cntraveler.com/story/most-visited-american-cities.

14. Larry Edelman, "Tourism De Force: How One Man Helped Make Boston a Top Travel Destination," *Boston Globe*, February 18, 2019, https://www.bostonglobe.com/business/2019/02/18/tourism-force-how-one-man-helped-make-boston-top-travel-destination/C8A6cAjpcLOXDxCCe31coJ/story.html.

15. Travel Market Insights, *China 3.0 Report* (Boston: Greater Boston Convention &Visitors Bureau, 2019), https://assets.simpleviewinc.com/simpleview/image/upload/v1/clients/boston/Scott_Johnson_China_3_0_Presentation_ea57aedd-d059-4f44-a0b5-318b564070de.pdf; Christopher Muther, "Could Boston's Tourism Industry Become a Victim of Coronavirus," *Boston Globe*, February 7, 2020, https://www.bostonglobe.com/2020/02/07/lifestyle/could-bostons-tourism-industry-become-victim-coronavirus/; "State Facts and Figures 2023: Massachusetts," Open Doors, accessed April 7, 2024, https://opendoorsdata.org/fact_sheets/state-fact-sheets/.

16. Bruce Ehrlich and Peter Dreier, "The New Boston Discovers the Old Tourism and the Struggle for a Livable City," in *The Tourist City*, Dennis R. Judd and Susan S. Fainstein, eds., (New Haven, CT: Yale University Press, 1999), 161.
17. "Domestic Tourism Visitation & Spending Rebounds in Massachusetts," Massachusetts Executive Office of Economic Development, July 25, 2023, https://www.mass.gov/news/domestic-tourism-visitation-spending-rebounds-in-massachusetts.
18. David O'Donnell, Vice President of the Greater Boston Convention and Visitor Bureau, Interview, November 22, 2019.
19. "Best Hospital Cities Ranking 2019," Medbelle, accessed June 28, 2022, https://www.medbelle.com/best-hospital-cities-world/; Mass General Patient Center, accessed June 28, 2022, https://www.massgeneral.org/international; "Why Has Boston Become a Mecca for Medical Tourism?" Mass General Patient Center, accessed June 28, 2022, https://www.massgeneral.org/international.
20. Peter Canellos, "Aerotropolis: The Rise of a Vibrant New Kind of City—and How Massachusetts Missed a Chance to Have One," *Boston Globe*, October 31, 2010, http://archive.boston.com/bostonglobe/ideas/articles/2010/10/31/aerotropolis/; John D. Kasarda & Greg Lindsay, *Aerotropolis: The Way We'll Live Next* (New York: Farrar, Straus, and Giroux, 2011).
21. "About John Kasarda," Aerotropolis, accessed April 24, 2023, https://aerotropolis.com/airportcity/index.php/about-john-kasarda/.
22. "Dubai Airport Annual Passenger Traffic Jumps 127%," *Reuters*, February 21, 2023, https://www.reuters.com/business/aerospace-defense/dubai-airport-annual-passenger-traffic-jumps-127-2023-02-21/.
23. John D. Kasarda, "Aerotropolis: Airport as the New City Center," *Sodexo 2015 Workplace Trends Report* (2015), http://aerotropolisbusinessconcepts.aero/wp-content/uploads/2016/01/8_Sodexo_Airports_as_the_new_city_center2.pdf.
24. John Kasarda maintains that many established cities in "the U.S. and Western Europe often view airports as nuisances and environmental threats rather than as critical infrastructure to compete and prosper. This has resulted in their neglecting airports while Asia and the Middle East invest heavily to leverage them." "About John Kasarda," Aerotropolis; Canellos, "Aerotropolis," *Boston Globe*, October 31, 2010.
25. John D. Kasarda, "Aerotropolis," *Wiley-Blackwell Encyclopedia of Urban and Regional Studies* (West Sussex, UK: John Wiley & Sons Press, 2017), https://onlinelibrary.wiley.com/doi/abs/10.1002/9781118568446.eurs0436.
26. Stephen J. Appold and John D. Kasarda, "The Airport City Phenomenon: Evidence from Large US Airports," *Urban Studies Journal*, 50(6), May 2013, 1245–246, https//:-DOI:10.1177/0042098012464401.
27. Steve Adams, "Port of Entry Reimagined for a Changing Economy," *Banker & Tradesman*, January 23, 2022, https://www.bankerandtradesman.com/port-of-entry-reimagined-for-a-changingeconomy/.
28. Saskia Sassen, *Cities in a World Economy*, 5th ed., (Thousand Oaks, CA: SAGE Publications, Inc. 2019), 225; Quoted in "Dublin Docklands Development Authority,"

Wikipedia, accessed October 11, 2021, https://en.wikipedia.org/wiki/Dublin_Dock lands_Development_Authority.
29. Boston Redevelopment Authority, *The Seaport Public Realm Plan* (Boston: 1999), 104.
30. Peter Canellos, "Aerotropolis"; Paul Goldberger, "The New Residential Vernacular"/"Glass Is the New White Brick," *Metropolis*, April 1, 2006, https://metropolismag.com/projects/the-new-residential-vernacular/.
31. Boston Redevelopment Authority, *Seaport Public Realm Plan*, 104.
32. *Radio Open Source* host Christopher Lydon has recalled an exchange he had with Mayor Thomas Menino when the Seaport development was getting underway. Lydon remarked about the Seaport architecture: "If you can't come up with something as good as the Back Bay, reproduce it brick-by-brick." Mayor Menino replied, defending the modernistic architecture: "I don't want to be remembered for old buildings." "Concrete Architecture and the New Boston," *Radio Open Source*, March 15, 2016, https://soundcloud.com/radioopensource/concrete-architectue/s-zpt1f.
33. "Institute of Contemporary Arts: Diller Scofidio+Renfro," *Architect: The Journal of the American Institute of Architects*, July 17, 2012, https://www.architectmagazine.com/project-gallery/institute-of-contemporary-art-318; Nicolai Ouroussoff, "Expansive Vistas Inside and Out," *New York Times*, December 8, 2006, https://www.nytimes.com/2006/12/08/arts/design/08ica.html.
34. District Hall, accessed April 24, 2023, https://districthallboston.org/about/.
35. "JLL Rethinks Global City Competitiveness for the Future," JLL, January 23, 2018, http://www.jll.eu/emea/en-gb/news/777/city-types-january2018.
36. "KKR Invests in 400 Summer Street Joint Venture in Boston Seaport," *Business Wire*, September 23, 2021, https://www.businesswire.com/news/home/20210923005285/en/KKR-Invests-in-400-Summer-Street-Joint-Venture-in-Boston-Seaport; Peter Grant and Esther Fung, "Boston Project Draws Chinese Insurance Firms' First U.S. Investments," April 7, 2015, *Wall Street Journal*, https://www.wsj.com/articles/boston-project-draws-chinese-insurance-firms-first-u-s-investments-1428437262.
37. St. Regis Residences, accessed August 1, 2022, https://www.srresidencesboston.com/; One Dalton Boston, accessed June 28, 2022, https://onedalton.com/. Urban scholar Göran Therborn argues that "the current global moment does entail a particular style of urbanism dominated by corporate skyscrapers in [glass-curtain] 'International Style.'" Göran Therborn, *Cities of Power: The Urban, The National, The Popular, The Global* (New York: Verso, 2017), 291, 317.
38. George Turner, "Switzerland, USA and Cayman Top the 2018 Financial Secrecy Index," Tax Justice Network, January 30, 2018. https://www.taxjustice.net/2018/01/30/2018fsi/; Chuck Collins and Emma de Goede, *Towering Excess: The Perils of the Luxury Housing Boom for Bostonians* (Washington, DC: Institute for Policy Studies, September, 2018), 2, 10–11, 27–28.
39. Tran Viet Duc, "Which Coastal Cities Are at Highest Risk from Damaging Floods? New Study Crunches the Numbers," The World Bank, April 19, 2013, https://www.worldbank.org/en/news/feature/2013/08/19/coastal-cities-at-highest-risk-floods.

40. David Abel and Ted Blanco, "Inundation District," 2023, https://vimeo.com/716779520; David Abel, "City Leaders Need to Make Billion-Dollar Decisions to Protect Boston from Sea Level Rise." *The Brink*, January 31, 2024, https://www.bu.edu/articles/2024/city-leaders-need-to-protect-boston-from-sea-level-rise/; Yvonne Abraham, "Stop Bad from Getting Worse," *Boston Globe*, September 5, 2021, https://www.bostonglobe.com/2021/09/04/metro/stop-bad-getting-worse/.
41. Andrew Ryan, "A Brand New Boston Even Whiter Than the Old," *Boston Globe*, December 11, 2017, https://apps.bostonglobe.com/spotlight/boston-racism-image-reality/series/seaport/; Jim O'Connell, Alex Koppelman, Ralph Willmer, "The Evolution of Boston's Seaport District," Virtual Mobile Workshop, American Planning Association National Conference, May 5–7, 2021, https://www.youtube.com/watch?v=D4IqwLPA3Ds&t=5s; Cameron Sperance, "Second and Third Chances," *Boston Sunday Globe*, September 12, 2021, https://bostonglobe.newspapers.com/image/764552333/; Devra First, "As Diners Return to Tables, Restaurants Reach for a Rebirth," *Boston Globe*, May 9, 2021, https://bostonglobe.newspapers.com/image/734029812/.
42. O'Connell, Koppelman, and Willmer, "The Evolution of Boston's Seaport District"; "Average Rent in Boston, MA," RentHop, accessed April 8, 2024, https://www.renthop.com/average-rent-in/seaport-district-boston-ma; "Boston, MA Real Estate Housing Market," Zero Down, accessed April 8, 2024, https://zerodown.com/housing-market-analysis/boston--ma; Cameron Sperance, "Boston Gets a Second and Third Chance to Build Affordable Neighborhoods. Will It? *Boston.com*, September 8, 2021, https://www.boston.com/real-estate/developments-construction/2021/09/08/boston-gets-more-chances-build-affordable-neighborhoods/. "Affordable" housing units in Boston are units that are designated for families earning between 50% and 120% of the area's median income, which was $112,150 in 2023. Tina Woodard, "Mattapan Station Housing Opens Its Doors," *Boston Globe*, April 25, 2023, https://www.bostonglobe.com/2023/04/25/metro/mattapan-station-housing-development-opens-its-doors/.
43. Beth Treffeisen, "Seaport Grows into Boston's Other High-End Retail Hot Spot," *Boston Business Journal*, August 18, 2021, https://www.bizjournals.com/boston/news/2022/08/18/seaport-boston-luxury-retail-back-bay.html.
44. Jon Chesto, "Harvard Owns Roughly One-Third of Allston. Now It Needs to Win Over the Residents," *Boston Globe*, September 4, 2021, https://www.bostonglobe.com/2021/09/04/business/harvard-owns-roughly-one-third-allston-now-it-needs-win-over-residents/.
45. "Suffolk Downs," HYM Investment Group, accessed April 24, 2023, https://www.hyminvestments.com/suffolk-downs/.

CHAPTER 6

1. Marc Levinson, *Outside the Box: How Globalization Changed from Moving Stuff to Spreading Ideas* (Princeton, NJ: Princeton University Press, 2020), 217.

2. Zheng Liu and Thuy Lan Nguyen, "Global Supply Chain Pressures and U.S. Inflation," Federal Reserve Bank of San Francisco, June 20, 2023, https://www.frbsf.org/research-and-insights/publications/economic-letter/2023/06/global-supply-chain-pressures-and-us-inflation/. The US inflation rate for 2021 was 4.7% and 8% for 2022. Hiranmaya Srinivasan, "U.S. Inflation Rate by Year: 1929–2024," Investopedia, May 2, 2024, https://www.investopedia.com/inflation-rate-by-year-7253832.
3. Walmart became a pioneer in outsourcing manufacturing to East Asia, when it sent its first buyers to Hong Kong and Taiwan in the late 1970s in search of cheap manufactured goods. By the mid-1980s, the company was contracting with factories in mainland China to provide the lowest-priced goods. These trade relations opened the way for companies to outsource manufacturing of various parts to the cheapest providers worldwide. In developing supply chains from Asia, Walmart also made logistics increasingly more efficient and less costly.
4. Winfield M. Thompson, "Leathers from Many Lands Sold in Boston," *Boston Globe*, May 8, 1904, https://bostonglobe.newspapers.com/image/431005380/.
5. H. Kent Bowen, Robert S. Huckman, Carin-Isabel Knoop, "New Balance Athletic Shoe, Inc.," Harvard Business School Case Study 9-606-094, June 30. 2008, https://www.hbs.edu/faculty/Pages/item.aspx?num=33243.
6. Kim Moody, "Why It's High Time to Move on from 'Just-In-Time' Supply Chains," *The Guardian*, October 11, 2021, https://www.theguardian.com/commentisfree/2021/oct/11/just-in-time-supply-chains-logistical-capitalism; Jon Chesto, "Escalating Trade War Hits Home for Many Local Businesses," *Boston Globe*, September 5, 2019, https://www.bostonglobe.com/business/2019/09/05/escalating-trade-war-hits-home-for-many-local-businesses/cYMy74ewKlY237rYhI8fvJ/story.html. In 2022, Amazon bought iRobot, which also makes military robots for surveillance and bomb disposal. iRobot is considered the "godfather," according to the *Boston Globe*, of Boston's robotics industry. Hiawatha Bray and Anissa Gardizy, "iRobot Roombas Its Way into Amazon's Arms, *Boston Globe*, August 5, 2022, https://www.bostonglobe.com/2022/08/05/business/amazon-acquire-irobot-17-billion-deal-local-robotics-firm-faces-challenges/.
7. Michael E. Porter, *Competitive Advantage: Creating and Sustaining Superior Performance* (New York: The Free Press, 1985), 45–48; Levinson, *Outside the Box*, 130.
8. Thomas L. Friedman, *The World Is Flat: A Brief History of the Twenty-First Century* (New York: Farrar, Straus, and Giroux, 2007), 457, 465. Another way of expressing this concept is the "global innovation network," which seeks to explain the web of collaborative interactions between different organizations engaged in knowledge production that is related to innovation. The "global innovation network" concept acknowledges how the technology development process has become more complex and globalized. Under the traditional paradigm, research was primarily undertaken within a corporation or at an affiliated university. Today, research can take place with various partners and sub-contractors at locations across the world, although usually in specialized research clusters. OECD, *The Links between Global Value Chains and Global Innovation Networks: An Exploration*, OECD Science, Technology and Innovation Policy Papers, No. 37, 2017, https://doi.org/10.1787/76d78fbb-en.

9. Jonathan Saltzman, "'Monumental': FDA Approves First CRISPR-Based Gene-Editing Drug, Marking Breakthrough for Sickle Cell Disease," *Boston Globe*, December 8, 2023, https://www.bostonglobe.com/2023/12/08/business/crispr-approved-fda-sickle-cell-gene-editing/.
10. Vertex Pharmaceuticals Incorporated, *Annual Report for the Year Ending December 31, 2019, to the U.S. Securities & Exchange Commission*, https://investors.vrtx.com/sec-filings/sec-filing/10-k/0000875320-20-000007, 32.
11. Barry Werth, *The Antidote: Inside the World of New Pharma* (New York: Simon & Schuster, 2014), 168.
12. Werth, *The Antidote*, 239.
13. The White House, *Building Resilient Supply Chains, Revitalizing American Manufacturing, and Fostering Broad-Base Growth: 100-Day Reviews under Executive Order 14017*, June, 2021, 9–10, https://www.whitehouse.gov/wp-content/uploads/2021/06/100-day-supply-chain-review-report.pdf.
14. Rena M. Conti, Yashna Shivdasani, Neriman Beste Kaygisiz, Ernst R. Berndt, "The Geography of Prescription Pharmaceuticals Supplied to the U.S.: Levels, Trends and Implications," National Bureau of Economic Research, Working Paper 26524, December, 2019, https://www.nber.org/papers/w26524; Rena M. Conti, Ernst R. Berndt, Neriman Beste Kaygisiz, Yashna Shivdasani, "We *Still* Don't Know Who Makes This Drug," *Health Affairs*, February 7, 2020, https://www.healthaffairs.org/do/10.1377/hblog20200203.83247/full/.
15. Conti, et al., "We Still Don't Know"; White House, *Building Resilient Supply Chains*, 15.
16. Newmark Knight Frank, "Boston Life Science Market, Research 2Q 2020," Newmark Knoght Frank, 2020, https://www.ngkf.com/storage/uploads/documents/2Q20-Boston-Life-Science-Market.pdf.
17. Cassie McGrath, "Six Takeaways from Moderna CEO on Covid, Future Treatments," *Boston Business Journal*, April 5, 2022, https://www.bizjournals.com/boston/news/2022/04/05/six-takeaways-from-with-moderna-ceo.html.
18. McGrath, "Six Takeaways from Moderna CEO"; Jennifer Kates, Cynthia Cox, and Josh Michaud, "How Much Could Covid-19 Vaccines Cost the U.S. after Commercialization?" Kaiser Family Foundation, March 10, 2023, https://www.kff.org/coronavirus-covid-19/issue-brief/how-much-could-covid-19-vaccines-cost-the-u-s-after-commercialization/; Eric Saganowsky, "After Nearly $1 Billion in Research Funding, Moderna Takes More than $1.5 Billion Vaccine Order from U.S.," Fierce Pharma, August 12, 2020, https://www.fiercepharma.com/pharma/after-nearly-1b-research-funding-moderna-takes-1-5b-coronavirus-vaccine-order-from-u-s.
19. "Why Norwood?: Background on Moderna Manufacturing," Moderna, March, 2020, https://www.modernatx.com/moderna-blog/moderna-manufacturing-why norwood.
20. "Moderna and Catalent Announce Collaboration for Fill-Finish Manufacturing of Moderna's Covid-19 Vaccine Candidate," Catalent, June 25, 2020, https://www.catalent.com/catalent-news/moderna-and-catalent-announce-collaboration-for-fill-finish-manufacturing-of-modernas-covid-19-vaccine-candidate/; "Moderna:

Spikevax," Covid-19 Vaccine Tracker, December 2, 2022, https://covid19.trackvaccines.org/vaccines/22/.
21. Naomi Kresge, "Moderna Vaccine Production Is Gearing Up, Partner Lonza Says," *Bloomberg*, November 19, 2020, https://www.bloomberg.com/news/articles/2020-11-19/moderna-vaccine-production-is-gearing-up-partner-lonza-says; Mark Gartsbeyn, "Most of Moderna's Covid Vaccine Will Be Made in Massachusetts, Co-founder Says," *boston.com*, December 1, 2020, https://www.boston.com/news/coronavirus/2020/12/01/moderna-coronavirus-vaccine-production-norwood-massachusetts.
22. "Covid-19," BioNTech, accessed September 8, 2020, https://biontech.de/covid-19; Erin Tiernan, "Massachusetts Drug Maker Pfizer Could Have 100 Million Doses of 'Most Advanced' Coronavirus Vaccine This Year," *Boston Herald*, July 20, 2020, https://www.bostonherald.com/2020/07/30/massachusetts-drug-maker-pfizer-could-have-100-million-doses-of-most-advanced-coronavirus-vaccine-this-year/; Chad P. Brown and Thomas J. Bollyky, "How Covid-19 Vaccine Supply Chains Emerged in the Midst of a Pandemic," *The World Economy*, February, 2022, https://www.ncbi.nlm.nih.gov/pmc/articles/PMC8447169/.
23. "Site Statistics, Cambridge, Massachusetts," Pfizer, accessed April 15, 2024, https://www.pfizer.com/und/science/research-development/centers/ma_cambridge.
24. "Pfizer Introduces New Logo in a 'Shift from Commerce to Science,'" PMLive, January 27, 2021, https://pmlive.com/pharma_news/pfizer_introduces_new_logo_in_a_shift_from_commerce_to_science_1360913/.
25. Carl Zimmer, "Inside Johnson & Johnson's Nonstop Hunt for a Coronavirus Vaccine," *New York Times*, January 13, 2021, https://www.nytimes.com/2020/07/17/health/coronavirus-vaccine-johnson-janssen.html; Jonathan Saltzman and Damien Garde, "Inside the Quest for a Vaccine," *Boston Globe*, November 10, 2020, https://www.bostonglobe.com/2020/11/10/metro/inside-quest-covid-19-cure/.
26. Massachusetts Biotechnology Council, *MassBio 2023 Industry Snapshot*, 2023, https://readymag.com/MassBio/4387300/.
27. MassBio, *State of Possible 2025 Report: Advancing Massachusetts Leadership in the Life Sciences*, June, 2020, 13, https://www.massbio.org/wp-content/uploads/2020/06/MassBio_State-of-Possible-2025-Report_FINAL-6-25-20.pdf.
28. MassBio, *State of Possible 2025 Report*, 23; Massachusetts Biotechnology Council, *MassBio 2023 Industry Snapshot*; "Modernizing the Way Drugs Are Made: A Transition to Continuous Manufacturing," US Food & Drug Administration, accessed October 29, 2020, https://www.fda.gov/drugs/news-events-human-drugs/modernizing-way-drugs-are-made-transition-continuous-manufacturing.
29. Henry Schwan, "Sanofi Opens 'Holy Grail' of Drug Manufacturing Facilities in Framingham," *MetroWest Daily News*, October 16, 2019; Sanofi Genzyme, accessed July 21, 2020, https://www.sanofigenzyme.com/en/about-us/our-history.
30. Jonathan Saltzman, "Thermo Fisher Just Opened a $180 Million Plant. Executives Are Already Talking about Expanding," *Boston Globe*, September 20, 2023, https://www.bostonglobe.com/2023/09/20/business/thermo-fisher-plainville-expanding/.
31. Ryan Cross, "The Broad Won the Biggest Patent Fight Yet, But the Rivalry over Gene Editing Is Still Simmering," *Boston Globe*, April 4, 2021, https://www.bostonglobe

Notes to Pages 132–140 **269**

.com/2022/04/04/business/broad-won-biggest-crispr-patent-fight-yet-rivalry-over-gene-editing-is-still-simmering/; "Vertex Expands into New Disease Areas and Enhances Gene Editing Capabilities through Expanded Collaboration with CRISPR Therapeutics and Acquisition of Exonics Therapeutics," Vertex, June 6, 2020, https://investors.vrtx.com/news-releases/news-release-details/vertex-expands-new-disease-areas-and-enhances-gene-editing; Edward Ingham, "CRIPR Therapeutics: I Sense a Long Bull Run as First Approval Approaches," *Seeking Alpha*, February 24, 2023, https://seekingalpha.com/article/4581813-crispr-therapeutics-long-bull-run-possible-first-approval-approaches.

32. "Paving the Way for Tomorrow's Cures," Pathway Devens MA, accessed February, 2023, https://devens.pathwayksp.com/. Of the project's first three tenants, two are in the climate tech field and one is in biotech. Greg Ryan, "Coming off Hat Trick, Devens Developer to Build a 4th Manufacturing Site, *Boston Business Journal*, May 17, 2024, https://www.bizjournals.com/boston/news/2024/05/17/devens-manufacturing-site.html.

33. Sharon Begley, "Bio-Innovation Center Will Aim to Protect State's Preeminence," *Boston Globe*, November 25, 2019, http://wwwo.bostonglobe.com/business/2019/11/25/bio-innovation-center-will-aim-protect-state-preeminence/81dUgro6Q79IHTjmOoBoxK/story.html.

CHAPTER 7

1. Sheldon Krimsky, *Genetic Alchemy: The Social History of the Recombinant DNA Controversy* (Cambridge, MA: MIT Press, 1982), 305–7.
2. Bryan Marquand and Jonathan Saltzman, "Pandemic Work Cements Broad's Legacy," *Boston Globe*, May 8, 2021, https://www.bostonglobe.com/2021/05/07/business/eli-broads-medical-research-legacy-will-touch-almost-whole-world/.
3. Peter Hall, *Cities of Tomorrow: An Intellectual History of Urban Planning and Design in the Twentieth Century*, 4th ed. (Hoboken, NJ: Wiley-Blackwell, 2014), 445.
4. Quoted in Robert Buderi, *Where Futures Converge: Kendall Square and the Making of a Global Innovation Hub* (Cambridge, MA: MIT Press, 2022), 252.
5. Merritt Roe Smith, "God Speed the Institute," in David Kaiser, ed., *Becoming MIT: Moments of Decision* (Cambridge, MA: MIT Press, 2010), 28.
6. Edward B. Robert & Charles Eesley, *Entrepreneurial Impact: The Role of MIT* (Kansas City, MO: Kauffman Foundation, 2009), 1, 6; Jonathan Saltzman and Damian Garde, "Inside the Quest for a Vaccine," *Boston Globe*, November 10, 2020, https://www.bostonglobe.com/2020/11/10/metro/inside-quest-covid-19-cure/; Michael Kuchta and Karen Weintraub, *Born in Cambridge: People and Ideas that Shaped Our World* (Cambridge, MA: MIT Press, 2022), 283.
7. Lynne G. Zucker, Michael R. Darby, and Marilyn B. Brewer, "Intellectual Human Capital and the Birth of U.S. Biotechnology Enterprises," *American Economic Review*, 88, No. 1 (March 1998), 290–306. Zucker and Darby contend that the United States has more than 50% of the world's biotechnology stars. Lynn G. Zucker and Michael R. Darby, "Movement of Star Scientists and Engineers and High-Tech Firm Entry,"

NBER working paper No. 12172 (April 2006, revised June, 2014), https://www.nber.org/papers/w12172.
8. Elizabeth Cooney, "I Find This Disease Just So Amazing," *Boston Globe*, March 10, 2021, https://bostonglobe.newspapers.com/image/719872581.
9. Robin Wolfe Scheffler, "Genetown: The Urbanization of the Boston Area Biotechnology Industry" (paper presented at Massachusetts Historical Society Environmental History Seminar, January 28, 2020), 27, 2, 9; Robin Wolfe Scheffler, "David Clem: Building Genetown," *The Metropolitan*, March 2023, https://themetropole.blog/2023/03/28/david-clem-building-genetown/.
10. Enrico Moretti, *The New Geography of Jobs* (Boston: Houghton Mifflin Harcourt, 2012), 15, 150–51, 182.
11. Walter Isaacson, *The Innovators: How a Group of Hackers, Geniuses, and Geeks Created the Digital Revolution* (New York: Simon & Shuster, 2014), 217, https://www.bostonindicators.org/-/media/indicators/boston-indicators-reports/report-files/bostons-booming-2018.pdf.
12. Massachusetts Biotechnology Council, *MassBio 2023 Industry Snapshot*, 2023, https://readymag.com/MassBio/4387300/; Mass General Brigham, *Economic Impact Report 2023*, accessed June 14, 2023, http://www.massgeneralbrigham.org/content/dam/mgb-global/en/about/documents/economic-impact-2023.pdf.
13. Massachusetts Biotechnology Council, *MassBio 2024 Industry Snapshot*, https://readymag.website/MassBio/2024IndustrySnapshot/44/; Rowan Walroth, "Mass Bio: 40K New Biopharma Jobs Predicated in Next 3 Years," *Boston Business Journal*, August 24, 2021, https://www.bizjournals.com/boston/news/2021/08/25/massbio-industry-snapshot-2021.html.
14. Massachusetts Biotechnology Council, *MassBio 2024 Industry Snapshot*, https://readymag.website/MassBio/2024IndustrySnapshot/44.
15. Startup Genome claims that the four most mature startup ecosystems in the world are Boston, Silicon Valley-Bay Area, New York, and London. Other top-rated biotech ecosystems are located in Tel Aviv-Jerusalem, Shanghai, and Beijing. Startup Genome, *Global Startup Ecosystem Report 2022*, https://startupgenome.com/report/gser2022; Luc Shuster and Peter Ciurczak, *Boston's Booming . . . But for Whom?: Building Shared Prosperity in a Time of Growth* (Boston: Boston Foundation, Boston Indicators, 2018), 38.
16. Startup Genome, *Global Startup Ecosystem Report 2019*, 57–65, https://startupgenome.com/reports/global-startup-ecosystem-report-2019; World Intellectual Property Organization, INSEAD, Cornell SC Johnson College of Business, and PwCStrategy, *The Global Innovation Index 2018*, 11th ed., 2018, xxxix, https://www.wipo.int/edocs/pubdocs/en/wipo_pub_gii_2018.pdf. Site selection consultants Hickey & Associates have ranked Boston #1 in the world for innovation as well as #1 for biotechnology and for pharmaceuticals and #2 for medical science. In state-oriented rankings for 2020, the Milken Institute *State Technology and Science Index* rated Massachusetts #1, while the *Bloomberg State Innovation Index* rated Massachusetts #2, after California. Hickey & Associates, *Global Innovation Hubs: 2019 Report*,

https://www.hickeyandassociates.com/globalinnovationhubs/; Milken Institute *State Technology and Science Index*, https://milkeninstitute.org/report/state-technology-and-science-index-2020; Shelly Hagan and Wei Lu, "California, Massachusetts Rank as Most Innovative States," *Bloomberg/Quint*, June 23, 2020, https://www.bloombergquint.com/global-economics/california-massachusetts-rank-as-most-innovative-u-s-states.

17. Thomas L. Friedman, *The World Is Flat: A Brief History of the Twenty-First Century* (New York: Farrar, Straus, and Giroux, 2007), 457, 465.

18. Yossi Sheffi, *Logistics Clusters: Delivering Value and Driving Growth* (Cambridge, MA: MIT Press, 2012), 54; Michael E. Porter, "Clusters and the New Economics," *Harvard Business Review* (November-December, 1998), https://hbr.org/1998/11/clusters-and-the-new-economics-of-competition. In an economic development strategy for Massachusetts, *The Competitive Advantage of Massachusetts* (1991), Michael Porter identified four primary clusters for the state to target for support: 1) healthcare (biotechnology was not yet consequential enough to merit specific attention), 2) knowledge creation services, 3) information technology, and 4) financial services. Michael Porter, *The Competitive Advantage of Massachusetts*, (Boston: Massachusetts Office of the Secretary of State, 1991), 53.

19. Sheffi, *Logistics Clusters*, 54. A study by MIT researchers of the Massachusetts biotechnology cluster stresses four primary factors driving innovation clusters: funding, human talent, legal protections, and social mores that encourage innovation. Mark R. Trusheim, Ernst R. Berndt, Fiona Murray, and Scott Stern, "American Entrepreneurial Chaos or Collaborative Industrial Policy: The Emergence of the Massachusetts Biotechnology Super-Cluster," *Proceeding of CONCORD 2020: 2nd European Conference on Corporate R&D*, February 25, 2010, https://www.researchgate.net/publication/308899856_CONCORDi_2010_Summary_Report/link/57f618a008ae8da3ce571e90/download; Lisa Pham, "UK's Cambridge Tries to Catch Up with Younger, Innovative Peer," *Bloomberg*, April 7, 2023, https://www.bloomberg.com/news/articles/2023-04-07/uk-s-cambridge-tries-to-catch-up-with-younger-innovative-peer.

20. Hall, *Cities of Tomorrow*, 447; Robert M. Krim with Alan R. Earls, *Boston Made: From Revolution to Robotics—Innovations That Changed the World* (Watertown, MA: Imagine Books, 2021), 2–15.

21. Robert D. Atkinson, Mark Muro, Jacob Whiton, *The Case for Growth Centers: How to Spread Tech Innovation across America* (Washington, DC: Brookings Institution, 2019), 38; Edward L. Glaeser, ed., *Agglomeration Economics* (Chicago: University of Chicago Press, 2010), 1; Edward L. Glaeser, *Triumph of the City: How Our Greatest Invention Makes Us Richer, Smarter, Greener, Healthier, and Happier* (New York: Penguin Group, 2011), 6, 28.

22. "Philips Research Cambridge—North America," Philips, accessed August 22, 2020, https://www.philips.com/a-w/research/locations/cambridge-north-america.html. Besides its location in Cambridge, Philips maintains "innovation hubs" in Eindhoven, Netherlands, Bangalore, and Shanghai.

23. Jon Chesto and Robert Weisman, "Cambridge Picked as National Hub for New Federal Health Research Agency," *Boston Globe*, September 26, 2023, https://www.bostonglobe.com/2023/09/26/business/cambridge-arpa-h-hub/.
24. Richard Florida, "Where US Tech Investment Is Growing the Most," Bloomberg, December 7, 2023, https://www.bloomberg.com/news/articles/2023-12-07/san-francisco-bay-area-nyc-boston-dominate-vc-investment-in-us; Massachusetts Biotechnology Council, *Massachusetts 2021 Biopharma Funding Report* (2022), https://www.massbio.org/industry-snapshot/2021-massachusetts-biopharma-funding-report/; Richard Florida and Ian Hathaway, *The Rise of the Global Startup City* (The Center for American Entrepreneurship, 2018), 18, https://startupsusa.org/global-startup-cities/; Massachusetts Biotechnology Council, *MassBio 2020 Industry Snapshot*, https://readymag.com/MassBio/2022IndustrySnapshot/2022-industry-snapshot-7/.
25. A valuable listing of Greater Boston venture capital firms is provided by The Capital Network, https://thecapitalnetwork.org/about/.
26. "Betting on Biotech," *Pitchbook*, July 8, 2020, https://pitchbook.com/news/reports/q3-2020-pitchbook-analyst-note-betting-on-biotech.
27. "Moderna, Inc." *Google Finance*, accessed August 31, 2021 and "March 4, 2025," https://www.google.com/finance/quote/MRNA:NASDAQ.
28. Third Rock Venture website, accessed November 10, 2020, https://www.thirdrockventures.com/; Luke Timmerman, "Third Rock Ventures. One of Biotech's Daring Investors, Raise $616M for More Startups, *Forbes*, October 31, 2016, https://www.forbes.com/sites/luketimmerman/2016/10/31/third-rock-ventures-one-of-biotechs-daring-investors-raises-616m-for-more-startups/; "Betting on Biotech," *Pitchbook*, July 8, 2020, https://pitchbook.com/news/reports/q3-2020-pitchbook-analyst-note-betting-on-biotech; Flagship Pioneering, accessed November 10, 2020, https://www.flagshippioneering.com/; Mark Terry, "Can Moderna Live up to the Hype?: mRNA Company Increases IPO Goal to $600 Million," *BioSpace*, November 29, 2018, https://www.fiercebiotech.com/biotech/bain-creates-1-1b-fund-for-fresh-round-life-science-bets; Mass General Brigham Innovation, accessed August 22, 2023, https://innovation.partners.org/; "Justine Hofherr, "10 Angel Groups Every Boston Entrepreneur Should Know," *Built in Boston*, January 20, 2020, http://www.builtinboston.com/2016/09/13/angel-groups-boston; MassChallenge, accessed February 12, 2022, https://masschallenge.org.
29. Mass General Brigham Ventures, accessed March 3, 2021, http://www.partnersinnovationfund.com/.
30. Paul Stephan, "Can Arena Bioworks Upend the Traditional Scientific Research Model in the US?" *Stat*, February 2, 2024, https://www.statnews.com/2024/02/02/arena-bioworks-scientific-research-model-funding-academia/.
31. MassChallenge, accessed February 12, 2022, https://masschallenge.org/startups.
32. Cambridge Innovation Center, accessed April 16, 2024, https://cic.com/cambridge/.
33. Hannah Green, "Tim Rowe, "Co-Founder and CEO of CIC, Talks of Latest Expansions," *Boston Inno*, https://www.bizjournals.com/boston/inno/stories/news/2022

/12/22/tim-rowe-cic-expansion-plans.html; Buderi, *Where Futures Converge*, 137–45; Rodrigo Martinez, Chief Marketing & Experience Officer, Cambridge Innovation Center, interview by author, March 1, 2023.
34. Wolf Greenfield, accessed February, 2022, https://www.wolfgreenfield.com/technologies/biotech.
35. Alexandria Real Estate Equities, Inc., "2020 Form 10-K Annual Report," US Securities & Exchange Commission, https://www.sec.gov/ix?doc=/Archives/edgar/data/1035443/000103544321000044/are-20201231.htm.
36. Alexandria Real Estate Equities, Inc., "2019 Form-10K Annual Report," US Securities & Exchange Commission, https://www.sec.gov/ix?doc=/Archives/edgar/data/1035443/000103544320000042/a4q1910-k.htm.
37. Rowan Walrath, "Building Bio: Massachusetts Has a Chance to Be a Manufacturing Leader. Can We Meet Our Moment?, *Boston Business Journal*, July 27, 2023, https://www.bizjournals.com/boston/news/2023/07/27/mass-biomanufacturing.html.
38. Tim Logan, "With Development Slowing, Life Science Sector a Bright Spot, *Boston Globe*, December 4, 2020, https://www.bostonglobe.com/2020/12/03/business/despite-development-slowdown-states-life-science-industry-keeps-building/.
39. Kate Sheridan, "For Charles River Labs, These Are Boom Times," *Boston Globe*, March 5, 2019; *Charles River Insights*, accessed July 21, 2020, https://www.criver.com/insights. For a map and inventory of all the contract research organizations in the world, see Contract Research Map, accessed February 25, 2021, https://www.contractresearchmap.com/.
40. Addgene, accessed April 16, 2024, https://www.addgene.org/; Anthony Regalado, "The Scientific Swap Meet Behind the Gene-Editing Boom," *MIT Tech Review*, April 8, 2016, https://www.technologyreview.com/s/601156/the-scientific-swap-meet-behind-the-gene-editing-boom; Daniel J. Monti, Laurel Smith-Doerr, and James McQuaid, *Immigrant Entrepreneurs in the Massachusetts Biotechnology Industry* (Malden, MA: Immigrant Learning Center, 2007), 9, https://www.immigrationresearch.org/system/files/Immigrant_Entrepreneurs_in_Biotech_final_5-25-07.pdf.
41. Massachusetts Life Sciences Center, accessed October 27, 2020, https://www.masslifesciences.com/.
42. "BIO Sets the BUSINESS WORLD RECORDS™ Title for the Largest Business Partnering Event," BIO, June 6, 2018, https://www.bio.org/press-release/bio-sets-guinness-world-records%E2%84%A2-title-largest-business-partnering-event; Boston-Paris Technology Summit™ website, May 18, 2017, https://bostonbiotechnologysummit.com/2017-event/.
43. AnnaLee Saxenian, *Regional Advantage: Culture and Competition in Silicon Valley and Route 128* (Cambridge, MA: Harvard University Press, 1996), 16–17.
44. Startup Genome, *Global Startup Ecosystem Report 2022*, 221; Yasmin Amer and Bart Tocci, "The Need for Equity in the Massachusetts Startup Economy," WBUR Radio Boston, https://www.wbur.org/radioboston/2023/02/07/the-need-for-equity-in-the-massachusetts-startup-economy.

45. Scott Kirsner, "Some 'Boston-Based' Companies Are Hardly Here, *Boston Globe*, November 28, 2021, https://www.bostonglobe.com/2021/11/28/business/some-boston-based-companies-are-hardly-here/; Scott Kirsner, "Who's Back in the Office? Who's Cutting Costs? We Surveyed the Boston Startup Scene," *Boston Globe*, September 6, 2022, https://www.bostonglobe.com/2022/09/06/business/we-surveyed-boston-startup-scene-about-future-work-heres-what-people-said/.
46. Daniel Faggella, "Artificial Intelligence in Boston: An Overview of Startups, Funding, and Trends," Emerj, October 14, 2019, https://emerj.com/ai-market-research/artificial-intelligence-boston-overview-startups-funding-trends/; The Innovation Institute at the Massachusetts Technology Collaborative, *The Annual Index of the Massachusetts Innovation Economy, 2021 Edition*, 2021, 33, https://masstech.org/index.
47. Massachusetts Technology Collaborative, *Insights & Indicators*, November, 2022, https://infogram.com/november-2022-index-newsletter-1h7g6k0q9q7go2o?live; Faggella, "Artificial Intelligence in Boston."
48. Will Knight, "Amazon's New Robots Are Rolling Out an Automation Revolution," *Wired*, June 26, 2023, https://www.wired.com/story/amazons-new-robots-automation-revolution/; Aaron Pressman, "Before the iRobot Acquisition, Massachusetts Was Already at the Forefront of All Things Robot," *Boston Globe*, August 15, 2022, https://www.bostonglobe.com/2022/08/15/business/amazon-irobot-how-massachusetts-became-leader-robotics-industry/; Lucia Maffei, "The iRobot Effect: The Roomba Maker Helped Turn the Bay State into a Robotics Hub over the Past Three Decades," *Boston Business Journal*, March 14, 2024, https://www.bizjournals.com/boston/news/2024/03/14/centerpiece_the-irobot-connection.html; Lucia Maffei, "The iRobot Diaspora: 15 Companies Started or Led by Former iRoboteers," *Boston Business Journal*, March 14, 2024, https://www.bizjournals.com/boston/news/2024/03/14/irobot-spinouts-startups-former-employees.html.
49. Boston Dynamics AI Institute, accessed July 10, 2022, https://theaiinstitute.com/.
50. MassRobotics, "5 Year Impact Report, 2017–2022," 2022, https://www.massrobotics.org/startups/5-year-impact-report/; MassRobotics, accessed July 9, 2023, https://www.massrobotics.org/; MassRobotics, "5 Year Impact Report, 2017–2022," 2022, https://www.massrobotics.org/startups/5-year-impact-report/.
51. David Scharfenberg, "The Most Interesting Startup in America Is in Massachusetts. You've Probably Never Hear of It," *Boston Globe*, June 1, 2023, https://www.bostonglobe.com/2023/06/01/opinion/vulcanforms-3-d-printing-additive-manufacturing/; Steve Lohr, "3-D Printing Grows Beyond Its Industrial Roots," *New York Times*, July 3, 2022, https://www.nytimes.com/2022/07/03/business/3d-printing-vulcanforms.html; Jörg Bromberger, Julian Ilg, and Ana Maria Miranda, "The Mainstreaming of Additive Manufacturing," McKinsey, March 15, 2022, https://www.mckinsey.com/capabilities/operations/our-insights/the-mainstreaming-of-additive-manufacturing.
52. Formlabs, accessed July 12, 2023, http://www.formlabs.com. Davide Sher, "Boston Is the Heart of Boston's New 3D Printing Sector," VoxelMatters, August 27, 2018, https://www.voxelmatters.com/boston-3d-printing-america/#.

53. Startup Genome, *The Global Startup Ecosystem Report: Cleantech Edition*, 2023, accessed November 30, 2023, https://startupgenome.com/article/global-cleantech-ranking-top-25-plus-runners-up.
54. The Engine, MIT, accessed June 3, 2022, https://www.engine.xyz/.
55. The Engine, accessed July 15, 2023, https://engine.xyz/; Massachusetts Clean Energy Center, *2022 Massachusetts Clean Energy Industry Report*, 2022, 7, 13, https://www.masscec.com/resources/2022-massachusetts-clean-energy-industry-report; Rowan Jacobsen, "Can Boston's Energy Innovators Save the World?" *Boston Magazine*, May 31, 2023, https://www.bostonmagazine.com/news/2023/05/31/boston-clean-green-energy-climate/.
56. Mark Muro, Julian Jacobs, Sifan Liu, "Building AI Cities: How to Spread the Benefits of an Emerging Technology across More of America," Brookings Institution, July 20, 2023, https://www.brookings.edu/articles/building-ai-cities-how-to-spread-the-benefits-of-an-emerging-technology-across-more-of-america/.
57. Scott Kirsner, "AI Talent Is Leaving Massachusetts. The State Is Hustling to Catch Up," *Boston Globe*, April 24, 2024, https://www.bostonglobe.com/2024/04/24/business/ai-talent-leaving-massachusetts/; Amazon Science, accessed April 15, 2022, https://www.amazon.science/locations/boston-cambridge-and-north-reading; "Google Research: Cambridge," Google Research, accessed April 15, 2022, https://research.google/locations/cambridge/ "Microsoft Research Lab—New England," Microsoft Research, accessed April 15, 2022, https://www.microsoft.com/en-us/research/lab/microsoft-research-new-england/.
58. MIT Schwarzman College of Computing, accessed June 3, 2022, https://computing.mit.edu/about/.

CHAPTER 8

1. Saskia Sassen maintains that immigration should be understood "as a set of processes whereby global elements are localized, international labor markets are constituted, and cultures from all over the world are de- and re-territorialized." This "puts them right there at the center along with the internationalization of capital, as a fundamental aspect of globalization." Saskia Sassen, *Cities in a World Economy*, 1st ed. (Thousand Oaks, CA: Pine Forge Press, 1996), 218.
2. Marie Price and Lisa Benton-Short, "Immigrants and World Cities: From the Hyper-Diverse to the Bypassed," *GeoJournal*, (June, 2007), https://www.researchgate.net/publication/226194363_Immigrants_and_world_cities_From_the_hyper-diverse_to_the_bypassed; Luc Shuster and Peter Ciurczak, *Boston's Booming . . . But for Whom?: Building Shared Prosperity in a Time of Growth*, https://www.bostonindicators.org/-/media/indicators/boston-indicators-reports/report-files/bostons-booming-2018.pdf; Marilynn S. Johnson, *The New Bostonians: How Immigrants Have Transformed the Metro Region Since the 1980s* (Amherst, MA: University of Massachusetts Press, 2015), 33-34. As of 2014, 43.6% of the foreign-born population

had achieved US citizenship, while 26.9% had legal permanent resident status, 4.0% were temporary residents with authorization to live in the country, and 25.5% were estimated to be undocumented. Ryan Nunn, Jimmy O'Donnell, and Jay Shambaugh, "A Dozen Facts about Immigration," The Hamilton Project/Brookings, October, 2018, 1, 5, https://www.brookings.edu/wp-content/uploads/2018/10/ImmigrationFacts_Web_1008_540pm.pdf.

3. "Emigration, 1801–1921," *The Encyclopedia of the Irish in America*, ed. Michael Glazier (Notre Dame, IN: University of Notre Dame Press, 1999), 260; Oscar Handlin, *Boston's Immigrants, 1790–1880: A Study in Acculturation* (New York: Atheneum, 1972), 49. https://docs.google.com/document/d/1f3k9IM8kq6YSxtszFgxAipq_EQcMa6pVDi2P1LLtuHg/edit?usp=sharing.

4. Johnson, *The New Bostonians*, 14–15. Boston attracted such a large number of Irish immigrants because it was the cheapest destination from Liverpool.

5. Michael Rawson, *Eden on the Charles: The Making of Boston* (Cambridge, MA; Harvard University Press, 2010), 157.

6. Thomas H. O'Connor, *The Boston Irish: A Political History* (Boston: Northeastern University Press, 1995), 76–77.

7. Handlin, *Boston's Immigrants*, 143.

8. Thomas H. O'Connor, *Civil War Boston: Home Front and Battlefield* (Boston: Northeastern University Press, 1997), 24–28; Martin Green, *The Problem of Boston: Some Readings in Cultural History* (New York: W.W. Norton & Co., 1966), 45–46.

9. Handlin, *Boston's Immigrants*, 219. Handlin wrote that "the old society felt a sense of *malaise* because newcomers did not fit into its categories, and resentment, because they threatened its stability. Uneasy, it attempted to avoid contact by withdrawing ever farther into a solid, coherent, and circumscribed group of its own, until in the fifties it evolved the true Brahmin who believed, with Holmes, that a man of family required 'four or five generations of gentlemen and gentlewomen' behind him." Handlin, *Boston's Immigrants*, 177.

10. John F. Stack, Jr., *International Conflict in an American City: Boston's Irish, Italians, and Jews, 1934–1944* (Westport, CT: Greenwood Press, 1979), 7.

11. John Gunther, *Inside U.S.A.* (Philadelphia: The Curtis Publishing Company, 1947), 513.

12. James O'Toole, "The Newer Catholic Races: Ethnic Catholicism in Boston, 1900–1940" *New England Quarterly*, March, 1992, 119.

13. William Foote Whyte, "Race Conflicts in the North End of Boston, *The New England Quarterly*, Vol. 12, December, 1939, 629.

14. Edward L. Glaeser, "Reinventing Boston, 1640–2003," NBER Working Paper 10166, December, 2003, 4, http://www.nber.org/papers/w10166. In 1920, immigrants and their second- and third-generation descendants made up two-thirds of the nation's manufacturing workforce. Nancy Foner, *One Quarter of the Nation: Immigration and the Transformation of America* (Princeton, NJ: Princeton University Press, 2022), 87.

15. Stephen Puleo, *The Boston Italians* (Boston: Beacon Press, 2007), 44.

16. James S. Pasto, "Immigrants and Ethnics: Post-World War II Italian Immigration and Boston's North End," in *New Italian Migrations to the United States, Volume I:*

Politics and History since 1945, eds. Laura E. Robert and Joseph Sciorra (Urbana IL: University of Illinois Press, 2017), 107; James S. Pasto, "Boston's North End: Post-World War II Italian Immigration, Segmented Assimilation, and the 'Problem of Cornerville,'" paper delivered at Massachusetts Historical Society, April 23, 2019, 16–17. The 1920 population figure marked the extreme high point, reflecting the Italian influx that occurred just before the federal draconian limitation of immigration that culminated in 1924. By 1940, the North End's population was 19,698; in 1960, 11,174; in 2014, 7,630. Over the decades, the proportion of Italians also declined. In 1970, 62% were Italian-born; by 2014, those claiming Italian ancestry amounted to 37%. Puleo, *The Boston Italians*, 47.
17. Puleo, *The Boston Italians*, 69–73.
18. Puleo, *The Boston Italians*, 91.
19. Puleo, *The Boston Italians*, 96.
20. Puleo, *The Boston Italians*, 15, 94; Whyte, "Race Conflicts," 631–32.
21. *Report of the United States Immigration Commission* (Washington, DC: Government Printing Office, 1911), quoted in Puleo, *The Boston Italians*, 77.
22. Russell A. Kazal, "Revisiting Assimilation: The Rise, Fall, and Reappraisal of a Concept in American Ethnic History," *American Historical Review*, Vol. 100, April, 1995, 438, https://www-jstor-org.ezproxy.bu.edu/stable/2169006?sid=primo&origin=crossref&seq=2#metadata_info_tab_contents.
23. Pasto, "Boston's North End," 12–13, 16.
24. Pasto, "Boston's North End," 4, 32, 34.
25. Ellen Smith, "'Israelites in Boston,' 1 840–1880," in *The Jews of Boston*, eds. Jonathan D. Sarna, Ellen Smith, and Scott Martin Kosofsky (New Haven, CT: Yale University Press, 2005), 56.
26. Herbert J. Gans, The *Urban Villagers: Group and Class in the Life of Italian-Americans* (New York: The Free Press, 1962), 7.
27. The Jewish population of Roxbury, Dorchester, and Mattapan dropped to 47,000 in 1960, to 15,800 in 1970, and to about 1,000 in 1980. Sarna, et al., *The Jews of Boston*, 344. They moved to such suburbs as Brookline, Newton, Sharon, Swampscott, Marblehead, and Framingham. For further background on the suburban settlement of Jews, see Gerald Gamm, *Urban Exodus: Why the Jews Left Boston and the Catholics Stayed* (Cambridge, MA: Harvard University Press, 1999).
28. William Braverman, "The Emergence of a United Community," Sarna, et al., *The Jews of Boston*, 75; Smith, "Israelites in Boston," 52.
29. Braverman, "The Emergence of a United Community," 78.
30. Thomas H. O'Connor, "The Jewish-Christian Experience," in Sarna, et al., *The Jews of Boston*, 333.
31. Foner, *One Quarter of the Nation*, 20; Karen Brodkin, *How Jews Became White Folks and What That Says about Race in America* (New Brunswick, NJ: Rutgers University Press, 1998), 40.
32. Johnson, *The New Bostonians*, 59; Andrew M. Sum, Johan Uvin, Ishwar Khatiwada, Dana Ansel, *The Changing Face of Massachusetts*, MassINC and Center for Labor

Market Studies, 2005), 31, https://massinc.org/research/the-changing-face-of-mass achusetts/.
33. Johnson, *The New Bostonians*, 79, 83.
34. Boston Indicators, Boston Foundation, UMass-Boston, and UMass Donahue Institute, *Changing Faces of Greater Boston* (Boston: Boston Foundation, 2019), 12, 17, https://www.bostonindicators.org/reports/report-website-pages/changing-faces-of-greater-boston; Foner, *One Quarter of the Nation*, 24.
35. Michael Liu, *Forever Struggle: Activism, Identity, and Survival in Boston's Chinatown, 1880–2018* (Amherst: University of Massachusetts Press, 2020), 190.
36. Johnson, *The New Bostonians*, 33–34; *Statistical Abstract of the United States: 1924*, 47th ed. (Washington, DC: US Department of Commerce, Bureau of Foreign and Domestic Commerce, July, 1925), 83, https://www.census.gov/library/publications/1925/compendia/statab/47ed.html.
37. Wendy Warren, *New England Bound: Slavery and Colonization in Early America* New York: Liveright Publishing, 2016); "Population in the Colonial and Continental Periods," US Census Bureau, 9, https://www2.census.gov/prod2/decennial/documents/00165897ch01.pdf.
38. Kerri K. Greenidge, *Black Radical: The Life and Times of William Monroe Trotter* (New York: Liveright Publishing Corporation, 2020), xv, xx.
39. Campbell Gibson and Kay Jung, *Historical Census Statistics on Population Totals by Race, 1790–1990, and by Hispanic Origin, 1970–1990, for Large Cities and Other Urban Places in the United States, Population Division, Working Paper No. 76* (Washington, DC: US Census Bureau, February, 2005), https://www.census.gov/content/dam/Census/library/working-papers/2005/demo/POP-twps0076.pdf; Peter Ciurczak; Luc Shuster, James Jennings, *Great Migration to Global Immigration: A Profile of Black Boston* (Boston: Boston Indicators, Boston Foundation, Embrace Boston, 2023), 28.
40. Gibson and Jung, *Historical Census Statistics*; Boston Indicators, *Changing Faces of Greater Boston*, 31; Boston Planning & Development Agency Research Division, "Further Insights from 2020 Census Redistricting Data," August 20, 2021, https://www.bostonplans.org/getattachment/8818db70-f9ca-4f48-944a-83f8a32c2cd1; Luc Shuster, "The Drop in Boston's Black Population May Be an Illusion," *Boston Globe*, November 19, 2021, https://www.bostonglobe.com/2021/11/17/opinion/drop-bostons-black-population-may-be-an-illusion/; Jim Vrabel, *A People's History of the New Boston* (Amherst: University of Massachusetts Press, 2014), 41.
41. Ana Patricia Muñoz, Marlene Kim, Mariko Chang, Regine O. Jackson, Darrick Hamilton, and William A. Darity Jr., *The Color of Wealth in Boston* (Boston: Federal Reserve Bank of Boston with Duke University and The New School, 2015), https://www.bostonfed.org/publications/one-time-pubs/color-of-wealth.aspx.
42. Richard Rothstein, *The Color of Law: A Forgotten History of How Our Government Segregated America* (New York: Liverwright Publishing Corporation, 2017); Catherine Elton, "How Has Boston Gotten Away with Being Segregated for So Long?" *Boston Magazine*, December 8, 2020, https://www.bostonmagazine.com/news/2020/12/08/boston-segregation/.

43. Vrabel, *A People's History*, 47–63.
44. Deanna Pan, "45 Years Ago, Black Protesters Tried to Desegregate Carson Beach. The Peaceful Demonstration Quickly Turned Violent," *Boston Globe*, July 13, 2020, https://www.bostonglobe.com/2020/07/13/metro/45-years-ago-black-protesters-sought-desegregate-carson-beach-its-racist-legacy-still-endures/.
45. Bill Russell, quoted in John Powers, "Celtics Legend Bill Russell, Towering Champion in Boston, Dies at 88," *Boston Globe*, July 31, 2022, https://ww.w.bostonglobe.com/2022/07/31/metro/celtics-legend-bill-russell-towering-champion-boston-dies-88/.
46. Brian MacQuarrie, "Slaying Threatens South Boston Gains," *Boston.com*, July 18, 2004, http://archive.boston.com/news/local/articles/2004/07/18/slaying_threatens_south_boston_gains?pg=full.

CHAPTER 9

1. Nancy Foner, *One Quarter of the Nation: Immigration and the Transformation of America* (Princeton, NJ: Princeton University Press, 2022), 3.
2. Bryan Baker and Sarah Miller, "Estimates of the Lawful Permanent Resident Population in the United States and the Subpopulation Eligible to Naturalize: 2022," (Washington, DC: US Department of Homeland Security, Office of Immigration Statistics, October, 2022), https://www.dhs.gov/sites/default/files/2022-10/2022_0920_plcy_lawful_permenent_resident_population_estimate_2022_0.pdf.
3. Jeanne Batalova, "Frequently Requested Statistics on Immigrants and Immigration in the United States," Migration Policy Institute, March 13, 2024, https://www.migrationpolicy.org/article/frequently-requested-statistics-immigrants-and-immigration-united-states#refugees-asylum.
4. Marilynn S. Johnson, *The New Bostonians: How Immigrants Have Transformed the Metro Region Since the 1980s* (Amherst: University of Massachusetts Press, 2015) 48.
5. Johnson, *The New Bostonians*, 65–68.
6. Johnson, *The New Bostonians*, 70.
7. Donna R. Gabaccia, *Foreign Relations: American Immigration in Global Perspective* (Princeton, NJ: Princeton University Press, 2012), 193; Niall McCarthy, "These Countries Are the World's Top Remittance Recipients." World Economic Forum, May 19, 2021, https://www.weforum.org/agenda/2021/05/infographic-what-are-the-world-s-top-remittance-recipients/.
8. Kelly Harrington, Luc Shuster, Anthony Capote, *Global Greater Boston: Immigrants in a Changing Region* (Boston: Boston Indicators and Immigration Research Institute, February, 2024), 10, https://www.tbf.org/-/media/indicators/boston-indicators-reports/report-files/bi_immigration_pages_reducedsize_2_13.pdf; Luc Shuster and Peter Ciurczak, *Boston's Booming... But for Whom?: Building Shared Prosperity in a Time of Growth* (Boston Foundation Indicators Project, 2018), 42.
9. Harrington, et al., *Global Greater Boston*, 13.

10. The chapter on "The Metropolitan Diaspora," in Marilynn Johnson's *The New Bostonians*, 74–105, provides a concise overview of the settlement patterns of new immigrant groups in Greater Boston. Ciurczak, et al., *Changing Faces of Greater Boston*, 54; "Foreign-Born Population in Boston Area Communities," *Global Boston: A Portal to the Region's Immigrant Past and Present*, Boston College, Department of History, accessed May 10, 2024, https://globalboston.bc.edu/index.php/interactive-map-1870-2010/. The *Global Boston* website has been developed by Professor Marilynn Johnson.
11. Harrington, et al., *Global Greater Boston: Immigrants in a Changing Region*, 13.
12. Johnson, *The New Bostonians*, 111, 124; Daniel J. Monti, Laurel Smith-Doerr, and James McQuaid, *Immigrant Entrepreneurs in the Massachusetts Biotechnology Industry* (Malden, MA: Immigrant Learning Center, 2007), 2, https://www.immigrationresearch.org/system/files/Immigrant_Entrepreneurs_in_Biotech_final_5-25-07.pdf; American Immigration Council, *Immigrants in Massachusetts* (Washington, DC: American Immigration Council, 2017), https://americanimmigrationcouncil.org/research/immigrants-in-massachusetts.
13. Johnson, *The New Bostonians*, 134.
14. Catholic parishes in Boston were originally undifferentiated by ethnic group. After the influx of Irish during the 1840s, their clergy and lay people dominated parishes across the Boston Archdiocese. As new ethnic groups using languages different from English settled in Boston in the late nineteenth century, the Archdiocese established ethnic parishes to serve French, German, Italian, Lebanese/Syrian, Lithuanian, Polish, and Portuguese residents. There were 64 ethnic parishes out of 288 by 1930. James O'Toole, "The Newer Catholic Races: Ethnic Catholicism in Boston, 1900–1940" *New England Quarterly*, March, 1992, 120.
15. Kim Parker, Juliana Menasce Horowitz, Rich Morin, and Mark Hugo, *Multiracial in America: Proud, Diverse and Growing in Numbers* Lopez (Washington, DC: Pew Research Center: June 11, 2015), 19–31, https://www.pewresearch.org/wp-content/uploads/sites/20/2015/06/2015-06-11_multiracial-in-america_final-updated.pdf.
16. "Tattered Dreams: Once in America, Some Asians Find Bigotry, Violence," *Boston Globe*, March 31, 1986, https://bostonglobe.newspapers.com/image/437631219/.
17. Marie Price and Lisa Benton-Short, "Immigrants and World Cities: From the Hyper-Diverse to the Bypassed," *GeoJournal*, June, 2007, 103–17, https://www.researchgate.net/publication/226194863_Immigrants_and_world_cities_From_the_hyper-diverse_to_the_Bypassed.
18. "U.S. States Hosting the Most International Students in the Academic Year, 2022/23," Statista, https://www.statista.com/statistics/237703/us-states-hosting-the-most-international-students/; The Institute of International Education, *Open Door Report 2023*, https://opendoorsdata.org/fact_sheets/state-fact-sheets/; New American Economy, "The Contributions of New Americans in Massachusetts" (New York: New American Economy, 2016), 23, https://www.newamericaneconomy.org/wp-content/uploads/2017/02/nae-ma-report.pdf.

19. Boston University Global Programs, accessed January 22, 2022, https://www.bu.edu/globalprograms/about/.
20. Thomas J. Sugrue and Dominic Vitiello, "Immigration and the New American Metropolis," in *Immigration and Metropolitan Revitalization in the United States*, eds. Thomas J. Sugrue and Dominic Vitiello (Philadelphia: University of Pennsylvania Press, 2017), 2–3. Without immigrants, metropolitan New York would have lost 600,000 people, Los Angles would have lost 200,000, and San Francisco 188,000. Harrington, et al., *Global Greater Boston: Immigrants in a Changing Region*, 9.
21. Alvaro Lima, Christina Kim, and Luc Shuster, *Powering Greater Boston's Economy: Why the Latino Community Is Critical to Our Shared Future* (Boston: Boston Indicators and Boston Planning & Development Agency, 2017), 5.
22. Marilynn, S. Johnson, "Revitalizing the Suburbs: Immigrants in Greater Boston since the 1980s," in *Immigration and Metropolitan Revitalization*, 69–70.
23. Michael B. Katz and Kenneth Ginsburg, "Immigrant Cities as Reservations for Low-Wage Labor," in *Immigration and Metropolitan Revitalization*, 92. For a thorough treatment of Lawrence's development as a Latino community, see Llana Barber, *Latino City: Immigration and Urban Crisis in Lawrence, Massachusetts, 1945–2000* (Chapel Hill, NC: University of North Carolina Press, 2017); Sugrue and Vitiello, "Immigration and the New American Metropolis," in *Immigration and Metropolitan Revitalization*, 2.
24. Johnson, *The New Bostonians*, 232–33.
25. American Immigration Council, "Immigrants in Massachusetts," 2023.
26. Bruno Lanvin and Paul Evans, *The Global Talent Competitiveness Index 2017: Talent and Technology*, INSEAD, 2017, 94, https://www.insead.edu/sites/default/files/assets/dept/fr/gtci/GTCI-2017-report.pdf.
27. Saskia Sassen, *Cities in a World Economy*, 5th ed. (Los Angeles: Sage Publications, 2019), 141.
28. Bruno Lanvin and Paul Evans, eds., *The Global Talent Competitiveness Index, 2015–2016: Talent Attraction and International Mobility* (Fontainebleau, France: INSEAD, Adecco Group, and Human Capital Leadership Institute, 2015), 93–95, https://www.insead.edu/sites/default/files/assets/dept/globalindices/docs/GTCI-2015-2016-report.pdf; Enrico Moretti, *The New Geography of Jobs* (Boston: Houghton Mifflin Harcourt, 2012), 240, 242; Natasha Mascarenhas, "Boston's Startup Community Vies for Entrepreneurs," Crunchbase News, October, 23, 2018, https://news.crunchbase.com/venture/bostons-startup-community-vies-for-immigrant-entrepreneurs/.
29. AnnaLee Saxenian, *The New Argonauts: Regional Advantage in a Global Economy* (Cambridge, MA: Harvard University Press, 2006), 11.
30. McKinsey Global Institute, *Digital Globalization: The New Era of Global Flows*, March, 2016, https://www.mckinsey.com/business-functions/mckinsey-digital/our-insights/digital-globalization-the-new-era-of-global-flows; Nunn, et al., "A Dozen Facts about Immigration," 10, https://www.brookings.edu/wp-content/uploads/2018/10/ImmigrationFacts_Web_1008_540pm.pdf.

31. Shuster and Ciurczak, *Boston's Booming . . . But for Whom*, 42; David Brooks, "The Eastern Germans of the 21st Century," *New York Times*, January 29, 2018, https://www.nytimes.com/2018/01/29/opinion/east-germany-immigration-usa.html; Thomas J. Miles and Adam B. Cox, "Does Immigration Enforcement Reduce Crime? Evidence From Secure Communities," *Journal of Law and Economics* 57, no. 4 (2014), 937–73, https://www.journals.uchicago.edu/doi/abs/10.1086/680935.
32. "NAE Cities Index," New American Economy, accessed February 7, 2022, https://www.newamericaneconomy.org/cities-index/interactive-index/--2021.
33. Cade Metz, "Toronto, the Quietly Booming Tech Town," *New York Times*, March 21, 2022, https://www.nytimes.com/2022/03/21/technology/toronto-tech-boom.html.
34. Ciurczak, et al., *Changing Faces of Greater Boston*, 69–70.

CHAPTER 10

1. The 21,000 migrants became the breeding stock for New England, which doubled in population every generation for two centuries. The number of people reached 100,000 by 1700 and more than one million by 1800. David Hackett Fischer, *Albion's Seed: Four British Folkways in America* (New York: Oxford University Press, 1989), 16–17.
2. Colin Woodard, *American Nations: A History of the Eleven Rival Regional Cultures of North America* (New York: Viking, 2011), 5, 173–82; David Hackett Fischer, *Albion's Seed*, 16–17.
3. Oliver Wendell Holmes, *The Autocrat of the Breakfast-Table* (Boston: James R. Osgood and Company, 1873), 143.
4. Lewis Mumford, "The Significance of Back Bay Boston," in *Back Bay Boston: The City as a Work of Art* (Boston: Museum of Fine Arts, 1969), 30; Alfred North Whitehead, quoted in Douglass Shand-Tucci, "Boston Granite, Heroic Concrete: A Speaking Aristocracy in the Face of a Listening Democracy," Mark Pasnik, Michael Kubo, and Chris Grimley, eds., *Heroic: Concrete Architecture and the New Boston, 1960–1976* (New York: Monacelli Press, 2015), 90.
5. Elizabeth Hardwick, "Boston," *A View of My Own: Essays in Literature and Society* (New York: Farrar, Straus and Cudahy, 1962), 148, 156, 158; John Gunther, *Inside U.S.A.* (Philadelphia: The Curtis Publishing Company, 1947), 520.
6. Quoted in Pasnik, Kubo, and Grimley, eds., *Heroic*, 101.
7. Neal R. Peirce, *The New England States: People, Politics, and Power in the Six New England States* (New York: W.W. Norton, 1976), 107.
8. Michael Kubo, Chris Grimley, and Mark Pasnik, "Futures: Expo Boston '76," Mas Context, accessed September 4, 2022, https://mascontext.com/issues/improbable/futures-expo-boston-76; Urban Design Department, Boston Redevelopment Authority, "United States Bicentennial World Exposition, Boston, 1967: New Community for Boston," August, 1968, 9, https://archive.org/details/preliminarysummaoobost/page/n1/mode/2up?view=theater.

9. Kubo, et al., "Futures: Expo Boston '76."
10. Stephen V. Ward, *Selling Places: The Marketing and Promotion of Towns and Cities, 1850–2000* (New York: Routledge, 1998), 191.
11. "Boston—Special Mention," Lee Kuan Yew World City Prize, accessed August 23, 2022, https://www.leekuanyewworldcityprize.gov.sg/about-the-prize/; Lee Kuan Yew World City Prize, "Reimagining Boston—A Collective Effort," February 3, 2023, https://www.leekuanyewworldcityprize.gov.sg/resources/features/reimagining-boston/; Boston Planning & Development Agency, "Boston Recognized by Lee Kuan Yew World City Prize, March 14, 2022, https://www.bostonplans.org/news-calendar/news-updates/2022/03/14/boston-recognized-by-lee-kuan-yew-world-city-prize.
12. A book has been written about the events surrounding this photograph—Louis P. Masur, *The Soiling of Old Glory: The Story of a Photograph That Shocked America* (New York: Bloomsbury Press, 2008).
13. Boston 2024 Partnership, *Boston 2024, Number 1: Overall Games Concept*, December 1, 2014, 14, 20, 36, https://www.masslive.com/news/boston/2015/01/read_the_bid_documents_boston.html.
14. Mark Arsenault and John Powers, "Boston Picked to Bid for Olympics," *Boston Globe*, January 8, 2015, https://www.bostonglobe.com/metro/2015/01/08/olympic-decision-boston-bid-could-come-thursday/6RHRYSTRGgsIlPImafWgRM/story.html; "Let the Olympic Dialogue Begin," *Boston Globe*, January 8, 2015, https://www.bostonglobe.com/opinion/editorials/2015/01/08/let-olympic-dialogue-begin/weWaRfTBnVOOcCV9FKIb2L/story.html; Dan Shaughnessy, "Like Many Others, USOC Was Captivated by Boston," *Boston Globe*, January 8, 2015, https://www.bostonglobe.com/sports/2015/01/08/like-many-others-usoc-was-captivated-boston/C5bOw3OKwdWr4PWAxzQ6AJ/story.html.
15. Chris Dempsey and Andrew Zimbalist, *No Boston Olympics: How and Why Smart Cities Are Passing On the Torch*, (Lebanon, NH: ForeEdge, 2017), 76.
16. Dempsey and Zimbalist, *No Boston Olympics*, 125, 150–60.
17. Dempsey and Zimbalist, *No Boston Olympics*, 136, 156; Beth Teitell, "We're Not Hosting the Olympics. Who's Luckier—Boston or the Olympics?" *Boston Globe*, February 20, 2022, https://www.bostonglobe.com/2022/02/20/metro/were-not-hosting-olympics-2024-whos-luckier-boston-or-olympics/.
18. Dempsey and Zimbalist, *No Boston Olympics*, 130.
19. Katharine Seelye, "Many in Boston Feel Relief as Olympic Bid Ends, but Others See a Stagnant City," *New York Times*, July 28, 2015, https://www.nytimes.com/2015/07/29/us/many-in-boston-feel-relief-as-olympic-bid-ends-but-others-see-a-stagnant-city.html. Both the USOC and the IOC looked askance at Olympic candidate cities holding referendums because they inevitably lost, fueled by controversies related to cost overruns.
20. Michelle Ye Hee Lee and Simon Denyer, "Japanese Taxpayers Were Shut Out from Olympic Venues. Now They Can View the Staggering Bill," *Washington Post*, August

15, 2021, https://www.washingtonpost.com/world/2021/08/15/olympics-tokyo-costs-japan/.
21. Kevin Cullen, "A Belated Thanks to Some Profiles in Courage" *Boston Globe*, February 17, 2022, https://www.bostonglobe.com/2022/02/17/metro/belated-thanks-some-profiles-courage/.
22. Ward, *Selling Places*, 200, 211, 217.
23. "Boston: Global City," Greater Boston Chamber of Commerce, May 16, 2016, accessed August 8, 2022, https://www.youtube.com/watch?v=cE9Ub_Ebhq0. It is worth noting that the *Greater Boston Chamber of Commerce Strategic Plan, 2019*, mentioned "global" matters only in a cursory manner, pledging to "keep Greater Boston a global competitor," without any detailed strategy. Greater Boston Chamber of Commerce, *Greater Boston Chamber of Commerce Strategic Plan, 2019*, 2019, https://bostonchamber.com/wp-content/uploads/2022/03/2019-Strategic-Plan.pdf.
24. It is worth noting that the *Imagine Boston 2030* plan recognizes the importance of employing metrics developed by global city benchmark studies to track the effectiveness of municipal operations and policies. City of Boston, *Imagine Boston 2030: A Plan for the Future of Boston*, 2017, 11–12, 402, 457, https://www.boston.gov/sites/default/files/embed/file/2018-06/imagine2oboston202030_pages2.pdf. To get a fuller appreciation of how cities can project "global" leadership, see the Brookings Institution's *The 10 Traits of Globally Fluent Metro Areas*. The "10 Traits" include Leadership with a Worldview, Legacy of Global Orientation, Compelling Global Identity, Culture of Knowledge and Innovation, and Adaptability to New Cycles of Global Change. Clark and Moonen, *The 10 Traits of Globally Fluent Metro Areas*, Brookings Institution and JPMorgan Chase, 2013, 20, https://www.brookings.edu/research/the-10-traits-of-globally-fluent-metro-areas/.
25. Göran Therborn, *Cities of Power: The Urban, The National, The Popular, The Global* (New York: Verso, 2017), 307–10. The term "world city" was being used just before World War I, when industrial Berlin adopted the moniker to claim similar status to London and Paris.
26. Tokyo Metropolitan Government, *New Tokyo. New Tomorrow: The Action Plan for 2020*, 2016, 21, 42, https://www.metro.tokyo.lg.jp/english/about/plan/documents/pocket_english.pdf.
27. "Announcement of Seoul Vision 2030 by Mayor Oh See-hoon to Restore the Hierarchical Mobility Ladder and City's Competitiveness," Seoul Metropolitan Government, September 17, 2021, https://english.seoul.go.kr/announcement-of-seoul-vision-2030-by-mayor-oh-se-hoon-to-restore-the-hierarchical-mobility-ladder-and-citys-competitiveness/.
28. Dubai, "Dubai 2024: Everything You Wanted to Learn about the Urban Master Plan," *The National UAE*, March 13, 2021, https://www.thenationalnews.com/uae/dubai-2040-everything-you-need-to-know-about-the-urban-master-plan-1.1183432. The Dubai Master Plan focuses on new development areas and projects. Social equity is not a concern, as its housing policy only mentions the need to "build and renovate

communities dedicated to Emiratis," not mentioning housing for workers from other countries.
29. "All Inclusive Boston" Marketing Campaign, 2021," City of Boston and Greater Boston Convention & Visitors Bureau, accessed August 20, 2022, https://www.bostonusa.com/allinclusivebos/.
30. The Innovation Trail of Greater Boston, accessed September 8, 2023, https://www.theinnovationtrail.org/.
31. HubWeek Fall Festival, accessed April 24, 2024, https://www.manifestboston.org/2020-hubweek-festival/; Globe Summit, 2023, https://www.youtube.com/playlist?list=PLvRt-9Whak2hipEc4iGvKtlNTgCLqf2OT.

CHAPTER 11

1. "Occupy Boston Shows Economic Anger Isn't Owned by the Right," *Boston Globe*, October 5, 2011, https://bostonglobe.newspapers.com/image/444153826/.
2. "Who Are the One Percent in the United States by Income and Net Worth?," *DQYDJ*, accessed August 19, 2021, https://dqydj.com/top-one-percent-united-states/. This piece used data from the 2019 Survey of Consumer Finances issued by the Federal Reserve Bank.
3. Karla Adam, "Occupy Wall Street Protests Go Global," *Washington Post*, October 15, 2011, https://www.washingtonpost.com/world/europe/occupy-wall-street-protests-go-global/2011/10/15/gIQAp7kimL_story.html.
4. Brian McGrory, "For Menino, Police, a 99 Percent Success," *Boston Globe*, December 11, 2011, https://bostonglobe.newspapers.com/image/444162708/.
5. Yvonne Abraham, "Lessons in Tent City," *Boston Globe*, December 4, 2011, https://bostonglobe.newspapers.com/image/444147319/.
6. Michael Levitin, "Occupy Wall Street Did More Than You Think," *The Atlantic*, September 14, 2021, https://www.theatlantic.com/ideas/archive/2021/09/how-occupy-wall-street-reshaped-america/620064/.
7. Saskia Sassen, *The Global City: New York, London, Tokyo* (Princeton, NJ: Princeton University Press, 1991), 13.
8. Jonathan Gruber and Simon Johnson, *Jump-Starting America: How Breakthrough Science Can Revive Economic Growth and the American Dream* (New York: Public Affairs, 2019), 126–27; Chuck Collins, *The Wealth Hoarders: How the Billionaires Pay Millions to Hid Trillions* (Medford, MA: Polity, 2021), 44; Thomas Piketty, *Capital in the Twenty-First Century* (Cambridge, MA: The Belknap Press, 2014), 247–49, 297.
9. David Harvey, *Spaces of Global Capitalism* (New York: Verso, 2006), 42–43; Carter C. Price and Kathryn A. Edwards, "Trends in Income from 1975 to 2018," RAND Education and Labor working paper, September, 2020, https://www.rand.org/pubs/working_papers/WRA516-1.html; Luc Shuster and Peter Ciurczak, "9 Key Findings about Wealth in 2022," Boston Indicators Racial Wealth Equity Resource Center, November 1, 2023, https://rwerc.org/9-key-findings-about-wealth-in-2022/.

10. Piketty, *Capital in the Twenty-First Century*, 243, 259, 261; Christopher Ingraham, "For the First Time in History, US Billionaires Paid a Lower Tax Rate Than the Working Class Last Year," *Washington Post*, October 8, 2019, https://www.washingtonpost.com/business/2019/10/08/first-time-history-us-billionaires-paid-lower-tax-rate-than-working-class-last-year/.

11. Luc Shuster and Peter Ciurczak, *Boston's Booming . . . But for Whom?: Building Shared Prosperity in a Time of Growth* (Boston: Boston Indicators, 2018), 16, 20, https://www.bostonindicators.org/-/media/indicators/boston-indicators-reports/report-files/bostons-booming-2018.pdf ; Katharine Swindells, "Income in US Cities Is Most Unevenly Distributed in Decades," *City Monitor*, December 22, 2022, https://citymonitor.ai/community/neighbourhoods/us-income-inequality-cities-revealed.

12. Shuster and Ciurczak, *Boston's Booming*, 26, 28.

13. Shuster and Ciurczak, *Boston's Booming*, 16.

14. Enrico Moretti, *The New Geography of Cities* (Boston: Houghton Mifflin Harcourt, 2012), 12, 100.

15. The 2018 Boston Indicators report expressed encouragement that Boston had declined from being #1 in inequality in 2014. This was achieved partially by increasing the state minimum wage from $8 an hour to $15 by 2023. This measure has boosted the incomes of 800,000 workers. Shuster and Ciurczak, *Boston's Booming*, 12,13, 16–20, https://www.bostonindicators.org/reports/report-website-pages/shared-prosperity. Also see Natalie Holmes and Alan Berube, *City and Metropolitan Inequality on the Rise, Driven by Declining Incomes*, Brookings, January 14, 2016, https://www.brookings.edu/research/city-and-metropolitan-inequality-on-the-rise-driven-by-declining-incomes/.

16. Ana Patricia Muñoz, Marlene Kim, Mariko Chang, Regine O. Jackson, Darrick Hamilton, and William A. Darity, Jr., *The Color of Wealth in Boston* (Boston: Federal Reserve Bank of Boston with Duke University and The New School, 2015), 2, 20.

17. A 2021 working paper published by the Federal Reserve Bank of Boston came up with a more expanded view of measuring wealth, arguing that defined benefit pensions and Social Security should be factored into a household's total wealth. Lindsay Jacobs, Elizabeth Llanes, Kevin Moore, Jeffrey Thompson, and Alice Henriques Volz, "Wealth Concentration in the United States Using an Expanded Measure of Net Worth," Federal Reserve Bank of Boston, Working Paper No. 21–6, April, 2021, https://doi.org/10.29412/res.wp.2021.06.

18. Anne Calef, "The Stubborn Persistence of the Gender Pay Gap in Massachusetts," Boston Indicators, March 31, 2022, https://www.bostonindicators.org/article-pages/2022/march/gender-pay-gap-20220331.

19. Claudia Goldin, "A Gender Convergence: Its Last Chapter," *American Economic Review*, April, 2014, 1093–1094, https://www.aeaweb.org/articles?id=10.1257/aer.104.4.1091.

20. Meera Raman, "Women Obtain More Executive Leadership Positions in Mass., but the Progress is 'Slow,' New Report Says," *Boston Business Journal*, December 5, 2023,

https://www.bizjournals.com/boston/news/2023/12/05/women-executive-progress-slow-in-massachusetts-b.html; MassBio, *Mass Bio's 2nd Biannual State of Racial, Ethnic, and Gender Diversity Report*, November, 2023, 13, https://www.massbio.org/wp-content/uploads/2023/11/2023-DEI-Report.pdf.

21. National Association of Realtors, "Change in Median Sales Price of Existing Single-Family Homes for Metropolitan Areas" 2nd Quarter, 2024, accessed October 14, 2024, https://www.nar.realtor/sites/default/files/documents/metro-home-prices-q2-2024-ranked-median-single-family-2024-08-13.pdf; Shuster and Ciurczak, *Boston's Booming*, 27; Barbara Lewis and Rita Kiki Edozie, "African Americans in Greater Boston: Challenges, Identities, Legacies and Movements," *Changing Faces of Greater Boston* (Boston: The Boston Foundation, 2019), 33, https://www.bostonindicators.org/reports/report-website-pages/changing-faces-of-greater-boston/changing-faces-of-greater-boston-report; John Avault, "Income Inequality in Boston," Boston Redevelopment Authority, Research Division, October 25, 2010; Katharine Swindells, "Income in US Cities Is Most Unevenly Distributed in a Decade," *City Monitor*, December 22, 2022, https://citymonitor.ai/community/equity/us-income-inequality-cities-revealed.

22. Chuck Collins and Emma de Goede, "Towering Excess: The Perils of the Luxury Real Estate Boom for Bostonians," Institute for Policy Studies, September, 2018, p. 10, https://inequality.org/wp-content/uploads/2018/09/Towering-Excess-Report-Final.pdf.

23. Metropolitan Area Planning Council (MAPC), *Homes for Profit: Speculation and Investment in Greater Boston* (Boston: Metropolitan Area Planning Council, 2023), 4–6 https://homesforprofit.mapc.org/report.

24. UBS, "UBS Global Real Estate Bubble Index," UBS, September 28, 2017, https://www.ubs.com/global/en/wealth-management/chief-investment-office/key-topics/2017/global-real-estate-bubble-index-2017.html; UBS, *UBS Global Real Estate Bubble Index 2021*, October, 2021, https://www.ubs.com/global/en/wealth-management/insights/2021/global-real-estate-bubble-index.html; Collins, *The Wealth Hoarders*, 124; Grant Welker, "Million Dollar Teardowns," *Boston Business Journal*, February 24-March 2, 2023, 14–19, https://www.bizjournals.com/boston/digital-edition?issue_id=21086; Rebecca Ostriker, "Reckoning with Boston's Towers of Wealth," *Boston Globe*, November 1, 2023, https://apps.bostonglobe.com/2023/10/special-projects/spotlight-boston-housing/boston-towers-of-wealth/.

25. The Boston Foundation, accessed December 7, 2023, https://www.tbf.org.

26. Roberto Mangabeira Unger, Harvard law professor and former Brazilian Minister of Strategic Affairs, has written that "a major cause of economic stagnation in the period since the early 1970s has been the confinement of the knowledge economy to relatively insular vanguards [high technology sectors] rather than its economy-wide dissemination." The primary reason technological advances have left large numbers of workers behind is that the innovations have been designed by and for those with advanced education. Roberto Mangabeira Unger, *The Knowledge Economy* (New York: Verso, 2019), 10. "Tech Hubs and the Labor Market: A Long-Read

Q&A with Enrico Moretti" podcast, AEI, November 22, 2019, http://www.aei.org/economics/tech-hubs-and-the-labor-market-long-read-qa-with-enrico-moretti/.
27. Massachusetts Business Roundtable, *A Talent Agenda to Drive Massachusetts' Competitiveness: Framing How to Attract, Retain, Develop, and Diversify Talent* (2022), 4, https://www.maroundtable.com/wp-content/uploads/2022/12/MBR_Talent Agenda2022.pdf.
28. "Make Your Dream of Higher Education a Reality," Office of Student Financial Assistance, Massachusetts Department of Higher Education, accessed April 23, 2024, https://www.mass.edu/osfa/programs/massreconnect.asp.
29. Larry Summers, "The Best Books on Globalization," Five Books, accessed August 23, 2021, https://fivebooks.com/best-books/larry-summers-globalization/.
30. Joseph E. Stiglitz, *Globalization and Its Discontents Revisited: Anti-Globalization in the Age of Trump* (New York: W.W. Norton & Company, 2018), xxvi.
31. See Stiglitz, "The Way Forward: What Is To be Done?" in *Globalization and Its Discontents Revisited*, 83–93.
32. Emily A. Shrider and John Creamer, "Poverty in the United States: 2022," United States Census Bureau, September 12, 2023, https://www.census.gov/library/publications/2023/demo/p60-280.html.
33. Bruce Katz, Max Nathanson, Chelsea Gaylord, "Can the UK Level Up? Early Signals and Key Lessons from the US," The New Localism, March 30, 2023, https://www.thenewlocalism.com/newsletter/can-the-uk-level-up-early-signals-and-key-lessons-from-the-us/; Justin Fox, "Comeback in Factory Jobs Appears to Be for Real," Bloomberg, February 9, 2023, https://www.bloomberg.com/opinion/articles/2023-02-09/comeback-in-factory-jobs-appears-to-be-for-real#xj4y7vzkg; "Fact Sheet: The Biden-Harris Administration to Kick Off Fourth Investing in America Tour to Highlight How the President Is Delivering for Communities in Every Corner of America," The White House, February 14, 2024, https://www.whitehouse.gov/briefing-room/statements-releases/2024/02/14/fact-sheet-biden-harris-administration-to-kick-off-fourth-investing-in-america-tour-to-highlight-how-the-president-is-delivering-for-communities-in-every-corner-of-america/.
34. "Remarks by Secretary of the Treasury Janet L. Yellen at the 2022 'Virtual Davos Agenda' Hosted by the World Economic Forum," US Department of the Treasury, January 21, 2022, https://home.treasury.gov/news/press-releases/jy0565; Jim Probasco, "How the Coronavirus Bills Affect You," *Investopedia*, February 6, 2022, https://www.investopedia.com/how-the-coronavirus-stimulus-bills-affect-you-4800404; Jim Probasco, "Understanding the Infrastructure Bills," *Investopedia*, January 16, 2022, https://www.investopedia.com/here-s-what-s-in-the-usd1-trillion-infrastructure-bill-passed-by-the-senate-5196817.
35. Richard Florida, *The New Urban Crisis: How Our Cities Are Increasing Inequality, Deepening Segregation, and Failing the Middle Class-and What We Can Do About It* (New York: Basic Books, 2017), 173–74.
36. Piketty, *Capital in the Twenty-First Century*, 297.

CHAPTER 12

1. Michael Wines and Amy Harmon, "What Happens When a Superspreader Event Keeps Spreading," *New York Times*, December 11, 2020, https://www.nytimes.com/2020/12/11/us/biogen-confereonce-covid-spread.html; WHO Coronavirus (Covid) Dashboard, accessed April 22, 2024, https://covid19.who.int/?mapFilter=deaths.
2. Sarah Lazare, "Top Weapons Companies Boast Ukraine-Russia Tensions Are a Boon for Business," *In These Times*, January 27, 2022, https://inthesetimes.com/article/ukraine-russia-raytheon-lockheed-martin-general-dynamics-weapons-industry); Raytheon Technologies, accessed April 15, 2022, https://www.rtx.com/.
3. City of Boston, *Climate Ready Boston*, December 2016, https://www.boston.gov/sites/default/files/file/2019/12/02_20161206_executivesummary_digital.pdf.
4. Melissa Hoffer, *Recommendations of the Climate Chief* (Boston: Massachusetts Office of Climate Innovation and Resilience, October 25, 2023), 67, https://www.mass.gov/info-details/recommendations-of-the-climate-chief.
5. City of Boston, *Boston Climate Action Fiscal Year 2021 Report*, October 2021, https://www.boston.gov/sites/default/files/file/2021/10/FY21%20Boston%20Climate%20Action%20Report_2.pdf; "Climate Justice," Michelle Wu for Mayor website, 2021, https://www.michelleforboston.com/issues/climate-justice.
6. David Abel, "After a Veto, Baker Signs Landmark Climate Bill," *Boston Globe*, March 26, 2021, https://www.bostonglobe.com/2021/03/26/science/baker-signs-climate-bill/; Bruce Katz, "The Reshaping of Cities and Metropolitan Economies: 5 Trends to Watch in 2023," Nowak Metro Finance Lab, Drexel University, January 11, 2023, https://drexel.edu/nowak-lab/publications/newsletters/five-trends-2023/.
7. Boston University Initiative on Cities, "Cities Joining Ranks: Policy Networks on the Rise," 2018, https://hdl.handle.net/2144/28865. Other international connections for Boston include bi-lateral Sister City relationships with Kyoto; Strasbourg; Barcelona; Hangzhou; Padua; Melbourne; Belfast; Beira, Mozambique; Taipei; Sekondi-Takoradi, Ghana; and Praia, Cape Verde. These relationships have tended to focus mainly on cultural exchanges, not on forging joint initiatives around urban issues or economic development.
8. The First Industrial Revolution was based upon water and steam power driving mechanized production. The Second Industrial Revolution was based upon electricity powering mass production. The Third Industrial Revolution used digital electronic and information technology systems. Klaus Schwab, "The Fourth Industrial Revolution: What It Means and How to Respond," *Foreign Affairs*, December 12, 2015, https://www.foreignaffairs.com/articles/2015-12-12/fourth-industrial-revolution. Jack Kelly, "Goldman Sachs Predicts That 300 Million Jobs Will Be Lost and Degraded by Artificial Intelligence," *Forbes*, March 31, 2023, https://www.forbes.com/sites/jackkelly/2023/03/31/goldman-sachs-predicts-300-million-jobs-will-be-lost-or-degraded-by-artificial-intelligence/; Richard Baldwin, "If This Is Globalization 4.0, What Were the Other Three?" World Economic Forum, 2018,

https://www.weforum.org/agenda/2018/12/if-this-is-globalization-4-0-what-were-the-other-three/.

9. Cade Metz, "Ray Kurzweil Still Says That He Will Merge with A.I.," *New York Times*, July 4, 2024, https://www.nytimes.com/2024/07/04/technology/ray-kurzweil-singularity.html.

10. Bruce Katz, "The New Localism: An Interview with Bruce Katz," *Brown Political Review*, October 23, 2022, https://brownpoliticalreview.org/2022/10/the-new-localism-an-interview-with-bruce-katz/.

11. "America's Top States for Business 2023," CNBC, July 11, 2023, https://www.cnbc.com/2023/07/11/americas-top-states-for-business-2023-the-full-rankings.html; Massachusetts Business Roundtable, *A Talent Agenda to Drive Massachusetts' Competitiveness* (Fall 2022), https://www.maroundtable.com/wpcontent/uploads/2022/12/MBR_TalentAgenda2022.pdf; Janelle Nanos, "'People Are Leaving': Massachusetts Has Lost 110,000 People Since Covid Began," *Boston Globe*, February 19, 2023, https://www.bostonglobe.com/2023/02/18/business/people-are-leaving-massachusetts-has-lost-110000-residents-since-covid-began-is-life-better-out-there/.

12. Alan Clayton Matthews, "Housing, Place, and Flexible Work: The Future of the New England Economy" (presentation, Federal Reserve Bank of Boston, January 19, 2023).

13. National Association of Realtors, "Median Sales Price of Existing Single-Family Homes for Metropolitan Areas," 2nd Quarter, 2024, accessed October 14, 2024, https://www.nar.realtor/sites/default/files/documents/metro-home-prices-q2-2024-ranked-median-single-family-2024-08-13.pdf; Andrew Brinker, "As Apartment-Hunting Season Ramps up, Finding a Place in Boston Is Harder Than Ever," *Boston Globe*, April 18, 2023, https://www.bostonglobe.com/2023/04/18/business/apartment-hunting-season-ramps-up-finding-place-boston-is-harder-than-ever/; *Zumper National Rent Report* (blog), accessed March 28, 2023, https://www.zumper.com/blog/rental-price-data/; "Budget Priorities," Citizens Housing & Planning Association, February 2023, accessed August 17, 2023, https://www.chapa.org/housing-policy/budget-priorities; Commonwealth of Massachusetts, "Affordable Homes Act–Overview," October 18, 2023, https://www.mass.gov/doc/affordable-homes-act-overview/download; "Governor Maura Healey Signs Most Ambitious Legislation to Address Housing Cost in State History," Mass.gov, August 6, 2024, https://www.mass.gov/news/governor-maura-healey-signs-most-ambitious-legislation-to-address-housing-costs-in-state-history.

14. City of Boston, *2020 Annual Housing Report for Housing Boston 2030*, 2021, 22–23, https://www.boston.gov/sites/default/files/file/2021/06/Annual%20Report%202020.pdf; The Boston Foundation, *The Greater Boston Housing Report Card 2021: Pandemic Housing Policy: From Progress to Permanence* (Boston: The Boston Foundation, 2021), 39–41, https://www.tbf.org/news-and-insights/reports/2021/jun/greater-boston-housing-report-card-2021.

15. Commonwealth of Massachusetts, Act Enabling Partnership for Growth, House No. 5250, January 6, 2021, https://malegislature.gov/Bills/191/H5250. This is the state's most far-reaching housing development policy requiring every community to do its share in providing housing since the Comprehensive Permit Act of 1969, popularly known as Chapter 40B. The earlier legislation allowed developers to override local zoning bylaws in communities having less than 10% of its housing defined as "affordable," as long as at least 20–25% of the proposed new units would have long-term affordability restrictions.
16. "Ridership on the T," Massachusetts Bay Transit Authority, accessed February 22, 2025, https://www.mbta.com/performance-metrics/ridership-the-t.
17. "Office Occupancy Rates and Remote Work," DC Policy Center, February 24, 2023, https://www.dcpolicycenter.org/publications/office-occupancy-remote-work-dc/; "Boston Office Insight Q4, 2023," JLL, January 11, 2024, https://www.us.jll.com/en/trends-and-insights/research/office-market-statistics-trends/boston; Mike Deehan, "How Downtown Boston's Pandemic Recovery Is Going," Axios, August 4, 2023, https://www.axios.com/local/boston/2023/08/04/boston-downtown-recovery-foot-traffic.
18. City of Boston, *Revive and Reimagine: A Strategy to Revitalize Boston's Downtown*, October 2022, https://www.boston.gov/sites/default/files/file/2022/10/Revive%20and%20Reimagine%20-%20a%20Strategy%20to%20Revitalize%20Boston%27s%20Downtown%20-%20Oct%202022.pdf.

Index

Page numbers followed by an f or t indicate a figure or table.

Abraham, Yvonne, 115, 223
Adams, Charles Francis, Jr., 61
Adams, John Quincy, 254n19
Adams, Samuel, 57
Advanced Research Projects Agency (ARPA), 92–93
Advanced Research Projects Agency for Health (ARPA-H), 127, 145–46
Afeyan, Noubar, 127, 148
African Americans and racial minorities: abolition, civil rights and discrimination, 182–84; Black Heritage Trail/Boston African American National Historic Site, 182; education and segregation, 184–85; improvements for, 185–86
Agassiz, Alexander, 64
air transportation: *Aerotropolis* (Kasarda, Lindsay), 107–12; airline companies, 99, 102–3, 105; Colonial Air Transport, 99; commercial air service, 98; international tourism, 100, 105–6; jet airplanes, 100; transatlantic commercial flights, 99–100
air transportation, Logan Airport: beginning of, 98–99; freight service, 103–4, 108; innovation districts and, 110; international hub, 103; International Terminal, 100–102; seafood processing industry and, 104–5; second airport proposal, 107–9, 264n24; Ted Williams Tunnel connection, 110
Albion, Robert G., 42–43
Allston, 6, 117, 136, 138, 153, 176

Amazon, 96, 157, 267n6
American Revolution Bicentennial Commission, 207–8
American Telephone & Telegraph (AT&T), 64
Ames, Frederick Lothrop, 61
Ames, Oakes and Oliver, Jr., 60–61
Aoun, Joseph, 217
Appold, Steven, 109
Arcadis, 22–23, 30t
Armory case (Mass. 1830), 66
Arroyo, Felix D., 194
artificial intelligence (AI), 95, 161–63, 241–42, 292n8
A. T. Kearney, 25t

Baker, Charlie, 153, 214, 245
Baker, Lorenzo Dow, 46
Baldwin, Richard, 242
Bancel, Stéphane, 125–26
Barouch, Dan, 129
Bates, Joshua, 63
Bell, Alexander Graham, 63, 85–87
Bell Telephone Company, 63–64, 87
Benton-Short, Lisa, 196
Berndt, Ernst R., 124
Berners-Lee, Tim, 5, 93–95
Biden administration, 120, 124, 158, 188, 235–36
Biomedical Advanced Research and Development Authority (BARDA) / Operation Warp Speed, 126, 129
Black Economic Council of Massachusetts, 186
Blanc, Ted, 115

Bloomberg, Michael, 20
Boston, population of, 38, 87, 205, 211
Boston as a global city: challenges, 242–44; climate leadership role, 292n7; history of, 204–6; image and reputation, 7–8, 203–4; innovation hubs, 2; literary epicenter, 205; post-Civil war influence, 205; stagnation period, 205–6; Transcendentalism and, 205
Boston Consulting Group, 24, 31t, 114
Boston Foundation, 9, 23, 201, 227, 232–33
Boston Foundation Indicators Project, 23, 227
Boston Globe, 12, 49, 107, 116, 158, 194, 209, 211, 219, 222
Boston Herald American, 211
Boston image: ethnic clashes and racial tension, 210–11; international image, 216–17; movie portrayals, 211–12; school desegregation, 211; tourism and, 218; urban blight and gangsters, 211
Boston Indicators report, 227, 288n15
Boston inequality gap: COVID-19 pandemic relief, 226, 235; economic mobility and, 228; ethnic groups and, 229; housing costs and, 230–32; MassReconnect, 234; neo-Keynesians and federal tax cuts, 235; social equity agenda, 232–33; socioeconomic inequality, 8–9, 227; up-skilling and education, 234, 290n26; wealth vs. income inequality, 229, 289n17; women's pay gap, 230
Boston Latin School, 169, 204
Boston Looks Seaward (Works Progress Administration), 40, 50, 52
Boston Made (Krim, Earls), 144
Boston port, antebellum period: East coast cities competition, 38; foreign trade, 39–41; railroads and, 42
Boston port, post-Civil War: decline and revival, 50, 52; domestic coastal trade, 45; foreign trade, 46, 49–50; imports and exports, 46; transportation and, 45, 49–50; waste material exports, 52–53
Boston rankings: airport, 101, 110; biopharma, 130, 272nn15–16; communications, 87; economics and finance, 20, 22, 24, 56, 72, 209, 243, 256n1; foreign tourism, 18, 105; global business, 17; higher education, 19, 21, 24, 143; housing, 232, 244; immigration destination, 5, 165, 189–90; inequality (Gini index), 9, 24, 227–28, 230, 288n15; innovation employment, 156; patents and scientific papers, 20, 143; per capita income, 16; population, 7, 204–5; sustainability, 23, 115; technology and computing, 19–20, 159; transportation, 22; venture capital, 21, 70
Boston Redevelopment Authority BRA), 111–12, 194, 207
Boston revitalization: athletic teams and activities, 209–10; Boston City Hall (1968), 206; events of, 206–7; Expo Boston '76 proposal, 207–8; Faneuil Hall-Quincy Market, 206; Fenway Park, 209–10; Government Center Urban Renewal project, 206; "Massachusetts Miracle," 154, 209, 217; New England Aquarium, 206; *Revive and Reimagine*, 246; Route 128 "America's Technology Highway," 208–9
Boston's Booming ... But for Whom? 23, 201, 227–28
Boston's Immigrants (Handlin), 167
Boston Wharf Company, 45
Boston While Black, 186
Bourla, Albert, 128
Braverman, William, 176
Brewer, Marilyn B., 139
British Navigation Acts, 35–36
Broad, Eli and Edythe, 137
Brodkin, Karen, 177
Brookings Institution, 14, 25t, 144, 227
Bucheli, Marcelo, 47
Building Resilient Supply Chains, 124
Bulfinch, Charles, 41
Bulger, James "Whitey," 211

Index   295

Bunting, W.H., 40
Bush, Vannevar, 69, 92, 141
Business Week, 74

Cabot, Paul, 74
Cabral, Andrea, 195
Calumet and Hecla Copper Mine, 60, 64
Cambridge-Boston life sciences biotech: Biogen, 135, 152, 238; biosafety code, 134–35; competition and threats to, 154–56; global biotech hub, 136–38, 140–41; law firms and real estate specialists, 152–53; Massachusetts Biotechnology Council (MassBio), 154; Massachusetts Life Sciences Center (MLSC), 153; Massachusetts Life Sciences Initiative, 153; Sanofi/Genzyme, 126, 128, 132, 135–36, 138; specialized scientific services, 153; supporting institutions, 150t; Whitehead Institute for Biomedical Research, 137, 140. *See also* Kendall Square (Cambridge)
Campbell, Andrea, 195
Campbell, John, 77
Canellos, Peter, 107–9, 112
Capital in the Twenty-First Century (Piketty), 225
Castells, Manuel, 17
Chan, Benjie, 153
Chan, Priscilla, 163
Changing Landscape of Disruptive Technologies, 28t
Chappe, Claude, 81
Chicago, Burlington & Quincy Railroad, 60
China Development Institute, 22, 30, 56
Chinese immigrants: Asian Community Development Corporation (CDC), 180; Chinatown and neighborhoods of, 178–81; Chinese American Civic Association, 180; Chinese Consolidated Benevolent Association, 179; Chinese Exclusion Act (1882), 178–79; unskilled labor, 178
Cities and the Wealth of Nations (Jacobs), 69

Cities Index (New American Economy), 201–2
Cities of Choice (Boston Consulting Group), 24, 31t
Citizens Housing & Planning Association, 244
City Momentum Index (JLL), 26t
Clark, Greg, 250n11
Clark, Katherine, 195
climate change: C40 Cities Climate Leadership Group, 241; climate tech, 159–61; Commonwealth Wind, 241; Glasgow Climate Pact (2021), 241; Inflation Reduction Act investments, 235–36; Paris Climate Accord (2015), 241; sea level threat, 115, 240; SouthCoast Wind Energy, 241
Climate Ready Boston, 115, 240
Cobb, Henry N., 112
Collins, John, 11
Common Ground (Lukas), 211
communications, colonial: newspapers and, 77; postal system, 77–78, 259nn3–5, 259n7; shipping and, 76–77
communications, development of: airmail, 80–81; Associated Press, 83; Boston Exchange Coffee House, 80; history of, 5; human voice transmission, 85–86; international mail, 79–80, 259n10, 259n13; International Telecommunications Union (ITU), 85; international telegraphy, 85; telegraphs and news, 81–84, 259n19; telephone, 86–88; telephone international, 89; Telstar and telecommunications satellites, 89–90; United States Post Office, 78–79; Western Union Company, 84
communications, globalization, 96–97
communications, Internet: 5G digital infrastructure, 96–97, 261n51; Advanced Research Projects Agency (ARPA), 92; Akamai Technologies, 95; artificial intelligence (AI), 95; Boston's continued role, 95–96; Boston's role in, 92; computer spreadsheets, 93, 261n39; email, 92–93; Facebook, 95;

communications (*continued*)
  Moore's Law and computing power, 91–92, 241; World Wide Web, 93–94, 261n45; World Wide Web Consortium (W3C), 94–95
The Competitive Advantage (Porter), 121
Compton, Karl, 69, 146
Condé Nast Traveler, 7, 100, 105
Condon, John, 123
Conti, Rena, 124
Cooke, Jay, 62
Cooke, William Fothergill, 82
Coolidge, Thomas Jefferson, 62, 256n8
Cotton Whigs, 53
Coughlin, Charles, 177
COVID-19 and vaccines: global supply chains, 4, 238–39; remote work and, 75, 96; tourism drop, 106. *See also* pharmaceutical and biopharma industry
Craig, Daniel H., 82–83
creative class, 20–21, 199
Credit Mobilier scandal, 60–61
Cunard, Samuel, 44, 80
Curley, James Michael, 169, 195, 206
Cushing, John Perkins, 41

Dame, Lawrence, 55
Darby, Michael, 139, 271n7
de Moura, Roberto Landell, 85
Dempsey, Chris, 213
Dertouzos, Michael, 94
Dexter, Philip, 66
DHL, 18, 103
DHL Global Connectedness Index 2016, 27t
Dicken, Peter, 96
Digital Equipment Corporation, 69, 154, 209
D'Isidoro, Anthony, 117
Doriot, Georges, 69, 146
Drapeau, Jean, 12
Drew, John E., 111
Driscoll, Kim, 195
Dukakis, Michael, 209
Dutch West India Company, 38

Earls, Alan, 144
East India Company, 33
Economist Intelligence (EIU), 30t
Edison, Thomas Alva, 84, 161
Edwards, Lydia, 116
Emerson, Ralph Waldo, 205
Entrepreneurial Impact (Kauffman Foundation), 139

Fairbanks, Richard, 76
Fan, Melina, 153
Federal Reserve Bank, San Francisco, 119
Federal Reserve Bank of Boston, 21, 184, 221–22, 229, 289n17
Fessenden, Reginald, 85
Fidelity Investments, 22, 57, 68, 70, 110
Field, Cyrus, 83
financial and professional services, 14, 43–44, 56
financial investments: foreign direct investment (FDI), 22; inequality and, 22–24; railroads and, 59–62. *See also* venture capital
financial sector: First National Bank of Boston, 57; investment management, 57; Massachusetts Bank (Bank of America), 57; New York comparison, 74; Stock & Exchange Board, 58
financial technology (fintech): DCU Fintech Innovation Center, 73; FinTech Sandbox, 73; importance of, 72; leading companies, 72–73; Mass Fintech Hub, 73
First, Devra, 116
Fish, John, 215
Fitzgerald, John "Honey Fitz," 169, 195
Fitzpatrick, John Bernard, 169
Flanders, Ralph, 69, 146
Florida, Richard, 9, 20–21, 23, 70, 146, 237
Flynn, Ray, 194
Food and Drug Administration (FDA), 122, 124–25, 127, 129, 135, 153, 268n9
Forbes, John Murray, 41, 59–60, 63, 86
Forbes, Robert Bennet, 41
Forbes, William Hathaway, 63

Index   297

foreign trade: Elder and Fyffes, 46; food importers, 46–48; Great Molasses Flood (1919), 47–48; triangle trade with Caribbean, 3, 34–37, 47; United States Industrial Alcohol Company, 48
Forry, Linda Dorcena, 195
Fort Point Channel warehouse district, 45–46, 48, 112
Foster, Hatherly, Jr., 67
Fowler, William, 52
Franklin, Benjamin, 77–78
Franklin, James, 77
Friedman, Tom, 121, 143
Friedmann, John, 13
Fuller, Margaret, 205
Future Cities (magazine), 108

Gardiner, Robert H., 66
Garrity, Arthur, 184–85
GaWC Research Network, 17–18, 28t
Gilbert, Walter, 135
Glaeser, Edward L., 21, 145
Global Cities Index 2022 (Schroders), 27t
Global Cities Index 2024 (Oxford Economics), 26t
Global Cities Report, 25t
global city: characteristics and performance of, 2, 14, 16, 250n11; connectivity and, 242; definition of, 13, 253n1; education in the, 21; financial investments, 21; Global cities ranking studies evaluating Boston, 16–17, 25t–31t; immigration destinations, 164–65; infrastructure of, 22; rankings reports, 114; reputation and, 24; sustainability, 22–23; world city distinction, 14
The Global City (Sassen), 13, 223–24, 250n9
Global City Talent Competitiveness Index, 28t
Global Connectedness Index (DHL), 18
global economy and financial services, 13–14, 250n9
The Global Financial Centres Index (Z/ Yen), 22, 30t–31t, 56, 72, 256n1

global inequality: former industrial cities and, 224; free market capitalism and, 1, 13, 224, 226; knowledge economy and, 223–24; Occupy Boston, 222–23; Trump tax cuts, 226; wealthiest people vs. bottom half of US population, 225–26
global innovation centers, 14
Global Innovation Hubs: 2022 Report, 29t
Global Innovation Index (WIPO), 20, 28t, 143
Globalization and World Cities Research Network (2018), 28t
The Global Liveability Index 2022 (EIU), 30t
Global Power City Index 2022 (Mori), 27t
Global Startup Ecosystem Report 2022, 29t
Global Urban Competitiveness Report, 19, 26t, 209
Goldberger, Paul, 112
Goldin, Claudia, 230
Goldman Sachs, 241
Gray, William, 87
Great Cities of the World Conference, 11–12
Great Depression, 50, 55, 65, 181
"A Great Dirty City" (Boston Globe), 12
Greater Boston Chamber of Commerce, 207, 217, 286n23
Greater Boston Labor Council (AFL-CIO), 222
Greenidge, Kerri K., 182
Grousbeck, Wyc, 70
Guardian, 121
Gunther, John, 169, 206

Hall, Peter, 84, 96, 137, 144
Hall, Samuel B., 40
Hancock, John, 36–37, 57
Handlin, Oscar, 167–68, 278n9
Hardwick, Elizabeth, 206
Harris, Benjamin, 76
Harvard University: admission limitations, 177; artificial intelligence (AI) at, 163; DNA research at, 134–37; history of, 204; North Allston

Harvard University (*continued*)
development, 117, 138; tech campus, 6; tourists and, 107, 218
Hathaway, Ian, 70, 146
Havemeyer, Henry Osborne, 48
Havemeyer Sugar Trust, 48
Healey, Maura, 153, 161, 195, 234, 244, 246
Hertz, Heinrich Rudolph, 85
Hickey & Associate Associates, 29t
Hicks, Louise Day, 208
Higginson, Henry Lee, 60, 64–65
Holmes, Oliver Wendell, 168, 205, 278n9
hospitals, federal research funding, 141–42
Houqua, 59
housing: affordability, 232, 234, 243–45; Affordable Homes Act (2024), 244; Boston rankings, 232, 244; discrimination and redlining, 183–84; Housing Boston 2030 Plan (2014), 245; Housing Choice legislation (2021), 245, 293n15; MBTA Communities Act, 245
Hubbard, Gardiner G., 86
Huxtable, Ada Louise, 12
Hynes, John, 11

IESE Cities in Motion Index, 22, 27t
Immigrant Learning Center, 153
immigration and immigrants: Americanization, 173–74; Black census, 183t; Black people and North Slope, 182; citizenship for foreign born, 277n2; Democratic Party and politics, 168–69; foreign born by city, 165t; globalization and, 277n1; history of, 5–6; "Know Nothing" party, 167, 169; National Origins Act (1924) and nativists, 167, 171–72, 181, 193, 278n16; seaport and, 166; Southern Black people and, 177; unskilled labor, 169–70, 172, 278n14; xenophobic treatment, 168; Yankee Brahmins, 168, 172, 278n9
immigration and immigrants (recent): benefits of, 200–202; Boston revitalization, 197–98, 283n20; business creation by, 192–93; churches role in, 193; community development corporations (CDC), 194, 196; effect of globalization on, 188–89, 196; European policies, 200; green cards or H-1B visa, 188, 197; immigrant occupations, 192t; Immigration Act (1965) reforms, 187, 191; Inquilinos Boricuas en Acción (IBA)/Puerto Rican Tenants in Action, 194; nativism and discrimination, 193–94; politics and minorities, 194; populism and "undocumented," 199–200; Refugee Act of 1980, 188; secondary migration, 189; well-educated immigrants, 192; working class neighborhoods, 190–91
Immigration Restriction League, 172
industries, colonial and antebellum: candy-making, 48; ice harvesting, 40, 254n16; leather tanning, 49; shipbuilding, 35, 44; textiles, 3, 53–54, 57–58
Innovation Geographies (JLL), 29t
innovation hubs: artificial intelligence (AI), 161–63; Boston and, 4; Boston technology industries, 18–20, 32, 96; climate tech, 159–61; commuter rail lines and, 246; Massachusetts and, 272n18; robotics, 156–58; Small Business Innovation Research & Small Business Technology Transfer Programs, 157; 3-D Printing, 156–59
INSEAD (Institut Européen d'Administration des Affaires), 28t
Inside U.S.A. (Gunther), 169
insurance companies, 17, 37, 41, 43, 56, 58, 69
international college students, 196
International Monetary Fund (IMF), 189, 224
investment banking: financing new industries, 62; leading banks, 4, 61, 63–65
investment management: alternative investment instruments, 65–66;

Index   299

Boston Safe Deposit and Trust Company, 66; family offices, 66–67; New England Trust Company, 66; trusts and trustees, 66–67
Irish: Catholicism of, 167–69, 282n14; cheapest destination, 278n4; effect on Boston, 168; Potato Famine (1845–1850) and, 166–67, 169
Isaacson, Walter, 94, 141
Italians: Catholicism of, 172, 282n14; criminal and anarchist reputation, 173–74; *Dillingham Commission Report* (1911), 173; homeland connection, 172; North End and, 170–74, 278n16

Jackson, Andrew, 168
Jackson, Patrick Tracy, 57
Jacobs, Jane, 69
James O. Welch Company, 48
Janey, Kim, 116
Jewish immigrants: antisemitism and, 177–78; housing and neighborhoods, 279n27; occupations of, 176; repressive Eastern European policies, 175; settlement areas, 175; support network of, 176
John, Richard R., 64
Johnson, Arthur M., 59
Johnson, Boris, 217
Johnson, Edward C., II, 68
Johnson, Edward C., III (Ned), 68
Johnson, Lyndon B., 187
Jones Lang LaSalle (JLL), 2, 16, 19, 25t–26t, 29t, 113–14
Jordan, Robert A., 12
Just, Ward, 67

Kasarda, John D., 108–9, 264n24
Katz, Bruce, 243
Kauffman Foundation, 139
Keith, Minor C., 46
Kendall Square (Cambridge): AI Institute, 157; big pharma and biotech at, 125, 128, 132, 135–36, 138–39, 143, 149; Cambridge Innovation Center (CIC), 20, 110, 130, 146, 150–52;

Flagship Pioneering venture capital t, 147; GE energy business at, 161; life sciences cluster, 138, 140, 144–45, 153–54, 156, 272n19; life sciences cluster financing, 146; National Aeronautics & Space Administration's (NASA) Electronics Research Center, 138; Philips Corporation, 145; technology center, 6, 96, 114
Kennedy, John F., 169, 207
Kidder, Henry P., 63
King, Mel, 194–95, 223
Kirsner, Scott, 219
KMPG, 28t
knowledge economy: Boston as a global city, 1, 4; Boston education and, 204; Boston technology industries, 55, 67, 243; Cambridge-Boston life sciences biotech, 137; cities' influence in, 13–14; effect on cities, 15–16; immigrants and, 200; inequality and, 23, 223–24, 227, 233–34; international students and, 196
Knox, Henry, 57
Koganti, Koushik, 117
Kollek, Teddy, 12
Kraft, Robert, 215
Krim, Robert, 144, 219
Krueger, Ivar, 65
Kurzweil, Ray, 242

Lander, Eric, 137
Langer, Robert, 139
Larson, Gloria, 215
Lawrence, revitalization, 198–99
Learoyd, Charles H., 67
Leffler, Edward G., 67
Lehane, Dennis, 211
Lehmann, Ruth, 140
Leighton, Tom, 94
Levitin, Michael, 223
Liberty Mutual, 58
Licklider, JCR, 92
Lincoln, Abraham, 60
Lindsay, Greg, 108
Liu, Michael, 180–81
Loh, Penn, 116

Loughborough University's (UK) GaWC Research Network, 17
Lowell, A. Lawrence, 177
Lowell, Francis Cabot, 53, 57
Lukas, J. Anthony, 211
Lydon, Christopher, 264n32
Lynch, Peter, 68

Marconi, Guglielmo, 85
Marion, Joseph, 37
Massachusetts Bay Company, 33, 36
Massachusetts Board of Railroad Commissioners, 61
Massachusetts Business Roundtable, 233–34
Massachusetts Institute of Technology (MIT): ARDC and, 21; artificial intelligence (AI) at, 161–63; climate tech and The Engine, 160–61; military and space government funding for, 141; research and entrepreneurial organization, 4, 139, 205; 3-D Printing development, 158; tourists and, 107. *See also* Kendall Square (Cambridge)
Massachusetts Port Authority/Massport, 5, 50, 52, 100, 102, 104–5, 108–10
master plans: *Can Seoul Become a World City?* 217; Dubai 2040 Master Plan, 218, 287n28; *Imagine Boston 2030*, 217, 286n24; London, 217; Tokyo, 217
Matthews, Alan Clayton, 244
McGrory, Brian, 222
McKay, Donald, 44
McKinsey Global Institute, 201
Medvedow, Jill, 113
Menino, Thomas, 8, 112–13, 195, 222–23, 245, 264n32
Metropolitan Area Planning Council, 231
Metropolitan Boston Communities (map), 15f
Michigan Central Railroad, 60
Miner, Rich, 150
Moretti, Enrico, 14–15, 140, 233
Mori Memorial Foundation, 2, 27t, 217
Morse, Samuel F. B., 5, 81–82, 84
Moynihan, Brian, 74

mutual funds: Incorporated Investors, 68; leading mutual funds, 67–68; small investors and, 67–68

National Institutes of Health (NIH), 125, 134, 141, 149
Navigating the Global Economy, 105
New American Economy organization, 201–2
Newell, Mary Ellen, 35
New England Comes Back (Dame), 55
New England Confectionery Company (NECCO), 48
New England-Israel Business Council, 103
New England Mutual Life, 58
The New Geography of Jobs (Moretti), 140
Newmark Knight Frank, 23, 26t, 113–14
The New Urban Crisis (Florida), 23, 237
New York & New England Railroad, 45
New Yorker, 112
New York rivalry, 37–39, 42, 74, 210
New York Times, 12, 61, 129

O'Connor, Thomas, 176
O'Donnell, David, 107
Olsen, Ken, 154
Opium Wars (1839–1842), 41, 254n19
Organisation for Economic Co-operation and Development (OECD), 115
O'Toole, James, 169
Ouroussoff, Nicolai, 113
Oxford Economics, 26t

Pagliuca, Stephen, 71, 215
Pasto, James, 174
Patrick, Deval, 102, 153
Peabody, Francis H., 63
Peabody, Oliver W., 63
Peirce, Neal, 207
Pelton, Lee, 233
Perham, Josiah, 62
Perkins, Thomas Handasyd, 41
Peterson, Mark, 35, 37
pharmaceutical and biopharma industry: Beth Israel Deaconess Medical Center,

Index **301**

4, 107, 125, 128–29, 133, 141, 176, 239; biopharma employers, 142t; biotech "stars," 271n7; COVID-19 vaccines, 4, 125–31, 139, 239; CRISPR Therapeutics, 122, 132; Dana-Farber Cancer Institute, 133; federal funding, 141; Johnson & Johnson, 4, 125, 128–29, 143, 147, 150, 239; Massachusetts Biomanufacturing Center, 131; Moderna, 4, 125–27, 129, 131, 139, 148, 152, 219, 239; Pfizer, 4, 125, 127–29, 131, 138, 143, 147, 239
Philips Corporation, 145, 273n22
Pierce, Samuel Stillman, 41–42
Piketty, Thomas, 225, 235, 237
Polk, James Knox, 82
Porter, Michael, 121, 144, 272n18
port of Boston: American Revolution and, 204; Atlantic trade, 204; Commercial Wharf (1819), 41; international trade, 34–35, 43, 48–49; maritime insurance business (1724), 37; shipbuilding, 35
port of New York: New England competition, 37–39, 42; New England personnel, 43
port of Philadelphia, 254n26
Pressley, Ayanna, 195
Preston, Andrew, 46
Preston, Paschal, 84
Price, Marie, 196
private equity and hedge funds: Bain & Company, 57, 71, 147; definition of, 70; leading companies, 71
public transit, 6, 22, 235, 245–46
Puleo, Stephen, 172
Puritans, 1, 11, 33–34, 36–38, 167, 204, 284n1
Putnam Investments, 22, 57, 69

railroads: Atchison, Topeka, and Santa Fe Railway, 62; Central Pacific Railroad, 60, 62; Mexican Central Railway, 62; Northern Pacific Railroad, 62; Santa Fe Railroad, 61; Union Pacific Railroad, 60–62
Railroads, Their Origins and Problems (C. F. Adams), 61

RAND Corporation, 226
Reagan, Ronald, 224, 234
real estate: biopharma manufacturing, 131; investments, 19, 114, 231–32; scientific spaces, 152–53; Seaport district, 7; urban development, 152–53. *See also* Jones Lang LaSalle (JLL); Kendall Square (Cambridge)
Redefining Global Cities (2016), 14, 19, 25t
Regional Advantage (Saxenian), 154
Resonance, 24, 31t
Revere, Paul, 57
Revive and Reimagine, 246
The Rise of New York Port, 1815–1860 (Albion), 42
The Rise of the Creative Class (Florida), 20
The Rise of the Network Society (Castells), 17
Rivera, Dan, 198
Rodrik, Dani, 18
Romney, Mitt, 71
Rosenbloom, Joshua, 58
Rowe, Tim, 151
Russell, Bill, 185
Russia, invasion of Ukraine, 239
Ryan, Andrew, 116

Salem, 39, 253n14
Sassen, Saskia, 13–14, 56, 223–24, 250n9, 277n1
Saxenian, AnnaLee, 154, 201
Scheffler, Robin, 140
Schroders, 27t
Seaport district: appearance and architecture of, 6–7, 111–12, 264n32; big pharma and biotech at, 138; Boston Convention Center, 113; criticism and positives, 115–17; Diller Scofidio+Renfro, 112–13; District Hall, 113; diversity and, 116–17; Institute of Contemporary Art (ICA), 112–13; "Inundation District" (film), 115; pollution cleanup, 111; real estate and gentrification, 113–16; sea level threat, 115

Shape of the City, 227
Sharp, Phillip, 135, 138
Shaughnessy, Dan, 213
Sheffi, Yossi, 143–44
The Singularity is Near (Kurzweil), 242
*The Singularity of Near*er (Kurzweil), 242
Smart Centres Index (Z/Yen), 29t
Smith, Merritt Roe, 139
social protection programs: American Rescue Plan, 236; Build Back Better Regional Challenge, 236; CHIPS and Science Act (2022), 235; Inflation Reduction Act (2022), 235–36; Infrastructure Jobs & Investment Act (2021), 235
South Boston Conley Container Terminal, 52
Spilka, Karen, 195
S.S. Pierce, ship provisions and importer, 41–42
Stack, John, 168
Standage, Tom, 84
Startup Genome, 21, 29t, 143, 155–56, 159, 272n15
State of Possible 2025 Report (MassBio), 131
State Street Corporation, 22, 57, 68, 74
steamships: Collins Line (New York), 44, 259n10; Cunard Line, 44, 50, 80; economics of, 44, 254n29; freight and passenger transport, 44–45, 50, 51f; North American Royal Mail Steam Packet Company, 44–45
St. Fleur, Marie, 195
Stiglitz, Joseph, 235
stock brokerages: Hayden, Stone, 65; Hornblower & Weeks, 65; Jackson & Curtis, 65; Paine, Webber, 65; Tucker, Anthony, 65
Storrow, James, Jr., 65
Street Corner Society (Whyte), 173–74
Sturgis, Russell, 63
Suffolk Downs, 109, 117–18, 138
Summer Olympics (2024) bid: Boston 2024 Partnership, 212–13, 215–16, 286n19; No Boston Olympics Committee, 213–14; US Olympic Committee (USOC), 212–15, 286n19
Summers, Larry, 234
Supple, Barry E., 59
supply chain: Amazon, 267n6; Boston companies and, 119–21; COVID-19 and, 4, 119–21, 124–25, 225; global innovation network, 2, 267n8; iRobot and, 267n6; life sciences and, 122; Massachusetts Biotechnology Council (MassBio), 130–31; pharmaceutical industry and, 125–32; shoe production management, 120–21; value chain, 121–22; Vertex Pharmaceuticals, 122–24; Walmart outsourcing, 267n3. *See also* foreign trade
Sustainable Cities Index (Arcadis), 22–23, 30t
Sustainable Development Goals (United Nations), 19, 23

Thatcher, Margaret, 224
Thayer, John Eliot, 63
Therbor, Göran, 265n37
Thoreau, Henry David, 205
Time magazine, 108
Tocqueville, Alexis de, 59
Tomlinson, Ray, 5, 92
tourism: Boston's attractions, 5–6, 106–7, 218–19; Chinese and, 105; Freedom Trail, 106–7, 218; HubWeek, 219; Innovation Trail, 219; medical tourism, 107
transportation. *See* air transportation; Boston port, post-Civil War; public transit
Trotter, William Monroe, 182
Trump, Donald, 188, 226
Tudor, Frederic, 39, 41

UBS Global Real Estate Bubble Index, 232
uncertainty and disruptions. *See* artificial intelligence (AI); climate change; COVID-19 and vaccines

Unger, Roberto Mangabeira, 290n26
UN-Habitat and Chinese Academy of
   Social Sciences, 19, 26t, 209
Universe of City Indices (JLL), 19, 25t

Vail, Theodore N., 88
Van Buren, Martin, 168
Velluci, Alfred, 134
venture capital: American Research
   and Development Corporation
   (ARDC), 21, 69, 146; angel investors,
   149; biopharma capital investors, 147;
   first example of, 21, 146; hospitals
   and, 148; leading companies, 69–70,
   147–48; MassChallenge accelerator,
   20, 73, 149; Silicon Valley and, 70;
   technology and biotech financing,
   69–70, 146, 148–49
Vidal, Luis, 101
Von Eckhart, Wolf, 206

Walsh, Marty, 195, 213–15, 245
Wampler, Jan, 207
Wang, Willis, 197
Ward, Stephen V., 209
Washington, George, 78
Washington Post, 206
Wealth Report (Knight Frank), 23, 26t, 114
Weaving the Web (Berners-Lee), 93

Welch, E. Sohier, 66
Whalen, Thomas, 215
Wheatstone, Charles, 82
White, Kevin H., 11–12, 204, 206, 247
White, William P., 40
Whyte, Dennis, 161
Whyte, William Foote, 173
Wiesner, Jerome, 141
Winsor, Robert, 64
Winthrop, John, 204
Worcester, Eldad, 41
World Bank, 115, 189, 224
"The World City Hypothesis" (Friedmann), 13
World Intellectual Property Organization, 2, 20, 28t, 143
The World Is Flat (Friedman), 121, 143
World's Best Cities Report (Resonance), 24, 31t
Wu, Michelle, 8, 195, 234, 240, 245–46

Yellen, Janet, 236
Yoon, Sam, 195

Zhang, Yong-Zhen, 128–29
Zimbalist, Andrew, 213
Zucker, Lynne G., 139, 271n7
Zuckerberg, Mark, 95, 163
Z/Yen Partners, 22, 29t–30t, 56

JAMES C. O'CONNELL, FAICP, teaches in the City Planning-Urban Affairs Program at Boston University. He has a BA from Bates College and a PhD in Urban History from the University of Chicago. He also has taught courses at the Boston Architectural College and UMass-Amherst. James has worked in urban planning positions at the Boston Regional Office of the National Park Service, the Cape Cod Commission, and in Springfield, MA. His books include *Dining Out in Boston: A Culinary History*, *The Hub's Metropolis: Boston's Suburban Development*, *From Railroad Suburbs to Smart Growth*, *Becoming Cape Cod: Creating a Seaside Resort*, and *The Pioneer Valley Reader*, ed. James was born and grew up in Springfield, MA, and currently lives with his wife Ann Marie in Newton, MA.

www.ingramcontent.com/pod-product-compliance
Lightning Source LLC
Chambersburg PA
CBHW022041230426
43672CB00008B/1032